THE EAST ASIAN CHALLENGE FOR HUMAN RIGHTS

The "Asian values" argument within the international human rights debate holds that not all Asian states can be or should be expected to protect human rights to the same degree due to varying levels of economic, political, and legal development and to differing cultural views on the virtues and necessity of freedom. This position of "cultural relativism," often used by authoritarian governments in Asia to counter charges of human rights violations, has been dismissed by many Western and Asian human rights advocates as a weak excuse. *The East Asian Challenge for Human Rights* moves beyond the politicized rhetoric that has dogged this debate to identify the more persuasive contributions by East Asian intellectuals to the evolving international debate on human rights.

The editors of this book argue that critical intellectuals in East Asia have begun to chart a middle ground between the extreme, uncompromising ends of this argument. The chapters form a collective intellectual inquiry into the following four areas: critical perspectives on the "Asian values" debate; theoretical proposals for an improved international human rights regime with greater input from East Asians; the resources within East Asian cultural traditions that can help promote human rights in the region; and key human rights issues facing East Asia as a result of financial development (and the more recent financial crisis) in the region.

This book emerges from a multiyear dialogue on human rights among prominent intellectuals – scholars, teachers, and activists – from North America and East Asia. The inclusion of so many East Asian voices, whose diverse perspectives on human rights have not often been articulated in the English-speaking world, makes the book an unusual and valuable contribution. The cultural case studies presented in Part IV are particularly vivid demonstrations of how Asian cultures can and do promote human rights on their own terms.

Joanne R. Bauer is the Director for Studies at the Carnegie Council on Ethics and International Affairs.

Daniel A. Bell is the author, most recently, of *East Meets West: Human Rights and Democracy in East Asia.* He is Associate Professor of Philosophy at the University of Hong Kong.

THE EAST ASIAN CHALLENGE FOR HUMAN RIGHTS

Edited by

Joanne R. Bauer

and

Daniel A. Bell

CAMBRIDGE
UNIVERSITY PRESS

PUBLISHED BY THE PRESS SYNDICATE OF THE UNIVERSITY OF CAMBRIDGE
The Pitt Building, Trumpington Street, Cambridge CB2 1RP, United Kingdom

CAMBRIDGE UNIVERSITY PRESS
The Edinburgh Building, Cambridge CB2 2RU, UK   http://www.cup.cam.ac.uk
40 West 20th Street, New York, NY 10011-4211, USA   http://www.cup.org

First published 1999

Printed in the United States of America

Typeset in 11/13 Garamond in QuarkXPress [GH]

*A catalog record for this book is available from
the British Library.*

Library of Congress Cataloging-in-Publication Data

The East Asian challenge for human rights / edited by Joanne R. Bauer,
Daniel A. Bell.
p.   cm.
Includes bibliographical references.
ISBN 0-521-64230-2 (hb)
1. Human rights – East Asia. 2. Human rights – Asia, Southeastern.
3. Political culture – East Asia. 4. Political culture – Asia,
Southeastern. 5. Economic development – Political aspects – East
Asia. 6. Economic development – Political aspects – Asia,
Southeastern. I. Bauer, Joanne R. II. Bell, Daniel A.

JC599.E18E37   1999
323'.095 – dc21   98-11653
                                                CIP

ISBN   0 521 64230 2   hardback
ISBN   0 521 64536 0   paperback

CONTENTS

CONTRIBUTING AUTHORS

Abdullahi A. An-Na'im is Professor of Law, Emory University (U.S.A.). He served as Executive Director of Human Rights Watch/Africa from 1993 to 1995. His publications include *Toward an Islamic Reformation: Civil Liberties, Human Rights, and International Law* (1990) and *Human Rights in Cross-Cultural Perspectives: Quest for Consensus* (editor, 1992).

Joanne R. Bauer is Director for Studies at the Carnegie Council on Ethics and International Affairs. She is a Japan specialist whose expertise is in the normative content of decision making in the areas of human rights, democratization, environment, and migration. Her current project is a comparative study of environmental values in the United States, Japan, India, and China.

Daniel A. Bell is Associate Professor, Department of Philosophy, University of Hong Kong. His publications include *Communitarianism and Its Critics* (1993), *Towards Illiberal Democracy in Pacific Asia* (1995, co-authored), and the forthcoming *East Meets West: Human Rights and Democracy in East Asia*.

Joseph Chan is Associate Professor in the Department of Politics and Public Administration, University of Hong Kong. He has published articles and book chapters on contemporary liberalism, Aristotle's political philosophy, Confucianism, and the Asian values and human rights debate. He is currently working on a book tentatively titled *Human Rights and Democracy – In Search of a New Confucian Perspective*.

Jack Donnelly is the Andrew W. Mellon Professor of International Relations at the Graduate School of International Studies, University of Denver. His most recent book is *International Human Rights* (2nd ed., 1998).

Yash Ghai is Sir Y. K. Pao Professor of Public Law at the University of Hong Kong. He was a consultant on the independence constitutions of Papua New Guinea, the Solomon Islands, and Vanuatu, and in 1996–7 he advised Opposition Parties in Fiji on the drafting of its new constitution, which was adopted in mid-1997. His recent publications include *Hong Kong's New Constitutional Order: The Resumption of Chinese Sovereignty and the Basic Law* (1997).

Mab Huang is Professor and Chair of the Department of Political Science at Soochow University (Taiwan). He formerly taught at the State University of New York at Oswego and was a visiting scholar at the Abo Institute of Human Rights, Finland. His recent publications include "Forty Years of the International Human Rights Movement" (in *The Chinese Intellectual*, Summer 1996).

Inoue Tatsuo is Professor of Philosophy of Law at the Graduate School of Law and Politics, the University of Tokyo. He was Fulbright Visiting Scholar at the Department of Philosophy, Harvard University, 1986–8. His publications include *Tasha eno jiyu: kokyosei no tetsugaku toshite no liberalizumu* (Freedom for the Other: Liberalism as a Philosophy of Public Legitimacy) (1998).

Benedict Kingsbury is Professor of Law at Duke University Law School (U.S.A.) and was previously a member of the law faculty at Oxford University. His recent publications include *Indigenous Peoples of Asia* (co-edited with R. H. Barnes and Andrew Gray, 1995) and *United Nations, Divided World* (co-edited with Adam Roberts, 2nd ed., 1993).

Onuma Yasuaki is Professor of International Law at the Graduate School of Law and Politics, the University of Tokyo. His publications include *A Normative Approach to War* (editor, 1993) and *Jinken, kokka, bunmei* (Human Rights, States and Civilizations) (1998).

Norani Othman is Associate Professor in the Department of Anthropology and Sociology, Universiti Kebangsaan Malaysia. She is a leading member of Sisters of Islam, an autonomous, nongovernment organization of Muslim women. Her recent publications include *Gender, Culture, and Religion* (1995) and *Shari'a Law and the Modern Nation-State: A Malaysian Symposium* (1994).

Suwanna Satha-Anand is Associate Professor and former Chair, Philosophy Department, at Chulalongkorn University, Bangkok. Her fields of interest are Buddhist philosophy, philosophy of women, and religion and social change. Her publications include *Mahayana Buddhism and Buddhadasa's Philosophy* (1993), *Currents in Chinese Philosophy* (1996), and "Buddhism on Sexuality" (forthcoming).

Amartya Sen is Master of Trinity College, Cambridge University. He received the Nobel Prize in Economic Science in 1998. He was formerly Lamont University Professor at Harvard University and Drummond Professor of Political Economy at Oxford University. His books address human rights and the social impact of economic decisions.

Dorothy J. Solinger is Professor of Politics and Society in the School of Social Sciences, University of California, Irvine and Adjunct Senior Research Scholar at the East Asian Institute, Columbia University. Her publications include *China's Transition from Socialism: Statist Legacies and Market Reforms* (1993) and the forthcoming *Peasant Sojourners and Social Change in Urban China: Migrants and Markets Enter the Cities*.

Kevin Y. L. Tan is Associate Professor at the Faculty of Law, National University of Singapore. He has published widely in constitutional and administrative law and is currently Chief Editor of the *Singapore Journal of International and Comparative Law,* as well as Executive Director of the Society of International Law, Singapore.

Charles Taylor is Chichele Professor Emeritus of Social and Political Theory at McGill University. He was formerly Professor of Social Theory at Oxford University. His publications include *Philosophical Arguments* (1995), *Multiculturalism and the Politics of Recognition* (1992), *The Malaise of Modernity* (1991), and *Sources of the Self* (1989).

PREFACE

This book is the product of a multiyear international project, The Growth of East Asia and Its Impact on Human Rights, part of the Human Rights Initiative of the Carnegie Council on Ethics and International Affairs, New York. The project, which ran from 1994 to 1998, was a collaborative study exploring how the people of East Asia, a region that has undergone rapid social and economic change, are coming to terms with human rights; how, under these circumstances, East Asians are giving meaning to and prioritizing rights (for the purposes of this project, we have defined East Asia as including Northeast and Southeast Asia). The study called upon intellectuals and activists from the region to reflect upon the principles and practice of human rights within their own countries.

The project's purpose was to improve understanding of human rights in East Asia while reducing confrontation between the West, particularly the United States, and East Asia. Revolving around a series of international workshops, it constituted the first sustained and structured dialogue on human rights between East Asians and the North Americans. The workshops were not designed to impose a particular point of view; rather, they were intended to provide opportunities for open, constructive dialogue and scholarly exploration of the realities of human rights across cultures. We also endeavored to widen the debate by bringing to it comparative political scientists, sociologists, development specialists, and other area scholars who have typically been on the sidelines of the human rights discourse.

As a basis for this dialogue, we commissioned research papers on specific topics that underscore competing conceptions of human rights as they relate to local realities. Keeping the focus on national conditions, the papers emphasized case studies drawn from project countries. It is from these papers, first presented at these workshops, that the chapters of this book were developed (it should be noted that the chapter by Inoue Tatsuo builds upon a paper written for an Asian Legal Philosophy Symposium in October 1996).

The workshops examined conceptions of human rights held by East Asian intellectuals and how these ideas are shaped by the dramatic political and economic changes taking place in the region. They raised such issues as the relationships among development, regime type, and human rights; the role of cultural traditions in both shaping conceptions of human rights and protecting human rights; competition among rights, especially during times of economic and political instability; and how conceptions of democracy and human rights are affected by entrenched political cultures. Where possible, we encouraged participants to explore also the successes and failures of democracy and human rights in the United States, a self-appointed standard-bearer for rights. In light of all this, the project explored how cooperation among nations on human rights can be made more constructive.

The first workshop was held in Hakone, Japan, in June 1995, and hosted by the Japan Institute for International Affairs (JIIA). It was structured around claims contained in the "Asian values" debate and explored through case studies the myths and realities of those claims. A March 1996 workshop in Bangkok, Cultural Sources of Human Rights in East Asia, examined in depth the civilizational/cultural aspects of human rights practice in these countries and the implications for the applicability of existing standards to the East Asian contexts under study. This workshop was jointly hosted by the Faculty of Law and Child Rights Asia Net of Chulalongkorn University. The third workshop, hosted by the Faculty Caucus for Social Justice in Seoul, Korea, in October 1996, focused on specific rights that are growing in political salience in the region – such as the rights of foreign workers, indigenous rights, and the right to a clean environment – and how they are being implemented. Participants reflected on both the philosophical bases and the political implications of these pertinent rights concerns.

In December 1996, a workshop was held at Harvard Law School, co-sponsored with the school's Human Rights Program. The two-day workshop accomplished the multiple goals of further exploring strategies for effective local implementation of rights in East Asia, synthesizing the work of the three-year project, and gaining critical feedback.

The project papers and workshop discussions were the inspiration behind the Carnegie Council's quarterly publication, *Human Rights Dialogue*. The eleven volumes issued in the course of the project contained articles contributed by East Asians, some of whom had been involved in the workshops, but many of whom had not. They highlighted a number of themes, including transitional justice; the role and assessment of economic, social, and cultural rights; and innovative local implementation strategies. Their aim was to expose a wider audience to the East Asian discourse on rights.

The project would not have been possible without the generous financial support of the Japan Foundation Center for Global Partnership, the Rockefeller Brothers Fund, the United States Institute of Peace, and the Ford Foundation Vietnam field office. Furthermore, the editors are indebted to the host organizations in Japan, Thailand, and South Korea, and at Harvard Law School, their directors and their staffs. We would like to express our particular appreciation to Amor Almagro, Han Sangjin, Hoshino Toshiya, Jennie Kim, Vitit Muntarbhorn, Apirat Petchsiri, Peter Rosenbluth, Shoji Ryuichi, and Henry Steiner for so freely giving of their time and efforts to make these events possible.

In conjunction with the workshops the project held public forums in each venue, a special NGO consultation in conjunction with the workshop in Seoul, South Korea, and a final policy conference in Washington, DC. For hosting these events, the Carnegie Council extends special thanks to the Ozaki Yukio Memorial Foundation (Tokyo) and its managing director, Hara Fujiko; the Association for the Promotion of International Cooperation (Tokyo) and its executive director, Yanagitsubo Hiroyuki; Lee Seong-hoon of the Korea Human Rights Network (Seoul); and David Little and Scott Hibbard of the United States Institute of Peace (Washington, DC). We also thank Andrew J. Nathan of Columbia University and the participants (especially Xu Xiaoqun and Orayb Najjar) in the 1997 National Endowment for the Humanities summer seminar, led by Professor Nathan, on The Asian Values Debate: Human Rights and the Study of Culture, for devoting an afternoon at the Carnegie Council to discuss draft versions of a number of the chapters.

We are especially grateful to all the individuals who participated in our workshops for the enthusiasm that kept the project moving forward and the insightful comments that informed these chapters: William Alford, Amor Almagro, Roger Ames, Aruga Tadashi, Gothom Arya, Daniel Bell (the distinguished American sociologist), Arief Budiman, Brian Burdekin, Cao Xuan Pho, Chan Hoiman, Tonya Cook, Jaran Cosananund, Clarence Dias, Maria Serena Diokno, Thomas Donaldson, Dzuong Chi Dzung, Donald Emmerson, Kek Galabru, Han Sangjin, Jonathan Hecht, Hirose Takako, Soraj Hongladarom, Hoshino Toshiya, Hashbat Hulan, Jomo K. S., Kawada Tsukasa, Ann Kent, Kim Bong Jin, Komatsu Jun'etsu, Lao Mong Hay, Lee Sang-Myun, Roderick MacFarquhar, David Maybury-Lewis, Vitit Muntarbhorn, Chandra Muzzafar, Nagai Shinya, Kassie Neou, Nguyen Thanh Chau, Matsunaga Nobuo, Nurcholish Madjid, Banthorm Ondum, Park Won Soon, Apirat Petchsiri, Pham Ngoc Uyen, Jefferson Plantilla, Rhee Jeong-Jeon, Joel Rosenthal, Benjamin Schwartz, Shoji Ryuichi, Sulak Sivaraksa, David Steinberg, Henry Steiner, Takagi Seiichiro, Jorge Tigno, Tu Wei-Ming, Boonthan Verawongse, Watanabe Akio, Surichai Wun'gaeo, Xia Yong, Xin Chunying, Yamada Tetsuya, Yokota Yozo, and Zheng Yong. Some of these individuals contributed papers to the workshops that greatly enriched our discussions. A special note of thanks is due to our committee of advisers – Watanabe Akio, Maria Serena Diokno, Donald Emmerson, Han Sangjin, Dorothy J. Solinger, Charles Taylor, Yokota Yozo, Xin Chunying – who provided valuable guidance throughout the project and brought consistency to the workshops.

We were fortunate to have the occasion to host several of our authors – Norani Othman, Dorothy J. Solinger, Abdullahi A. An-Na'im, Yash Ghai, and Onuma Yasuaki – at the Carnegie Council for afternoon seminars where their papers were presented. Additionally, the project and several of the authors were featured at panels at the American Political Science Association (1995), the International Studies Association (1996), and the Association of Asian Studies (1996) conferences. We thank the individuals who attended those seminars and sessions for their interest and critical feedback.

There is not the space to thank all the many people who provided invaluable advice and who assisted us in identifying potential East Asian participants, but we would like to recognize Peter Geithner, Jeannine Guthrie, Jonathan Hecht, Sidney Jones, R. William Liddle, Andrew J. Nathan, Song Bong, Xiao Qiang, and Phyllis Chang, Mark Sidel, and others in the field offices of the Ford Foundation and the Asia Foundation.

We are indebted to a number of people at the Carnegie Council: Susan Burgerman for lending us her keen editorial skills in assisting with the chapters at the final hours; Deborah Field Washburn, director of publications, for her expert management of the business matters related to the manuscript; Tonya Cook, program officer for Studies, for her sharp insights that helped to shape the agendas of the final workshops; and Joel Rosenthal, Carnegie Council president, for his unfailing encouragement and enthusiasm throughout the project. And we wish to thank the Carnegie Council program assistants and interns, Justin, Peralman, Erik Kuhonta, Baldwin Robertson, Randy Chamberlain, Mara Davis, Adam Berg, Patrick Ferry, and Magdalena Bryneson, for their able handling of the myriad details that arise in organizing workshops with participants from so many countries.

Finally, we would like to acknowledge the thoughtful attention and guidance of Mary Child, our editor at Cambridge University Press.

March 1998

EDITOR'S NOTE

In this volume all Cambodian, Chinese, Japanese, Korean, and Vietnamese names appear with family name preceding given name, except in a few cases for Chinese names of authors who are based in the West and use the Western style of family name last. The conventional system of transliteration for Japanese is used. Mandarin Chinese terms from Mainland China are presented in the Pinyin system of romanization. Chinese proper names or terms originating from Taiwan appear in the Wade-Giles system of romanization. The system of Arabic transliteration is based on that of the *International Journal of Middle East Studies.* The symbol ' is used to indicate an *ayn* and ' for a *hamza.* We have omitted all diacritical marks. Thai names are cited and alphabetized by family name in the notes and index. After the first appearance of the full name in the text, however, the given name is used according to Thai practice.

THE EAST ASIAN
CHALLENGE
FOR HUMAN RIGHTS

INTRODUCTION

JOANNE R. BAUER AND DANIEL A. BELL

This book is an exploration of how the experiences of the people of East Asia – a highly dynamic and diverse region – can contribute positively to the evolution of international human rights principles. Hence, our choice of title: *The East Asian Challenge for Human Rights.* The challenge is about seeing how inclusive the rights regime can become while still realizing its essential purpose: to promote and protect vital human interests. The East Asian challenge for human rights is thus not a challenge *to* human rights in the sense that it is trying to displace human rights in favor of some other set of principles. Rather, it is a question of whether the existing regime is flexible enough to accommodate fully the needs of the non-Western, in this case East Asian, peoples. And the challenge for East Asians is to locate themselves in the discourse of universality, which many observers see as originating in and largely shaped by Western experience.

The East Asian discourse on human rights has been growing since the 1993 Bangkok Declaration on human rights, when parallel regional networks of governments and nongovernmental organizations (NGOs) first appeared. It has been spurred by a combination of factors. First, political opening allows for the growth of civil society as educated citizenries confront economic development in an era of intense global competition. Next, East Asians are seeking out local attachments to recover a sense of belonging and trying to come to grips with a postcolonial identity, while at the same time identifying with larger, international (human rights) movements. Third, new social, political, and economic tensions come with greater income stratification and the breakdown of the community and the safety net it provided. Finally, networks of people throughout the region with shared human rights concerns are continually expanding. The new human rights discourse is also a reaction to the increasing pressure on East Asian governments to comply with international human rights norms. This pressure comes from an international community that has heightened expectations for a part of the world that has become irrevocably integrated into global markets.

Most widely publicized in the world's media have been the pronouncements of senior Asian officials, notably Lee Kuan Yew of Singapore and Prime Minister Mahathir Mohamad of Malaysia, which are offered as justifications for the curtailment of "Western-style" human rights in the name of economic development and social harmony. These claims have been met by receptive audiences throughout the region, a reaction that underscores a public mood in Asia of disgruntlement with the West. Yet faced with political repression and economic dislocation, not all East Asians endorse the assertion of an "Asian Way." East Asian activists, opposition political parties, and intellectuals are challenging the human rights claims of their own governments (if given the opportunity) and fighting for government transparency, economic and social justice, and democratic rights. At the same time they are being prompted to reflect on and debate about how East Asians can contribute to a human rights discourse in which they have not heretofore played a substantial part. Though less provocative than those of their governments, these "unofficial" East Asian viewpoints on human rights are contributing to a genuine dialogue that goes to the heart of the debate: the meaning of "universality" and the areas of justifiable difference.

It is clear that these individuals and the groups they lead have already begun to have a profound impact on the international human rights discourse, most notably in the areas of group rights and economic, social, and cultural rights. Through active participation in the last six UN conferences – Rio (environment), Vienna (human rights), Cairo (population), Copenhagen (social exclusion), Beijing (women's rights), and Istanbul (human settlements) – Asian spokespersons have placed these rights on the international agenda, thereby giving them more prominence than they might otherwise have had. Regardless of how we judge the current condition of the Pacific Rim – whether it is the formidable force to be reckoned with that had been portrayed throughout the early to mid-nineties, or whether the region is weakening as a result of the weighty financial crisis of 1997–8 – promoting human rights that do not seriously engage East Asian perspectives on these issues risks widening misunderstanding and setting the stage for hostility that could otherwise have been avoided. But even beyond this fact, it is important to understand East Asian positions on human rights because they address concerns that all societies, including Western capitalist democracies, share as they confront the underside of globalization.

This book emerged from a multiyear dialogue on human rights among prominent intellectuals – scholars, activists, and policy practitioners – from

North America and East Asia. Workshops were held in Japan, Thailand, and South Korea, with a final wrap-up session at Harvard Law School. It includes fourteen of the papers presented at these workshops. Contributors were asked to focus primarily on the economically successful countries of Northeast and Southeast Asia and to explain how the rapidly changing societies of the region are coping with the notion of human rights: how, given the realities of their lives today, East Asians give meaning to and prioritize rights. In this way the authors seek to sweep away the self-serving rhetoric of the "Asian Values" debate and uncover areas of commonality and difference between Asia and the West as well as within Asia.

The aim of the book is to combine normative and theoretical inquiry with sensitivity to the social and political realities in East Asia. It addresses questions that are just beginning to be covered in courses on human rights, political theory, and East Asian studies, but that require more substantial and evidentiary material. Most empirically informed works in political theory draw on examples from Western societies, and most Western authors writing about East Asia habitually inject their own values into their studies without considering alternative normative standpoints. Works on human rights tend to be either sophisticated philosophical treatises written at a high level of abstraction or descriptive accounts of case histories in East Asia and elsewhere. We hope that this volume will help set the terms for debate on the topic of East Asia and human rights for many years to come, and moreover that it will contribute to the evolution of an international human rights regime that responds to the needs of all societies and that all cultures can embrace.

The collection is organized around four themes: critical perspectives on the "Asian values" debate; theoretical proposals for an improved international human rights regime with greater input from East Asians; the resources within East Asian cultural traditions that can help promote human rights in the region; and solutions proposed by East Asians to the key human rights issues they are facing as a result of rapid economic growth in the region. The book concludes with some reflections on the future of the human rights debate.

CRITICAL PERSPECTIVES ON THE "ASIAN VALUES" DEBATE

"Asian values" is a term devised by several Asian officials and their supporters for the purpose of challenging "Western-style" civil and political freedoms. Asians, they claim, place special emphasis upon family and social harmony, with the implication that those in the "chaotic and crumbling" societies of the West should think twice before intervening in Asia for the sake of promoting human rights. As Lee Kuan Yew put it, Asians have "little doubt that a society with communitarian values where the interests of society take precedence over that of the individual suits them better than the individualism of America."[1] The sustained interest in the Asian values debate among scholars and political activists both Asian and Western testifies to the fact that this is no passing intellectual fad. Although politically inspired, the debate has given way to a developing area of knowledge and has opened up an opportunity for serious reflection on what is at stake in this debate and what direction this new area of scholarship is taking. Part I of the book is devoted to an assessment of the rhetoric and the substance of the Asian values debate and whether the debate itself requires us to reconceive the terms of international standards.

Contributions by Inoue Tatsuo and Jack Donnelly assess the arguments against human rights most often put forth by proponents of Asian values. In doing so, both authors defend the applicability of the reigning concept of human rights, arguing that it is flexible enough to allow for cultural differences.

Inoue, a professor of law at Tokyo University, shows that Asian values proponents aiming to denounce liberal democracy as a specifically Western value system alien to Asian culture ironically rely on Western normative language and "West-centric" misperceptions of Asia. For example, to silence voices calling for human rights they invoke state sovereignty, a distinctly Western concept in origin. In the same vein, the assumption that Asia has its own cultural essence fundamentally different from that of the West owes its roots to Western intellectual imperialism, that is, "Orientalism," the very force that is being criticized by Asian critics of human rights.

Inoue also seeks to shatter the dichotomy between an individualist West and a communitarian Asia. He points out that communitarian elements can be found in Western social practices and political theories, and that Asian cultural traditions uphold individualistic values. Moreover, he argues, liberal rights and communitarian values are not necessarily antithetical. In contemporary Japanese society, for example, individual rights may contribute to a rich and mature form of communality.

According to Jack Donnelly, the Asian arguments challenging the universality of human rights norms "represent the most prominent contemporary attack on what for the last two decades most states and human rights activists have taken to be authoritative international standards." But Donnelly, a political scientist at the University of Denver, argues against the attempt to dismiss human rights on the grounds of their "foreign" origin. The fact that

---

1. Quoted in the *International Herald Tribune,* November 9–10, 1991.

human rights ideas first emerged in early modern Europe does not prove that these ideas are any less applicable in East Asia. Those ideas and practices were designed to protect individuals and families against "the power of ever more intrusive states and the grueling indignities of free market capitalism." The same social forces – powerful states and free markets – are penetrating and changing the social fabric of Asian societies today even more than in the past, and there is no reason why human rights should not also function to protect vulnerable groups and dispossessed individuals in these contexts.

Nor is it necessarily the case, Donnelly argues, that Westerners place special emphasis upon civil and political rights whereas Asians care more about social and economic rights. Although the United States tends to neglect certain social and economic rights, the welfare states of Western Europe have a relatively good record of implementing such rights. Donnelly makes the case that even though some economically successful Asian societies, such as Japan, Taiwan and South Korea, have done well at achieving a relatively egalitarian form of economic development, other Asian states, including China and even Singapore, sacrifice economic and social rights – which are concerned with the distribution of goods, services, and opportunities – to the pursuit of market-driven rapid growth.

Thus, both Inoue and Donnelly deny that claims about Asian "cultural essences" justify the systematic denial of human rights. But only part of the Asian values debate is actually about culture. Much of the debate turns on the practical issue of how to promote economic development or how to deal with the perceived necessity to suspend certain civil and political rights during an alleged temporary crisis. This position is also put forward by Singapore's Lee Kuan Yew, who has argued that political leaders in Asia should be committed to the eradication of poverty above all else: "As prime minister of Singapore, my first task was to lift my country out of the degradation that poverty, ignorance and disease had wrought. Since it was dire poverty that made for such a low priority given to human life, all other things become secondary."[2] If factional opposition threatens to slow down the government's efforts to promote economic development or to plunge the country into civil strife, then in Lee's view tough measures can and should be taken to ensure political stability.

Amartya Sen, Master of Trinity College at Cambridge University and Professor Emeritus at Harvard University, casts doubt on the validity of this position with two arguments. He shows that rights have intrinsic value, regardless of their economic and social consequences. Most obviously, individuals

2. Nathan Gardels, "Interview with Lee Kuan Yew," *New Perspectives Quarterly* vol. 9, no. 1 (Winter 1992).

have the right not to be killed in the process of exercising their civil rights. For example, the outrage at the events at Tiananmen Square in 1989 cannot be explained solely (or primarily) by the bad consequences of such an action. Second, he argues that there is little empirical evidence that civil and political rights lead to disastrous outcomes. Systematic cross-national statistical studies do not support the claim that there is a correlation or a causal connection between authoritarianism and economic success. Civil and political rights in fact help to safeguard economic security in the sense that such rights draw attention to major social disasters and induce an appropriate response:

> Whether and how a government responds to needs and sufferings may well depend on how much pressure is put on it, and the exercise of political rights (such as voting, criticizing, protesting, and so on) can make a real difference.
>
> For example, one of the remarkable facts about famines in the world is that no substantial famine has ever occurred in any country with a democratic form of government and a relatively free press.

At the Hakone workshop, however, several participants noted that East Asian governments also present narrower justifications for curbing *particular* rights in *particular* contexts for *particular* economic or political purposes. These actions are said to be taken as a short-term measure to secure a more important right or more of that same right in the long term. Justifications for the temporary suspension of rights are usually put forward by government officials, but they often attract significant local support. Widespread Malaysian support for the suppression of the local Al-Arqam group, as discussed in Chapter 6, and the tendency of older South Koreans to support suppression of pro–North Korea political activism, are two cases in point.[3]

Such trade-off arguments for rights violations cannot be refuted solely by appealing to general principles. Social critics can question the premise that the society under question is actually facing a crisis requiring immediate political action or the idea that curbing rights is the best means of overcoming it. But to be effective the critic must be armed with detailed and historically informed knowledge of that particular society. Even if it turns out that (1) the social crisis is real and (2) curbing rights is the most effective way of overcoming it, such local justifications for the denial of rights are, as Donnelly puts it, "at best a short-run excuse." There is nothing uniquely East Asian about this sort of trade-off argument: International human rights instruments such as Article 4 of the ICCPR (1966) explicitly allow for temporary derogation of certain rights when necessary to overcome a state emergency.

---

3. See the other examples discussed by participants at the Hakone workshop in Daniel A. Bell, "The East Asian Challenge to Human Rights: Reflections on an East–West Dialogue," *Human Rights Quarterly* vol. 18, no. 3 (August 1996), pp. 646–7.

This leads us to conclude that the "Asian values" debate is something of a misnomer. Some government arguments for curtailing rights turn solely on the validity of empirical facts, not on culture. These arguments are sometimes used to call for curtailing rights in such a way that traditional cultural values are actually violated. As Amartya Sen observed at Hakone, the Chinese government justifies its one child per family policy by claiming (erroneously, in Sen's view) that it is necessary to deal with the population crisis. In fact, the resulting policy violates, not honors, a deeply held cultural preference for siring male children.

The contributors to Part I show that "Asian values" do not undermine the quest for a truly universal human rights regime: Cultural arguments for the systematic denial of basic civil and political rights, as well as economic, social, and cultural rights, cannot withstand critical scrutiny, even allowing for justifiable political differences and for plausible accounts of situation-specific curtailment of particular rights. But for the effective implementation of these norms and for a genuine understanding of what rights really mean to people in different cultural contexts, we cannot stop there. We must acknowledge the widespread perception that most international human rights groups interpret and prioritize rights according to Western liberal ideals and that international human rights instruments have not yet adequately incorporated non-Western views.[4] The two contributions to Part II describe this alleged West-centric bias and propose remedies that draw on the positive – potential and realized – contributions of East Asians.

TOWARD A MORE INCLUSIVE HUMAN RIGHTS REGIME

Onuma Yasuaki, professor of international law of the University of Tokyo, articulates many of the negative reactions of Asian citizens to the style and substance of Western intervention. He argues that Western governments and Western-based transnational NGOs have failed to recognize the importance of psychological factors at play in East Asian societies. One such factor is the "humiliating" colonial past endured by countries whose governments are now serious human rights violators and the targets of international criticism. This factor is behind the "excessively sensitive" responses of East Asian officials to well-meaning efforts by the international community. Onuma writes, "For those who have experienced colonial rule and interventions under such beautiful slogans as 'humanity' and 'civilization', the term 'human rights' looks like nothing more than another beautiful slogan by which great powers rationalize their interventionist policies."

---

4. See, for example, Amitai Etzioni, *The New Golden Rule* (New York: Basic Books, 1996), p. 36.

Similarly problematic and often counterproductive is the Western tendency to judge and criticize other countries while assuming their own superiority and ignoring human rights problems at home. According to Onuma, this type of action elicits resentment from within East Asian societies, where cultural norms dictate against behavior that is perceived as aggressive. Thus, blanket criticism of human rights practices that does not take local customs and social realities seriously and in which the critic ignores the shortcomings of his or her own society is often perceived as self-righteous in East Asia, even by dissident intellectuals.

Onuma goes on to criticize the Western biases inherent in the application of the existing human rights regime and in the quest to universalize it. He asserts that Westerners miscast the human rights debate within the framework of universality versus particularity, as though "Islam" and "Confucianism" represent particularity whereas "Christianity" and "the European way" necessarily express universal values. There is little room left, Onuma notes, to think that something non-Western can be universally valid and that Western outlooks may be unique to particular societies.

Most serious, Onuma criticizes a tendency of the American human rights discourse to define human rights solely in terms of civil and political rights. Economic, social, and cultural rights, he notes, are usually referred to only in passing, if at all, and most Americans have been reluctant to do more than pay lip service to these rights, let alone fully accept them as human rights. The main point that needs to be acknowledged if human rights are to have salience in non-Western societies is that problems related to economic and social rights are very real, particularly in these countries as they contend with the pressures of development in a globalized context.

Major European and American-based international human rights NGOs, Onuma argues, frequently make the same mistake. Human rights reports by Amnesty International, Human Rights Watch, and Freedom House, according to Onuma, betray a tendency to deal almost exclusively with violations of civil and political rights, and to neglect the material conditions necessary for the realization of vital human interests. To remedy these flaws, Onuma proposes an "intercivilizational approach to human rights" that would entail dialogue between members of "civilizations" with the aim of achieving the widest possible consensus on human rights. This approach would also involve improving the major human rights protection instruments so that they provide comprehensive standards to evaluate economic, social, and cultural rights as well as civil and political rights.

Onuma's chapter is important because it reflects a widespread view that human rights assessments need to be more transparent and balanced. But other workshop participants noted that the prospect of the intercivilizational dialogue he envisions as a solution presents new unresolved issues. For example, the boundaries between "civilizations," if they exist at all, are never easy to delineate, especially when considering the fact, noted elsewhere in this book, that there are serious disputes over these issues even within particular traditions. In addition, it raises the question of who should participate. Should the dialogue involve diplomats, international lawyers, leaders of religious traditions, academics, NGO representatives, ordinary citizens, or a combination of these? Inclusiveness can have a positive effect on such deliberations, but it may make it difficult to arrive at any conclusive resolution.

Like Onuma, Charles Taylor, a professor of philosophy at McGill University, begins by observing that the Western rights tradition rests on assumptions about human nature and the human good that may not be shared by all societies. The notion of a "subjective right" – the idea that an individual has rights that in principle he or she can waive and has a role in enforcing – is crucial to the Western tradition and has been an important part of its jurisprudence since the Middle Ages. Subjective rights have supported a philosophical view that greatly privileges an individual's freedom and the right to consent to the political arrangements under which he or she lives, a view that has underpinned much of Western democratic theory over the last three centuries.

Taylor contrasts this tendency with the case of Buddhism in Thailand to show that there are other ways to arrive at human rights norms. For Thai Buddhists, a human rights outlook is grounded in the notion that each individual must take responsibility for his or her own enlightenment by adhering to the doctrine of nonviolence, rather than in the dignity of human beings, as in the West.[5] Furthermore, Taylor maintains, the protection of rights need not always take a legal form. Whereas the notion of a fundamental law has a long tradition in Western societies and its judicial guardians have often played a crucial role in securing rights, in Thailand rights have most recently been protected by a king who can draw on the immense moral prestige of the monarchy to end military repression and restore constitutional rule.

What this means, according to Taylor, is that it may be possible to arrive at a "genuine, unforced consensus" on human rights norms, but that given certain unbridgeable differences in how societies function, it is important to

5. Although reformist Buddhism can support "minimal human rights," it does not necessarily support the democratic right to participate in government. Relatively benign paternalistic regimes, such as Hong Kong in the 1980s and the Republic of Venice several centuries ago, have also provided the freedom of religion and other civil freedoms that individuals need in order to take responsibility for their own enlightenment. Similarly, nondemocratic regimes can also rule with what Taylor calls a "minimal use of coercion in human affairs," as demanded by the doctrine of nonviolence. Taylor is appropriately critical of "the cramping of the democratic political process in Singapore," but defenders of the Singaporean government can reply that their regime does provide freedom for those who stick to their own religious, economic, and family affairs, and it is unclear on what grounds a Buddhist reformer might criticize Singapore-style paternalism.

allow for disagreement on the justification of these norms as well as possible variations in the legal institutions and practices of enforcement. It is counterproductive to try to export Western assumptions about individual freedom and the overriding importance of the judicial process. Not only does this approach tend to produce a backlash against "Western intellectual imperialism," about which Onuma writes, but it would also foreclose the possibility of mutual learning from each other's "moral universe." It is from mutual learning that an unforced consensus can be expanded and enhanced.

Taylor admits that sometimes consensus is not as readily attainable as the foregoing example of reformist Buddhism might lead one to think. He argues, for example, that equality – a notion that stems from Natural Rights Law and has become deeply embedded in rights talk over the last two centuries – is hard to export to societies that define themselves in terms of a hierarchical cosmic order. Taking the example of gender equality, Taylor notes that shedding one's traditional identity without having access to an alternative identity can produce alienation rather than liberation, as "the loss of the traditional identity is disorienting and potentially unbearable." In such cases, he warns especially against supporting a "brutal break" from the past and suggests that it may be necessary to reverse the order of consensus making through first establishing "sympathetic understanding" to bring the different worlds into closer proximity. This will require to a large extent the ability of Westerners to see their culture as "one among many."

Still, an international rights regime, even one that emerges from a consensus-building dialogue, cannot do all the work. Many rights battles will be fought within societies according to local norms and customs. Moreover, building human rights on traditional cultural resources – on the customs and values that people use to make sense of their lives – is more likely to lead to long-term commitment to human rights ideas and practices.

CULTURE AND HUMAN RIGHTS

The struggle to promote human rights is more likely to be won if it is fought in ways that speak to local cultural traditions. This leads to the question: Can East Asian cultural traditions provide the resources for local commitment to values and practices similar to those in Western countries? In the Asian values debate, culture is often no more than a convenient excuse deployed by authoritarian leaders to violate rights. But it is also a reality, a worldview that shapes the way individuals and communities interact and give meaning to human rights, and that, in the words of contributing author Abdullahi An-Na'im, "is integral to the formulation and implementation of all state policies."

Against the claim that human rights ideas and practices must be founded on the Western liberal tradition, contributors to Part III take Charles Taylor's "unforced consensus" one step further to try to show, by means of detailed examples, that cultural traditions within East Asia also provide the resources for local justifications of rights. The examples are drawn from the three major traditions in the region: Islam, Buddhism, and Confucianism.

Abdullahi An-Na'im, a professor at Emory University School of Law, argues that the "cultural mediation" of human rights is needed if universality is to be taken seriously. Cultural mediation calls for an open discourse about the meaning and implications of relevant cultural norms and institutions. An-Na'im challenges the reader by selecting the 1994 case of government suppression of the Al-Arqam Islamic sect in Malaysia, a group that itself is charged with human rights abuses, particularly toward women and children.

An-Na'im argues that the government action to arrest Al-Arqam leader Ashaari Muhammad without trial under the International Security Act and to ban the group was wrong because it was not in accordance with either the rule of law or the essence of Islam. First, it violated the rule of law because the state improperly "assumed the mantle of guardian of the beliefs of its citizens" in declaring Al-Arqam "deviationist" and overstepped its mandate to maintain national security and public safety by staking its charge on "vague and unsubstantiated claims." Although An-Na'im does not endorse the positions of the group, he argues that the act to suppress it was a betrayal of international human rights because in making an arbitrary decision, the government and the many who supported its actions denied the application of rights to marginalized groups, the very groups that most need it. Second, the government misused Islam for the purpose of condemning Al-Arqam and violating its rights. An-Na'im notes, for example, that deviationism is unknown to any orthodox formulation of *Shari'a* (Islamic Law) and that the government failed to conform "to the demands of the principle of legality and rule of law under *Shari'a* itself."

It is An-Na'im's belief that both culturally specific and universal norms must be recognized and validated for an international human rights regime to be effective. But although appeals to local culture are important in promoting rights ideas, An-Na'im recognizes that dominant interpretations about the tradition itself (Islam) may sometimes need to be challenged. There are aspects of Islamic belief, such as apostasy – repudiating one's faith in Islam – to which the Malaysian government made reference in its accusation of Al-Arqam, that may not be compatible with human rights in the punishment assigned (sometimes death). Human rights advocates, Muslim and non-Muslim, need to be prepared to challenge these ideas, but they must do so within the culture and on the basis of local beliefs. The *Shari'a* is consistent with human rights, albeit using different terminology, in the principles that ought to have governed this case – namely, toleration and the respect for dignity of all human beings. It is on these grounds, according to An-Na'im, that the case can and should be argued by human rights advocates.

An-Na'im's argument turns on the problem of abuses of power that take place in defining cultural norms and institutions, whether by the West in its historical hegemony over international law making, by Asian governments toward their citizens, or by a religious institution itself. Cultural mediation, involving "the widest possible multiplicity of voices," can check this power. In effect, to gain local commitment to human rights, An-Na'im argues for freedom of speech and democracy, the former so that pro–human rights cultural interpretations could persuade the majority and thus become *socially* dominant, and the latter so that pro–human rights interpretations could eventually become *politically* dominant.

Human rights activists tend not to question the need for changing a tradition so that it allows minority viewpoints to become socially and politically dominant, but this does not always translate into unequivocal support for "American-style" freedom of speech. Consider the case of Dr. Sulak Sivaraksa, a leading prodemocracy activist in Thailand and a nominee for the Nobel Peace Prize, who participated in the Bangkok workshop. In 1991, the Thai ruler, General Suchinda Kraprayoon, pressed charges against Sulak for lèse-majesté – derogatory remarks directed at the royal family – and for defaming him (the general) in a speech given at Thammasat University in Thailand. Fearing for his life, Sulak fled the country but returned in 1992 to face the charges after the Suchinda government had fallen. In court, Sulak did not deny that he had attacked the "dictator" Suchinda, but he did deny the charge of lèse-majesté, referring to the many services he had performed for the Royal Family. Sulak explains:

> I did not . . . stake my ground on an absolute right to free speech. My defense against the charge of lèse majesté was my innocence of the charge; my defense was my loyalty to the King and the Royal Family and, even where I discussed the use of the charge of lèse majesté in current Siamese political practice, it was to highlight abuse and to point to the ways in which abuse might undermine the monarchy, rather than to defend any theoretical right to commit this action. I am not affirming, nor would I affirm, a right to commit lèse majesté. This aspect of the case is particularly concerned with my being Siamese and belonging to the Siamese cultural tradition.[6]

In other words, Sulak aimed to persuade fellow citizens that the dominant political system should be replaced with an alternative, relatively democratic political structure, but he made it explicit that this did not mean advocating the removal of the existing constraint on direct criticism of the Thai king. Perhaps Sulak, like many Thais, would feel deeply offended, if not personally

---

6. Sulak Sivaraksa, "Buddhism and Human Rights in Siam," unpublished paper presented at the Bangkok workshop, March 24–27, 1996. On file with the editors.

harmed, by an attack on the king. Here is a case where a constraint on freedom of expression is endorsed by both defenders and critics of the status quo. It suggests that it is important to fight the human rights battles where there will be the least resistance and in ways that are locally acceptable, even if this requires some constraint on freedom of expression.[7]

However, there are areas in which dominant cultural interpretations clearly need to be challenged by human rights activists. Women's human rights is one such area, and for activists throughout East Asia it is a question of how to achieve emancipation for women without seeming to impose unwelcome foreign ideas. In their contributions, both Norani Othman, a sociologist at Universiti Kebangsaan Malaysia, and Suwanna Satha-Anand, a professor of philosophy at Chulalongkorn University, argue against the mainstream views in their societies about their cultural traditions, asserting that they are distortions and that in fact these traditions can be invoked to promote the cause of women's human rights.

Othman focuses on the case of Islam in Malaysia and Indonesia, the predominantly Muslim countries of Southeast Asia. Islam has often been used to justify patriarchal practices in Asia and elsewhere, but Othman maintains that such actions carried out today in the name of Islam often contravene Islam's central ideas and animating principles. The central *Qur'anic* notion of a common human ontology, *fitnah,* for example, supports arguments for gender equality and the rights of women and counteracts the prevailing tendency to define rights and obligations of citizens on the basis of gender and faith.

Othman, like An-Na'im, emphasizes the politics behind cultural interpretation, arguing that women's rights are inherent in Islam and have been distorted by the increasingly powerful conservative faction of Muslims influenced by the "dominant parochial views of Islam's Middle Eastern heartlands." By drawing on examples of actual disputes over gender equality in Malaysia, Othman shows that the modernist Islamic challenge to "traditional" antifeminism has important political implications. Her Kuala Lumpur–based group, Sisters in Islam, tries to advocate women's equality in religious terms that are locally persuasive and authentic, a strategy the group finds the most effective for ending women's subordination in the Malaysian context. In this way, women's movements can avoid being branded as "merely an imposition of outside Western cultural ideals" in contradiction to locally binding and morally superior religious norms, requirements, and laws.

Satha-Anand argues that in predominantly Buddhist Thailand, feminist reinterpretations of key Buddhist passages can help change the cultural con-

---

7. This argument against "American-style" free speech is not distinctly "Asian." As Charles Taylor pointed out at the Harvard Law School workshop, Canada has relatively uncontroversial laws against hate speech.

ditions that contribute to the pervasive problem of female prostitution. She discusses the national and global economic "pull" forces that play a key role in the flesh trade, but she argues that traditional religious values that justify the subordination of girls also play a crucial "push" role. Most prostitutes in Thailand, for example, send money back to their families, presumably on the understanding that sacrificing themselves for the sake of "superior" male family members is a moral duty.

Malaysia provides a contrasting example within Asia, as pointed out by Chandra Muzaffar, director of Just World Trust in Penang, at the Bangkok workshop. Notwithstanding the presence of the same kind of global and national economic conditions in Malaysia as in Thailand, the Muslim community in Malaysia is not similarly plagued by the problem of female prostitution. Muzaffar suggested that this phenomenon may be related to an important cultural difference between the two countries: Whereas Islam celebrates sex within marriage and condemns it outside marriage, Buddhism tends to denigrate the sexual act no matter what the context. The implication is that for Buddhists prostitutes may not be all that much worse morally than those engaged in marital sex.

In any case, Satha-Anand notes that female prostitutes in Thailand cannot even begin to articulate rights claims for reasonable control and determination of their own lives so long as Buddhism continues to support the view that girls have been created for the enjoyment and convenience of the male species. Hence, challenging patriarchal attitudes is necessary for changing the cultural conditions that support the prostitution business in Thailand. Like both An-Na'im and Othman, Satha-Anand argues that this reinterpretation of traditional religious values must be done in ways that are locally persuasive, meaning in the Thai context that feminist perspectives and rights discourse must be injected into key Buddhist passages. Satha-Anand shows how this can be done in the case of the popular *Vessantara jataka* tale, which can then be taught along with other revised Buddhist passages in schools, local plays, and religious institutions.

The chapter on the Confucian tradition by Joseph Chan, a professor of politics at the University of Hong Kong, is a departure from the other contributions in Part III. Here Chan explores how Confucianism may in certain cases justify a different moral standpoint vis-à-vis the human rights regime typically endorsed by Western governments, scholars, and human rights activists. He begins with an argument that many key elements in Confucianism are compatible with the idea of human rights, but he goes on to show that Confucianism's understanding of civil liberties differs from that of certain dominant strands of Western liberalism. In some cases, Confucians would advocate *narrowing* the scope of rights. For example, Confucians would affirm freedom of speech for instrumental rather than intrinsic reasons: Freedom is a means for society to correct wrong ethical beliefs, to prevent people from committing vices, and to ensure that rulers would not indulge in wrongdoing. What this means, Chan points out, is that Confucians would be reluctant to recognize that people have a basic moral right to speech that does not serve these purposes, such as pornographic magazines, which appeal to "people's prurient or debased interests." In other areas, however, Confucians would want to *widen* the scope of vital human interests to be protected by a rights regime. Here Chan explores the notion of the rights of the elderly, a right that does not receive mention in any of the major human rights instruments.

Such attempts as these by Othman, Satha-Anand, and Chan to root human rights in cultural traditions give rise to the question of legitimacy and who is qualified to speak for a tradition. In An-Na'im's words, "How and by whom are social values defined and prioritized in practice and to what ends? Who determines the standards of conformity with cultural values and 'national' objectives? What are the possibilities and consequences of contesting prevailing perceptions of social values and priorities and their human rights implications?" Conservatives often regard those advocating more progressive interpretations of a religious text, for example, as insincere and opportunistically and dangerously exploiting local tradition for the sake of progressive social goals, such as feminism or human rights. In the case of East Asia, and no doubt other non-Western societies, conservatives regard these as damaging attempts to replace local traditions with a modernist, secular, "Western" agenda.

This criticism can be deflected by distinguishing between the tradition's "core" and "contingent" aspects, as Othman attempts to do in her contribution:

> The transitory and contingent texts enunciate specific rules or guidelines for Muslims during the Prophet's lifetime . . . particularly for the Muslim community in Medina. . . . The permanent texts refer to those verses revealed in Mecca, or outside Medina, that happen also to be general rules or principles about equality, morality, virtue, and social justice.

No doubt these criteria are enormously difficult to discern and will vary from one tradition to another. For example, some traditions place relatively more value upon pronouncements contained in The Book. But making these criteria explicit will help to remove the doubt that a certain amount of arbitrariness informs the process of picking and choosing between "good" and "bad" elements of a tradition.

ECONOMIC DEVELOPMENT AND HUMAN RIGHTS

Of course, some rights issues have little if anything to do with reflection upon cultural sources. In some cases, rights violations occur as adverse consequences of economic development, and excessive focus on culture can only detract attention from the underlying structural economic forces that need to be challenged by rights advocates. Part IV focuses on how East Asia's experience of rapid development has brought certain rights issues to the fore and how East Asians are making sense of these rights in this context.

We begin with Yash Ghai's argument that East Asia's greater integration in the global economy has had negative effects overall in terms of human rights, particularly with respect to the protection of social and economic rights. Ghai, a law professor at the University of Hong Kong, argues that globalization, which has accelerated in the last few decades, has given new legitimacy to transnational corporations and market-oriented rights. The state is no longer the main framework for economic policy making, and governments have been forced to accommodate outside pressures that adversely affect the living standards of ordinary citizens. Ghai notes that the situation can only get worse with the economic crisis currently facing the region. He invokes China's experience since its shift to the market, which "illustrates well the sharp decline in social and economic rights that can flow from an adherence to the market. There is little doubt that a large number of people live in harsher economic circumstances than they did when China still practiced socialist policies." Ghai notes that economic survival today depends principally upon reducing the costs of production, which is generally achieved by increasing the exploitation of labor or dispensing with it. The recent attempt by the South Korean government to boost competitiveness by curtailing workers' rights shows that even governments elected under free and fair elections sometimes respond to global economic pressures by acting in ways that undermine human rights.

This means, Ghai argues, that human rights advocates should abandon their state-centric conceptions of human rights. Many rights are at the mercy of corporations, but the traditional national methods of controlling corporations that violate rights are no longer sufficient. Ghai suggests that corporations should additionally be made subject to international courts and tribunals.

Kevin Tan, in contrast, discusses the positive effects of globalization on the protection of human rights in East Asia. Focusing on the island "tiger" economies of Taiwan and Singapore, Tan discusses the role of law in underpinning rapid economic growth in the two countries. Tan, a professor at the National University of Singapore, recognizes that Taiwan and Singapore sacrificed some civil and political rights for the sake of development and security, concerns related to ethnic conflict and communist oppression, but he points out that both countries nonetheless had a stable and relatively predictable legal system in the area of commercial law. In the long term, Tan argues, greater prosperity, education, and international communications mean that the case for the curtailment of civil and political rights also loses its force.

Tan's argument is borne out in the case of Taiwan, which has largely abandoned political repression to emerge "as perhaps the first truly democratic Chinese society in history." Singapore, however, continues to clamp down on civil and political rights, an action it justifies on the grounds of internal "security threats," a pattern Tan sees as continuing, at least for the short term. Tan, however, notes that Singaporeans value civil and political rights to a greater extent than Singapore's political leaders would have us believe, and he predicts that generational change and the increased globalization of society will eventually lead to greater respect for civil and political rights.

Ghai and Tan are not so much offering competing answers to the question of the impact of economic development on human rights as they are highlighting different rights within different time frames. Social and economic rights seem particularly vulnerable as societies move toward integration in a global marketplace, whereas this same transformation may contribute to greater protection for civil and political rights in the long run. No doubt there are exceptions to this rule, and this debate cannot be resolved without detailed discussions of the impact of particular forms of economic development on particular rights. This is the approach of the remaining contributors to this section: Solinger, Huang, and Kingsbury all focus in depth on a specific rights issue related to economic development.

Dorothy Solinger, a political scientist from the University of California–Irvine, examines the impact of economic development on the rights of China's migrant workers. Solinger notes that between 60 million and 100 million Chinese peasants have migrated to urban areas in search of better work opportunities and higher earnings following Deng Xiaoping's economic reforms. These migrants, however, have been subjected to a variety of human rights abuses, including restrictions on their freedom of movement, on the rights of assembly, association, and political participation, and on the right to decent treatment at work.

The source of the problem, Solinger argues, rests upon a politically sanctioned hereditary distinction between those born in rural and in urban households. Urban household registrants are granted an extra share of rights and entitlement, and migrants are precluded from partaking of these benefits as a result of their rural backgrounds, regardless of how long they have actually lived in urban areas. Solinger argues that the plight of China's migrant workers can be compared to that of foreign "guest workers" in Japan and Germany, who are similarly prevented from enjoying full citizenship rights as a result of their background. Solinger notes that guest workers in Japan and Germany actually receive better treatment than Chinese internal migrants. She recognizes, however, that much depends on the unit of comparison.[8] But even so, she points out that in other developing countries migrant workers are granted basic political rights (such as the right to vote) and basic civil rights (such as the right to move freely) that Chinese migrants are denied. Solinger concludes with the prediction that the plight of Chinese peasants in urban areas will improve with economic development, increased interaction between urbanites and migrant workers, new labor laws, and greater economic interaction with Western, law-based states.

Mab Huang, a political science professor at Soochow University, turns his attention to the impact of economic growth on the environment, an important new issue in East Asian human rights that has not been well documented. Focusing on the case of the anti–nuclear power movement in Taiwan, Huang shows that the Taiwanese government pushed for rapid industrialization, including the promotion of nuclear power, as its claim to legitimacy shifted in the 1970s from anticommunism to rapid economic development and the promise of a more comfortable life for the people. Rapid economic development did succeed in bringing higher living standards to most people, but only at the cost of severe environmental damage.

In response, environmental protest movements, spearheaded by the anti–nuclear power movement, sought to challenge the "no-holds barred" approach to economic development. Although the anti–nuclear power movement has succeeded in making the right to a clean environment a subject of public debate in Taiwan, Huang suggests that progress has been limited as a result of the continuing intransigence of business and government leaders. Huang also discusses two distinctive features of the anti–nuclear power movement in Taiwan. First, the academic community played an important role in leading the movement, perhaps drawing on a Confucian tradition of respect for the *engagé* intellectual. Second, several members of the main opposition party began their political careers as activists within the anti–nuclear power movement (if only because environmental protest was one of the few legitimate avenues for protest in the 1980s), which contrasts with the widespread view that the struggle for basic civil and political liberties normally takes precedence over demands for "postindustrial" rights (such as the right to a clean environment). In fact, Huang concludes that "environmental activism has . . . contributed to securing the rights to free expression, assembly, and association, indirectly adding impetus to Taiwan's democratization and the strengthening of civil society."

Benedict Kingsbury, a professor at Duke University School of Law, dis-

---

8. Several workshop participants observed that China's migrant workers seem to be better off in many ways than migrant workers inhabiting the shanty towns of Brazil, Mexico, India, and Indonesia, countries closer to China's level of economic development than either Japan or Germany.

cusses the plight of indigenous peoples in Asia suffering from the negative effects of development projects. Rapid economic development may benefit substantial sectors of society, but for indigenous peoples "development" has often meant brutal exploitation and the dispossession of their ancestral homes and lands. Kingsbury, a leading international lawyer, argues that a more rigorous definition of indigenous peoples and concomitant codification of their rights in particular contexts will improve the situation.

Kingsbury points out that the governments of China and India claim that their societies do not include indigenous peoples, who have experienced a special history of gross human rights abuses. The official position in these countries is that the question of indigenous peoples is a product of the common experience of European invasion settlement, whereas their societies are still by and large composed of the "original" inhabitants. Denying the existence of indigenous minorities, Kingsbury suggests, has the effect of isolating those groups, who do have distinctive histories and vulnerabilities, from the benefits of international advocacy and limiting their national, political, and legal salience. Kingsbury argues that international lawyers must respond by broadening the legal concept of indigenous peoples so that it refers to more than groups subjected to European colonialism. He does this by invoking a set of definitional "essential requirements" and "relevant indicia" that broaden the concept of indigenous peoples while preserving the existing and highly functional international political distinction between indigenous peoples and minority groups.

This sort of conceptual clarification is fundamental to international efforts to monitor and protect the rights of indigenous populations, particularly under circumstances in which they find themselves resisting the homogenization and social dislocations that have accompanied modernity. Kingsbury presents five case studies – in India, Bangladesh, Myanmar, Taiwan, and Indonesia – of indigenous mobilization that, to varying degrees, grew out of confrontation with their governments' single-minded pursuit of large-scale development strategies. These cases highlight the interactions between indigenous peoples' movements and governments, international financial institutions, and transnational NGO communities.

By means of such detailed investigations of the impact of economic development on rights consciousness and practice, Solinger, Huang, and Kingsbury lend support to Ghai's argument that globalization brings with it substantial human rights violations. But Solinger and Huang also share Tan's optimism that economic development will eventually improve the rights situation by both raising rights consciousness and providing the political space for activism on behalf of rights. Moreover, each of these essays reveals how East Asians are responding to the political and economic changes in the world around them, and in their case-specificity they point to means for more effective human rights implementation both by local NGOs and by the international community.

The central concern of this volume is how the voices of East Asians can be more fully incorporated into the international human rights regime. Although the official rhetoric dominating the Asian values debate has raised questions about the validity of the existing human rights norms, standards, and instruments, all of the contributors share a recognition that some universal requirements that rest on a common humanity are needed to guarantee equal concern and respect from the state as well as from nonstate violators. And they recognize that the existing regime is at least an important first step in an evolving process toward universal requirements.

The project found that to a large extent it is the question of rights trade-offs that underlies the Asian values debate and that this is the source of many of the points of contention over rights. To determine the validity of these trade-off arguments, in which officials in the East are claiming to give higher priority to economic, social, and cultural rights than to civil and political rights, one needs to look at their empirical basis. However, until recently the empirical analysis has by and large been lacking from the main body of the human rights literature, as have the particularities of implementation policies.[9] And without any systematic and effective monitoring and assessment of the full range of rights in question, as Onuma Yasuaki discusses in Chapter 4, how can such arguments be challenged? Targeted East Asian states can easily cite in their defense arbitrary human rights assessments that do not account for economic, social, and cultural rights. This book is an attempt to begin to fill the knowledge gap in order to make the human rights discourse more constructive.

Bringing the debate down to the community level, one finds that there is a rights enunciation and implementation process in East Asia that is far removed from the Asian values debate engaged in by elites in certain countries. The process is occurring in the real-life struggles of people to achieve basic dignity and human security, and is taking the forms of education, people-initiated legal and social reforms, and indigenous NGOs. What was striking about the workshop in Seoul, where the chapters of the last section of this volume were first presented, was how many of the salient social issues raised by participants were in fact being discussed locally in rights terms, and furthermore, how many of the rights areas discussed – foreign worker

---

9. For a thoroughgoing discussion of the study of human rights in the post–cold war era, see Jack Donnelly, "Post–Cold War Reflections on the Study of International Human Rights," *Ethics & International Affairs* vol. 8 (1994), pp. 97–117.

rights, indigenous peoples' rights, minority rights, women's rights, the right to a clean environment, and democratic rights – involved new claimants in the form of local groups and new nonstate violators, such as corporations.[10] In other words, local concern for rights is often an indigenous process and a reaction to new global realities, not simply a function of Western pressure.

As this book's contributors show, these concerns, which entail equal consideration of economic, social, and cultural rights and of civil and political rights, and a recognition of group rights in addition to individual rights, represent ground still contested internally within countries as well as internationally. Yet these may not be the only contested areas. Participants in the Bangkok workshop cited examples of rights that are not spelled out in universal charters. The rights of the elderly, which Chan discusses in his contribution, is one case. Other examples include the rights accorded to the dead in Islam, rights that are treated lightly by international declarations, such as the Buddhist reverence for nature and the environment, and even rights that seem to contradict capitalist (and Western) notions of property, such as the right of cultural communities to their ancestral domain, as was recently enunciated by groups in the Philippines. To widen the consensus on norms and achieve greater respect for rights generally, the rights community needs to be responsive to the needs and experiences of all peoples; and this requires a continuing and constructive dialogue to improve human rights.

One important insight that has emerged from our years of dialogue is that the impact of economic globalization on vulnerable members of society has produced strikingly similar social problems on both sides of the Pacific, such as poverty, inadequate housing, lack of access to health care, environmental degradation, and weakening security nets. This phenomenon points to the possibility of a new approach to human rights policy between Asia and the West, particularly the United States, one based on a recognition of mutuality and a desire for cooperation, rather than confrontation.

---

10. See "Innovative Human Rights Strategies in East Asia," *Human Rights Dialogue* vol. 9. (June 1997).

PART I

CRITICAL PERSPECTIVES ON THE "ASIAN VALUES" DEBATE

CHAPTER 1

LIBERAL DEMOCRACY AND ASIAN ORIENTALISM

INOUE TATSUO*

INTRODUCTION: THE POST–COLD WAR CHALLENGE FROM ASIA

The collapse of communist regimes in East Europe and the former USSR has induced many people to regard liberal democracy as the victor in the global war of ideologies.[1] They may grant this recognition jubilantly or grudgingly, depending on their political sympathies. In either case, they assume a Liberal–Marxist dichotomy and share the understanding that, owing to the failure of Marxism–Communism, liberal democracy is now the only ideological option adequate to the discipline and challenges of modern industrial civilization. Mixed ideologies such as social democracy, according to this understanding, must be sobered up from their "socialist hangover" and redefined as more or less revisionist variants of liberal democracy if they are to survive.

This understanding has been contested by the political leaders and spokespeople of several Asian governments.[2] They reject the assumption of a Liberal–Marxist dichotomy and advocate a third alternative: "the Asian way."

* This is a revised and expanded version of the paper that I presented at a conference, held at the University of Tokyo on October 10, 1996, which was part of the Asian Legal Philosophy Symposium on Law in a Changing World: Asian Alternatives, organized as the Fourth Kobe Lecture by the Japan Association of Legal Philosophy and the Japan Section of International Association of Legal and Social Philosophy, and cosponsored by Egusa Foundation. Another version of the original paper, shorter than this one, is to appear in *Archiv für Sozialphilosophie.*

My thanks go to Yang Seungdoo, Onuma Yasuaki, Daniel A. Bell, Joanne Bauer, Michael Mosher, and many others for their helpful comments on the earlier versions of this paper.

1. For a typical expression, see Francis Fukuyama, *The End of History and the Last Man* (New York: The Free Press, 1992).
2. Singapore's ex-premier, Lee Kuan Yew, and Malaysia's premier, Mahathir Mohamad, are among the most vocal Asian challengers to the "hegemony" of liberal democracy. See, for example, Lee Kuan Yew, "Jinken gaiko wa machigatteiru [Human Rights Diplomacy Is Wrong]," in *Shokun,* September 1993, pp. 140–9; Mahathir Mohamad and Ishihara Shintaro, *'No' to ieru Ajia: tai obei eno hosaku* [The Asia That Can Say "No": Cards Against the West] (Tokyo: Kobunsha, 1994).

This is a combination of capitalist economy and "Asian values," which they claim are embedded in traditional Asian cultures and are incompatible with the core values of liberal democracy: civil and political liberties, especially the right to criticize and to change the government, and minority rights. To put it another way, it is a strategy based on economic modernization without political modernization.

To be sure, some serious thinkers expound more sophisticated and nuanced visions of the third way for Asian countries. I have no procrustean desire to use this characterization of the Asian way to oversimplify or distort their views. On the contrary, I think that their perspective is fundamentally compatible with the aforementioned core values of liberal democracy. They are endeavoring to tap Asian cultural resources to develop some distinctive variants of liberal democracy that could appeal to Asian people's sensitivities and imagination.[3] In this chapter, however, I am concerned with the views of those who use the discussion of "the Asian way" to reject basic civil and political liberties as being culturally inadequate to Asian societies.

Their strategy now appears to be successful, owing to the remarkable economic growth achieved by several authoritarian capitalist countries in Asia, including China, whose official communist creed was undermined when the economy was unleashed while political activity was clamped down on even more tightly. It is true that the current crises of their economies revealed their vulnerabilities. But it does not mean that their past achievements were nullified. Although they have to cope with many difficulties, they will never be what they were before their economic take-off. Their current big recession may well be regarded as proof that they have grown to be big or sizable economies. Short-term fluctuations, even if sharp ones, are no definitive reason to deny the long-term growth tendency.

This situation has important implications for many Asian people who harbor deep resentment against the West for its past colonialism and who have an inferiority complex in regard to Western civilization. Given this ambivalent attitude toward the West, it is natural that Asia's economic success and growth potential should enhance people's self-confidence and incite them to challenge Western hegemony in international norm setting and to require that the West pay due respect and attention to the Asian voice. This is the

---

3. For a recent notable example, see Daniel A. Bell, "A Confucian Democracy for the Twenty-First Century," presented at the international symposium on Asian legal philosophy held at the University of Tokyo on October 10, 1996. Bell incorporates the Confucian ideal of rule by the virtuous into democracy in his proposed model of bicameral representative democracy in which the upper house consists of members selected through examination. I think this model is closer to the spirit of liberal democracy than is J. S. Mill's design of representative government, which gives plural votes to the better educated, provided the examination offers fair equal opportunity to everybody and brings into focus not just technical ability but civic virtue and moral sensitivity to human rights.

historical–psychological background against which the talk of the Asian way has emerged and obtained general currency.

The psychology of the Asian way is quite understandable, but what about its objective merits? Can it claim more than the recognition of economic merits? Does its confrontation with liberal democracy have a normatively sound and philosophically tenable basis? Is the Asian way a real alternative that has sufficient distinctness and moral weight to compete with liberal democracy? To ask a more bluntly skeptical question: Is it anything more than the ruling establishment's attempt to perpetuate its power by taking advantage of people's resentment against the Western world? The answer to this set of questions depends on the credibility of the concept of "Asian values" as the moral basis of the Asian way. Here I aim to argue that this is a misguided and perverse concept and that liberal democracy is not a sheer West-centric idea but an appropriate response to the human conditions that we also find in Asia.

My argument is twofold. First, I will point out in "The Inauthenticity of 'Asian Values'" that the concept of Asian values does not convey Asian voices in their full complexity and diversity, nor does it represent genuine Asian initiatives. Rather, it depends on, or even abuses, the West-centric frameworks that it claims to overcome. Second, I will show in "Beyond Dichotomies: Asian Contexts for Liberal Democracy" that there are points of contact between Asian voices and liberal democracy – not simply that there are some Asian voices sympathetic to liberal democracy, but that the latter can give us intellectual and institutional resources that we need in order to accommodate the internal diversity and conflict among Asian voices and to resolve the problems raised by them.

In arguing this way, I do not assume that the current version of liberal democracy is the ultimate form of human thought or "the end of history." The collapse of Marxism should not blind us to the fact that liberal democracy is now exposed to a fundamental critique, such as the argument offered by communitarians, in the very Western societies (especially in the United States) where it is prevalent. I consider liberal democracy to be an unfinished project, not only in the sense that it has yet to be fully implemented, but in the deeper sense that its foundations, principles, and institutional devices leave much to be clarified, refined, and developed. Asian voices can and should be incorporated into this process.

THE INAUTHENTICITY OF "ASIAN VALUES"

The idea of Asian values derives its appeal from its anti-West-centric stance. The underlying message is this: Liberal democracy is a specifically Western value system alien to Asian culture and therefore the Western attempt to impose it on Asian countries must be denounced as cultural imperialism. A typical form of the critical response to this argument is to show that the core principles of liberal democracy are indeed applicable to Asia. I will offer my own version of this response in the next section. Here I want to present a different critical perspective. My purpose is to undermine the appeal of the Asian values discourse by demonstrating that its anti-West-centric stance is specious. Ironically enough, this discourse abuses Western normative language and is dominated by a West-centric perception, or misperception, of Asia.

The Abuse of Western Priorities

The Asian values rhetoric is primarily a rebuttal to the charges brought against Asia by Western human rights diplomacy. To be effective, it utilizes the moral language of those it addresses. The apologia of Asian values thus looks to the Western vocabulary of political morality for "trump" cards to play against the Western demand for human rights implementation and distorts their meaning in a manner convenient to its purposes.

Among the most bluntly abused principles are state sovereignty and socioeconomic rights to decent means of subsistence. I will make a brief examination of the way they are abused.

The sanctification of state sovereignty. The philosophical origins of the concept of sovereignty are found in the thoughts of Machiavelli and Jean Bodin; its current usage was elaborated by the doctrines and practices of modern European domestic and international law. Thus, according to Richard Falk, "[i]n origins and evolution, sovereignty is definitely a Western concept, and was not shared by other regions until this century."[4]

Although the Asian values discourse criticizes the Western concept of human rights, it accepts the Western concept of sovereignty without reservation. In fact it sanctifies sovereignty as an omnipotent talisman for silencing annoying human rights demands. For instance, the 1993 Bangkok Declaration,[5] which diluted the Asian values talk with diplomatic euphemisms and the seeming moderation of the "balanced approach,"[6] paid lip service to all the major international human rights instruments officially ratified by Asian countries, only to defang them by emphasizing "the principles of respect for

---

4. Richard Falk, "Sovereignty," in Joel Krieger, ed., *The Oxford Companion to Politics of the World* (New York: Oxford University Press, 1993), p. 851.
5. For an overview of the background and impact of this declaration and discussions of the issues involved, see Michael C. Davis, ed., *Human Rights and Chinese Values: Legal, Philosophical, and Political Perspectives* (Hong Kong: Oxford University Press, 1995). For my subsequent quotations from this declaration I refer to its reprint in the appendix of this book.
6. Davis, ed., *Human Rights and Chinese Values,* p. 205.

national sovereignty and territorial integrity as well as non-interference in the internal affairs of States, and the non-use of human rights as an instrument of political pressure."[7]

This rhetorical maneuver is unwarranted not only because the alleged "balanced approach" to human rights disguises an unbalanced reliance on state sovereignty, but also because the disproportionate emphasis on sovereignty betrays a lack of understanding about the close connection between sovereignty and human rights. It is to be noted here that the development of the sovereignty principle has been accompanied by the parallel development of human rights in Western history. This is no coincidence. There are internal connections between the two. The following three nexuses deserve our special attention.

First, the equal and autonomous status of the sovereign state in international relations is a conceptual extrapolation of the equality and autonomy of the individual rights holder in interpersonal relations. The principle of sovereignty protects minor and weaker states against the oppression of major and hegemonic states, just as human rights protect weaker individuals and minorities against stronger political and social forces. Both sovereignty and human rights normatively redistribute unequal power resources among agents by imposing the "fiction" of their equal and autonomous status.[8] This partly explains why the developing countries in Asia and other regions that still have fresh memories of their struggles against Western and Japanese colonialism are more adamant in the assertion of sovereignty than are the powerful nations, in which one can find a fashionable tendency to look down upon the idea of sovereignty as being obsolete.

The conceptual homology of sovereignty and human rights not only requires people in the developed countries to be more sensitive to the importance of sovereignty for the developing countries, it also reveals the deceptiveness of those leaders of developing states who use sovereignty to shield themselves from their response to their own violations of human rights. It is a moral if not a logical contradiction to uphold a devout faith in sovereignty as the normative resort for weaker states in the international context while being cynical about the demands for human rights pressed by weaker individuals and groups in the domestic context.

---

7. Davis, ed., *Human Rights and Chinese Values*, p. 206.

8. This equalizing function of rights is one of the main reasons why Japanese "modernist" jurists engaged in the postwar enlightenment movement regarded the concept of rights and their judicial implementation as essential to democratization in Japan. See Kawashima Takeyoshi, *Nihonjin no hoishiki* [The Legal Consciousness of the Japanese] (Iwanami Shoten, 1967). Although his explanation of the Japanese aversion to litigation in terms of the lack of rights-consciousness and his idealization of Western civil society have invited criticism from many quarters, I think that his insight into the equalizing function of rights is still illuminating and relevant.

Second, human rights are the functional complement of sovereignty. The centralization of power in the modern sovereign state encroached upon the medieval system of power dispersed among various authoritative organizations (churches, guilds, cities, and so on) each of which had its own status-specific privileges and vested rights. As a result, individuals were divested of the protective shield provided by these bodies and exposed defenseless to the power of the state. Human rights as well as the modern principle of the separation of powers have developed to replace the destroyed medieval safeguards against state tyranny. The same compensatory requirement for a system of human rights applies to those Asian countries that are now, in the process of their own state building, undermining more or less autonomous village community structures and other traditional buffers against the power of the central government.[9]

I should hasten to add that the medieval European system also had a dark side. Although the various centers of authority in this system functioned as safeguards against state tyranny, their own social tyranny (internal oppression and status discrimination) was left unchecked. This leads us to appreciate the third connection between sovereignty and human rights: Human rights are the moral basis for sovereignty.

The sovereign state emerged not only as a potential violator but also as a powerful protector of human rights. By dissolving and controlling diffuse intermediary social powers, the sovereign state liberated individuals from the oppression and discrimination inherent in these social structures, although it exposed them to the new threat of its own. The French Revolution is one of the main historical sources of the idea that the sovereign state is the liberator of individuals from their feudal fetters. To be sure, this Enlightenment theory of the state exalted the hubris of the leaders of the Revolution, which led to the Terror. Nevertheless, the idea of the state as the defender of the individual's human rights against social oppression has an important role to play in contemporary societies plagued with social tyranny and social discriminations by various informal powers.[10]

Accordingly, sovereignty needs human rights not just as a functional compensation for what it undermined but also as a positive justification for its emergence, so it is no wonder that the modern social contract theories based on natural rights emerged as the legitimating ideologies of the sovereign state building. Apart from the many theoretical problems involved in them,

9. For a view that emphasizes this point to show the usefulness of human rights for developing countries see Onuma Yasuaki, "In Quest of Intercivilizational Human Rights: 'Universal' vs. 'Relative' Human Rights Viewed from an Asian Perspective," *Occasional Paper No. 2* (The Asia Foundation's Center for Asian Pacific Affairs, 1996), pp. 8ff.

10. For a development of this perspective, see Higuchi Yoichi, *Kindai kokuminkokka no kenpo kozo* [The Constitutional Structure of the Modern Nation State] (Tokyo: The University of Tokyo Press, 1994).

their basic assumption remains relevant today: Such a formidable leviathan as the sovereign state should be allowed to exist only insofar as human rights are its creator and master. Sovereignty is not an independent concern overriding human rights but a high-risk adventure only justifiable as an effective means of their protection.

We have seen that both the international and domestic aspects of sovereignty are closely connected with human rights. Given the conceptual, functional, and moral connections shown earlier, we must conclude that it is illegitimate and inconsistent for the Asian values advocates to use the concept of sovereignty to counter claims of human rights. It should be added, however, that we would make the same mistake in a converse way if we opposed human rights to sovereignty and rejected the latter in favor of the former. Moreover, such a view fails to see the important role that sovereignty can play, especially for developing countries, in equalizing their normative status vis-à-vis the developed countries and empowering their governments to protect human rights against informal social pressures. The proper critical response to the sanctification of sovereignty is not to reject the principle outright, but to confirm that human rights are the internal constraint on sovereignty. "Sovereignty or human rights?" is not the way the debate should be formulated; what we need to convey is "no sovereignty without human rights."

In Chapter 2, Jack Donnelly argues that international pressure for human rights by "all ordinary means of foreign policy" short of the threat or use of force is legitimate and not a violation of sovereignty. My point is stronger and more controversial than his; I argue not only that international concern for human rights is compatible with the principle of state sovereignty, but that human rights are normative constraints inherent in sovereignty. However, in another sense, my view may be considered weaker or more qualified. As my criticism of Orientalism in the sections to follow indicates, I believe in Asia's endogenous potential to develop human rights and democracy while being critical of Westerners' complacency about their own record in implementing these values. Although Western countries can legitimately exercise nonmilitary political influence over human rights practices in Asia, they should not act like a moral teacher punishing intractable pupils, but show the kind of compassionate concern and readiness to advise that equally fallible friends show each other. Positive incentives and encouragement, as well as expressions of disapproval offered with due respect, are more appropriate and effective means of influence than punitive sanctions, except in cases of grave violation of human rights. The same discretion is required of Japan, which is in a position to use its economic leverage to influence human rights practices in other Asian countries while having its own marred human rights record and history of having emulated Western imperialism in Asia. With this reservation, however, I have to emphasize that those Asian countries that have poor human rights records are not excused for their wrongs just because the Western countries (and Japan) also did wrong: Two wrongs do not make a right.

The primacy of subsistence over freedom. The "balanced approach" of the Bangkok Declaration disguises another imbalance: It gives the right to subsistence priority over other rights. This approach claims to reaffirm "the interdependence and indivisibility of economic, social, cultural, civil and political rights, and the need to give equal emphasis to all categories of human rights."[11] In fact, however, as this ordering suggests, economic and social rights are given top priority whereas civil and political rights are ranked lowest. The rationale is that "economic and social progress facilitates the growing trend towards democracy and the promotion and protection of human rights."[12]

The underlying motive is more straightforwardly expressed by the Chinese government's official human rights doctrine[13] and by Singaporean ex-Premier Lee Kuan Yew's "good governance" theory,[14] both of which influenced the Bangkok Declaration. The argument can be summarized this way: The civil and political rights constitutive of liberal democracy are luxuries that only the developed countries can afford to enjoy; for developing countries, the most urgent task is to guarantee their peoples' right to the means of subsistence by economic and social development, which requires that their governments exercise strong leadership and efficient management at the cost of the peoples' civil and political rights. With the social maladies of contemporary American society in mind, Lee goes so far as to suggest that good governance in the Asian fashion is not just a political compromise needed at a certain developmental stage, but in fact an alternative principle morally superior to Western liberal democracy.[15]

The right to subsistence, or more generally the concept of socioeconomic rights as distinct from civil and political rights, has a powerful rhetorical attraction for Western audiences because the concept has been developed by the Western countries themselves since the late nineteenth century, as part of

11. Davis, ed., *Human Rights and Chinese Values*, pp. 205ff.
12. Davis, ed., *Human Rights and Chinese Values*, p. 206.
13. My source is the official Chinese report published in Japan as "Chugoku no jinken jokyo [Human Rights in China]" in *Pekin shuho* [Beijing Weekly] No. 44 (1991), pp. 8–41.
14. See Lee, "Jinken gaiko wa machigatteiru [Human Rights Diplomacy Is Wrong]."
15. Lee, "Jinken gaiko wa machigatteiru [Human Rights Diplomacy Is Wrong]," p. 146. See also Mahathir and Ishihara, *'No' to ieru Ajia: tai obei eno The hosaku* [The Asia That Can Say "No": Cards Against the West], pp. 113ff.

their endeavor to cope with the class struggle. After the Second World War, socioeconomic rights prevailed as a supraparty consensus in the Western welfare states until the Reagan–Thatcher revolution, and even then the basic social net was not fully dismantled.

To be sure, there may be some Asian cultural resources for developing these rights – for example, the Confucian idea of public ownership of the public realm is said to be a historical source for Chinese socialism[16] – but this merely demonstrates that socioeconomic rights are not alien to Asian traditions, not that they are peculiar to these traditions. The peculiarity lies in how the Asian values discourse exploits this concept, by resorting to socioeconomic rights as an excuse to restrain political liberties. In the social democratic tradition, these rights support arguments for regulation of the market, not arguments against political participation.

Furthermore, there are serious flaws in this peculiar use of socioeconomic rights by Asian values advocates. The first flaw is that they fail to see the importance of political liberties for the realization of rights to subsistence. Amartya Sen has offered a powerful argument for this point with reference to the problem of famine, as he discusses in Chapter 3.

Here I want to focus on another flaw I find in the subsistence rhetoric: It is self-deceiving. Socioeconomic rights emerged later than civil and political rights in the history of human rights in Europe. Why did they develop later? The reason is not just that it took Western moral consciousness more time to notice their importance. The fundamental reason is that it took Western capitalism time to accumulate an adequate level of social surplus. If a society is to assure the needy access to a publicly provided subsistence as an entitlement, it must have developed its economy to the point at which government controls greater material resources than are necessary to supply basic public goods such as crime control, defense, and industrial infrastructure.

Therefore, it is through faulty reasoning that Asian developing countries claim that subsistence precedes freedom. The truth is that socioeconomic rights rather than civil and political rights are luxuries that only the developed countries can afford to implement adequately. As far as the economic cost is concerned, civil and political rights are more accessible to developing countries. Civic education involves some costs, but they are not prohibitively high. Anyway, the best school for democracy is democracy itself, as we learn from Alexis de Tocqueville.[17]

By way of rebuttal, it may be argued that the more serious economic costs

16. See Mizoguchi Yuzo, *Hoho tosihteno Chugoku* [China as Method] (Tokyo: The University of Tokyo Press, 1989), pp. 12–23.
17. See Alexis de Tocqueville, *Democracy in America,* trans. G. Lawrence (New York: Anchor Press, 1969), esp. vol. 1, part U, chapter 6; vol. 2, part R, chapters 4–8.

of political rights lie elsewhere: Democratization tends to obstruct economic growth because, given the power to influence policy making, people are bound to use it to pursue their myopic special interests to the detriment of capital accumulation and productivity enhancement.[18] With respect to Asian countries, this hypothesis is falsified by a remarkable counterexample: Japan's postwar history, in which it simultaneously underwent democratization and miraculous economic growth out of total devastation. To be sure, democratization generally involves to a greater or lesser degree the drawbacks of interest group politics. Japan's postwar democracy has its own share of these problems, but it proves that even a democracy riddled with interest group politics can contribute to economic growth by redistributing its benefits, if not to the extent of the welfare state ideal, then at least in such a way that the discontents and uneasiness of those affected by rapid social change are allayed and a national consensus on the priority of economic development is formed and stabilized.[19]

Democratic consensus formation can facilitate the pursuit of developmentalist policies because it enhances the government's legitimacy in requesting from its citizens the self-discipline and patience essential to economic growth. An authoritarian regime, on the other hand, brings its own structural obstacle to economic development: Members of the ruling class, who are unchecked by democratic controls, have an incentive to interfere politically in the market economy to advance their own private interests. This impedes efficient resource allocation, undermines public trust in the fairness of the system, and lowers productivity and morale.

Civil and political rights are therefore not economically infeasible for developing countries, but we have to understand that these countries may encounter economic difficulties in adequately implementing socioeconomic rights. As a matter of fact, some Asian developing countries that rhetorically emphasize the primacy of subsistence rights are actually placing their highest priority on building the material and institutional infrastructure of a market economy and on fostering their own industries. They are now more eager to boost their economies by releasing market forces than to burden them with the cost of adequate social welfare for needy citizens. They also restrain another important element of socioeconomic rights, that is, workers' rights to form independent unions and strike; this is not surprising because the low cost of labor is one of their major competitive advantages over developed countries.

---

18. See Jon Elster, "The Necessity and Impossibility of Simultaneous Economic and Political Reform," in D. Greenberg, et al., eds., *Constitutionalism and Democracy: Transitions in the Contemporary World* (New York: Oxford University Press, 1993), pp. 267–74.

19. See Kyogoku Junichi, *The Political Dynamics of Japan,* trans. Ike Nobutaka (Tokyo: The University of Tokyo Press, 1987), pp. 96–132.

The socioeconomic rights incorporated in social democracy and welfare state liberalism are intended to ensure that individuals receive their fair share of the means for a decent human life and to reinforce the workers' bargaining power even if economic growth and efficiency are thereby rendered suboptimal. The primacy-of-subsistence rhetoric of some Asian developing countries conceals a contradictory practice: The national goal of economic growth is given primacy, not only over political liberties but also over individual rights to a decent share and collective labor rights.

This said, I do not belittle the Asian developing countries' aspiration to economic and social progress. My points are the following: The rhetoric of socioeconomic rights conveys a deceptive self-image that runs counter to their true aspirations and needs. Further, their developmental needs may provide them a temporary excuse for failing to adequately implement social and economic rights, but not for trampling on civil and political rights.[20]

The Spell of Orientalism

The Asian values discourse does not confine itself to a strategic manipulation of Western principles. It goes further to assert Asian cultural uniqueness, based on the old dualism of Asia as the Orient and Euro-American countries as the Occident. This dualism enables Asian values advocates to make charges of cultural imperialism in response to Western human rights concerns and to make the cultural relativist response: "Asia will go its own way." I want to show that these arguments are dominated and misguided by the very West-centrism that they criticize, because their dualist assumptions are themselves the products of the Western intellectual imperialist construct referred to as Orientalism.

Two critiques of West-centrism. First of all I want to distinguish two different critical perspectives of West-centrism. For this purpose it is necessary to articulate West-centrism's logical structure. West-centrism, in the sense relevant to our discussion, can be formulated as the following inference:

P1: Western societies played a leading role in the historical development of democracy and human rights.

P2: Irrespective of their historical pedigree, democracy and human rights have a universal scope in terms of their normative validity, so they must also be realized in Asia.

P3: Despite its recent remarkable economic growth, Asian political structure is

---

20. Whereas Donnelly argues in this volume that the "liberty trade-off" and "equity trade-off" are both problematic, my point is that the liberty trade-off is far less excusable than the equity trade-off.

dominated by premodern, traditional culture, which is essentially incompatible with Western principles, so it lacks the endogenous will and competence to develop democracy and human rights. The Hegelian perception of Asian ahistorical stagnancy[21] remains true of Asian politics, and its political stagnation contributes to making its savage capitalism undisciplined and unruly.

P4: Therefore, Western leadership and interference are indispensable to the establishment of democracy and human rights in Asia.

The two anti-West-centric perspectives to be discussed here concur in rejecting the conclusion, P4, of this inference, but they differ as to which premise should be denied. The first perspective, which I will call "the critique of value dominance," rejects P4 by denying P2. The second, which I will call "the critique of epistemic hegemony," does so by denying P3.

The Asian values discourse represents the critique of value dominance. Whether it resorts to cultural relativism or, more aggressively, claims Asian superiority, it denies universal validity of Western concepts of human rights and democracy in order to undermine the normative foundations of Western pressure.

On the other hand, the critique of epistemic hegemony rejects the epistemic matrix that differentiates Asia from the West by disclosing its hegemonic nature. The most eloquent expression of this perspective can be found in Edward Said's critique of Orientalism.[22] His critique is mainly concerned with the Western perception of the Islamic world in the Middle and Near East, but it is relevant to Asia in general.[23] Although his expansive analysis of the Orientalist literature is controversial in parts, his basic insight, as I interpret or reinterpret it, throws a fresh light on the nature of West-centrism. It can be reconstructed for our purposes in the following way: Asia, as the Orientalists see it, is essentially different from the West. They claim that the overall system of Asian language, culture, religion, politics, economy, and history can be unifyingly explained by its heterogenous essence. Moreover, they assume that only the West, which has developed its tradition of Oriental studies through the colonization of Asia, has the intellectual competence and resources to understand and conceptualize this essence of Asia and thereby to lead it. The West is the knowing agent and Asia is the object to be known, which cannot have a clear self-perception without having its own meaning determined through the Orientalist matrix of the West.

At a deeper level, Orientalism is motivated by the West's desire to estab-

---

21. See Georg W. F. Hegel, *Lectures on the Philosophy of World History,* trans. H. B. Nisbet (London: Cambridge University Press, 1975). In his notorious foreword for the chapter on China, Hegel places China and India outside the scope of world history on the grounds that these countries experience no dialectical change whatever but merely repetition of the same pattern.

22. See Edward W. Said, *Orientalism* (New York: Georges Borchardt Inc., 1978).

23. For an attempt to incorporate a critique of Orientalism into the study of Chinese history, see Paul Cohen, *Discovering History in China* (New York: Columbia University Press, 1984).

lish its own identity as the historical agent that created the modern spirit and civilization. To establish this identity, the West needed Asia as the Other. Asia must be the negative background against which the West presents its own positive figure. The West represents Modernity, and Asia must ipso facto represent Countermodernity. Furthermore, as long as the West legitimatizes its domination of Asia by its historical mission of promoting modernity and seeks to perpetuate this status, Asia's countermodernity must be its perennial essence.

Orientalist dualism is disguised as an empirical generalization, but in fact it is a transcendental scheme for interpreting data that justifies the observer in disregarding any counterexample as a meaningless anomaly and thus blinds him or her to the internal diversity and dynamic potential. It is an epistemological device for guaranteeing Western hegemony over Asia.

The critique of epistemic hegemony aims to undermine the Orientalist dogma as presented here and rejects P3 as a typical expression of it. P3 ascribes to Asia a cultural essence incompatible with the values of modernity (i.e., human rights and democracy). Although my presentation of the epistemic hegemony critique is inspired by Said, it is adapted for the purpose of understanding the Asian potential to develop these values.[24] The epistemic hegemony critique intends to undermine, not the values themselves, but the Western claim to a spiritual monopoly over them.

The trap of identity. If we compare the two forms of anti-West-centrism, the value dominance critique may appear to be the more radical, in that it rejects or at least relativizes "Western" principles of human rights and democracy. I think, however, that the epistemic hegemony critique is more profound and illuminating, because it reveals that the position taken by the Asian values discourse parasitically adheres to Orientalist dualism and is thus dominated by West-centric intellectual hegemony.

When Asian values advocates reject civil and political rights, which form the core of human rights and democracy, as being specifically Western and culturally inadequate to the Asian context, they ascribe the same homogeneous cultural essence to Asia that Orientalists utilize to contrast Asian society with the Western self-portrait of "Civil Society." They change the evaluative connotation of this essence from negative to positive (or equivalent) but keep its cognitive content unchanged. For an Asian identity they look to the stereotype that Orientalists imposed on Asia to establish a superior Western identity.

This is ironical but understandable. It is the same psychological mechanism found in practices of social discrimination. When the discriminatory

---

24. Said's analysis does not elaborate on this issue, so I do not claim that the epistemic hegemony critique in my sense is faithful to his perspective.

stereotype is deeply held, the groups who are discriminated against are induced to convert it into a basis for self-esteem. This occurs not so much because, given the persistence of such a stereotype, it is strategically easier to turn it to their own advantage rather than destroy it, as because the conversion strategy promises to heal a people's wounded self-respect more powerfully than does the strategy of destroying the stereotype. Kwame Anthony Appiah, the Ghana-born professor of philosophy at Harvard, has a clear and profound explanation for this phenomenon: "It will not even be enough to require being treated with equal dignity despite being Black, for that will require a concession that being Black counts naturally or to some degree against one's dignity. And so one will end up asking to be respected as a Black."[25] Here we find the source of the claim: "Black is beautiful." We can criticize the demand for a positive recognition of the black identity as reproducing the racial categorization used to discriminate against them, but we have to understand that it is a natural response for those African Americans who want to disassociate themselves from the presumption of racial inferiority that the practice of discrimination has imposed on them. They positively affirm their black identity because to detach their identity from being black in order to prove their equal status vis-à-vis whites would make them accomplices to the presumption of inferiority.

To the deep-seated Orientalist prejudice, the Asian values advocates seeking to increase their self-esteem offer an analogous response: "Asia is beautiful." Although some government leaders who resort to Asian values rhetoric may do so partly or mainly to perpetuate their power, much of the appeal this discourse holds for the wider Asian audience comes from its healing effect on people's self-esteem. Their legitimate claim to equal respect vis-à-vis the West turns into an ironic affirmation of the imposed Asian identity.

Although understandable, this reverse use of the imposed Asian identity is wrong and dangerous. Although sympathetic to the assertions of gay and black identity, Appiah warns that they will easily turn into a tyrannical imposition of the "proper ways of being black and gay."[26] The same warning applies to the assertion of Asian identity. It represses the recognition of Asia's internal diversity and potential for endogenous transformation, and tempts one to discourage and even to oppress Asian demands for human rights and efforts at democratization,[27] just as advocates of a black identity often castigate those members of the community whom they consider to be mimicking

25. K. A. Appiah, "Identity, Authenticity, Survival," in A. Gutmann, ed., *Multiculturalism: Examining the Politics of Recognition* (Princeton, NJ: Princeton University Press, 1994), p. 161.

26. Appiah, "Identity, Authenticity, Survival," pp. 162–3.

27. This is exemplified by the contemptuous way in which Lee Kuan Yew criticizes democratization in the Philippines and other Asian countries. See Lee, "Jinken gaiko wa machigatteiru [Human Rights Diplomacy Is Wrong]," pp. 142–4.

whites by stigmatizing them as "oreos."[28] The cult of Asian identity has even produced the label "bananas" to express contempt for yellow-skinned Asians mimicking the values of whites. This cult will reinforce the Orientalist prejudice that Asian culture is inadequate for human rights and democracy, just as the black identity cult reinforces racist essentialism: "Blacks are blacks."

The epistemic hegemony critique enables us to get out of this trap of Asian identity by dissolving the Orientalist dualism. It does not require that Asians be considered capable of human rights and democracy *despite* being Asians. Rather, this critique undermines the assumption of a monolithic Asian cultural essence. In this way it also undermines the Asian identity assertion of those who are asking to be respected *as Asians,* as people identified with "Asian values" as distinct from "Western" principles of human rights and democracy.

This does not mean that the epistemic hegemony critique uncritically idealizes Western practices of human rights and democracy as a model for Asia. On the contrary it reveals that such an idealization comes from the Western self-deception generated by Orientalism, which seeks to sanctify the West's historical identity by portraying it as being based on a sublime mission to embody the principles of modernity.

This self-portrait suppresses or rationalizes abominable Western practices past and present, such as colonialism, slavery, racism, fascism, anticommunist crusades (McCarthyism, Vietnam War), and so on. It is distorted not just in what it blurs but also in what it highlights. Critical reexamination and revision have been made of the standard Western historical narrative in which democracy and human rights are said to be victoriously established through the Euro-American bourgeois revolutions in the seventeenth and eighteenth centuries. In this context, it is interesting to note that comparative political science indicates that democratization, defined by a set of empirical indexes such as the ratio of voters to total population, took place only recently even in Western countries: normally in this century, never in the "Great Eras" of the Glorious Revolution, the American Revolution, and the French Revolution.[29] For example, it was not until the second decade of this century that the proportion of voters to the total British population exceeded 10 percent. The United States enacted constitutional prohibition against discriminatory restrictions of female suffrage only in 1920.[30]

---

28. The political implication of this expression is critically analyzed in connection with politics of difference in Michael A. Mosher, "On the Philosophical Foundations of Multiculturalism" (unpublished paper presented at the Faculty of Law, University of Tokyo, July 16, 1996).

29. See Robert A. Dahl, *Democracy and Its Critics* (New Haven: Yale University Press, 1989), chapter 17 (especially Figure 17.1 at pp. 236–8).

30. However, the year 1920 also marked the hysterical Red Hunt persecution and the Sacco–Vanzetti case, spoiling the monumental significance that this year could have held for democracy and human rights in the United States.

These facts demonstrate that the polarizing drive of Orientalist dualism traps the West as well as Asia in a distorted perception of self-identity. The value dominance critique denies the universal validity of democratic and human rights principles on the grounds that these are specifically Western values, thereby accepting not only the Orientalist stereotype of Asia, but also the West's own Orientalist self-sanctification. By contrast, the epistemic hegemony critique undermines Orientalist dualism to deny that Asia is essentially inadequate to develop these values and to remind the West of its own suppressed grim record in terms of democracy and human rights. The critique of epistemic hegemony, therefore, directs both Asia and the West away from the cage of their deceptively polarized identities. In the next section I will proceed to criticize more specific distorted dichotomies and to explore Asian contexts for liberal democracy.

BEYOND DICHOTOMIES: ASIAN CONTEXTS FOR LIBERAL DEMOCRACY

Among the major dichotomies typically assumed by the Asian values discourse are "Christian (or Judeo-Christian) West" versus "Confucian (or Confucian–Islamic) Asia," and "individualist West" versus "communitarian Asia."[31] A critical dissolution of these dichotomies would enable us to see that liberal democracy, by which I mean democracy with due respect not only for economic freedoms but also for civil and political liberties and minority rights, is not alien to but in fact appropriate to conditions in Asia. There are endogenous and contextual reasons for liberal democracy to develop in Asia.

Religious and Cultural Diversity

Beyond the "clash of civilizations." It is obviously impossible to characterize Asia and the West as two distinct civilizations solely with reference to their religious foundations, for if there is anything we can speak of as a general truth about Asia, it would be its religious and cultural diversity. In this respect Asia's internal heterogeneity is much greater than that of the West. All of the major world religions with their various denominations have habitats and competitive influence in Asia, to say nothing of the myriad of minor indigenous religions.

---

31. See Lee, "Jinken gaiko wa machigatteiru [Human Rights Diplomacy Is Wrong]," pp. 145–8; Mahathir and Ishihara, "'No' to ieru Ajia: tai obei eno hosaku [The Asia That Can Say 'No': Cards Against the West]," pp. 112–27.

It is unjustifiable even as a caricature to depict Asia as a Confucian or Confucian–Islamic civilization, as opposed to the Judeo-Christian West. First, other major religious traditions, such as Hinduism and Buddhism, have a comparable presence in Asian spiritual practices. In particular, Buddhist influence is pervasive throughout Asia. Second, the difference between secular Confucianism and monotheistic Islam is extremely deep. On the other hand, Judaism, Christianity, and Islam compete with each other as sequentially diverging monotheistic traditions with partially overlapping religious narratives, so in a sense their rivalry could be called sectarian strife or even a family dispute. Accordingly, it would be theologically scandalous to unite Confucianism and Islam into a civilizational alliance opposed to the Judeo-Christian world, and still more so to merge Islamic Asia into Confucian Asia. Third, Christianity has penetrated Asia and exerted strong social and political influence, especially in the Philippines and arguably in South Korea.

This division of civilization spheres according to religion is not just wrong, it is also politically dangerous. It is an accomplice of the current version of the Orientalist geopolitics on the Western side, such as Samuel Huntington's perception of "the clash of civilizations."[32] It characterizes Asia (excluding Japan as a sui generis civilization) as a Confucian–Islamic connection and as a civilizational threat to the Judeo-Christian sphere of Western democracies. Unlike the earlier imperialism, this theory does not prescribe conquering the "alien civilization" but argues the necessity of containing it and consolidating the Western sphere of influence. This difference is, however, more a matter of strategy than of principle. It is not hard to see that the geopolitical strategy with this Orientalist perception of civilizational confrontation could at any time change from a defensive to an aggressive one if the military and economic conditions should change to the advantage of the West. The religio-civilizational dichotomy of the Asian values talk reinforces and rationalizes the dangerous misperception of the Western counterpart.

What is more important, Asia's religious and cultural diversity is not compartmentalized by national borders. Many Asian countries, including China, Malaysia, Singapore, and Indonesia, whose governments are very vocal in the Asian values debate, are multireligious, multicultural, and even multinational. The increased human mobility resulting from economic development has contributed to this internal diversity. For this reason, domestic conflicts resulting from the internal religiocultural diversity of Asian countries, rather than the supposed "clash of civilizations" between Asia and the West,

---

32. See Samuel Huntington, "The Clash of Civilizations," *Foreign Affairs* vol. 72, no. 3 (1993).

are the important factors that we have to consider in discussing what political structures would be appropriate for these countries.

Toward a liberal pluralism. Their internal diversity requires Asian countries to develop liberal democracy to accommodate the sharp conflicts and tensions it generates. There can be no long-term peaceful coexistence among different religious and cultural groups without the establishment of a generally accepted common basis for political legitimacy. Liberal democracy is the political system that has shown the greatest concern for establishing such a basis for legitimacy, because it separates politics and religion, assures all religious and cultural groups of equal rights to civil and political liberties, and protects minorities against legal and social discrimination. I want to develop this thesis by responding to some important opposing arguments.

First, it may be objected that the destabilizing effect of religious and cultural diversity requires not liberal democracy but an oppressive regime to "silence" discontented minorities. As a matter of fact, nonliberal governments, including some Asian governments, cite the need for political stabilization as an excuse for oppressing minorities. But the oppressive system does not dissolve but rather suppresses the discontent of minorities, and their pent-up indignation and hatred increase the instability of the system from a long-term point of view. Even if it were able to destroy resistance by overwhelming power, stabilization by naked power lacks legitimacy and so involves the huge maintenance costs of coercion.

On the other hand, liberal democracy is, in principle, capable of stabilizing culturally divided societies by establishing a basis of legitimacy, although the actual practices of liberal-democratic countries have often failed to realize these principles. Constitutional designs intended to achieve stability in diverse societies vary from country to country, and we need not regard the American constitutional system with its emphasis on judicial review as being the only paradigm. For example, the European political systems Arend Lijphart described as "consociational democracies" coped with the task of accommodating religious and cultural diversity by developing mechanisms for legislative power sharing and consensual decision making,[33] but the essential purpose is the same: to ensure all groups equal access to effective political participation and to establish institutional safeguards against the tyranny of the majority.

The core of liberal tolerance is fairness, not "orderliness" based on compelled silence, and fairness, not compelled silence, will truly stabilize the

---

33. See Arend Lijphart, *Democracy in Plural Societies* (New Haven: Yale University Press, 1977); Lijphart, *Democracies: Patterns of Majoritarian and Consensual Government in Twenty-One Countries* (New Haven: Yale University Press, 1984).

political system in the long run. To be sure, the stability of political regimes is a matter of empirical assessment, but we can at least say this: There is no reason to presume that an oppressive system is more effective than liberal democracy in securing long-term stability. Moreover, the former's stablity is at the mercy of military power balance whereas the latter's is not necessairly so.

The second objection that could be raised to my thesis is that liberal democracy is not the only attempt to achieve religious tolerance and that the Islamic world has its own historically successful alternative form of religious tolerance: the millet system.[34] To be sure, this system endowed some non-Muslim minorities in the Ottoman Empire, such as the Greek Orthodox, the Armenian Orthodox, and the Jews, with the collective right to observe their faiths and to govern their internal affairs. This tolerance for non-Muslims is quite remarkable when compared with the Christian persecution of Muslims, Jews, and Gypsies in the Iberian Peninsula following the *Reconquista*.

Under this system, however, non-Muslim minorities could only practice their religions within their self-governing communities (millets) and were deprived of the right to propagate their religions and the freedom to build churches without permission. What is more important, religious liberty was a collective right enjoyed by the community as a whole, not an individual right to religious autonomy, so non-Muslim minorities as well as Muslims persecuted heretics and apostates within their own communities.[35] The millet system admittedly institutionalized religious tolerance to a certain degree, but it did not accommodate religious diversity and freedom to the extent granted by liberalism. It was not fair enough even to the officially recognized non-Muslim minorities and was gravely unfair to unauthorized minorities and heretics.

We can say, then, that the millet system is not so much a full-fledged moral alternative to liberal tolerance as it is a preliminary step toward the latter. The pursuit of the common fair basis of legitimacy for multireligious society expressed itself in the millet system only in the inchoate form, but this germinal form had a potential to open the way for liberal tolerance. As Will Kymlicka reports, "There were many periods during the 500-year history of the millets in which liberal reformers within each community pushed for constitutional restrictions on the power of the millet's leaders. And in the second half of the nineteenth century, some of the millets adopted liberal constitutions, in effect converting a religious theocracy into a secular system

---

34. I wish to thank Daniel A. Bell for reminding me of this as a potential objection. For illuminating accounts of this system, see Will Kymlicka, *Multicultural Citizenship* (Oxford: Oxford University Press, 1995), pp. 156–8, 162–5, 183–4; Benjamin Braude and Bernard Lewis, eds., *Christians and Jews in the Ottoman Empire: The Functioning of a Plural Society* (New York: Holmes and Meier, 1982).
35. Kymlicka, *Multicultural Citizenship*, p. 157.

of liberal-democratic self-government for the various national groups in the Empire."[36] We should add that in the background of these intramillet reforms there were liberal reform movements within the Muslim regime, such as the thirty-first Sultan, Abdul Mejit's "benevolent reforms" *Tanzimat,* which recognized the social equality of non-Muslims, and the Young Turkish Party's movement for constitutionalist reforms. All this constitutes the historical source for contemporary Turkey's secular constitutional democracy. What we should learn from the history of the millet system, therefore, is to break down the contemporary Orientalist stereotype of "Islam as the fanatic fundamentalism" and appreciate the Islamic potential for liberal tolerance.

The last objection to be considered comes from some multiculturalists who criticize liberal individualism for obstructing religious and cultural minorities' rights to collective survival and self-rule.[37] Such promotion of group over individual rights is incompatible with liberal tolerance insofar as it denies an individual member the right to criticize and attempt to revise the dominant beliefs and practices of her own cultural community and to move out if she loses faith in it. However, it is doubtful whether the denial of such individual rights can be justified as necessary to protect the culture, for culture is not a fossilized way of life but rather a living organic form of human interaction that grows through a metabolic process of renovation activated over time by internal criticism. It would not protect but rather asphyxiate a culture to stem this vital process. If, on the other hand, it is the case that socioeconomic factors, such as employment opportunity, structurally distort the "natural selection" of competing cultures in such a way that minority cultures are doomed to extinction, then preferential treatment of cultural minorities can be accommodated by the liberal concern for the value of individual autonomy.[38]

I have argued that liberal democracy is capable of coping with the legitimacy crisis inherent in culturally divided societies. If my arguments are sound, Asian countries confronted with tensions generated by diversity have good reason to develop some form of liberal democracy. This is not surprising because the liberal pursuit of popular legitimacy originated in the doctrines of religious tolerance and secular natural law that emerged from the catastrophic folly of the sixteenth- and seventeenth-century religious wars in Europe.[39]

---

36. Kymlicka, *Multicultural Citizenship,* p. 157. See also Braude and Lewis, eds., *Christians and Jews in the Ottoman Empire,* pp. 18, 23, 28–31.
37. For surveys of these debates, see Will Kymlicka, ed., *The Rights of Minority Cultures* (Oxford: Oxford University Press, 1995); Gutmann, ed., *Multiculturalism.*
38. For a notable example, see Will Kymlicka, *Liberalism, Community and Culture* (Oxford: Oxford University Press, 1989); Kymlicka, *Multicultural Citizenship.*
39. For a recent confirmation of this point, see John Rawls, *Political Liberalism* (New York: Columbia University Press, 1993), pp. xxiv–xxx. A classic example of the toleration doctrine as the source of liberalism is John Locke's *A Letter Concerning Toleration,* 1689.

It certainly cannot be said that Western practice has admirably reflected the principle of liberal tolerance or that it has been completely fair in accommodating the tensions of religious and cultural diversity. We may say, however, that Western practices, as well as the development of the millet system in Islamic history, indicate that the basic principles of liberal democracy have served and will continue to serve to regulate the ongoing expansion of the circle of tolerance and the exploration of new schemes for mutual respect, justified in terms of a fair common basis of legitimacy within religiously and culturally divided societies.

This pluralist nature of liberal democracy has recently been reaffirmed by John Rawls.[40] In *Political Liberalism* he reminds us that liberal democracy is not just a mixture of market economy and popular vote, but is in fact a more challenging enterprise that seeks to establish a reasonable common basis of legitimacy for societies deeply divided by competing and even incommensurable religions, cultures, and other "comprehensive" world views.

I think that his recent theory correctly identifies the task of liberal democracy, but I must make some critical reservations about his method of tackling this task and the related tendency in the recent discourse on liberalism. Rawls claims to "apply the principle of tolerance to philosophy itself."[41] This means that he expands the separation of politics and religion into the separation of politics and philosophy. To avoid commitment to any controversial philosophical doctrine, he gives up the philosophical validity claim for his liberal conception of justice and turns, for its substitute basis, to "the overlapping consensus" among the reasonable comprehensive doctrines adapted to democratic political culture.[42]

The implication of Rawls' conventionalist turn for our discussion is that he denies the universal applicability of liberal democratic principles to non-Western countries that lack political traditions comparable to Western constitutional democracy. In his recent paper on international justice,[43] Rawls recognizes the legitimacy of states he calls "the well-ordered hierarchies," which are not aggressive toward other states but lack secular democratic institutions and officially enforce hierarchical discrimination of different religious groups and social classes. These states maintain consultation systems to channel popular grievances and give minimum protection to oppressed religious and social groups as long as these groups remain obedient to the hierarchical regime.

Although he asserts that such a regime can have "legitimacy in the eyes of its own people,"[44] Rawls avoids discussing conflicts among the different social

40. Rawls, *Political Liberalism*. 41. Rawls, *Political Liberalism*, p. 10.
42. Rawls, *Political Liberalism*, pp. 13–14, 134–72.
43. Rawls, "The Law of Peoples," in Stephen Shute and Susan Hurley, eds., *On Human Rights: The Oxford Amnesty Lectures 1993* (New York: Basic Books, 1993), pp. 41–82.
44. Rawls, "The Law of Peoples," p. 61.

classes and religious–cultural groups constituting the "people," and even fails to ask whether such a regime could be considered fair from the perspective of the religions and classes discriminated against. The liberal pursuit of a common fair basis of legitimacy should not degenerate into a mere reconstruction of the conventional political culture, which often conceals a society's internal conflicts and suppresses dissenting voices in order to forge a specious consensus. The virtue of the liberal pursuit inheres in its critical and transformative power to undermine the complacent self-rationalization of the dominant regime. This virtue is inseparable from the philosophical commitment to the unattenuated human rights principles.

I do not deny, however, that the concept of overlapping consensus can be adapted for the international context in a different way: It may be used not to weaken the requirements of democracy and human rights but to offer alternative cultural justifications for these principles. Charles Taylor develops this approach in his discussion of Thai Buddhist Reformism in Chapter 5 of this book, although I have to add that he is not completely free from the conventionalist inclination to rationalize social discrimination (such as gender discrimination) on the pretense of cultural identity.

The tendency toward the cultural relativization of liberal democracy is more straightforwardly expressed in John Gray's avowal of "post-liberalism."[45] Gray declares that liberal philosophy is dead, but resurrects its substance (i.e., civil and political liberties and the rule of law) as the tradition of Western civil society, proclaiming: "That our way of life is ours gives us good enough reason to defend it."[46] Claiming that civil society is "an invention of Western cultures," he rejects the demands made of other cultures to adopt it as "Western cultural imperialism" and urges respect for "the constraints of local cultural traditions."[47]

Here we see the stance: "We live our own way, and let them live their own way." This may appear to be a sensible extension of liberal tolerance to the international setting, but it amounts to a condescending deference to the Asian values discourse and indulges in the Orientalist identity script: the self-complacent sanctification of Western traditions achieved by ascribing a contrary cultural essence to the non-Western world. Ernest Gellner further articulates this Orientalist script when he contrasts "Civil Society" with its post-Marxist "rivals," the Islamic "Umma" and the communitarian developmentalist states in Asia: "So, all in all, Civil Society is justified at least in part by the fact that it seems linked to our historical destiny. . . . But what point is there in vaunting our values, and condemning the commitment of

---

45. See Gray, *Post-Liberalism: Studies in Political Thought* (New York: Routledge, 1993), pp. 238–50, 283–328.

46. Gray, *Post-Liberalism*, p. 325.   47. Gray, *Post-Liberalism*, p. 317.

others to absolutist transcendentalism or demanding communalism? They are what they are, and we are what we are: if we were them, we would have their values, and if they were us, they would have ours."[48]

This We-and-They dualism leads Gellner to treat Turkey's struggle for secular constitutional democracy as "the curious case" and to declare that it is doomed to eternal instability.[49] To be sure, Turkey has been suffering from political instability owing to the conflicts between the "proreligious" populist movement and the Kemalist military, but it also has civilian forces that support secular democracy. Moreover, the Western countries have also been confronted with the crises of liberal democracy generated by religious and ethnic conflicts and "fundamentalist" populism.[50] Gellner, however, does not sympathetically see in Turkey the same kind of difficulties and vulnerabilities that have afflicted the Western countries. He simply assumes that "our values" are secured for "us" as "our historical destiny" whereas "they" are doomed to eternal Sisyphean labor if "they" seek for "our values." Why? Because "we" are not "them" and "they" are not "us."

In sum, I have argued that the tendency in recent Western political philosophy to show apparent deference to "non-Western" political cultures, which are presumed to be insusceptible to liberal democracy, is not so much an extension of liberal tolerance as a retelling of the Orientalist narrative. This conventionalist turn seeks to cleanse Western self-perception of its stains, such as deep-seated religious intolerance and social discrimination, and to dump the "waste" from this self-purification into the space assigned to "non-Western cultures" or "Asian civilization."

The pluralist sensibility of liberalism should be exercised, not to polarize the West and Asia, but to bridge the exaggerated gap by highlighting the internal religious and cultural diversity of Asian countries and by recognizing their need, and actual or potential capacity, to join in the liberal pursuit of fair accommodation of diversity. The perception that "they, Asians" share common problems with "us, Westerners" will enable "us" to show not specious, condescending deference, but genuine respect and concern for "them" and to form a sympathetic understanding of "their difficulties" as being "our own." Asian people, for their part, should not exploit the Western failure to carry out the liberal enterprise in order to castigate the enterprise itself. The greater and deeper internal diversity of Asian societies puts an even heavier burden to pursue this venture upon their own shoulders.

48. Ernest Gellner, *Conditions of Liberty: Civil Society and Its Rivals* (London: Hamish Hamilton, 1994), pp. 213–14.
49. Gellner, *Conditions of Liberty*, p. 200.
50. See, for example, Ronald Dworkin, *A Bill of Rights for Britain* (London: Chatto and Windus, 1990); also Sasaki Takeshi, *Amerika no hoshu to liberaru* [Liberals and Conservatives in America] (Tokyo: Kodansha, 1993).

Individualist–Communitarian Tensions

The dichotomy of individualistic West versus communitarian Asia may sound more plausible than the religious dichotomy, but I hold that it is also untenable. The difference between Asia and the West in this respect is not so deep and unbridgeable as to justify the claim that liberal democracy is alien to Asia.

The communitarian West and individualist Asia. First of all, the communitarian threads can also be found in the fabric of Western civil society. This is eloquently emphasized by the contemporary communitarian movement,[51] which has become part of the Western intellectual mainstream, especially in the United States, the country regarded as the land of rugged individualism. Communitarians object that liberal individualism is not only philosophically inadequate but also incorrectly interprets the history of the American tradition.

They hold that American democracy depends for its vitality on active forms of communal life, such as small townships, religious communities, clubs, and various intermediary associations, which function as the seedbed of civic virtue, defined as the capacity and willingness to undertake responsibility for the common good. They deplore the erosion of civic virtue, for which they blame liberalism, and aim to revive what they consider to be the best elements of the democratic tradition.

I argue that the communitarians' critique of liberalism is unfair in that they misrepresent it by a crude characterization of atomistic individualism that liberals themselves would reject. They are also misguided in denouncing individual rights as antithetical to community.[52] However, their insight into the communal basis of civil society nicely counterbalances the misrepresentation of civil society as consisting of atomistically isolated individuals. The antiatomist perception of civil society, emphasizing the role of intermediary communities, is widely shared beyond the circle of contemporary communitarians.

Let me turn to the Asian side of the dichotomy, which is no more tenable than the Western side. Elements of individualism are not alien to Asia.

---

51. Although a number of reputable scholars are associated with the communitarian movement, such as Charles Taylor, Michael Walzer, and Alasdair MacIntyre, I find that Michael Sandel's work most clearly represents the movement's motivation and philosophical perspective. See Sandel, *Liberalism and the Limits of Justice* (Cambridge: Cambridge University Press, 1982); Sandel, *Democracy's Discontent: America in Search of a Public Philosophy* (Cambridge, MA: Harvard University Press, 1996). For a witty dialogic presentation and defense of the communitarian perspective, see Daniel A. Bell, *Communitarianism and Its Critics* (Oxford: Oxford University Press, 1993).

52. For my argument, see Inoue, "Kyodotai no yokyu to ho no genkai [The Claims of Community and the Limits of Law]," *Chiba Journal of Law and Politics* vol. 4, no. 1 (1989), pp. 121–71; also "The Poverty of Rights-Blind Communality: Looking Through the Window of Japan," *Brigham Young University Law Review* vol. 1993, no. 2 (1993), pp. 517–51.

Confucianism, for example, is too rich and complex to be presumed ignorant of the value of individuality. William Theodore de Bary, an authority on Chinese intellectual history, thus finds an individualistic and even liberal tendency in the Neo-Confucian movement that, according to de Bary, emphasized the worth of individual self-development and the importance of an independent, critical, and creative attitude toward the Confucian texts and their authoritative exegeses.[53] He holds that "Neo-Confucian liberalism" found its culmination in the seventeenth-century scholar Huang Tsung-hsi, who not only criticized despotism but also noted the limitations of the sage's rule as a traditional Confucian ideal. Huang Tsung-hsi emphasized the importance of rule of law and the necessity of institutional reforms to encourage free critical discussion and to ensure moral checks on political activity.[54]

This interpretation of the Neo-Confucian movement is certainly not uncontroversial.[55] Generally speaking, however, the Confucian commitment to moral control of political power has two competing tendencies. Confucians who want to moralize politics are tempted to politicize morality, identifying themselves with political power and using it to impose their doctrines on their rivals and critics in an authoritarian way. On the other hand, this moral commitment also cultivates the critical spirit toward political power and the courage to resist persecution, which indicates the moral autonomy and independent political agency of one who has internalized moral principles as the basis of identity. When the authoritarian tendency corrupts and erodes the moral and intellectual vigor of Confucianism, the critical tendency emerges as a countermovement for its rebirth. Without this dynamic process Confucianism could not have preserved its life as an intellectual legacy of global stature, so it is irrelevant to argue over whether Confucianism is essentially antiliberal or proliberal. The important point is that Confucianism has developed through conflicting interpretations of its own tradition and that this tradition is rich enough to lend itself to a liberal interpretation like that of de Bary.

The individualist tendency can be found, perhaps even more vividly, in Buddhism. Apart from Amartya Sen's interesting remark that "Ashoka, whose inscriptions from the third century B.C. emphasize tolerance and lib-

---

53. See Wm. Theodore de Bary, *The Liberal Tradition in China* (New York: Columbia University Press, 1983).
54. See de Bary, *The Liberal Tradition in China*, pp. 67–90.
55. We might say that Huang Tsung-hsi is more republican than liberal, or more like Rousseau than Locke, judging from his emphasis on the cultivation of individual civic virtue and his intolerance of Buddhism and other non-Confucian religions. But this does not obviate the fact that he encouraged individuals to criticize and control the political authorities. See Yamanoi Yu, ed., *Ko sogi* [Huang Tsung-hsi] (Tokyo: Kodansha, 1983).

erty as central values of a good society,"[56] what might be called a transcendental individualism is a deep-seated mentality. While rejecting obsession with the ego, Buddhists stress self-reliance in spiritual awakening and regard the pleasures of family love and other communal attachments as disturbing earthly passions (*klesa*). As is revealed in the concept of *pravrajya* (leaving home), detachment from familial and communal encumbrances for the sake of the self-disciplined and self-reliant search for spiritual truth is a step toward true salvation for the individual.

This is typically the case with Theravada Buddhism, but the life of Buddha, which exemplifies detachment and independence, has not lost its paradigmatic meaning for the more secularized Buddhist traditions, either. A well-known Buddhist scripture reports that, at the point of death, Buddha said to his disciple, Ananda, "Whoever makes himself his isle and depends on none other than himself, whoever makes *dharma* his isle and depends on nothing other than *dharma,* shall be at the highest stage as my monk – no matter who he may be."[57] Buddha repeatedly demanded a self-reliant quest of dharma, the Principle of the Universe, in his last words. Maeda Sengaku, a Japanese authority on Buddhism, thus indicates that "converting to one's self," by which he means the quest of the true self, identified exclusively with dharma, and spiritually independent from the authority of any existing religion or saint, even from Buddha's authority, has a central place in Buddhist thought.[58]

It is often said that in the West, Protestantism supplied a religious source for individualism, but the aspects of Confucianism and Buddhism just presented show that a spiritual individuality is not monopolized by, nor did it originate in, the Protestant tradition. The Islamic world also has its own version of Protestantism: Sufism, a mystical tradition that emerged around the end of the eighth century. Sufism is now characterized as having been a reform movement protesting the way in which the Islamic faith had been reduced to a shell and rendered a mere formalistic observance of Islamic law (*Shari'a*) by the *ulama,* or official scholars, who enjoyed the Caliph's protection. Sufi, the leaders of this movement, rejected the knowledge of the *ulama* (*'ilm*) in favor of their own new form of knowledge (*ma'rif ah*), which is an individual understanding based on the direct, unmediated communicative unification of the self with the Deity, achieved through ascetic practices.

---

56. A. Sen, "Thinking About Human Rights and Asian Values," *Human Rights Dialogue* vol. 4 (March 1996), p. 2.

57. *Mahaparinibbana-suttanta,* chapter 2, §26. My English translation is based on Nakamura Hajime's Japanese translation from the Pali original text: *Buddha saigono tabi* [Buddha's Last Travel] (Tokyo: Iwanami Shoten, 1980), p. 64.

58. See S. Maeda, *Buddha wo kataru* [Tokyo: Talking About Buddha] (Tokyo: Nihon Hoso Shuppan Kyokai, 1996), pp. 223ff., 337–48.

Here we see the general dynamics of faith in which the individual desire for direct communion with the divine truth brings about a spiritual autonomy that transcends the fetters of the earthly order. Although vulgar worship of Sufi involved superstitious pursuit of secular interests, an important factor of the popularization of Sufism is said to be people's desire and attempt to live like Sufi.[59]

In addition to individualist elements in the major Asian religious traditions, we have to consider the socioeconomic diversity in Asia. We should avoid the fallacy of looking to peasant communities that maintain a strong social cohesion for a historical prototype of Asian society. This is a source of the polarized image of communitarian Asia, but the model of peasant community oversimplifies Asian societies, even as a historical prototype.

For example, in the Muromachi and Edo periods (from the end of the fourteenth century through the mid-nineteenth century), the Japanese merchant class developed its own individualistic urban culture, which emphasized aesthetic self-expression and that formed a cultural resource for contemporary Japanese social development.[60] The concept of justified resistance was traditionally familiar to Chinese courtiers and gentry whose shared Confucian learning included Mencius's theory of Heaven-ordained revolution (*yi xing ge ming*). This Confucian potential of dissent and rebellion, according to Maruyama Masao, permeated even the Japanese *bushi* class (warriors), whose official ideology urged that "even if the lord is not lordly, the subjects should not cease to be subjects." The impossibility or difficulty of disengaging themselves from loyalty to their lords turned their moral energy to active engagement in critical control of their lords from within in the form of remonstrance.[61] Their strong sense of honor also cultivated the moral courage to refuse self-degrading servility to the order without cause even at the cost of their lives. Durkheim notwithstanding,[62] their practice of seppuku (self-disembowelment) was not so much a savage ostentation of defiance of death as an honorable way of taking responsibility for their actions, which include what we would now call conscientious objection and civil disobedience.

Finally, we have to pay attention to social change in contemporary Asia.

59. For an illuminating account of these aspects of Sufism, see Nakamura Kojiro, *Isuramu: shiso to rekishi* [Islam: Its Thought and History] (Tokyo: The University of Tokyo Press, 1977), pp. 195–231.
60. See Yamazaki Masakazu, *Nihon bunka to kojinshugi* [Japanese Culture and Individualism] (Tokyo: Chuokoronsha, 1990), pp. 3–95.
61. See Maruyama Masao, *Chusei to hangyaku* [Loyalty and Rebellion] (Tokyo: Chikuma Shobo, 1992), pp. 7–57.
62. "The readiness of the Japanese to disembowel themselves for the slightest reason is well known. A strange sort of duel is even reported there, in which the effort is not to attack one another but to excel in dexterity in opening one's own stomach." Emile Durkheim, *Suicide: A Study in Sociology,* trans. John Spaulding and George Simpson (New York: The Free Press, 1951), p. 222. How was a serious and profound sociologist like Durkheim content to make such a flippant and superficial observation on seppuku? Orientalism may well be part of the answer.

The rapid economic development in this region is now accompanied by an accelerated urbanization, the infiltration of market exchange in communal relationships, the dissemination of a meritocratic and competitive mentality, the enlargement of educational opportunity, technological if not institutional improvements in popular access to information, and so on. We may well say that these social changes are bound to enlarge the social and economic habitat for people with more or less individualistic value orientations.

Accommodating the tensions. The points that I have made far from exhaust the range of issues relevant to the dichotomy in question, but I hope I have said enough to undermine its plausibility. What does all this add up to? I want to emphasize the following implications for the acceptability of liberal democracy in Asia.

First, my reference to "the communitarian West and individualist Asia" is rhetorical. The examples given earlier are not meant to prove the reverse of Orientalist essentialism, but rather that individualist–communitarian tensions run not between the West and Asia but within each of them. No society is free of these tensions. To be sure, the relative force of individualist and communitarian elements can vary, generating different problem situations in different societies at different times, but the difference in their relative force has nothing to do with any essential difference between Asia and the West, not just because it is merely a matter of degree, but also because the pattern of tension varies locally and historically within both the West and Asia. Even if we assume, for the sake of argument, that liberal democracy is ultimately based on individualism, it does not follow that liberal democracy is essentially alien to Asia because of Asia's incapability of appreciating and respecting the worth of individuality.

Second, this assumption needs to be qualified. The communitarians in contemporary political theory remind us that democracy requires intermediary communities to cultivate civic and cooperative virtues and that our communal identification with a larger society is invigorated by our experience of democratic participation.[63] This insight implies two things. On the one hand, the communitarian aspect of Asian societies, which we should recognize without exaggerating, is not necessarily adverse, but rather conducive, to democracy. On the other hand, Asian countries need democratization if they are to reinforce communitarian virtues, such as the willingness to undertake responsibility for the common good, in a social context larger than the family, and especially at the national level.

63. See Sandel, *Democracy's Discontent;* Benjamin Barber, *Strong Democracy: Participatory Politics for a New Age* (Berkeley: University of California Press, 1984).

The former point is likely to invite the objection that "premodern" communities in Asia are too different from "modern" intermediary communities constituting Western Civil Society to be a basis for democracy. Like other Orientalist dichotomies, however, this objection idealizes the historical communal sources for Western democracy as much as it slights Asian communities. The Puritan communities of colonial New England that are now characterized as the roots of American democracy, for example, were more fundamentalist than, and at least as intolerant as, the "old"-world societies they had fled. The 1692 Salem witch-hunt illustrates their fanaticism and superstition. Even in the mid-eighteenth century, nine out of the thirteen colonies still had established churches, and the historical success of Thomas Paine's *Common Sense* in getting wide popularity in New England and instigating the American Revolution is partly explained in terms of its abundant Biblical references that appealed to the naive grassroots faith.[64] Tocqueville, the great French analyst of the nineteenth-century American democracy, did not fail to remark upon the social tyranny and religious intolerance of the small townships, which he regarded as a seedbed of civic virtue.[65]

Just as unenlightened and intolerant religious communities can provide the solidarity that promotes democratic practices, so Asian communities of "premodern" origin also have democratic potential. For example, I have argued elsewhere[66] that in postwar Japan, the communal cohesion mediated by popular attachment to *Tenno* (the Emperor), who has "authority without power," as the symbol of Japanese national culture and history has proven to be not just compatible with democracy but also capable of promoting grassroots participation both in local self-rule and in national politics. Attachment to the Emperor reinforces people's identification with and concern for the fate of their own communities and of the nation. I have also emphasized that such communal cohesion involves the persistent danger of social tyranny and discrimination against the individuals and minorities who refuse to identify themselves with the dominant community or nation, such as Korean residents in Japan. But this is a universal problem that every democratic community faces in some way.

Concerning the second point, that Asian countries need democracy in order to build and maintain national community, Daniel A. Bell addresses the fact

---

64. See Saito Makoto, "Amerika kakumei no haikei toshiteno daikakusei [The Great Awakening as a Background of the American Revolution]," *Nihon Gakushiin Kiyo* [Transactions of the Japan Academy] vol. 51, no. 2 (1997), pp. 31–134, 142–4.

65. See Tocqueville, *Democracy in America*, pp. 41–3, 246–61, 290–4.

66. See Inoue Tatsuo, "Tennosei wo Tou shikaku: minshushugi no genkai to liberalizumu [What Is Wrong with the Emperor System? Liberalism and the Limits of Democracy]," in Inoue, Nawata yoshihiko and katsuragi takao, *Kyosei eno Boken* [Adventure for Conviviality] (Tokyo: Mainichi Shinbunsha, 1992), pp. 37–121.

that the government of Singapore, one of the most confident in advocating Asian values, is concerned about "Singaporeans feeling little attachment to the country and its people" and about "the gap between the rhetoric of communitarianism and the more individualistic reality."[67] For authoritarian capitalist regimes, such a gap is difficult to avoid because their capitalist economies encourage self-interested pursuits while their authoritarian politics deprive people of the democratic experience of participating in their nation's public affairs, thereby confining them to the world of private concerns. These countries need democracy to redeem their own communitarian commitments.

Finally, the liberal component of liberal democracy is individualistic in that it emphasizes the importance of individual rights, which often compete with the collective goals of national and subnational communities, and protects individuals from the social tyranny latent in communal cohesion and from the arbitrary exercise of state power. The communitarian argument I developed earlier for democratization in Asia should not be understood to exclude this liberal concept of individual rights. Daniel A. Bell and other scholars hold that illiberal democracy, meaning a nonneutral (moralistically interfering), technocratic, and managed democracy, will be the model for political change in Pacific Asia.[68] I would argue that if this model excludes the establishment of individual rights in this region, then it is not adequate.

I am somewhat skeptical of the illiberal democratic model's predictive power. For the ruling elite sticking to their power, undemocratic liberalism is easier to swallow than illiberal democracy. Liberalization will bind their hands, but democratization may cut off their heads. Even the managed democracy will become sooner or later unmanageable and fell down the initial managers. This is evidenced by the recent political developments in the Republic of Korea.

So the authoritarian rulers are more likely to accept liberalization than democratization as a political concession for canalizing increasing popular discontents and allaying foreign investors' anxiety. I guess, for example, this will be the way China will go in the foreseeable future.

The more fundamental issue, however, is whether individual rights are morally acceptable to the Asian people, in light of their unique aspirations and dilemmas. I think the answer is yes. We have seen that Asian countries have their own share of individualist–communitarian tensions, and individ-

67. See Daniel A. Bell, "Democracy in Confucian Societies: The Challenge of Justification," in Daniel A. Bell, David Brown, Kanishka Jayasuriya, and David M. Jones, *Towards Illiberal Democracy in Pacific Asia* (New York: St. Martin's Press, 1995), p. 39.
68. See Bell, Brown, Kanishka, and Jones, *Towards Illiberal Democracy in Pacific Asia,* pp. 163–7.

ual rights would naturally be acceptable to people who have individualist tendencies, but they also are for people with communitarian aspirations.

Elsewhere I have argued, with reference to the communitarian dilemmas of contemporary Japanese society, that individual rights are necessary for the enjoyment of a rich and mature form of communality.[69] The same individual belongs to different spheres of communality: family, friends, neighborhood, workplace, religious community, local and national communities, and so on. Conflicts occur, therefore, not just between individual freedom and communal responsibility but also between different communal responsibilities. If we give too much of ourselves to one communal sphere, then we neglect our responsibilities for other spheres. Such closed communality erodes social maturity and has haunted contemporary Japan in various forms. The most banal form is workers' devotion to the firm as an identity-constituting community that involves not only self-sacrifice but also neglect of the family and escape from civic responsibilities. The most bizarre form is the fanatic cult groups that completely absorb members' personalities and make them turn their backs on the outer society – for example, Aum Shinrikyo, the cult that recently committed acts of terrorism and murderous purges.

People with communitarian aspirations need individual rights to escape from the pitfall of anticommunality, rather than to enjoy unlimited freedom of the unencumbered self. Individual rights entitle them to exercise a veto over the demands of one communal sphere and to reserve their moral energy for other spheres that are also essential to their personal development. In other words, individual rights enable one to strike the right balance between competing communal responsibilities and to cultivate a more inclusive and mature form of communality.

Here I want to make a related point about the internal connection between individual rights and communality. Many scholars argue that individual rights are inseparable from the confrontational mode of dispute resolution peculiar to Western litigious culture and so are inapplicable to Asian culture, which prefers a consensual mode of dispute resolution.[70] This argument is coterminous with the individualist West versus communitarian Asia

---

69. See Inoue, "The Poverty of Rights-Blind Communality."

70. Onuma presents a qualified version of this theme to argue for the necessity of developing alternatives to human rights (Onuma, "In Quest of Intercivilizational Human Rights," p. 13). The Bangkok Declaration demands that "the promotion of human rights should be encouraged by cooperation and consensus, and not through confrontation and the imposition of incompatible values" (Davis, ed., *Human Rights and Chinese Values,* p. 205). Kawashima Takeyoshi was an influential source of the idea that the consensual mode of dispute resolution prevalent in Japan indicates a lack of rights consciousness, although his aim was to reconstruct Japanese culture rather than to reject the concept of rights (Kawashima Takeyoshi, *Nihonjin no hoishiki* [The Legal Consciousness of the Japanese] (Tokyo: Iwanami Shoten, 1967)).

dichotomy and is subject to the same critique developed earlier in this chapter. Tension between the two modes of dispute resolution runs not between the West and Asia but within each region.[71] Beyond this point, I want to emphasize the close connection between individual rights and consensus.

The veto power conferred by individual rights limits the degree of legitimate coercion imposed upon individuals, so there is a logical connection between individual rights and consensus,[72] to which systems for judicial remedy give substance. Given the unequal distribution of socioeconomic power, the consensual mode of dispute resolution disguises virtual coercion in the name of consensus. Judicial implementation of individual rights protects individuals against this coercion by ensuring that cases are adjudicated by independent and neutral judges following the fair procedures. It gives the weaker individual a state-sponsored negotiating tool and so reinforces his or her bargaining power as a prerequisite for conflict resolution to be truly consensual. Lacking effective access to a "confrontational" judicial remedy, to which individuals can resort when a reasonable consensus cannot be achieved through negotiation, "consensual" dispute resolution will easily turn into coercion and exploitation of those in a weaker bargaining position. Accordingly, if people who profess an "Asian communal virtue of harmonization through mutual concession" really want to cultivate this virtue, if they do not want it to become debased as a deceptive catchword concealing coercion and exploitation, then they should secure the judicial implementation of individual rights. Existing judicial institutions admittedly have many defects – for example, delays in judgment, high costs and risk factors, and asymmetries in legal knowledge and other resources between parties. That institutions are defective is not a reason to deny the importance of judicial remedy, but rather is an urgent reason to carry out institutional reforms to ensure people's access to effective judicial remedy.

To conclude, individualism is not alien to Asia, but it is not only individualist Asians who need liberal democracy. Communitarian Asians also need individual rights and democratic political institutions if they are sincerely committed to their communitarian aspirations. Liberal democracy is not exclusively based on individualism or on communitarianism; it rather combines these two competing perspectives so as to make the tension between them productive. There are neither pure individualists nor pure communitarians in the West or in Asia. The two perspectives create conflicts within

71. For a development of this point, see Oki Masao, *Nihonjin no hokannen: seiyoteki hokannen tono hikaku* [The Japanese Notion of Law: Comparison with the Western Concept of Law] (Tokyo: The University of Tokyo Press, 1983).

72. Ronald Dworkin has clarified this point to show that Rawlsian contractarianism presupposes a rights-based theory as its deep theory. See Dworkin, *Taking Rights Seriously* (Cambridge, MA: Harvard University Press, 1977), pp. 168–77.

each of us: The enterprise of liberal democracy has so much the more univer-sal significance.

CONCLUSION

In this chapter, I have shown the inauthenticity of the Asian values discourse and criticized its underlying dichotomies, and I have argued that Asia has contextual and endogenous reasons to develop liberal democracy. Let me con-clude by making two remarks about how Asian voices can contribute to the unfinished project of liberal democracy.

First, although both Asian and Western publics are not free from the spell of Orientalism, Asians might be said to be generally in a better position to break it, because it is easier for the targets of stereotypes to destroy it than for its perpetrators. By breaking this spell, Asian countries can communicate that the West can be no more complacent about its own record in developing liberal democracy than Asia can be contemptuous of this ideal. This should clear the way for a sincere critical dialogue and a sympathetic understanding between them concerning the follies, failures, difficulties, and aspirations that they share.

Second, Asian conditions challenge liberal democracy to complete two fundamental tasks: to identify a reasonable and fair common basis of legiti-macy for divided societies without giving up the commitment to basic human rights, and to enrich the concepts of individual rights and democracy so as to accommodate individualist–communitarian tensions in a principled way. I have tried to suggest some promising approaches to these issues but am far from solving them conclusively. However, I hope I have shown that conditions in Asia demand a resolution to these questions, and that it is espe-cially in these problem areas that Asian voices can be expected to contribute to the unfinished project of liberal democracy.

CHAPTER 2

HUMAN RIGHTS AND ASIAN VALUES: A DEFENSE OF "WESTERN" UNIVERSALISM

JACK DONNELLY*

I came to the collective project that led to this book not, obviously, as an Asian, nor even as a specialist on Asian politics or society. Rather, I am an American who has spent most of his academic career studying the theory of human rights and international human rights practices. Having long been interested in questions of cultural relativism,[1] I eagerly accepted the opportunity to address recent arguments advocating a distinctive "Asian" approach to human rights.

That I largely reject these Asian arguments is a sign not of disrespect but of disagreement. I may be incorrect in arguing that international human rights standards can and should be applied directly and pretty much in their entirety to the countries of contemporary Asia. I do believe, though, that I have given appropriately careful and detailed scrutiny to Asian arguments to the contrary. My tone may be exceedingly harsh to Asian ears – although the statements of Malaysia's Prime Minister Mahathir Bin Mohamad certainly suggest that combative public rhetoric is not foreign to the region, but I believe that the important substantive issues raised by, and the passion behind, many recent Asian arguments deserves an equally strong and impassioned reply from those who would defend the universal application of international human rights standards.

* I thank Joanne R. Bauer, Daniel A. Bell, Rhoda Howard, and Dorothy Solinger for their helpful comments on an earlier draft. And I thank the participants in the Hakone and Bangkok meetings leading up to this book – especially Daniel A. Bell, Joseph Chan, Jomo K. S., and Chandra Muzaffar – for valuable conversations and insights.
1. See Jack Donnelly, *Universal Human Rights in Theory and Practice* (Ithaca: Cornell University Press, 1989), chapters 3–8.

THE CONCEPT OF HUMAN RIGHTS

Human rights[2] are, if we take the term literally, the rights that one has simply because one is human. This deceptively simple notion has profound implications.

"Right" in English has two principal (moral and political) senses: "rectitude" and "entitlement." In the most general sense of rectitude, we speak of something *being* the right thing to do, indicating conformity with a standard of action. Entitlement is a narrower sense of "right." When one *has* a right, she is entitled to something and therefore armed with claims that have a special force. The focus is on the relationship between right-holder and duty-bearer, rather than duty-bearer and standard of rectitude.

If Anne has a right to *x* with respect to Bob, it is not simply desirable, good, or even merely right that Anne enjoy *x*. She is *entitled* to it. Should Bob fail to discharge his obligations, beyond acting improperly and harming Anne he violates her rights. This makes him subject to special claims and sanctions that she controls.

Anne is not a mere beneficiary of Bob's obligation. She is actively in charge of the relationship, as suggested by the language of "exercising" rights. Anne may assert her right to *x* in order to try to assure that Bob discharges his obligation. If he fails to do so, she may press further claims against Bob (or excuse him), largely at her own discretion. Beyond benefiting their holders, rights empower them.

To claim that there are human rights is to claim that all human beings, simply because they are human, have rights in this sense. Such rights are universal, held by all human beings. They are equal: One is or is not human, and thus has or does not have (the same) human rights, equally. And they are inalienable: One can no more lose these rights than one can stop being a human being, no matter how inhuman the treatment one may be forced to endure.

Against whom are such rights held and exercised? Conceived as rights in rem – that is, rights to particular things that hold against all possible duty bearers – every person and group would have human rights obligations to every human being. Although logically plausible, and in some ways morally attractive, this has not been the standard interpretation. Throughout their history, human rights have been seen to hold primarily against the state and society of which one is a member. Human rights require the state to provide certain protections, goods, services, and opportunities to every citizen.[3]

---

2. This section draws heavily on the second chapter of Donnelly, *Universal Human Rights in Theory and Practice.*
3. See Jack Donnelly, "The Social Construction of International Human Rights," in Timothy Dunne and Nicholas Wheeler, eds., *Human Rights in Global Politics* (Cambridge: Cambridge University Press, 1998).

In what follows, I take this understanding of human rights as given, not because I endorse it (although I do) but because it is the standard sense of "human rights" in contemporary international discussions. Asian and other critics are certainly correct to note that this understanding is not morally and politically neutral, but it is the dominant conception in contemporary international society. The issue, of course, is whether it is justifiable or desirable to apply universal standards based on this understanding of human rights to the countries of contemporary Asia.

A (VERY) BRIEF HISTORY OF HUMAN RIGHTS

The idea that all human beings, simply because they are human, have inalienable political rights was foreign to all major premodern societies. This section focuses on the West. The following section will consider traditional Asian societies.

One searches in vain for human rights in (Western) classical and medieval political theory or practice. For example, the Greeks distinguished between Hellenes and barbarians (non-Greeks), whom they considered congenitally inferior. The Romans recognized rights based on birth, citizenship, and achievement, not mere humanity, and in the millennium following the fall of Rome, most Christian political theorists sharply distinguished the ways society ought to treat believers and nonbelievers. Furthermore, the equality of all believers did not extend to political equality.

In the premodern West, rulers were obliged to further the common good. This duty, however, arose from divine commandment, natural law, tradition, or contingent political arrangements. It did not rest on the rights (entitlement) of all human beings to be ruled justly. In a well-ordered society, the people would benefit from the political obligations of their rulers, but they had no (natural or human) rights that could be exercised against unjust rulers. The reigning idea was natural right (in the sense of rectitude) not natural rights (entitlement).[4]

Natural or human rights entered the mainstream of Western political theory and practice in the seventeenth century. John Locke's *Second Treatise of Government* (1688) is conventionally, and with some justification, seen as the first fully developed natural rights theory consistent with later human rights ideas.[5] In addition to natural law injunctions to rule justly, Locke saw rulers as bound by the natural rights of their citizens to life, liberty, and estates.

4. For an extended argument to this conclusion in the case of Aquinas, see Jack Donnelly, "Natural Law and Right in Aquinas' Political Thought," *Western Political Quarterly* vol. 33 (December 1980).
5. See Richard Tuck, *Natural Rights Theories* (Cambridge: Cambridge University Press, 1979); and Donnelly, *Universal Human Rights in Theory and Practice*, chapter 5.

Government thus can be considered legitimate insofar as it furthers the effective enjoyment of the human rights of its citizens. And citizens are entitled to such a government. They hold rights against the state and society – in extreme cases, even a right to revolution.

These ideas first emerged in early modern Europe in response to the social disruptions of modernity. Political and economic centralization, industrialization, and the growing penetration of the market created (relatively) autonomous individuals and families, who were left (relatively) alone to face the power of ever more intrusive states and the grueling indignities of free-market capitalism. Individual natural rights were their most enduring response.[6]

These same social forces also led to the rise of the middle classes, who found in natural rights ideas powerful arguments against aristocratic privilege. But the close connection between the rising bourgeoisie and natural rights arguments gave most seventeenth-, eighteenth-, and even nineteenth-century accounts a distinctive bias. For example, despite the apparent universalism of natural rights, Locke sought to protect only the rights of propertied European males. He did not see women, "savages," servants, and wage laborers as right-holders.

Once the claim of equal and inalienable rights held by all had been advanced, however, the burden of proof shifted to those who would deny these rights to other members of the species *Homo sapiens*. Privilege could be defended by appeals to racial superiority, the natural rational infirmities of women, or superior acquired virtue. It was protected through force. But dominant elites found it increasingly difficult to evade the egalitarian logic of human rights.

Many of the great political struggles of the past two centuries have revolved around expanding the recognized subjects of human rights. For example, efforts to extend the right to vote beyond a small propertied elite provoked intense controversy in most European countries in the nineteenth century. The rights of working men led to often violent political conflict in nineteenth- and early twentieth-century Europe and North America. The rights of colonized peoples were a major global political issue during the 1950s, 1960s, and 1970s. Struggles to eliminate discrimination based on race and gender have been prominent in many countries over the past thirty years.

The essence of the argument of each dispossessed group was that we, no less than you, are human beings and as such are entitled to the same basic

---

6. Compare Rhoda E. Howard, *Human Rights and the Search for Community* (Boulder, CO: Westview Press, 1995), chapters 1, 2, and 5.

rights. And each group has used the rights they did enjoy to press for legal recognition of human rights being denied them. For example, workers used their votes, along with what freedom of the press and freedom of association were allowed them, to press for eliminating legal discrimination based on wealth or property. They also demanded new rights that would bring true liberty, equality, and security to working men (and later women), initiating the process that led to today's welfare-state societies. Racial, ethnic, and religious minorities, women, and peoples suffering under colonial domination have likewise used the rights that were allowed them to press for full participation as equal members of society and for legal and political recognition of their special needs, interests, and rights.

Human rights, however, entered international relations quite late. For example, they are not mentioned in the Covenant of the League of Nations. Only in the immediate aftermath of World War II did human rights enter the mainstream of international relations, beginning with their prominent inclusion in the Preamble and Article 1 of the United Nations Charter.

The most notable result of this change in attitude was the adoption by the United Nations General Assembly of the Universal Declaration of Human Rights on December 10, 1948, supplemented by the 1966 International Human Rights Covenants. The rights specified in these documents, which are often referred to collectively as the International Bill of Human Rights, are summarized in Table 2.1.

Today these norms are accepted, at least in word, by nearly all states. Furthermore, human rights have become a regular subject on multilateral and bilateral international agendas. Recent Asian arguments challenging the universality of these norms represent the most prominent contemporary attack on what for the last two decades most states and human rights activists have taken to be authoritative international standards.

TRADITIONAL ASIA AND HUMAN RIGHTS

"The protection of human rights is an integral part" of the traditions of Asian societies.[7] "All the countries of the region would agree that 'human rights' as a concept existed in their tradition."[8] "The idea of human rights developed very early in China."[9] In China, "human rights ideas appeared as

---

7. See Anwar Ibrahim, Luncheon Address (unpublished, delivered at JUST International Conference, Rethinking Human Rights, Kuala Lumpur, 1994), p. 2.
8. See Radhika Coomaraswamy, "Human Rights Research and Education: An Asian Perspective," in UNESCO, *International Congress on the Teaching of Human Rights: Working Documents and Recommendations* (Paris: UNESCO, 1980), p. 224.
9. Chung-Sho Lo, "Human Rights in the Chinese Tradition," in UNESCO, *Human Rights: Comments and Interpretations* (New York: Columbia University Press, 1949), p. 186.

TABLE 2.1 Internationally Recognized Human Rights

The International Bill of Human Rights recognizes the rights to:

- Equality of rights without discrimination (D1, D2, E2, E3, C2, C3)
- Life (D3, C6)
- Liberty and security of person (D3, C9)
- Protection against slavery (D4, C8)
- Protection against torture and cruel and inhuman punishment (D5, C7)
- Recognition as a person before the law (D6, C16)
- Equal protection of the law (D7, C14, C26)
- Access to legal remedies for rights violations (D8, C2)
- Protection against arbitrary arrest or detention (D9, C9)
- Hearing before an independent and impartial judiciary (D10, C14)
- Presumption of innocence (D11, C14)
- Protection against ex post facto laws (D11, C15)
- Protection of privacy, family, and home (D12, C17)
- Freedom of movement and residence (D13, C12)
- Seek asylum from persecution (D14)
- Nationality (D15)
- Marry and found a family (D16, E10, C23)
- Own property (D17)
- Freedom of thought, conscience, and religion (D18, C18)
- Freedom of opinion, expression, and the press (D19, C19)
- Freedom of assembly and association (D20, C21, C22)
- Political participation (D21, C25)
- Social security (D22, E9)
- Work, under favorable conditions (D23, E6, E7)
- Free trade unions (D23, E8, C22)
- Rest and leisure (D24, E7)
- Food, clothing, and housing (D25, E11)
- Health care and social services (D25, E12)
- Special protections for children (D25, E10, C24)
- Education (D26, E13, E14)
- Participation in cultural life (D27, E15)
- A social and international order needed to realize rights (D28)
- Self-determination (E1, C1)
- Humane treatment when detained or imprisoned (C10)
- Protection against debtor's prison (C11)
- Protection against arbitrary expulsion of aliens (C13)
- Protection against advocacy of racial or religious hatred (C20)
- Protection of minority culture (C27)

Note: This list includes all rights that are enumerated in two of the three documents of the International Bill of Human Rights or have a full article in one document. The source of each right is indicated in parentheses, by document and article number. D = Universal Declaration of Human Rights. E = International Covenant on Economic, Social, and Cultural Rights. C = International Covenant on Civil and Political Rights.

early as 2,000 years ago."[10] Such claims, I will argue, confuse human rights with human dignity or well-being,[11] or with the enjoyment of goods, services, and opportunities that in the contemporary world are recognized as human rights. Human rights were as foreign to traditional Asian societies as they were to their Western counterparts. For convenience, I will focus here on traditional China.[12] Consider the following representative argument.

> Human rights under the traditional Chinese political culture were conceived to be part of a larger body of morally prescribed norms of collective human conduct. . . . The Confucian code of ethics recognized each individual's right to personal dignity and worth, but this right was "not considered innate within each human soul as in the West, but had to be acquired" by his living up to the code.[13]

This right clearly is not a *human* right. It had to be earned, and could be lost. The ground of the right was not the fact that one was a human being. The dignity and worth in question are not seen to be inherent in the person.

"In a broad sense, the concept of human rights concerns the relationship between the individual and the state; it involves the status, claims, and duties of the former in the jurisdiction of the latter. As such, it is a subject as old as politics, and every nation has to grapple with it."[14] However, not all institutionalized relationships between individuals and the state are governed by, related to, or even consistent with human rights. What the state owes to those it rules is indeed a perennial question of politics. Human rights, however, provide but one answer. Divine right monarchy offers another. The dictatorship of the proletariat, the principle of utility, aristocracy, theocracy, democracy, and plutocracy are still different answers.

The traditional Chinese theory of the Mandate of Heaven viewed political power as a heavenly grant to assure harmony, order, and prosperity. Maintaining this mandate was contingent on the ruler's proper discharge of his office. If he systematically failed to carry out his obligations, Confucian civil servants, as the authorized representatives of society, were obliged to remon-

10. See Han Yanlong, "Legal Protection of Human Rights in China," in Peter R. Baehr, Fried van Hoof, Liu Nanlai, Tao Zhengua, and Jacqueline Smith, eds., *Human Rights: Chinese and Dutch Perspectives* (The Hague: Martinus Nijhoff, 1996), p. 93.
11. See Donnelly, *Universal Human Rights in Theory and Practice,* chapters 3 and 4.
12. I am well aware of the dangers of a simplified, static vision of any long established social and political tradition, let alone one as ancient as China's. But as those against whom I am arguing advance an even more abstracted vision of "Asia" – compare Inoue's useful discussion of "Orientalism" in Chapter 1 – I hope that I can be excused this gross oversimplification. For parallel arguments dealing with Islam and with Hindu India, see Donnelly, *Universal Human Rights in Theory and Practice,* pp. 50–3, 126ff.
13. See Tai Hung-Chao, "Human Rights in Taiwan: Convergence of Two Political Cultures?" in James C. Hsiung, ed., *Human Rights in an East Asian Perspective* (New York: Paragon House Publishers, 1985), p. 88. Tai Hung-Chao is quoting John King Fairbank, *The United States and China,* 3rd ed. (Cambridge, MA: Harvard University Press, 1972), p. 119.
14. See Tai Hung-Chao, "Human Rights in Taiwan," p. 79.

strate with the ruler, and if the ruler proved recalcitrant and unusually vicious, popular resistance was authorized. In fact, widespread resistance was evidence that the ruler had lost his mandate.

These limitations, however, did not rest on the inalienable rights of the Emperor's subjects. Limited government in general should not be confused with government limited by the human rights of its citizens, and irregular political participation in cases of extreme tyranny should not be confused with a human right to political participation.

Individuals may have held rights as members of families, villages, and other groups. But the purpose of political rights "was not to protect the individual against the state but to enable the individual to function more effectively to strengthen the state."[15] Such rights may be of great value and importance. They are not, however, human rights, as that term is conventionally used today.

Many commentators seem uncomfortable with this fact. For example, Lo Chung-Sho notes that "there was no open declaration of human rights in China, either by individual thinkers or by political constitutions, until this concept was introduced from the West. In fact, the early translators of Western political thought found it difficult to arrive at a Chinese equivalent for the term 'rights'."[16] Personal and political ethics stressed duty and a transcendental harmony that was to be realized through practices centered on notions such as filial piety, not personal rights. "East Asian societies as a whole preoccupied themselves not with the rights of individuals but with their duties."[17]

However, Lo continues, "this of course does not mean that the Chinese never claimed human rights or enjoyed the basic rights of man."[18] How they managed to claim human rights without the language to make such claims certainly is obscure. It is not surprising then that Lo's examples show only a divinely imposed duty of the ruler to govern for the common good, not rights of the people. This is not a "different approach to human rights,"[19] it is an approach to human dignity or well-being that does not rely on human rights.

"Different civilizations or societies have different conceptions of human wellbeing. Hence, they have a different attitude toward human rights issues."[20]

---

15. See Andrew J. Nathan, "Sources of Chinese Rights Thinking," in R. Randle Edwards, Louis Henkin, and Andrew J. Nathan, *Human Rights in Contemporary China* (New York: Columbia University Press, 1986), p. 148.
16. See Chung-Sho Lo, "Human Rights in the Chinese Tradition," p. 186.
17. See Lee Manwoo, "North Korea and the Western Notion of Human Rights," in Hsiung, ed., *Human Rights in an East Asian Perspective*, pp. 132–3.
18. See Chung-Sho Lo, "Human Rights in the Chinese Tradition," p. 186.
19. Chung-Sho Lo, "Human Rights in the Chinese Tradition," p. 188.
20. See Lee Manwoo, "North Korea and the Western Notion of Human Rights," p. 131.

Even this is significantly misleading. Unless societies possess a concept of human rights they are unlikely to have *any* attitude toward human rights. They may have (similar or different) attitudes toward issues that *we* consider in terms of human rights. To fail to respect this important conceptual distinction is not to show cultural sensitivity, respect, or tolerance, but rather to impose an alien human rights framework.

Consider also James Hsiung's effort "to develop a definition of human rights that is compatible with a country's cultural legacy."[21] There is no obvious reason why this should be possible, let alone desirable. Some cultural legacies are incompatible with any plausible idea of human rights. For example, racism, sexism, and anti-Semitism were for many centuries – many would argue still are – deeply entrenched elements of the cultural and political legacy of the West. One of our principal human rights achievements has been precisely to challenge, in theory and in practice, this legacy and to help to create another.

The equal and inalienable rights of all people, simply because they are human – human rights – is a distinctive principle of social and political organization. Human rights are compatible with only a limited range of practices. They are not, and should not be, neutral with respect to political forms or cultural traditions.

The International Bill of Human Rights rests on an implicit model of a liberal democratic (or social democratic) welfare state.[22] The legitimate state, as envisioned by internationally recognized human rights norms, is democratic: Political authority arises from the sovereignty of the people. It is liberal: The state is seen as an institution to establish the conditions for the effective realization of the rights of its citizens. It is a welfare state: Recognized economic and social rights extend well beyond the libertarian right to property. And all three elements are rooted in the overriding and irreducible moral equality of all members of society and the political equality and autonomy of all citizens.

Whether this late-twentieth-century human rights approach is best for every contemporary society is a matter of legitimate debate, but unless the distinctive nature of that approach is recognized, that debate will be, at best, vacuous or misguided.

The list of internationally recognized human rights certainly includes many values sought by both Western and Asian societies for centuries, but even where "the same" values are pursued, their grounds and the means to

21. James C. Hsiung, "Human Rights in an East Asian Perspective," in Hsiung, ed., *Human Rights in an East Asian Perspective*, p. 20.
22. Compare Rhoda E. Howard and Jack Donnelly, "Human Rights, Human Dignity, and Political Regimes," *American Political Science Review* vol. 80 (September 1986).

realize them may differ radically. Violations of rights are a special kind of injustice, with a distinctive force and remedial logic. For example, protection against arbitrary execution is today an internationally recognized human right, but the duty of a ruler not to execute subjects arbitrarily may have no connection to a right of the ruled. It may rest, for example, on a divine injunction to the ruler. When subjects lack a right, they are protected differently. Furthermore, whether the right is a legal right, contingently granted by the state, or a human right, independent of the state and its interests, dramatically alters the relationship between states and subjects.

To avoid misunderstanding, I want to emphasize that the "Western" origins of human rights ideas and practices is a simple historical fact. It is not a matter for praise (or blame). Human rights initially emerged – were created or "discovered" – in Europe not because of superior Western virtue or insight but because, for better or worse, modern states and capitalism first appeared there. This history does not make these rights any more irrelevantly "Western" than the origins and initial spread of both Newtonian and quantum physics makes them "Western" physics inapplicable to Asia. Whatever applicability – or inapplicability – internationally recognized human rights have is independent of their place of origin.

Historical contingency and cultural diversity are facts, not answers to the problems of cross-cultural analysis and judgment. Recognizing these differences, we need to ask whether internationally recognized human rights, "Asian traditions," or any other set of practices "make sense" today. That will be my focus in the remainder of this chapter.

The thrust of my argument will be that contemporary Asian individuals, families, and societies face the same threats from modern markets and states that Western societies do, and therefore need the same protections of human rights. In principle, Asians, Africans, or Latin Americans – or, for that matter, Europeans or North Americans – may be able to devise effective alternatives. In practice, however, I do not see "soft" authoritarianism, party-state dictatorship, or paternalism, the principal Asian alternatives advanced in recent debates, as involving morally defensible political regimes, let alone plausible conceptions of human rights.

I hasten to add that my argument does not imply cultural suicide, or even sacrifice. In fact, in the last section of this chapter I stress the space available for distinctively Asian implementations of internationally recognized human rights. But this space is within a general framework of (relatively) "universal" rights, laid out in the Universal Declaration and other authoritative international human rights instruments, that respond to the global threats posed to human dignity by powerful and ever more intrusive modern states and increasingly difficult to control national, regional, and global markets.

SOVEREIGNTY AND INTERNATIONAL HUMAN RIGHTS

One standard argument against the application of international human rights standards rests on sovereignty.[23] Chinese officials and scholars in particular have insisted that "sovereignty is the foundation and basic guarantee of human rights,"[24] the implication being that "the rights of each country to formulate its own policies on human rights protection in light of its own conditions should . . . be respected and guaranteed."[25] Taken at face value, this amounts to a claim that whatever a country does with respect to human rights is its business and its business alone. Rather than a defensible conception of human rights, this would subordinate human rights to the competing rights and values of sovereignty.

The record of Western (and Japanese) colonial rule in Asia (and elsewhere) certainly suggests that sovereignty is a necessary condition for a rights-protective regime, but it is by no means a sufficient condition. Sovereignty removes some international impediments to the implementation of internationally recognized human rights. It does little to address issues of *internal* human rights protection and violation. Far from being a guarantee of human rights, sovereignty is typically the mantle behind which rights-abusive regimes hide when faced with international human rights criticism.

Mahathir Mohamad recently complained that "it would seem that Asians have no right to define and practice their own set of values about human rights."[26] This is to a considerable extent true, not just for Asians, but for all groups of countries. Authoritative international human rights norms govern internationally defensible definitions of human rights, especially in countries that are parties to the Covenants and other international human rights instruments.

The Bangkok Declaration on Human Rights, adopted at the Asia and

---

23. For a complementary, and more deeply theoretical, discussion of sovereignty and human rights, see Chapter 1 in this volume. For an unusually open attempt by a Chinese scholar to address the competing claims of sovereignty and human rights, see Xin Chunying, "Can the Pluralistic World Have a Unified Concept of Human Rights?" in Baehr, van Hoof, Nanlai, Zhengua, and Smith, eds., *Human Rights: Chinese and Dutch Perspectives,* pp. 54–6.

24. See Xie Bohua and Niu Lihua, "Review and Comments on the Issue of Human Rights" (unpublished paper presented at JUST International Conference, "Rethinking Human Rights," Kuala Lumpur, 1994), p. 1; compare People's Republic of China, *Human Rights in China* (Beijing: Information Office of the State Council, 1991), pp. 57–61; and People's Republic of China, "Statement by H. E. Mr. Liu Hiaqui to the Second World Conference on Human Rights" (unpublished, Vienna, June 15, 1993), p. 4.

25. See People's Republic of China, "Statement by H. E. Mr. Liu Hiaqui to the Second World Conference on Human Rights," p. 5; compare statement by the representative from Indonesia to the Second World Conference on Human Rights" (unpublished, Vienna, June 15, 1993), p. 11; and see John F. Cooper, "Peking's Post-Tiananmen Foreign Policy: The Human Rights Factor," *Issues and Studies* vol. 30 (October 1994), p. 69.

26. Mahathir Bin Mohamad, Keynote Address (unpublished, delivered at JUST International Conference, "Rethinking Human Rights," Kuala Lumpur, 1994), p. 9.

Pacific regional preparatory meeting for the Vienna Conference, reiterates the indisputable international legal right of all countries "to determine their political system," but there is also a substantial body of international human rights law. The authority of the Universal Declaration and the Covenants is reaffirmed by both the Bangkok Declaration and the Vienna Final Document, and they severely restrict the range of internationally defensible definitions of human rights.

"Imposing the human rights standard of one's own country or region on other countries or regions is an infringement upon other countries' sovereignty and interference into other countries' internal affairs."[27] The standards being "imposed" on China, however, are simply those of the Universal Declaration of Human Rights. These are not distinctively Western, as even many critics of the West emphasize. "All the countries of the region are party to the U.N. Charter. None has rejected the Universal Declaration."[28]

"They threaten sanctions, withdrawal of aid, stoppage of loans, economic and trade boycotts and actual military strikes against those they accuse of violating human rights."[29] Military strikes by one state in response to human rights violations in another would almost certainly violate sovereignty and territorial integrity, but Mahathir conveniently neglects to mention even a single example of such (exceedingly rare) acts. In fact, he criticizes the West for *failing* to use force on behalf of the Iraqi Kurds and Bosnian Muslims,[30] and the other activities of which he complains are entirely legitimate.

Why shouldn't a country withdraw aid if it objects to a recipient's human rights practices? Why must it loan money to tyrants? Were a state or group of states to claim "a right to impose their system of Government," or "[arrogate] to themselves the right to intervene anywhere where human rights are violated,"[31] they would indeed be guilty of serious international offenses. But it is completely legitimate for a country to use its financial and political resources on behalf of internationally recognized human rights.

Human rights are a legitimate matter of international concern. Sovereignty requires only that states refrain from the threat or use of force in trying to influence the human rights practices of other states. Short of force, states are free to use most ordinary means of foreign policy on behalf of internationally recognized human rights.

27. See Xie Bohua and Niu Lihua, "Review and Comments on the Issue of Human Rights," p. 1. Compare People's Republic of China, *Human Rights in China*, p. 61.
28. See Bilahari Kausikan, "Asia's Different Standard," *Foreign Policy* vol. 92 (1993), p. 25.
29. See Mahathir Bin Mohamad, "Rethinking Human Rights," Keynote Address, p. 7.
30. Mahathir Bin Mohamad, "Rethinking Human Rights," Keynote Address, pp. 5, 6, and 8.
31. Mahathir Bin Mohamad, "Rethinking Human Rights," Keynote Address, pp. 4 and 8.

THE DEMANDS OF DEVELOPMENT

In Asia as elsewhere, it is often argued that systematic infringements of internationally recognized human rights are necessary, and thus justifiable or even desirable, to achieve rapid economic development. Two particular rights-development trade-offs are commonly advanced. What I have called the liberty trade-off holds that civil and political rights introduce so many inefficiencies in government that they must be systematically infringed by a state seeking rapid economic development. What we can call the equity trade-off sacrifices economic and social, not civil and political, rights. The argument is that immediate satisfaction of basic needs for all or the achievement of a relatively egalitarian income distribution excessively retards the pace and progress of development. Elsewhere, I have argued at length against such blanket trade-offs.[32] Here I have space only to raise questions about their plausibility and relevance to cross-cultural discussions of human rights.[33]

We can begin by noting that there is nothing distinctively Asian to such arguments. The liberty trade-off has been a mainstay of developmental dictatorships of all stripes. The equity trade-off, a staple of many capitalist development strategies, is part of the new orthodoxy preached (and imposed) by the International Monetary Fund and other (Western-dominated) international financial institutions. Rather than rely on culturally relative Asian values, these trade-offs appeal to a universal developmental imperative that overrides both culture and human rights.

Furthermore, these trade-off arguments justify only temporary human rights infringements. It is perhaps true that "when poverty and lack of adequate food are commonplace and people's basic needs are not guaranteed, priority should be given to economic development."[34] But this is at best a short-run excuse. Regimes that sacrifice either civil and political rights or economic, social, and cultural rights to development do not represent an inherently desirable form of government. Such sacrifices ought to be a matter of profound regret and discomfort. They are to be endured, in the hope of a better life for one's children, not celebrated.

Therefore, we must be especially wary of arguments for categorical sacrifices of human rights. For example, U.S.-style interest-group politics may inappropriately favor certain special interests over the general welfare or introduce unacceptable political and administrative inefficiencies, but this

---

32. Donnelly, *Universal Human Rights in Theory and Practice,* chapters 9 and 10.
33. In Chapter 3, Amartya Sen also critically evaluates arguments for subordinating human rights to "development."
34. See People's Republic of China, "Statement by H. E. Mr. Liu Hiaqui to the Second World Conference on Human Rights," p. 3.

does not justify wholesale denial of freedom of speech, assembly, and association, let alone practices such as against arbitrary arrest and detention or outlawing opposition political movements and parties.

We also need to be skeptical of the empirical basis of trade-off arguments. The equity trade-off is especially problematic in the East Asian context. Japan, Taiwan, and South Korea have achieved rapid economic growth with considerable equity. Aggressive state efforts to support equitable terms of trade and to develop human capital brought extraordinary growth without creating a wildly unequal income distribution, at the same time that basic needs satisfaction improved dramatically. And although no state has achieved sustained, rapid development at an early stage of growth under a rights-protective government, the necessity of repression, as opposed to its convenience for the wealthy and powerful, is not clear.

Many standard exercises of civil and political rights may be economically inefficient. Free, fair, and open elections may induce a government to pursue policies aimed at delivering short-term material benefits at the cost of long-term development. Freedom of association may be used by powerful social groups to further their special interests over the needs and interests of society as a whole.

The economic costs of the *denial* of civil and political rights, however, must also be considered. Officials who need not justify their performance to the electorate easily become corrupt and uncaring. A free press provides information from the population to decision makers that may mitigate the inefficiencies of bureaucracies and counterbalance the special interests of bureaucrats. "By not giving vent to the voices of dissent, wrongs cannot be made right and remedies for failures cannot be made available."[35] "The link between authoritarianism and economic failure is only too evident in many parts of Asia."[36]

The standard trade-off arguments seem to envision incorruptible and unusually effective political leaders who must be protected from the selfish or foolish desires of the populace. The reality, however, is often one of foolish and corrupt, or just plain fallible, leaders and planners. "Authoritarian rule more often than not has been used as a masquerade for kleptocracies, bureaucratic incompetence, and worst of all, for unbridled nepotism and corruption."[37]

Particular infringements of internationally recognized human rights may be justified in the pursuit of rapid economic development, but the burden of proof lies on those who would resort to the obvious prima facie evil of denying rights. Even when trade-offs are justified, governments must be forcefully

---

35. See Ibrahim, "Rethinking Human Rights" Luncheon Address, p. 4.
36. Ad Hoc Coalition, 1993.
37. Ibrahim, "Rethinking Human Rights," Luncheon Address, p. 4.

reminded that such sacrifices are no more than a tragic necessity that must be kept to an absolute minimum in number, duration, and severity.

ECONOMIC AND SOCIAL RIGHTS

"The central issue in the contemporary discourse on human rights is not so much whether it is Western or Eastern in origin but rather the balance between civil and political rights on the one hand, and societal and economic rights on the other."[38] Critics typically argue that in the West civil and political rights are overemphasized while economic, social, and cultural rights are systematically denigrated.[39]

The West may have neglected or resisted economic and social rights in the nineteenth and early twentieth centuries,[40] but that anyone looking at the welfare states of Western Europe could take such claims seriously today is, to put it bluntly, mind-boggling. Western Europe is the sole region of the world that has over the last several decades forcefully and consistently acted on the premise of the interdependence and indivisibility of all internationally recognized human rights. Even the United States – the Western country with the worst record of state action to implement internationally recognized economic and social rights – devotes considerable effort and money to social welfare programs.

Conversely, it is not clear that contemporary Asian societies give unusual emphasis to economic and social human rights. For example, many Asian governments seem willing, even anxious, to sacrifice economic and social rights to the pursuit of rapid growth. Dorothy Solinger's discussion of China's "floating people" in Chapter 12 tells a story that is sadly reminiscent of that of market-driven urban immigrants in eighteenth- and nineteenth-century Europe. Too often in Asia – as in other regions – an alleged concern for economic and social rights is in fact a concern for growth/development irrespective of its distributional/rights consequences.

A developmental perspective is aggregate and focuses on production. It is concerned with the whole of society, and only secondarily, if at all, with its individual members. Economic and social rights, by contrast, are concerned

---

38. Ibrahim, "Rethinking Human Rights," Luncheon Address, p. 2.
39. See, e.g., Kausikan, "Asia's Different Standard," p. 35. This is a common argument in cross-cultural discussions of human rights. The most cited English language version of the argument is Adamantia Pollis, "Liberal, Socialist and Third World Perspectives on Human Rights," in Peter Schwab and Adamantia Pollis, eds., *Toward a Human Rights Framework* (New York: Praeger Publishers, 1982).
40. Even then, the problem was less an underemphasis on economic rights than an exceedingly narrow list of economic rights, extending scarcely beyond the right to property. In fact, one might argue that in the United States, with its peculiar legal doctrine of freedom of contract, the real problem was an excessive emphasis on property rights – which are economic, not civil or political, rights – to the detriment of civil and political rights such as the freedom of association.

with *distributions* of goods, services, and opportunities, which must be guaranteed to every person even when pursuing the most noble social goals. Consider the example of Singaporean social welfare policy.

> It is the PAP government's policy not to provide direct funds to individuals in its "welfare" programs. Instead, much is spent on education, public housing, health care and infrastructure build-up as human capital investments to enable the individual and the nation as a whole to become economically competitive in a capitalist world. . . . For those who fall through the economic net . . . public assistance is marginal and difficult to obtain. . . . The government's position is that "helping the needy" is a moral responsibility of the community itself and not just of the state. So construed, the recipients of the moral largesse of the community are to consider themselves privileged and bear the appropriate sense of gratitude.[41]

Whatever the merits of this approach, it clearly does not emphasize economic and social human rights. A system based on "moral largesse" that sees assistance as a privilege has little to do with human rights.

Setting aside issues of comparative practice, I want to argue against calls emanating from Asia for an overriding emphasis on economic and social rights. For example, at the Vienna Conference, China argued that "the major criteria for judging the human rights situation in a developing country should be whether its policies and measures help to promote economic and social progress."[42] Such claims reflect a sadly impoverished view of human dignity. A life constantly subject to arbitrary power is one that a human being may learn to settle for, but not one to which she ought to aspire.

Jiang Zemin's argument that the "right of survival of China's population is more important that political rights"[43] may have some attractions in extraordinarily poor societies. If the denial of political rights will bring physical survival, a free people may choose survival (although even this is not entirely obvious). But to reduce human rights to a guarantee of mere survival is a perverse betrayal of any plausible conception of human dignity. A state forced to make such a choice acts under a tragic necessity. Its policies represent, at best, triage. And if after more than forty years in power, a regime must still rely on arguments of mere survival, it is hard not to conclude that the poor are being forced to suffer doubly for the poverty to which their government has condemned them.

Such judgments do not reflect Western romanticism or ethnocentrism.

41. See Beng-Huat Chua, "Australian and Asian Perceptions of Human Rights," in Ian Russell, Peter Van Ness, and Beng-Huat Chua, *Australia's Human Rights Diplomacy* (Canberra: Australian National University Press, 1992), p. 95.
42. People's Republic of China, "Statement by H. E. Mr. Liu Hiaqui to the Second World Conference on Human Rights," p. 3.
43. Quoted in Cooper, "Peking's Post-Tiananmen Foreign Policy," p. 56.

The Bangkok Declaration reaffirms "the interdependence and indivisibility of economic, social, cultural, civil and political rights, and the need to give equal emphasis to all categories of human rights." At Vienna, Korea's Minister of Foreign Affairs argued that "it is neither justifiable nor appropriate to deny some human rights in order to guarantee others." And the Ad Hoc Coalition of Asian NGO Participants at Vienna strongly rejected the argument "that the enjoyment of civil and political rights be deferred until economic development has been achieved."

Whatever the cultural differences between East and West, I am aware of no evidence that Asians value protection from arbitrary government any less than their Western counterparts or that Asians do not highly value the opportunity for families and individuals to make important choices about their life and future. "Tyranny and injustice are repugnant to civil society wherever they may occur, and to cite cultural differences or Asian values in order to deflect from ourselves criticism against human rights violations is an affront to our moral sense."[44]

INDIVIDUALS AND SOCIETY

Another cluster of arguments centers on a critique of excessive individualism in the Western practice of human rights. Asian and other Third World critics argue that Western human rights practices reflect a corrosive, hedonistic individualism that gives inadequate attention to social duties and is incompatible not only with traditional values but with any plausible conception of human dignity and decency. At the end of this chapter I will argue that international human rights norms are sufficiently broad to accommodate most Asian desires for more communitarian practices. Here I will focus on extreme communitarian arguments that amount to denials of human rights.

For example, Mahathir Mohamad argues that "governments, according to the liberal democrats, cannot in any way act against the personal wishes of the individual in society. . . . [I]ncest to them is not wrong . . . if that is what is desired by the individuals."[45] This obviously misdescribes practice in the West, where rape, murder, theft, assault, incest, and a great variety of other behaviors resting on desire are prohibited and punished. Rhoda Howard describes such arguments as examples of "The Central Park Thesis": Human rights have returned the Western world to an anomic, Hobbesian state of nature best represented by New York's Central Park at night.[46] They reflect

44. See Ibrahim, "Rethinking Human Rights," Luncheon Address, pp. 1–2.
45. Mahathir Bin Mohamad, "Rethinking Human Rights," Keynote Address, p. 6.
46. Howard, *Human Rights and the Search for Community,* p. 23.

what she aptly labels "Occidentalism" – a caricature of a static, monolithic, Western "other" – among cultural critics of the West.[47]

However, beneath this caricature lies a common misunderstanding of human rights as absolute rights. "There are no absolute rights and freedoms in the world. The individual rights and freedoms must be subjected to the requirement and provisions of the law."[48] It is true that one function of law is to delimit the range of rights, but a central function of human rights is to set limits on the state and its laws. For example, arbitrary arrest and detention are prohibited even if the law explicitly allows unlimited incommunicado detention without charges. Legally sanctioned racial discrimination is especially reprehensible, not permissible.

Many internationally recognized human rights do require the state not to interfere with the pursuit of individual desires, for example, to speak one's mind, choose and practice a religion, associate with whomever one pleases, and raise a family, but none of these rights is absolute. Freedom of religion does not extend to human sacrifice. Freedom of association does not cover conspiracy to commit ordinary crimes. Family relations are constrained by rules to protect the health and safety of children.

What is at stake here is a society's understanding of the proper balance between individual and community rights and interests.

> The view of society as an organic whole whose collective rights prevail over the individual, the idea that man exists for the state rather than vice versa and that rights, rather than having any absolute value, derive from the state, have been themes prevailing in old as well as new China. . . . The idea of the individual was not absent: but it was of an order of importance secondary to a family-based community system which differentiated between roles and abilities.[49]

To the extent that this description is correct – "man exists for the state rather than vice versa" – this Chinese conception of social order denies the very idea of human rights.

> Any emphasis on individual human rights, apart from the rights of the community in which this individual lives, is sheer nonsense. In real history, human rights for the community come first, and human rights for any individual are conditioned by a healthy social environment and appropriate social institutions.[50]

47. Howard, "Occidentalism, Human Rights, and the Obligations of Western Scholars," *Canadian Journal of African Studies* vol. 29, no. 1 (1995).
48. See Xie Bohua and Niu Lihua, "Review and Comments on the Issue of Human Rights," p. 4.
49. See Ann Kent, *Between Freedom and Subsistence: China and Human Rights* (Hong Kong: Oxford University Press, 1993), pp. 30–1.
50. See A. M. Hussein, "The Impact of Western Hegemonic Policies upon the Rights of People in West Asia and North Africa" (unpublished paper presented at JUST International Conference, "Rethinking Human Rights," Kuala Lumpur, 1994), p. 1.

This too amounts to a denial of human rights. The rights of the community, whatever priority we give to them, are not human rights (any more than the sovereignty rights of the state are human rights). Active *enjoyment* of individual human rights will be greatly fostered by a healthy social environment and supportive social institutions. But if society is the source of all individual rights, such an individual has no *human* rights.

The Chinese claim at Vienna that "individuals must put the state's rights before their own"[51] is incompatible with *any* plausible conception of human rights. An individual may often be legitimately asked, even required, to sacrifice or defer the exercise or enjoyment of her rights. But there have been many states whose rights merited little respect from individuals, and sometimes it is society that must give way to the basic rights of individuals.

"No one is entitled to put his individual right above the interest of the state, society, and others. This is the universal principle of all civilized society."[52] This is roughly equivalent to having no rights at all. And a society in which self must always be categorically subordinated to other simply cannot be considered "civilized" in the late twentieth century.

RIGHTS AND DUTIES

As we saw earlier, traditional Asian societies were structured around duties, not rights, and any rights held by individuals, families, or communities were largely dependent on the discharge of duties. Essential to any plausible conception of human rights, however, is the claim that all human beings have certain rights prior to and irrespective of their discharge of social duties. Therefore, "Western" rights and their exercises often conflict with traditional duty-based values and practices, which from a duty-oriented perspective appear wildly, even destructively, individualistic. Once more, I will focus on the incompatibility of extreme versions of such arguments with international human rights norms, leaving for the final section of this chapter more moderate arguments that suggest distinctively Asian ways to implement these rights.

"The rights and obligations of the citizens are indivisible and interrelated."[53] This commonly expressed view is either false or merely trivially true. Rights do have correlative duties. Many (but not all) duties have correlative rights, but particular rights and duties may stand in a great variety of relations to one another, and many rights are held independently of the dis-

---

51. Quoted in Cooper, "Peking's Post-Tiananmen Foreign Policy," p. 69.
52. Xie Bohua and Niu Lihua, "Review and Comments on the Issue of Human Rights," p. 4.
53. Xie Bohua and Niu Lihua, "Review and Comments on the Issue of Human Rights," p. 4.

charge of duties. Anne has a right to being repaid the ten dollars that Bob borrowed simply because he borrowed it. One has human rights simply because one is a human being.

It simply is not true that "freedom of speech entails a corresponding duty not to disseminate lies, not to incite communal and religious hatred, and generally not to undermine the moral fabric of society."[54] A right to free speech has no logical connection to an obligation not to disseminate lies. Society and the state may legitimately punish me for spreading vicious lies that harm others. Those penalties, however, rest on the rights or interests of those who I harm, not my right to free speech. If I slander someone, I do not lose my right to freedom of speech – if we conceive of it as a human right. Incitement to communal or religious hatred may be legitimately prohibited and punished, but even the most vocal hate monger still has a right to express his views on other subjects – if free speech is a human right.

Defensible limits on the exercise of a right should not be confused with duties inherent in the possession of a right. When irresponsible exercises of a recognized right threaten interests that are legitimate matters of social or political regulation, they may be legitimately prohibited. These restrictions, however, are separate from the right – unless the right in question is granted on the condition of accepting those restrictions, in which case it is not a human right.

TRADITIONAL ORDER AND HUMAN RIGHTS

Arguments against individualism and in favor of duty feed into a broader critique stressing social order and harmony. Again I will take traditional China as an illustrative reference point.

Traditional Chinese society was dominated by the pursuit of harmony (*he*) at all levels, from the cosmic to the personal.[55] The path to harmony was *li*. Although often translated as "propriety," that term, in contemporary American English at least, is far too weak to encompass *li*'s force, range, or depth. *Li* prescribes a complex set of interlocking, hierarchical social roles and relations centered on filial piety (*xiao*) and loyalty (*zhong*). Deference and mutual accommodation were the ideal. Personal ethics emphasized self-cultivation in the pursuit of *ren* (humanness), achieved by self mastery under the guidance of *li*.

This system of values and social relations is incompatible with the vision

---

54. Ibrahim, "Rethinking Human Rights," Luncheon Address, p. 5.
55. See Kent, *Between Freedom and Subsistence*, pp. 31–40; John Y. Fenton, Norvin Hein, Frank E. Reynolds, Alan L. Miller, and Niels C. Nielsen, *Religions of Asia* (New York: St. Martin's Press, 1983), chapters 14–16; Yu-Wei Hsieh, "The Family in Confucian Society," *Areopagus* (Advent, 1994), pp. 16–19.

of equal and autonomous individuals that underlies international human rights norms. In fact, the "Western" emphasis on individual rights is likely to seem little short of moral inversion. Asian critics of demands for "Western" (internationally recognized) human rights argue that they have developed alternative political ideals and practices that aim to preserve traditional values of family, community, decorum, and devotion to duty. As an absolute minimum, they are committed to avoiding the excesses of the rights-obsessed West: "guns, drugs, violent crime, vagrancy, unbecoming behavior in public – in sum, the breakdown of civil society."[56]

Such arguments can easily run to a myopic romanticism that sees none of the faults of the traditional nor any of the virtues of the modern. There is also the danger of ignoring the fluid nature of culture.[57] The most interesting arguments for an Asian third way, however, guard against such problems by advocating a selective adoption of "Western" values and practices to produce an Asian version of modernity. For example, Singapore's former prime minister Lee Kwan Yew advocates a dynamic (if cautious) melding of the indigenous and the exotic. "Let me be frank; if we did not have the good points of the West to guide us, we wouldn't have got out of our backwardness. We would have been a backward economy and a backward society. But we do not want all of the West."[58]

Consider also Chandra Muzaffar's call to move "from Western human rights to universal human dignity."[59]

> Mainstream human rights ideas . . . have contributed significantly to human civilization in at least four ways. *One,* they have endowed the individual with certain basic rights such as the right of free speech, the right of association, the right to a fair trial and so on. *Two,* they have strengthened the position of the ordinary citizen against the arbitrariness of power. *Three,* they have expanded the space and scope for individual participation in public decision-making. *Four,* they have forced the State and authority in general to be accountable to the public.[60]

Implicit in this list of contributions is a powerful critique of traditional society for inadequate attention to individual equality and autonomy. But

---

56. See Fareed Zakaria, "Culture Is Destiny: A Conversation with Lee Kuan Yew" *Foreign Affairs* vol. 73 (March/April 1994), p. 111.

57. This issue is at the heart of the debate I have had with Roger Ames, arising out of the initial version of this chapter. See Ames, "Continuing the Conversation on Chinese Human Rights" *Ethics & International Affairs* vol. 11 (1997); Donnelly, "Conversing with Straw Men While Ignoring Dictators: A Reply to Roger Ames" *Ethics & International Affairs* vol. 11 (1997).

58. Zakaria, "Culture Is Destiny," p. 125.

59. Chandra Muzaffar, "From Human Rights to Human Dignity" (unpublished paper presented at JUST International Conference, "Rethinking Human Rights," Kuala Lumpur, 1994), p. 4.

60. Muzaffar, "From Human Rights to Human Dignity," p. 1.

Muzaffar sees human rights (and democracy),[61] particularly in their characteristic Western implementations, as inadequate to achieve the broader and higher goal of human dignity.

Such arguments cannot be rejected out of hand. It is for the people of Asia, individually and collectively, to resolve these issues as they see fit. Within certain fairly broad limits, a free people is free to order its life as it sees fit. This is the fundamental implication of the rights to self-determination and political participation. Nonetheless, I am skeptical of projects for an Asian third way.

Many are politically naive. For example, Muzaffar argues that the remedy to "the crass individualism and self-centredness which both capitalism and democracy (as it is practised) tend to encourage" lies in the "much cherished ideal in all religious traditions" of "sacrificing one's own personal interests for the well-being of others." "Religion integrates the individual with society in a much more harmonious way."[62] This borders on a utopian denial of the notorious problems of linking religion and politics. Critics of the destructive unintended consequences of Western practices must confront the problems of implementing their alternative visions. To compare existing Western practices with a vague, never-yet-implemented ideal is unfair and unilluminating – as is underscored by the deviation between Western ideals and practice on which so much Asian criticism rests.

A different form of political naivete can be seen in the assumption of the continuing relevance of traditional practices in modern conditions. Is an authoritarian leader backed by the immense capabilities of the modern state really all that similar to traditional leaders? What has happened to traditional local autonomy in the face of economic and political integration in a modern nation state? How relevant to modern urban life are practices developed for rural societies with little social mobility or demographic change? Can consensual community decision making and dispute resolution through nonlegal means really work in the absence of relatively closed and close-knit face-to-face communities? What would they even look like in sprawling urban centers inhabited by strangers and migrants? These are only rhetorical questions, not arguments, but they are the sorts of questions that need to be answered before we can accept denying internationally recognized human rights in the name of traditional culture.

I am especially skeptical of such claims because most of the arguments being made about Asian differences could have been made equally well in

61. Chandra Muzaffar, "Asian Economies: Development, Democracy and Human Rights" (unpublished paper presented at a conference on "Development and Democracy" at the Southeast Asia Center, Bochum, Germany, 1994).
62. Muzaffar, "Asian Economies: Development, Democracy and Human Rights," pp. 10, 11.

eighteenth-century Europe. Although Asians need not follow the same path of development, I think it is legitimate to ask why they are likely to respond to similar conditions in very different ways.

Arguments for an Asian alternative rest on the claim that Asian peoples do not want to live in a liberal democratic welfare state. "Popular pressures against East and Southeast Asian governments may not be so much for 'human rights' or 'democracy' but for good government: effective, efficient, and honest administrations able to provide security and basic needs with good opportunities for an improved standard of living."[63] Even granting that this is true – and in fact I think this is a description of the minimum people are willing to accept or tolerate rather than that to which they aspire – I would suggest that good government is unlikely in the absence of human rights.

Even if a country is fortunate enough to get an efficient and relatively benevolent and incorruptible despot or ruling elite, I am skeptical that Asians will prove more successful than Westerners in keeping the successor generation from succumbing to corruption without reliance on human rights – especially with the immense wealth made available by economic growth. The spread of money politics throughout the region, which increasingly distances people from rulers and makes politics not merely venal but predatory, raises serious questions about the future of even minimal good government in regimes that do not open themselves to the often adversarial popular scrutiny of "Western" human rights. Asian authoritarianism, like its Western counterpart, lacks the powerful internal mechanisms of self-correction and continued rededication to the common good provided by human rights.

Human rights, in contrast to traditional (Eastern and Western) political practices, provide clear and powerful mechanisms for ascertaining whether rulers' claims about popular preferences are true. For all their shortcomings, free and open periodic elections carried out in an environment with few restrictions on freedoms of speech, press, assembly, and association do provide a relatively reliable gauge of popular political preferences. Alternative schemes based on duty, deference, or hierarchy often do not.

Consider, for example, the argument of Indonesia's Foreign Minister at the Vienna Conference. "When it comes to a decision by a Head of State upon a matter involving its [the State's] life, the ordinary rights of individuals must yield to what he deems the necessities of the moment."[64] But what if the people disagree with their ruler's judgment of the necessities of the moment? Electoral accountability provides at least some sort of test once the (alleged)

---

63. See Kausikan, "Asia's Different Standard," p. 37.
64. Quoted in Fried van Hoof, "Asian Challenges to the Concept of Universality: Afterthoughts on the Vienna Conference on Human Rights," in Baehr, van Hoof, Nanlai, Zhengua, and Smith, eds., *Human Rights: Chinese and Dutch Perspectives*, p. 6.

crisis has passed. Individual rights to freedom of political speech provide a mechanism for immediate dissent. Traditional mechanisms of remonstrance, by contrast, have little relevance in a world of powerful, intrusive, centralized states and modern political parties. Party cadres are hardly analogous to traditional Confucian bureaucrats.

If the problem in the West is that too many people and institutions are guarding the guardians, the problem with traditional Asian alternatives to human rights, at least as they seem to operate in their contemporary variants, is that too few are guarding, and they have inadequate power. It is not surprising that I suggest that if we must err it should be on the side of human rights. I say this, however, not simply as a Westerner who is comfortable with liberal democracy, but as a believer in universal human rights who is convinced that if the differences between East and West truly are as claimed, Asians can be trusted to exercise internationally recognized human rights in responsible ways that make the proper allowances for their cultural values.

HUMAN RIGHTS AND "ASIAN VALUES"

In the preceding sections I have argued that where traditional practices conflict irreconcilably with internationally recognized human rights, traditional practices usually must give way – just as traditional Western practices such as racial and gender discrimination and the persecution of religious deviants have been required to give way. Sovereignty, development, and traditional conceptions of social order do not absolve Asian governments from the requirement to implement internationally recognized human rights. But this does not mean that Asian societies ought to follow "Western" models blindly. Quite the contrary, internationally recognized human rights leave considerable space for distinctively Asian implementations of these rights.

Elsewhere I have described this approach to human rights as "weak cultural relativism."[65] Human rights are treated as essentially universal, but substantial space is allowed for variations in implementing these universal norms. Core rights "concepts" laid down in authoritative international documents, such as equal protection and social security, should be considered largely invariant. But they are subject to differing "interpretations," within the range laid down by the concept. And concrete "implementations" of these interpretations have a wide range of legitimate variation.

Consider two examples, drawn somewhat arbitrarily from the Universal Declaration of Human Rights. "No one shall be subjected to torture or to cruel, inhuman or degrading treatment or punishment." (Article 5)

65. Donnelly, *Universal Human Rights in Theory and Practice,* chapter 6.

Whether, for example, caning or killing convicted criminals falls under this prohibition is a matter of legitimate disagreement and variation. "Everyone is entitled to full equality to a fair and public hearing by an independent and impartial tribunal." (Article 10) "Independent" and "impartial" certainly are subject to a variety of legitimate – and illegitimate – interpretations. And although "full equality" would seem to require some sort of right to competent legal advice, the particular form may vary with differing national conceptions of fairness (as well as differing levels of available resources).

Internationally recognized human rights concepts may be interpreted and implemented in significantly divergent ways. Different states and societies may even weigh particular rights differently. But legitimate variations are limited to the (relatively narrow) range specified by the core concept of the right in question, and countries cannot legitimately pick and choose among internationally recognized human rights.

Consider a few Asian examples. James C. Hsiung presents the Northeast Asian practice of permanent employment as a distinctively Asian style of implementing economic and social rights.[66] Likewise, families in Asia are often seen as bearing social welfare obligations that in the West today fall more on the state. International human rights standards leave Asians entirely free to follow these preferences, so long as the state assures that firms and families discharge their obligations and that people who are not adequately cared for by these preferred mechanisms have another recourse.

Deference to seniority and hierarchy is often presented as characteristic of Asian societies. As Lawrence Beer notes of Japan, "ranking may stifle the free expression of individual thought."[67] But this deference is largely a matter of informal social sanction, not government policy. It is a matter of how people in Japan typically choose to interact with one another, how they choose to exercise their rights of free speech – which are legally guaranteed. As Beer himself emphasizes, despite such cultural differences in standard patterns of verbal interaction, "freedom of expression is viable and protected in Japan."[68]

"Rulers in Korea have always been father figures. A super-father figure like Kim Il-sung . . . is not an accidental phenomenon, for the principles of hierarchy and deference to superiors remain deeply ingrained in the behavior of all Koreans."[69] Citizens may exercise their political rights to select and

---

66. Hsiung, "Human Rights in an East Asian Perspective," in Hsiung, ed., *Human Rights in an East Asian Perspective,* pp. 20–1.
67. Lawrence W. Beer, "Freedom of Expression in Japan, with Comparative Reference to the United States," in Richard P. Claude, ed., *Comparative Human Rights* (Baltimore: The Johns Hopkins University Press, 1976), p. 105.
68. Beer, "Freedom of Expression in Japan, with Comparative Reference to the United States," p. 99.
69. See Lee Manwoo, "North Korea and the Western Notion of Human Rights," p. 136.

defer to a patriarchal leader (although, of course, this was not the case with Kim Il-Sung). If free and equal citizens consent and defer to relatively paternalistic political systems, they are entirely defensible – as they were, for example, in many immigrant wards of large American cities for much of this century.

The Asian preference for consensual decision making is likely to have a major impact on party politics. Consider, for example, Japan's system of de facto one-party rule. So long as peaceful political activity by opposition parties and groups is unhindered and the rules by which elections are contested are generally perceived by all sides as fair and impartially executed, the choice of voters to return candidates predominantly from a single party cannot be legitimately questioned or denied.

Gender equality is often a particularly sensitive matter in cross-cultural discussions. International standards do require that all human rights be available to men and women without discrimination, but that does not require the elimination of differential gender roles. For example, women cannot be denied the right to run for political office. They do, however, remain free to choose not to see that as their role, and voters of both sexes are at liberty to treat sex as a relevant consideration in selecting candidates. Everyone has the right to work and to free choice of employment. (Universal Declaration Article 22) Therefore, women cannot be prevented from working outside the home. They are, however, free to choose not to. Similarly, women cannot be prevented from speaking in public, although they remain free to keep a deferential silence.

I realize that this talk of freedom to choose is somewhat forced. Women are under immense social pressure to conform to traditional gender roles in Asia (as in all other regions of the world), but that is precisely why insisting on the right to choose is so crucial. The right to nondiscrimination not only precludes the state from sanctioning or imposing gender discrimination, it requires the state to protect those who flout convention. "Free" choice rarely is without costs, but so long as the choice is a matter of human rights, those costs must not be imposed by the state.

The right to nondiscrimination allows women to determine – in conjunction with those with whom they associate, intimately as well as casually, in a great variety of circumstances – the extent to which they will conform to, reject, or modify traditional gender roles. If they choose traditional roles, that choice is protected, no less – but no more – than the choice to challenge conventional definitions of what they ought to be and how they ought to act. Human rights simply seek to assure that no group of human beings is authorized to use the apparatus of the state to impose on any other group of human beings a set of standards, rules, or roles that they do not also impose on themselves.[70]

Human rights empower those individuals and groups who will bear the consequences to decide, within certain limits, how they will lead their lives. Therefore, differences in implementing international human rights are not merely justifiable, they are to be expected. For example, Asian children would be expected to give much greater weight to the views and interests of their families in decisions to marry. Confrontational political tactics will be less common (and less effective). There will be greater social constraints on deviant public speech and behavior of all sorts.

These examples, however, illustrate individuals exercising their internationally recognized human rights in a particular fashion, not a different conception of human rights, and they do not suggest the legitimacy, let alone the necessity, of coercively prohibiting the "Western" style of exercising these rights. If Asians choose to exercise their rights in "Western" ways, that too is their right.

Children cannot be legally prohibited from marrying the partner of their choice – unless we are to deny the human right to marry and found a family. Families may sanction their choices in a variety of ways, but it is not the role of the state to enforce family preferences on adult children. Members of minority religious communities may legitimately suffer social sanctions or even ostracism. But unless we deny the human right to freedom of religion, the state has no business forcing the religious preferences of some on others. If individuals and groups who make unpopular choices are willing to accept the social sanctions associated with "deviant" behavior, their decisions, whatever their relation to cultural tradition, must be not merely tolerated but protected by the state – or we must abandon the idea of human rights.

A human rights approach assumes that people probably are best suited, and in any case are entitled, to choose the good life for themselves. If Asians truly do value family over self, they will exercise their personal rights with the consequences for their family in mind. If they value harmony and order, they will exercise their civil liberties in a harmonious and orderly fashion. International human rights norms do not require or even encourage Asians to give up their culture – any more than Locke, Paine, or Jefferson asked their contemporaries to give up their culture.

---

70. This is obviously an exaggeration. Any system of law involves imposing social values. Nonetheless, human rights seek to specify domains of personal autonomy in which the values of others are legitimately held at bay, no matter how widely or deeply they are shared by the mainstream of society. Debates over lists of human rights are about how to define these protected domains. The idea of human rights, however, rests on the claim that there are important and substantial areas in the lives of individuals from which the state and society are legitimately excluded.

However, human rights also empower people to modify or reject parts of their traditional culture. Cultural traditions are socially created legacies. Some are good. Others are bad. Still others are simply irrelevant. And what is considered to be the content of a tradition changes with time. Tradition legitimately governs and limits fundamental life choices covered by human rights guarantees only to the extent that individuals and groups choose to follow, and thus reproduce, that tradition.

To the extent that traditions continue to have valued meanings, they are likely to be reproduced, but if people choose not to conform to tradition, so much the worse for tradition. In particular, so much the worse for those who hold political power who insist that tradition must be followed. For example, the fact that the Chinese tolerated, accepted, or even embraced often arbitrary imperial rule for centuries is no reason why they should embrace repressive party rule today. The people, not their rulers, must decide what they value.

So long as individual and group choices are protected by and within the limits laid out by international human rights standards, they must be respected – both by foreigners and by Asian governments and elites. Anyone, anywhere, who denies these choices, must be opposed. And once we recognize that Asian values need not be sacrificed in the name of human rights, many of the arguments I have considered earlier appear in their true light, namely, as efforts by rapacious Asian ruling elites to manipulate public fear and understandable resentment against an often arrogant and overbearing West to shore up their predatory rule and to deflect attention from their own responsibility for the sufferings of their fellow citizens.

One of the things that makes us human is our capacity to create and change our culture. Cultural diversity has in recent years increasingly come to be valued in itself. Westerners have in recent centuries been especially insensitive in their approach to such differences. Nonetheless, the essential insight of human rights is that the worlds we make for ourselves, intentionally and unintentionally, must conform to relatively universal requirements that rest on our common humanity and seek to guarantee equal concern and respect from the state for every person.

Human rights, as specified in the Universal Declaration and Covenants, represent the international community's best effort to define the social and political parameters of our common humanity. Within these limits, all is possible. Outside of them, little should be allowed.

CHAPTER 3

HUMAN RIGHTS AND ECONOMIC ACHIEVEMENTS

AMARTYA SEN*

INTRODUCTION

I have been asked to write on "the economic costs and benefits of rights violations." Some would rebel against applying something as mechanical and contingent as cost-benefit analysis to a subject as deeply basic and foundational as human rights. I imagine the intention is not so much to apply some mechanical method of cost-benefit analysis to respecting or violating rights, but to examine in general terms the merits and demerits of giving priority to the demands of rights. In this context, we must also be clear about the limitations of "economic" costs and benefits seen on their own – divorced from other, noneconomic considerations that are legitimate to consider.

There is a more immediate issue: cost-benefit analysis is typically used to evaluate something – such as an investment – that is only *instrumentally* important, with no intrinsic value. But it is surely not eccentric to claim that human rights might well be *intrinsically* important – valued for their own sake, and not just as a means to some other end. Human rights can't really be like investing in a mining shaft, which could be reasonably subjected to cost-benefit analysis to check whether its costs are justified by the benefits it would generate (the shaft itself is not seen typically as a benefit *on its own* – but valued derivatively and only to the extent that it promotes something that is intrinsically valued). It may indeed be asked whether the topic assigned to me is not based on a "category mistake" – treating human rights like a mining shaft?

The answer must surely lie in broadening the conception of cost-benefit

* For helpful comments and suggestions, I am grateful to an anonymous referee of the publisher, to Joanne R. Bauer and Daniel A. Bell, and to the other participants of the Hakone workshop on The Growth of East Asia and Its Impact on Human Rights, organized jointly by the Japan Institute of International Affairs and the Carnegie Council on Ethics and International Affairs, in June 1995.

analysis to take us well beyond what occurs in industrial project evaluation and to treat human rights as having possible instrinsic importance in addition to instrumental functions. If human rights are taken to be valuable in themselves, then there is no reason why this valuation cannot be incorporated within a broadly conceived system of costs and benefits of promoting human rights. The analogy with the mining shaft will then not hold, but this would not entail that the basic program of paying attention to all relevant benefits and costs has been abandoned. What are the intrinsic values of relevance to such an analysis? Universalists would demand that attention be paid to the fundamental importance of human rights irrespective of locality and region; cultural ethicists would suggest looking at the valuations championed in the local culture; I shall have to discuss both. These noninstrumental concerns take us beyond the purely instrumental appraisal of rights and liberties, which also raise difficult issues of assessment.

There has been a good deal of discussion in recent years on the far-reaching importance of "Asian values" in the economic success of Asia. Even though the evident thrill in the power of Asian values has somewhat diminished with the financial and economic troubles that the East Asian economies have faced during 1997–8, enough has been achieved in this region – both absolutely and in relation to the record of other regions – to make it legitimate to continue to celebrate the economic performance of East Asia over the decades. What is relevant in the present context is the claim – often made – that the so-called Asian values have actually played a crucial role in the economic success of this region over the last few decades. These values are taken to imply some disregard, in general, of human rights (focusing more on duties and discipline than on rights and entitlements), and deep skepticism, in particular, of political liberty and civil rights (focusing more on economic conditions than on political freedom). Indeed, the economic success of East Asia is often seen as being, in no small measure, directly fostered by the ability of these economies to downplay political and civil liberties in favor of no-nonsense economic growth. The thesis that political authoritarianism may be helpful for economic growth, which is sometimes called the "Lee thesis" (after arguments in that direction presented by Lee Kuan Yew, the influential ex-Prime Minister of Singapore), has gained considerable political backing and support.

Although instrumental issues have been in the forefront of the claims in favor of "Asian values," it would be a mistake to think that the proponents of these values have confined themselves only to instrumental reasoning. The heritage of Asia has been much invoked, and the reading of traditional Asian values has influenced the nature of the argument for adherence to these allegedly ancestral norms and mores in that region. The focus on discipline as opposed to rights has received support not merely from the supposed effectiveness of that priority, but also from the importance of being true to Asia's "own traditions."

The vocal advocates of following "Asian values" have tended to look primarily to East Asia as the region of greatest relevance. The generalizations are meant to apply particularly to the east of Thailand, even though there is also a larger claim that the rest of Asia is quite "similar" too. Lee Kuan Yew, for example, has supplemented his assertion about "the fundamental difference between Western concepts of society and government and East Asian concepts" by explaining "when I say East Asians, I mean Korea, Japan, China, Vietnam, as distinct from Southeast Asia, which is a mix between the Sinic and the Indian, though Indian culture itself emphasizes similar values."[1] Thus, these claims are rather extensive in terms of regional coverage and ideologically versatile in incorporating both intrinsic and instrumental reasoning.

These arguments and claims in favor of Asian values raise three different types of question:

1. What evidence is there in favor of the *instrumental* claim that these allegedly Asian values – with their focus on discipline and authoritarianism against rights and liberties – are particularly efficient in promoting economic development?

2. In going beyond instrumental reasoning, is it appropriate only to consider what *local* values are traditional in a region, and ignore any *universal* importance that may be attached to some basic values – such as liberty – in assessing social arrangements and institutions?

3. Is the much-repeated historical reading of Asian values vindicated by a critical examination of the *actual history of ideas in Asia,* in contrast with those elsewhere?

I shall address these questions in turn.

POLITICAL RIGHTS AND THEIR ECONOMIC CONSEQUENCES

The relevance of basic political liberties and civil rights in poor countries is often disputed on the ground that they allegedly hinder economic and social progress, which can be carried out much more effectively when the government's efforts are not frustrated by factional opposition. This view is defended with a variety of arguments, but perhaps the most powerful con-

---

1. Fareed Zakaria, "Culture Is Destiny: A Conversation with Lee Kuan Yew," *Foreign Affairs* vol. 73 (March/April 1994), p. 113.

tention is based on a much-repeated belief – the "Lee thesis" – that political and civil rights hamper economic growth. Support for the Lee thesis is often anecdotal and casual, but there have been arguments that build empirically on an alleged negative correlation between economic growth and civil and political rights.

What empirical evidence is there in favor of the Lee thesis?[2] Certainly, some relatively authoritarian states (such as South Korea, Lee's own Singapore, and recently China) have had faster rates of economic growth than some less authoritarian ones (such as India, Costa Rica, or Jamaica). But the overall picture is much more complex than these isolated observations might initially suggest, and systematic statistical studies give no real support to the claim that there is a general conflict between political rights and economic performance.[3] That relationship seems conditional on many other circumstances, and indeed the hypothesis that there is no relation between them in either direction is very hard to reject on the basis of the empirical evidence that exists. Indeed, the case for democracy and civil rights cannot be based on their likely *positive* impact on economic growth, nor can that case be demolished by their likely *negative* effect on economic growth. If these rights have value of their own, then this value, it appears, can be obtained at little or no cost to economic growth.

The "Lee thesis" is really based on very selective statistics, rather than on a general statistical test over the wide-ranging information that is available. We should not take the high economic growth of South Korea or Singapore in Asia as proof that authoritarianism does better in promoting economic growth any more than we should conclude the opposite on the basis of the fact that one of the fastest growing countries in the world – Botswana – with the best consistent record of economic growth in Africa has been a real oasis of democracy in that continent. The selective anecdotal evidence goes in contrary directions, and the general statistical picture does not yield any clear relationship at all.

---

2. The discussion here draws on my earlier attempts to deal with these issues in "Freedom and Needs," *The New Republic* (January 10 and 17, 1994), and "Legal Rights and Moral Rights: Old Questions and New Problems," *Ratio Juris* vol. 9 (1996).

3. See Adam Przeworski et al., *Sustainable Democracy* (Cambridge: Cambridge University Press, 1995); and Robert J. Barro, *Getting It Right: Markets and Choices in a Free Society* (Cambridge, MA: MIT Press, 1996). See also Robert J. Barro and Jong-Wha Lee, "Losers and Winners in Economic Growth," *Working Paper 4341* (New York: National Bureau of Economic Research, 1993); Partha Dasgupta, *An Inquiry into Well-Being and Destitution* (Oxford: Clarendon Press, 1993); John Helliwell, "Empirical Linkages Between Democracy and Economic Growth," *Working Paper 4066* (New York: National Bureau of Economic Research, 1994); Surjit Bhalla, "Freedom and Economic Growth: A Vicious Circle?" (unpublished, presented at the Nobel Symposium in Uppsala on Democracy's Victory and Crisis, August 1994); Adam Przeworski and Fernando Limongi, "Democracy and Development" (unpublished, presented at the Nobel Symposium in Uppsala just cited).

Furthermore, from the point of view of economic analysis, we have to look not only at statistical connections, but also at the *causal* processes that might be involved. In fact, the processes that led to the economic success of, say, East Asian economies are by now reasonably well understood. In this process of economic development, a variety of factors played their part, involving the use of international markets, openness to competition, a high level of literacy, successful land reforms, and the provision of selective incentives to encourage growth and exports. There is nothing whatsoever to indicate that these social policies were inconsistent with greater democracy and had to be sustained by the elements of authoritarianism actually present in South Korea or Singapore. The temptation to see the positive role of authoritarianism seems to be based on taking the post hoc to be also propter hoc; it is not really founded on any systematic establishment of cause and effect relations.[4]

Furthermore, in examining the economic costs and benefits of alternative political arrangements, we cannot confine our investigation only to the effects on the average rates of growth of gross national product or real national income. Economic development involves much more that. For example, development also involves the promotion of greater economic security in the lives of people. In examining economic security, we also have to explore, as I have tried to argue elsewhere,[5] the connection between political and human rights, on the one hand, and the prevention of major social disasters, on the other. Civil and political rights give people the opportunity not only to do things for themselves, but also to draw attention forcefully to general needs and to demand appropriate public action. Whether and how a government responds to needs and sufferings may well depend on how much pressure is put on it, and the exercise of political rights (such as voting, criticizing, protesting, and so on) can make a real difference.

For example, one of the remarkable facts in the terrible history of famines in the world is that no substantial famine has ever occurred in any country with a democratic form of government and a relatively free press. This applies not only to the affluent countries of Europe and America, but also to poor but broadly democratic countries (such as India, Botswana, Zimbabwe).[6] Also, we have intertemporal evidence in the same direction when a country undergoes *transition* to democracy. For example, India continued to have famines right up to the time of independence in 1947 (the Ben-

---

4. On this see also my joint study with Jean Drèze, *Hunger and Public Action* (Oxford: Clarendon Press, 1989).
5. See my "Development: Which Way Now?" *Economic Journal* vol. 93 (1983); reprinted in *Resources, Values and Development* (Oxford: Blackwell, and Cambridge, MA: Harvard University Press, 1984). See also my joint book with Jean Drèze, *Hunger and Public Action,* and also my presidential address to the American Economic Association, "Rationality and Social Choice," *American Economic Review* vol. 85 (March 1995).
6. For the empirical evidence for this relationship, see Drèze and Sen, *Hunger and Public Action.*

gal famine in 1943 killed between 2 and 3 million people), and then it stopped quite abruptly with independence and the installation of a multi-party democratic system. No government can afford to face elections after a major social calamity, nor can it deal easily with criticism from the media and opposition parties while still in office. The incentive effects of these connections can be very powerful.[7]

When economic policies go smoothly, the protective role of democracy may not be much missed. However, when things go wrong for one reason or another, democratic and civil rights provide incentives for rapid correction that authoritarian forms of government do not have. For example, when the so-called Great Leap Forward proved to be a major policy mistake in China, the disastrous policies were not corrected for three full years, through 1958 to 1961, while 23 to 30 million people died. No democratic country with opposition parties and a free press would have allowed that to happen.

To conclude this section, the connection between political rights and economic growth is ambiguous and contingent, but there is certainly little evidence to vindicate the Lee thesis. Not much of a case *against* democratic rights can be established on the basis of their allegedly negative effects on economic growth. The observed international contrasts make it hard to reject the view that these rights do not hinder economic growth in any significant way, and a causal analysis provides further reasons for skepticism about a negative relationship. Furthermore, because development involves much more than mere economic growth, the instrumental contribution of political liberty and civil rights goes much beyond the connection with economic growth. The importance of political and civil rights in guaranteeing economic security and in preventing major disasters is particularly relevant in this context.

HUMAN RIGHTS, RELEVANCE AND UNIVERSALITY

I have concentrated in the last section on the *instrumental* arguments for and against political and civil rights. Even when economic objectives are viewed very narrowly in terms of economic growth, the instrumental argument against these rights based on the "Lee thesis" does not seem to work, because the Lee thesis is empirically so dubious and misleading. When the economic

---

7. See my *Resources, Values and Development;* Drèze and Sen, *Hunger and Public Action;* Drèze and Sen, *The Political Economy of Hunger* (Oxford: Clarendon Press, 1990), especially the paper by N. Ram; Article 19, *Starving in Silence: A Report on Famine and Censorship* (London: Article 19 International Centre on Censorship, 1990), with articles by Frances D'Souza, Alex de Waal, and an anonymous Chinese scholar; Human Rights Watch, *Indivisible Human Rights: The Relationship between Political and Civil Rights to Survival, Subsistence and Poverty* (New York, 1992); International Federation of Red Cross and Red Crescent Societies, *World Disaster Report 1994* (Geneva, 1994).

objectives are seen in adequately broad terms, then some contrary claims emerge powerfully.

What about *non*instrumental arguments? There are claims in that direction too, as was mentioned earlier, based on the value of being "true" to "Asian values." This raises the question, on the one hand, of how much importance should be attached to the preservation of values that have dominated in the past (when such values can be clearly identified), and the question, on the other hand, whether the reading of "Asian values" by their official interpreters – who are often governmental spokesmen rather than historians or classicists – is in fact correct. I shall postpone these questions to the next section.

There is, however, a more general argument that is clearly noninstrumental and plausibly relevant, to wit, the pervasive importance of rights no matter what values might or might not have flourished in the past of particular regions. If rights and freedoms are taken to be valuable everywhere, not only in particular regions and localities, then surely there must be an issue of intrinsic importance that transcends regional and local values. There are indeed weighty arguments in that universalist direction when it comes to the valuation of personal liberty or autonomy, with possible application also to elementary civil and political freedom, and reasonings of this type can be found in the writings of a variety of authors, ranging from Aristotle to John Stuart Mill and John Rawls.[8]

This is not to dispute that some authors have explicitly denied that rights can have any intrinsic importance or noninstrumental relevance. For example, Jeremy Bentham argued that the idea of "natural rights" was nonsensical, and the concept of "natural and imprescriptible rights" was "nonsense on stilts." Bentham's own interest in legal rights, which was considerable (he was one of the earliest theorists of the typology of rights), was purely instrumental. Legal rights were seen as being contingently useful institutional means that can in many circumstances help the promotion of intrinsically valuable objectives such as utilities. But many of Bentham's contemporaries took quite a different view; immediate illustrations can be found, for example, in Tom Paine's *Rights of Man,* or Mary Wollstonecraft's *The Vindication of the Rights of Women,* both published in 1792, just around the time when Bentham was producing his great utilitarian works. This contrast of basic beliefs regarding intrinsic importance can be seen in contemporary debates as well.

This is not the occasion to try to settle a foundational argument in politi-

---

8. Aristotle, *Politics;* John Stuart Mill, *On Liberty* (1859); John Rawls, *A Theory of Justice* (Cambridge, MA: Harvard University Press, 1971).

cal and moral philosophy, but I have tried to examine these issues elsewhere.[9]
I have argued that it is hard to accept the utilitarian presumption that all
normative issues can be reduced *entirely* to the calculus of utilities. No matter
how utility is defined (as pleasure, or desire fulfillment, or the numerical representation of choice), there would seem to be some need for going beyond
an exclusive reliance on this limited informational base.

I shall not repeat these arguments, which suggest that there is an important need to go beyond utilities in the valuational exercise and also that the
universal relevance of elementary freedoms permits a significant enriching of
the normative perspective. To the extent that these lines of reasoning are
accepted, some concepts of human rights or of elementary freedoms would
have an importance that is not purely instrumental. They have to be accommodated in judging the placing of human rights, over and above the considerations that would emanate from instrumental reasoning, and also over and
above the concerns that may emerge as being relevant on the basis of our
readings of local cultures and history.

Contemporary political debates often accommodate these perspectives
quite powerfully. For example, at the height of the Vietnam war, when four
protesters were shot and killed by the guards at Kent State University, the
badness of the consequence could scarcely be seen simply as four people
dying prematurely; that happens too frequently all the time, somewhere or
other. Nor can the moral outrage aroused by that act be explained by relating
it to the actual political impact that these four students would probably have
had if they were left unharmed, and not mowed down. It could even be
argued that these four had more influence as martyrs than they would have
had as living protesters.

It was mainly the unacceptability of political violence and victimization,
by the state against political dissidents, that this outrage reflected. This issue
relates directly to the intrinsic importance of elementary rights, including
preeminently the right not to be killed in the process of exercising one's civil
rights. The outrage at the events at Tiananmen Square in 1989 can be analyzed along similar lines. The unacceptability relates first and foremost to the
importance of these elementary rights themselves.

There is, in addition, the *constructive* role of elementary civil and political
rights in promoting public discussion, which helps citizens to form their values in an informed way and to scrutinize their conceptions of needs. It can be
argued that not only does the exercise of basic political rights make it more

9. In particular, in my *Collective Choice and Social Welfare* (San Francisco: Holden-Day, 1970; republished,
   Amsterdam: North-Holland, 1979); "Utilitarianism and Welfarism," *Journal of Philosophy* vol. 7 (September 1979); "Well-Being, Agency and Freedom: The Dewey Lectures 1984," *Journal of Philosophy*
   vol. 82 (1985).

likely that there will be a policy response to transparent economic needs (a purely instrumental argument that was considered in the last section), but also that the conceptualization and comprehension of economic needs may require the exercise of such rights. It can indeed be argued that a proper understanding of what economic "needs" are – their content and their force – requires discussion and exchange.

Human beings suffer from miseries and deprivations of various kinds – some more amenable to alleviation than others. The totality of the human predicament would be an impossible basis for the social analysis of needs. For example, there are many things that we might have good reason to value if they were feasible – such as complete immunity from illnesses of all kinds, or even immortality – but we do not, indeed cannot, see them as *needs*. Our conception of needs relates to our analysis of the nature of deprivations and to our understanding of what can or cannot be done about them. Political rights, including freedom of expression and discussion, are not only pivotal in inducing political response to economic needs, they are also central to the conceptualization of economic needs themselves, and this constructive role can be seen to be a central aspect of the importance of elementary rights that make it possible for citizens to interact and to form values and priorities.

Even though this constructive role works *through* a political and moral process), it cannot be seen as purely instrumental, because it is a part of the valuational process and takes us beyond the ways and means of promoting *given* values. Certainly, the constructive argument radically extends the relevance of political freedom and civil rights. The need to go beyond purely instrumental assessment as well as beyond purely regional culture and values is further strengthened by this constructive aspect of political and civil freedom.

EVALUATION OF RIGHTS AND "ASIAN VALUES"

I turn now to the postponed issue of the reading of "Asian values." Although it is not altogether clear what "Asian values" exactly are, they seem to have gained a place in the standard analysis of contemporary events. In a provocative essay, titled "Japan's Nice New Nationalism," published not long before the Hakone workshop where this essay was first presented, *The Economist* poses a question in a rather stark form – a query that has often been stated, albeit less clearly: "Is the combination of nationalist confidence and a growing economic interest in Asia likely to pose a threat?"[10] The threat referred relates to the concerns of the Western countries. The reference here is not only to – not even primarily to – Japan's dominance in trade and world markets, but to

10. "Japan's Nice New Nationalism," *The Economist*, January 14, 1995, p. 13.

Japan's possible role in tolerating and supporting some policies and practices in Asia that may be quite unacceptable in the West. *The Economist* identifies "human rights and press freedoms" as "the most frequent battlegrounds."

This way of seeing the "clash of cultures" is increasingly prevalent now, but to see the conflict over human rights as a battle between Western liberalism, on one side, and Asian reluctance to go along with that, on the other, is to cast the debate in a form that distracts attention from the central issues, which concern Asia itself. In the battle over the role of human rights and such matters as press freedom (a battle that is certainly forceful in contemporary Asia), the primary parties are Asians of different beliefs and convictions, even if occasionally a visiting American might get caned in an Asian country. This is not to deny that America or Europe may have legitimate reasons to worry about the outcome of this and related contentions about ideas and politics in Asia (I have nothing against *The Economist* posing this "Western" question – one of some interest to its readers), but this dispute over principles and practice is really about the lives of Asians – their beliefs and traditions, their rules and regulations, their achievements and failures, and ultimately their lives and freedoms. The Western concern – legitimate on its own – may even contribute to misspecifying the central features of the debate.

There is a further reason for removing this debate from the perspective of Western anxiety about Asian practice. That often-invoked perspective gives the immediate impression that the primacy of human rights is a fundamental and ancient feature of Western culture, and one not to be found in Asia. It is, as it were, a contrast between the authoritarianism allegedly implicit in, say, Confucianism vis-à-vis the respect for individual liberty allegedly deeply rooted in Western culture. There are good historical reasons to doubt each of the two claims implicit in the contrast. In answer to the question, "at what date, and in what circumstances, the notion of individual liberty . . . first became explicit in the West," Isaiah Berlin has noted: "I have found no convincing evidence of any clear formulation of it in the ancient world."[11] Also, insofar as we do find arguments championing freedoms *in some generic sense* in ancient Greek treatises (as we clearly do, for example in Aristotle's *Politics* and also in the *Nicomachean Ethics*), it is not hard to discover comparable championing of generically described freedoms in the writings of many Asian theorists, such as the Indian emperor Ashoka who was among the first

---

11. Isaiah Berlin, *Four Essays on Liberty* (Oxford: Oxford University Press, 1969), p. xl. Even as far the idea of democracy itself is concerned, as Benjamin Schwartz notes, "In China, the model of the natural and sacred hierarchy of the patrilinear family may have lent its own coloration to the concepts of hierarchy and authority, but we must again remember that even in the history of the West, with its memories of Athenian 'democracy', the notion that democracy cannot be implemented in large territorial states requiring highly centralized power remained accepted wisdom as late as Montesquieu and Rousseau," *The World of Thought in Ancient China* (Cambridge, MA: Harvard University Press, 1985), p. 69.

– in the third century B.C. – to tackle the difficult issue of protecting minority rights in a multicultural and multireligious polity.

Indeed, the rhetoric of freedom is abundantly invoked in many of the Asian literatures. Buddha even explains "nirvana" in the language of "freedom," to wit, freedom from the miseries of life. If there is a real gap today in the acceptance of freedom and liberty in the West vis-à-vis those in Asia, the roots of a hard division lie much closer to our times.

Nor is it helpful to see the contrast in terms of the practical traditions of "Oriental despotism" that so fascinated European scholars in the heyday of the historical emergence of democratic commitments of the West. If the despots of the Orient were more despotic than those in the West (it is not obvious that this was always – or even typically – the case), the political limits of today's Asia are clearly not bound by those traditions any more than the political possibilities in Europe are confined by the heritage of Spanish inquisition or the history of Nazi genocide.

Many Western commentators find it deeply unacceptable that some people who argue against human rights in Asia try to gain inspiration from specific interpretations of "Asian values." This is an understandable concern, but that search for inspiration is a close cousin of the tendency in the West to see ideas of democracy and liberty specifically in terms of "Western" traditions. Even the language used in recommending to Asia what is called "Western democracy" imposes a geographical mode of divisiveness that springs not only from Asian intransigence but also from a Western "priority complex." If the grabbing of "Asian values" by the champions of authoritarianism has to be effectively and fairly questioned, what is needed is not the claim – often implicit – of the preeminence of what are taken as "Western values," but a broader historical study of Chinese, Sanskrit, Arabic, and other Asian literatures (in relation to corresponding writings in the Western classics).[12] Nearer our times, acknowledgement would have to made to the contributions of national leaders such Mahatma Gandhi or Dr. Sun Yat-sen, who were, already a hundred years ago, cogently vocal in defense of the widest forms of democracy and political and civil rights.

I would not dispute that at a truly deep level, cultural comparisons based on real history could be extremely interesting in diagnosing the contrast of focal concerns in different regional traditions in the world in dealing with

12. In my Morgenthau Memorial Lecture, Human Rights and Asian Values, at the Carnegie Council on Ethics and International Affairs (New York), given on May 1, 1997, I illustrated the varieties of political philosophy that have been championed in the past in different Asian countries. The text of the lecture has been published by Carnegie Council as *Human Rights and Asian Values* (New York: Carnegie Council on Ethics and International Affairs, 1997), and also in *The New Republic*, July 14 and 21, 1997.

the principles and reasonings that have a bearing on the contemporary formulations of human rights, but neither the rapid invoking of "Asian values"
in defense of suppressing human rights nor the expression of Western anxiety
and consternation about "Asian ways" helps to advance critical scrutiny of
the role of human rights and their consequences in Asian societies. The subject has a contingently regional dimension, but it is not a foundationally
regional issue.

This last claim supplements the substantive analysis I have tried to present earlier in this chapter. The case *for* human rights, including political and
civil rights, rests on (1) their *intrinsic* importance, (2) their *consequential* role
in providing political incentives for economic security, and (3) their *constructive* role in the genesis of values and priorities. The case is no different in Asia
than it is anywhere else, and the dismissal of this claim on the ground of the
special nature of Asian values does not survive critical scrutiny. Values that
have been championed in the past of Asian countries – in East Asia as well as
elsewhere in Asia – include an enormous variety, just as substantial variations
are seen in the history of ideas in the West. To see Asian history in terms of a
narrow category of authoritarian values does little justice to the rich varieties
of thought in Asian intellectual traditions. Dubious history does nothing to
vindicate dubious politics.

PART II

TOWARD A MORE INCLUSIVE HUMAN RIGHTS REGIME

CHAPTER 4

TOWARD AN INTERCIVILIZATIONAL APPROACH TO HUMAN RIGHTS

Onuma Yasuaki*

INTRODUCTION

As we approach the end of the twentieth century, the problem of human rights has emerged as a subject of fierce international debates. Are human rights universal, or are they culturally relative? Should developing nations first pursue economic development and then move to the realization of human rights, or should both be pursued in tandem?[1] In developing countries, should civil and political rights enjoy a privileged status as they do in most developed countries, or do economic and social rights, such as the right to subsistence, deserve greater priority? The increased salience of these debates is due to the following factors.

First, there has been a steady increase in the significance of human rights in the United States in recent decades. In the 1960s, the problem of the civil rights of African Americans became one of the major political issues. In the late 1970s, Jimmy Carter's "human rights diplomacy" was the subject of controversy in the international political arena. Since then, racism, sexism, and domestic problems such as drugs and crime have been discussed in relation to human rights. Today, it is not only lawyers, traditionally the main participants in debates over human rights, who are tackling these issues: Philosophers, political scientists, anthropologists, and religious and political leaders as well as journalists have been involved. Because the United States has tremendous influence in setting the contemporary agenda in international society, human rights have become a major global issue.

---

* The author is deeply grateful to Professor Daniel A. Bell, who kindly edited this chapter. A longer version of this article will be published in the *Asian Yearbook of International Law* vol. 7 (forthcoming).

1. Here the term "human rights" is understood as referring to civil and political rights. The problematic nature of equating civil and political rights with human rights in general will be fully discussed in this chapter.

Second, the end of the Cold War opened a more serious path to the treatment of various nonsecurity issues. During the Cold War period, the strategic confrontation between the United States and the USSR, which seemed to directly threaten the survival of the human species, was regarded as vitally important. With the end of the Cold War, however, international economics, human rights, religious and ethnic conflicts, and the environment have also come to be treated as major global issues. On the normative plane, the West has regarded the end of the Cold War as the triumph of the "free market," "democracy," and "human rights." As a consequence, these ideas have come to be strongly asserted by Western powers in the 1990s.

The problem, however, is that the increased prominence of human rights in the international arena has not always led to desirable results. In the East Asian region, "human rights diplomacy" has often been ineffective or counterproductive. Partly, of course, this is caused by bad faith on the part of the region's authoritarian governments. But conflicts over human rights are also caused by politically influential West-centric perspectives that tend to ignore or marginalize local perspectives.[2] Instead, what is needed is a comprehensive framework within which one can understand issues of human rights as expressions of truly global concerns. This chapter will begin by describing the phenomenon of West-centrism, followed by a discussion, albeit in an abstract and incomplete manner, of a comprehensive, *intercivilizational* framework meant to remedy the flaws of the current West-centric human rights regime.

WEST-CENTRIC PERSPECTIVES

Lack of Understanding of the Psychological Legacy of Imperialism and Colonial Rule

In developed countries, where people generally enjoy a high standard of living, a quest for economic well-being is not always the highest priority. Instead, a quest for "human rights," understood mainly as civil and political rights, and the "environment" is attracting a greater number of people. The voice of those who claim that they should not tolerate serious human rights violations has become stronger and stronger. This voice demands their governments to intervene and stop human rights violations, even if they are committed in foreign countries. This phenomenon, which is most obvious in the United States today, can also be witnessed in other developed countries. It will continue to spread.

The problem, however, is that most nations with serious violations of

2. "Eurocentrism" is the term that is generally used to designate a tendency to approach natural and social phenomena from a perspective that assumes the Western way of thinking as the standard framework. However, it is the American, not the European way, that is decisively influential in today's world. That is why I use the term "West-centrism," rather than "Eurocentrism."

human rights and that are thus the targets of criticism were once under colonial rule and the victims of military intervention and economic exploitation by developed countries. Because of this humiliating past, they tend to respond to criticism by the developed countries in an excessively sensitive manner. For those who have experienced colonial rule and interventions under such beautiful slogans as "humanity" and "civilization,"[3] the term "human rights" looks like nothing more than another beautiful slogan by which great powers rationalize their interventionist policies.[4]

To say that such a claim is a convenient excuse of the leaders of authoritarian regimes is certainly true, at least in part. No nation is monolithic. Even in countries that do not respect the freedom of expression, dissenting voices can be heard criticizing the official view of the ruling party or government. It is necessary to encourage such dissenting voices. However, does it follow that in these countries it is the voice of such dissenting activists, rather than the view of the government, that represents the people as a whole? Not necessarily. Here lies a difficult problem.

It is true that the Chinese Communist Party, the Vietnamese Communist Party, the government of Singapore, and some other Asian regimes suppress the voice of certain intellectuals and citizens who demand respect for freedom. Moreover, it is not likely that these regimes can be maintained indefinitely in their present form: The desires of a large number of people seeking more freedom will bring about a regime that respects more freedom than today. However, these facts and expectations do not necessarily mean that the present regimes have not represented the will of their people. It is even less true to say that in these countries human rights activists represent the will of the people as a whole.

Unlike socialist regimes in Eastern Europe, these regimes were not imposed by an outside power. Most of them grew spontaneously from struggles against colonial rule, poverty, and privileged ruling classes of the past. Despite many shortcomings such as authoritarian rule, corruption, and abuses of human rights, these regimes were chosen by their own people to struggle against the violence and misery of the past. As such, they have a certain legitimacy.[5] Moreover, the

---

3. The idea of *mission civilisatrice* was used to rationalize imperialistic policies by the Western powers from the late nineteenth to the early twentieth century. The idea of "humanitarian intervention" was frequently resorted to by Western powers when they intervened militarily in Turkey and other Afro-Asian states in the same period. See, for example, J. Kunz, "Zum Begriff der 'nation civilisée' im modernen Völkerrecht," *Zeitschrift für offentliches Recht* vol. 7 (1928), pp. 86–99 and 111–63; Jörg Fisch, *Die europäische Expansion und das Völkerrecht* (Stuttgart: Steiner, 1984), pp. 258, 274–6, 283–379, 422, 488–91, 499, 502.

4. See, for example, Yi Ding, "Opposing Interference in Other Countries' Internal Affairs Through Human Rights," *Beijing Review* vol. 32, no. 45 (1989), pp. 10–12.

5. For a similar view, see Watanabe Akio, "Kokusai josei hendoki ni okeru nihon no gaiko seisaku no kettei katei," *1990 nen dai ni okeru nihon no senryakuteki kadai* [Japan's Strategic Priorities in the 1990s] (Tokyo: Nihon Kokusai Mondai Kenkyujo, 1993), pp. 5–6.

overcoming of domestic diversity is a vital task in the process of nation building. Although today's developed countries have already carried out this task in a violent manner up to the early twentieth century, most developing countries must face this task now and in the future.[6]

Given these facts, it is too simplistic to assert that regimes in these countries are merely rationalizing human rights abuses. It is rather self-complacent to say that the voice of the human rights activists represents the true will of their people. Resistance to criticism by developed countries, whether by their governments or nongovernmental organizations (NGOs), is not limited to the ruling elites. Grudges and animosities against colonial rule, external intervention, economic exploitation, racial discrimination, and religious prejudices by the formerly imperial, developed countries of today are widely shared by the popular masses in many developing countries.[7] In such situations, "human rights diplomacy" and criticism by NGOs in developed countries are likely to be perceived as arrogant interventions or pressures. Thus, even a legitimate criticism cannot fulfill its proper task of improving human rights conditions in the developing countries.

Lack of Self-Criticism

Many East Asian nations have achieved economic development and social stability in the latter half of the twentieth century. Japan is already on par with the United States and Western European countries in terms of human development indices. Taiwan, Singapore, and Hong Kong are catching up with them. Although still undeveloped in many respects, China is taking a path to becoming the largest economic power.[8] Many of these nations have generally achieved a more equitable distribution of wealth than the United States and many Western European countries.[9] These increases in power, eco-

---

6. See Onuma Yasuaki, *Wakoku to kyokuto no aida* [Between the Country of "Wa" and the "Far East"] (Tokyo: Chuo Koronsha, 1988), pp. 198–9.

7. When the Chinese government is criticized for human rights violations, it often tries to offset the criticism by referring to the imperialistic policies by the Western powers and Japan since the Opium War. It is true that they are "diplomatic cards" against the Western nations and Japan. However, it is because there do exist the historical facts of Western imperialism and Japanese aggression, as well as deeply rooted rancor among the Chinese people, that Chinese leaders can use these diplomatic cards. Such rancor is shared by many developing nations.

8. Although the late 1990s have seen economic confusion in the region, when viewed from a longer perspective, overall economic development is likely to continue.

9. In terms of income share, the ratio of the highest 20 percent to the lowest 20 percent is 4.3 in Japan, 5.7 in South Korea, 5.8 in Germany, 7.5 in France, 8.7 in Hong Kong, 8.9 in the United States, and 9.6 in Singapore and the United Kingdom (1981–93 for Korea, Hong Kong, and Singapore and 1981–91 for the rest). See UNDP, *Human Development Report 1996* (New York: Oxford University Press, 1996), pp. 170–98. Homicide cases per 100,000 from 1991 to 1994 are 1.0 in Japan, 4.6–4.9 in France, and 9.0–9.8 in the United States. Other indexes in criminal cases indicate basically similar tendencies. See *Homu sogo kenkyujo, Hanzai hakusho* [Criminal White Papers] (Tokyo: Okurasho Insatsukyoku, 1996), pp. 26, 241, 361, 379.

nomic prosperity, and social stability of East Asian nations are in many ways based on the introduction of Western ideas and institutions. However, they also owe a great deal to their own cultural heritage and social underpinnings. It is natural for these nations to become more confident in their own ways and more critical of the self-righteous and assertive ways of Western, particularly American, diplomacy and NGO activity.

One of the major counterarguments held by some East Asians against Western human rights advocates is that contemporary Western societies, especially the United States, are suffering from various social diseases such as crime, drugs, and the degradation of family and community ethics. They argue that these diseases may well be a consequence of excessive legalism[10] and individual-centrism.[11] These are major components of the idea of human rights.

The mechanism of human rights has developed hand in hand with the development of individualism and the establishment of legal mechanisms stressing the importance of rights (Charles Taylor explains this process in Chapter 6 in this volume). Until recently, a modernist framework that sees only positive aspects of this development has been predominant. The more individualistic a person becomes, the more liberated he or she is from various constraints such as the family, feudalistic ties, rural communities, and religious authorities. The more firmly a legal mechanism can protect citizens from the power of states, the more their values and interests will be secure. Although such a naive, modernist perception is no longer held by many experts in developed countries, it is still strong among the masses, and even among intellectuals in non-Western societies, because of a persistent image of "the developed, rights-oriented and individualistic West" versus "the underdeveloped, non-legalistic and collectivist non-West."[12]

Legalization in terms of rights and individualization is certainly important and useful in societies where modernization has only recently begun. However, the negative aspects of these phenomena are also becoming evident. In the last couple of decades we have witnessed the emergence of communitarians and virtue-oriented philosophy as opposed to the individual-centered and

---

10. Here legalism refers to a way of thinking in which people think highly of law and legal enforcement mechanisms of social values, and their behavior is highly influenced by such ideas as "law," "rights," "justice," and "the juridically enforced realization of values." See also Judith Shklar, *Legalism* (Cambridge, MA: Harvard University Press, 1964).

11. This term refers to a way of thinking in which people think highly of individuals who are independent from the society and their natural environment and then deny the dependence of individuals upon other people, collectivities, and nature.

12. One of the reasons why developing countries have emphasized the importance of collective rights, including the right of self-determination, is their sense of alienation from the discourse on human rights. Had the notion of human rights not taken up the issue of collective human rights deprivation of those under colonial rule, it would have been of little value to them. Although one cannot deny certain cultural differences between the "individualist" West and the "collectivist" East, it would be wrong to explain the emphasis on collective rights by Afro-Asian intellectuals solely from cultural perspectives.

rights-oriented philosophy in developed countries, particularly in the United States. This is not to deny that the United States has made real human rights progress in recent decades, especially in terms of its efforts to make the country less racially divided and to counter gender discrimination, but continuing problems do suggest that a reappraisal of the dominant approach to human rights is needed.

Nor should we deny the importance of such basic rights as the prohibition of torture. Few would tolerate dying from starvation. As Jack Donnelly argues, differences in culture or religion and the principle of nonintervention under international law cannot justify violations of basic human rights (see Chapter 2 in this volume). Nonetheless, if those critical of such violations looking from the outside are ignorant of religions, cultures, and social customs in local communities, and lack self-criticism of their own behavior, their criticism may be regarded as an arrogant intervention by external powers. Even when the criticism has legitimate grounds, it may well invite antagonism from local people. Since some nations targeted as violators of human rights today, such as China, are steadily increasing their economic power, even a legitimate criticism may be counteracted by this economic power. This would be a serious setback for the cause of human rights.

West-Centric Universalism

It has frequently been asked whether human rights were solely of European origin or whether they existed in other regions as well. Some intellectuals in developing countries, although they criticize the universalist discourse of human rights by the West, claim that their own civilizations, religions, and cultures had human rights from ancient times (we can call this view the theory of universal origin).[13] This view is often shared by those in developed countries as well. Why has this question been repeatedly asked and answered in the affirmative?

First, there is a naive interest among Western intellectuals in whether Western ideas and practices also existed in non-Western societies. Many of them are rather ignorant of the history of non-Western societies and may ask such questions as whether a market economy existed in premodern China. How about colleges in the Tokugawa Japan? Or democracy in ancient India? It is not surprising that those interested in human rights ask: Did human rights exist in the teachings of Islam, Confucianism, or Buddhism?

Second, one should consider various unfavorable factors surrounding intellectuals or human rights advocates in many non-Western societies. The term

---

13. See, for example, Y. Tyagi, "Third World Response to Human Rights," *Indian Journal of International Law* vol. 21 (1981), pp. 119–40.

"human rights" invites certain suspicions and antipathies from the government, the military, religious leaders, or influential persons in local communities. It is still alien to a majority of the population. Under these circumstances, it is understandable for intellectuals or human rights advocates in these societies to argue: "Look, human rights are not alien. They are already in the teachings of *our* religion (culture, customs, etc.)." In order to propagate the idea of human rights in many non-Western societies, it is often effective to resort to the theory of universal origin.

Third, several non-Western intellectuals are critical of the view that anything good or desirable in human history originated in the West. If such a good thing as human rights existed in Europe, they argue, it should also have existed in their own culture or religion.[14] There is a psychological background to this way of thinking. The pride of many intellectuals in developing countries is hurt by the contemporary realities surrounding them, such as poverty, dictatorship, and corruption. It is understandable that some make rather self-contradictory arguments, severely criticizing the Western universalist discourse of human rights, and yet claiming that human rights – something good – has existed in their own nations' histories, cultures, and civilizations.

Fourth, there is an element of guilt on the part of certain intellectuals in developed countries. It is true that they are generally critical of human rights abuses in developing countries. However, at least some of them are concerned with the wide gaps between North and South, their nations' past colonial rule, and their resource-consuming lifestyles. They are also sensitive to the criticism of Eurocentrism. For them, it is somewhat difficult to assert that human rights – a good guy! – existed exclusively in Europe. Nodding to the assertion that human rights existed in Islam, Hinduism, Confucianism, and so on, is much easier than refuting it.

In this way, both developed and developing countries have substantive and psychological factors that give rise to the theory of universal origin. However, it is difficult to support it. Non-European civilizations had their own mechanisms to pursue the spiritual and material well-being of humanity, but they were not characterized as human rights. These mechanisms protected the interests of people in various ways, and may be characterized as the ontological or functional equivalents of human rights, but not as human rights per se.[15] Even in Europe, the idea of human rights did not exist in premodern days. What existed were specific rights or privileges belonging to specific

14. For example, Professor Tyagi claims that it has been asserted that the history of human rights began with the Magna Carta, that the human rights movement was initiated by Western scholars or statesmen, that the civilized nations of the Western world fought two world wars for the reinstatement and protection of human rights, and such. He argues that "all these assertions reflect a typical Western 'monopoly of wisdom'" (Tyagi, "Third World Response to Human Rights," p. 119).

15. This point is discussed by Jack Donnelly in Chapter 2.

groups or classes. For example, rights guaranteed in the Magna Carta were not rights of persons per se, they were the special rights or privileges or specific persons such as peers, feudal lords, and the clergy. Rights characterized as those of individuals abstracted from specific belongings were born only after *corps intermédiares* were dissolved in the formation of sovereign states.[16]

Moreover, even after human rights came to be defined as the rights that a human being has simply because he or she is a human, the "human" in this definition was required to meet certain qualifications.[17] As suggested by certain European languages designating a human (a man, *un homme*), this term was in Europe for a long time identified with men, excluding women. It was only after 1945 that the very term "human rights" became predominant instead of "rights of man." In the French language, *droits de l'homme* rather than *droits humains* is still used today. The propertyless classes and "people of color" were also excluded from enjoying many human rights.[18]

Prior to the twentieth century, the history of human rights is the history of qualifications. The male-dominated French National Assembly of 1792 denied the Declaration of the Rights of Women, and the West-centric Versailles Conference of 1919 rejected the Japanese proposal for including a racial equality clause in the Covenant of the League of Nations.[19] The century and a half following the American Declaration of Independence and the French Declaration of the Rights of Man and Citizens, two of the most famous human rights declarations, witnessed the peak of colonization by Western powers. People under colonial rule were generally denied the enjoyment of the rights proclaimed in these declarations.

However, since human rights are defined simply as rights based on humanity, it is almost inevitable that those implicitly excluded from the rights will claim: "We too should be entitled to these rights." It is difficult to deny the universalizing potential of human rights. Explicit qualifications have gradually been rectified, first in theory and then in practice. The Universal Declaration of Human Rights of 1948 and the two International Covenants of Human Rights of 1966 accepted the equality of sex and race.[20] The successful developments in civil rights for "people of color" in the United States, worldwide decolonization, and the rise of feminist movements

---

16. See my essay "In Quest of Intercivilizational Human Rights," *Occasional Paper No. 2* (San Francisco: The Asia Foundation's Center for Asian-Pacific Affairs, 1996), pp. 7–9 and 16 ns. 50, 52, 54.

17. See H. von Senger, "From the Limited to the Universal Concept of Human Rights: Two Periods of Human Rights," in W. Schmale, ed., *Human Rights and Cultural Diversity* (Golbach: Keip Publishing, 1993), pp. 47–100.

18. See von Senger, "From the Limited to the Universal Concept of Human Rights," pp. 52–66.

19. Onuma, "Harukanaru jinshu byodo no riso [The Unreachable Ideal of Racial Equality]," in Onuma Yasuaki, ed., *Kokusaiho, kokusai rengo to nihon* [International Law, the United Nations and Japan] (Tokyo: Kobundo, 1987), pp. 447–56.

20. Article 2 of the UDHR, as well as Articles 2 and 3 of the ICESCR and the ICCPR, explicitly provide for the prohibition of discrimination based on race and sex, as well as for equality of men and women.

have gradually lessened the barriers of sex, property, race, religion, and other qualifications in a more substantial manner.

As suggested by the history just described, the universality of human rights was claimed by the exploited and marginalized groups who had been prevented from enjoying human rights. Western powers, in contrast, were inclined to deny the universal nature of human rights by resorting to differences in color, sex, religion, culture, or social custom. The Western powers' reluctance to recognize the universality of human rights can also be seen in the attitudes of states toward international mechanisms for the protection of human rights. For three decades after the establishment of the United Nations, the United States was reluctant to strengthen its human rights mechanisms. Although thousands of petitions were sent to the U.N. Human Rights Commission to deal with concrete human rights abuses, it refused to take up these petitions until the late 1960s. A major reason for this negative attitude was the reluctance of the major powers, especially the United States.[21] The United States was also extremely reluctant to ratify the international human rights covenants of 1966 and other human rights treaties. It ratified the ICCPR only in 1992, with reservations, understandings, and declarations substantially nullifying its effect, and has yet to ratify the ICESCR.

Today, however, the Western powers tend to assert the universality of human rights, and anti-universalist arguments based on cultural or religious differences are mainly put forward by leaders of Asia and Africa.[22] Non-Western intellectuals and leaders often criticize Western human rights discourse or diplomacy to rebut external criticism of human rights conditions in their own countries. Constant resort to the principle of nonintervention or domestic jurisdiction reveals this motivation. However, such politically motivated criticism reinforces, rather than diminishes, the strength of Western claims. Moreover, despite their criticism of the West's preoccupations and biases, they themselves unconsciously share West-centric ways of thinking because of the global influence of American information and culture, these leaders' own educational backgrounds, and their Westernized way of life.[23]

When human rights is criticized by appealing to "particularity," the "Asian way," "Islam," the "social customs of Hinduism," the "ethics of Confucianism," and the like are invoked as specific examples. But the "European

21. The U.S. government was reluctant to establish an effective mechanism for human rights in the United Nations partly because it was concerned that race problems in the United States might be taken up in the United Nations. American NGOs, in contrast, were generally eager to strengthen the mechanism.
22. See Part I of this book.
23. As to the huge influence of American information and culture, see, for example, Edward Said, *Orientalism* (New York: Vintage Books, 1979); Joseph S. Nye, Jr., *Bound to Lead: The Changing Nature of American Power* (New York: Basic Books, 1990), pp. 188–201; John Tomlinson, *Cultural Imperialism: A Critical Introduction* (Baltimore: Johns Hopkins University Press, 1991).

way" and "Christianity" are seldom referred to as examples of such particularity! It is almost always assumed that what is universal is something Western whereas particularity refers to something non-Western. This is very strange given the fact that an overwhelming majority of the world's population are non-Westerners.[24] So long as one relies on the dichotomy between "Western universalism" and "non-Western particularism," there is little room left to think that something non-Western, whether it be Asian, African, Islamic, or Confucian, can be universally valid.

The point here is that the idea of human rights has almost always been qualified, whether in its "Eastern" or "Western" variants. Rather than worry about the origin of human rights, it is more useful to think about how to further universalize human rights. Nor is it just a question of universalizing the same set of "original" human rights. When ideas or institutions expand from their place of origin to other regions, they inevitably transform their original nature or characteristic features in order to be accepted by the inhabitants of the regions to which they spread. Human rights were born in Europe for protecting individuals from the abuse of power of states, but they have transformed themselves and become more comprehensive, including social and economic rights as well. They have come to protect humans not only from the power of states, but also from nonstate actors. Today, the mechanism of human rights is an essential tool for realizing the well-being of humanity under the modern system of sovereign states and capitalist economies. It must be adopted by all nations in this system, irrespective of their civilizational backgrounds. Precisely because of this global significance, West-centric biases must be overcome, and the raison d'être of human rights must be grounded in a broader, intercivilizational perspective.

Civil and Political Rights – Centrism

One of the most serious flaws in contemporary human rights discourse is the identification of civil and political rights with human rights in general. This is not limited to a view that "real" or "authentic" human rights are civil and political rights.[25] An overwhelming majority of the human rights discourse

---

24. It is true that the universality of an idea is different from the universality of those who share the idea. However, the very fact that some 1.5 billion share Confucian culture, or that 1.1 billion believe in Islam, suggests that there are some universal factors in these belief systems.
25. M. Cranston, *What Are Human Rights?* (New York: Basic Books, 1963); M. Bossuyt, "La distinction juridique entre les droits civils et politiques et les droits économiques, sociaux et culturels," *Revue des droits de l'homme* vol. 8 (1975), pp. 783–820; E. Vierdag, "The Legal Nature of the Rights Granted by the International Covenant on Economic, Social and Cultural Rights," *Netherlands Yearbook of International Law* vol. 9 (1978), pp. 69–105. See also Robert Nozick, *Anarchy, State and Utopia* (New York: Basic Books, 1974), pp. 167–74.

has been founded on this implicit identification.[26] Economic, social, and cultural rights are referred to only in passing or as a supplement. This tendency is especially strong in the United States, which has regarded freedom from the arbitrary powers of the state as most important and has been reluctant to accept economic, social, and cultural rights as human rights.[27] As Jack Donnelly also points out (see Chapter 2 in this volume), the situation is less problematic in Western European states, which generally take a more comprehensive approach to human rights. However, this bias is also evident in the discourse of many major human rights NGOs, the majority of whose operations depend on the support of people in the North. Their activities are widely reported, and their claims are generally regarded as more reliable than official governmental publications because of their independent status and their devotion to the cause of human rights, so their objectivity and reliability must be scrutinized.

Let us first take the *Amnesty International Report,* the best-known annual report.[28] It starts with an introduction and a few essays dealing with such issues as campaigns, human rights education, and work with international organizations. It then reports human rights conditions country by country, spending between half a page and four pages per country. The 1997 Report covers 150 countries, and the method is purely descriptive. The report deals almost exclusively with civil and political rights, although by statute it recognizes that human rights are indivisible and interdependent.[29] With regard to the method through which it selects countries, allocates pages, and describes each country's human rights conditions, as well as the bases for judgments included in the descriptions, it provides few explanations. It is difficult for readers to judge its standards and procedures in these critical areas.

The *Human Rights Watch World Report,* which covers some 65 countries in its 1996 version, has similar characteristics.[30] It starts with an introduction and surveys human rights conditions country by country within regional groupings, with brief overviews of each region. It ends with brief descriptions

---

26. In fact, because of the prominence of the "liberal paradigm" in human rights discourse, human rights have often been equated mainly with civil rights, rather than civil and political rights. The oft-employed terminology "human rights and democracy" demonstrates this tendency. In this expression, "human rights" represents civil rights, while political rights are expressed by "democracy." See, in this respect, an interesting observation by J. Habermas, "Human Rights and Popular Sovereignty," *Ratio Juris* vol. 7 (1994), pp. 1–13.

27. For a critical analysis, see Philip Alston, "U.S. Ratification of the Covenant on Economic, Social and Cultural Rights," *American Journal of International Law* vol. 84 (1990), pp. 365–93.

28. In what follows, I am referring to the *Amnesty International Report 1997* (London: Amnesty International Publications, 1997).

29. *Amnesty International Report 1997,* p. 355.

30. Human Rights Watch, *Human Rights Watch World Report 1996* (New York: Human Rights Watch, 1996).

of specific projects such as the arms project, the children's rights project, and the women's rights project. Again the method is descriptive, with sporadic value judgments embedded in the description of human rights conditions it takes up. Like the Amnesty report, it does not satisfy the requirements of accountability and transparency in its judgment. Moreover, it deals almost exclusively with civil and political rights, showing little concern with economic, social, and cultural rights. This may be justified to a certain extent because both Amnesty International and Human Rights Watch may have good strategic reasons for limiting their mandate and they can still perform an excellent job by doing so. However, it cannot be denied that this contributes to the prevalent perception that only civil and political rights are human rights.

Freedom in the World (1996 version) by Freedom House is different from the former two reports in the following respects. First, it evaluates the political and civil rights of 191 nations and 57 related territories by grading 1 (most free) to 7 (least free) and classifies countries as "free," "partly free," and "not free." Second, it provides information on economic systems, purchasing power parities, life expectancy, and the population percentage of ethnic groups of most countries it covers. Third, it contains a table of social and economic comparisons composed of real GDP per capita and life expectancy.[31]

However, it shares with the Amnesty International and Human Rights Watch reports the characteristic features of a strong emphasis on civil and political rights. References to socioeconomic factors are limited to crude statistical data of respective nations as a whole (as opposed to the socioeconomic rights of individuals).[32] It also shares the problematic feature of the lack of accountability in its observations and judgments. In this respect, its problem is even more serious because, unlike the Amnesty International and Human Rights Watch reports, *Freedom in the World* not only observes human rights conditions in countries, but also dares to rate countries according to its own standard.

In order to rate countries by human rights standards one must have sophisticated methods that are endorsed from a number of perspectives. First, they must reflect the major human rights instruments, including the Universal Declaration of 1948, the ICESCR, the ICCPR, and the Vienna Declaration on human rights of 1993, in a comprehensive and well-balanced manner. Second, they must also reflect intercivilizational legitimacy. Third, they must satisfy basic requirements from a perspective of statistical methodology.[33] They must

---

31. Freedom House Survey Team, *Freedom in the World: The Annual Survey of Political Rights and Civil Liberties 1995–1996* (Freedom House, 1996), pp. 530–8 and the first page of the respective countries reviewed.
32. Freedom House, *Freedom in the World 1995–1996*, pp. 539–40.
33. See R. Barsh, "Measuring Human Rights," *Human Rights Quarterly* vol. 15 (1993), pp. 87–121.

make explicit the ways and procedures used to reach ratings such as the data and materials they use, who operationalizes them and in what capacity, the methods adopted to minimize their inevitable biases and preconceptions, and other requirements for accountability. The survey methodology in *Freedom in the World* is far from satisfactory in these essential requirements. Although it shows checklists of civil and political rights, it does not elaborate by what specific standards and procedures it classifies countries from the most to the least free. It claims that "Freedom House does not have a culture-bound view of democracy" but does not demonstrate the basis for this assertion.[34]

This argument is not intended to deny that these NGOs have played an indispensable role in mitigating cruelties of human rights violations around the world for years. Moreover, some human rights may be intrinsically difficult to measure, and my criticisms of these groups' methods may be too harsh. However, given their enormous influence, their activities must be constantly scrutinized, their flaws must be rectified, and their intercivilizational legitimacy must be strengthened. Otherwise, it would be difficult to respond to the criticism of "cultural imperialism" or biased self-righteousness of the West often made by people in the Third World.

Charles Humana's *World Human Rights Guide* is far less influential than the reports by major rights NGOs.[35] However, from a theoretical perspective, it is much more interesting because it elaborates the method of assessment in an explicit manner. It basically covers states with a population exceeding one million and assesses forty rights in these countries. Its main sources of information are major Western human rights NGOs and the Western mass media.[36] It classifies the degree of protection of rights into four categories: (1) unqualified respect for rights; (2) qualified satisfactory answers due to occasional breaches thereof; (3) frequent violations thereof; and (4) a constant pattern of violations thereof. In the assessment, it weighs seven sorts of violations of freedoms involving physical suffering. In this way, it assesses human rights conditions in respective countries with a rating from 100 percent to 0 percent. Humana's assessment was adopted by the

---

34. *Freedom in the World 1995–1996*, p. 531. See critical remarks in R. Goldstein, "The Limitations of Using Quantitative Data in Studying Human Rights Abuses," in Thomas B. Jabine and Richard P. Claude, eds., *Human Rights and Statistics: Getting the Record Straight* (Philadelphia: University of Pennsylvania Press, 1992), p. 48; and in D. Gupta et al., "Creating a Composite Index for Assessing Country Performance in the Field of Human Rights," *Human Rights Quarterly* vol. 16 (1994), pp. 137–8.

35. Charles Humana, *World Human Rights Guide*, 3rd ed. (New York: Oxford University Press, 1992).

36. More specifically, Humana draws almost exclusively from American, British, and French NGOs and mass media. Although some of them may claim an international character, no one can deny that they are led, supported, and financed by Western activists and capital. Not only does he ignore NGOs and media institutions in developing countries, whose population accounts for more than 80 percent of the world's total, but even those in developed countries other than the United States, the United Kingdom, and France are ignored.

United Nations Development Programme as an index indicating political freedoms in the Human Development Report 1991.[37] However, this decision was severely criticized by developing countries and was abandoned in subsequent versions.[38]

Although I agree that human development indexes should have human rights perspectives, I believe that the decision to use Humana's indexes is wrong. They have a fundamental problem common to the major human rights reports described earlier: failure to embrace human rights in a comprehensive and well-balanced manner, with an excessive focus on civil and political rights. Humana's West-centric narrowness is evident in his very definition of human rights: "Human rights are the laws, customs, and practices that have evolved over the centuries to protect ordinary people, minorities, groups, and races from oppressive rulers and governments."[39] It is evident that this does not reflect the internationally accepted definition of human rights, which includes not only civil rights, but also economic, social, cultural, and political rights.

Humana claims that he adopted "human rights which can be clearly assessed" as its criterion. However, he includes few economic, social, and cultural rights. Only three out of the forty rights come from the ICESCR. He justifies this selection by arguing that "the articles [of the ICESCR] usually refer to vague guarantees such as 'recognizing the right of' or 'taking steps towards' respecting a particular right." By citing Article 12(2) of the ICESCR, he says that "[s]ince promises and aspirations cannot be measured, . . . the questionnaire could make only limited use of the articles of the ICESCR."[40] However, this argument cannot be maintained.

Article 12(2) provides the right for the enjoyment of the highest attainable standard of health. To achieve the full realization of this right, it provides for such steps as the reduction of the still-birth rate and of infant mortality; the improvement of environmental and industrial hygiene; the prevention, treatment, and control of epidemics and other diseases; and the creation of conditions assuring medical service and medical attention in the event of sickness. One can measure the extent to which states meet their obligations by invoking objective indexes such as the rates of stillbirths, of infant mortality, of epidemic mortality, and so on. These can be used to mea-

---

37. UNDP, *Human Development Report 1991* (New York: Oxford University Press, 1991), pp. 19–21.

38. UNDP, *Human Development Report 1993* (New York: Oxford University Press, 1993), p. 105. See also Barsh, "Measuring Human Rights," pp. 87–90.

39. Humana, *World Human Rights Guide,* p. 4.

40. Humana, *World Human Rights Guide,* pp. 7–8. In making this argument, Humana ignored earlier studies such as Goldstein's, which had demonstrated that the area of economic and social rights has far more reliable and operationalizable data than the area of civil and political rights. Goldstein, "The Limitations of Using Quantitative Data in Studying Human Rights Abuses," pp. 40ff.

sure the improvement or degradation of human rights conditions in individual countries, or as indexes for comparison across countries.

The same is true for other economic, social, and cultural rights. For example, Humana does not address the protection of and assistance to the family (Article 10 of the ICESCR), the right to an adequate standard of living (Article 11), and the right to education (Article 13). The enjoyment of these rights can be assessed with greater objectivity than the rights he examines. For example, a question of whether and how adequately a state accords to mothers paid leave or leave with adequate social security benefits can at least prima facie or indirectly be assessed by inquiring into the amount and period of such payments or security benefits. The same can be said of data on daily caloric intake per person, the literacy rate, and the like. It is true that there is room to argue whether and to what extent these figures adequately indicate the degree to which individual rights are enjoyed. Most existing data are collected and provided by economists and economic institutions or for development studies without reference to human rights experts or institutions. They are expressed as aggregate figures, and therefore cannot be used as standards for assessing individuals' enjoyment of human rights.

However, the problem of arbitrary judgment is not limited to economic, social, and cultural rights. It is even worse in the case of the civil and political rights that the existing literature endeavors to assess.[41] For example, Humana fails to give specific criteria in judging human rights conditions according to four categories, which range from unqualified respect to constant violation. Moreover, Humana gives triple weight to seven items, the violation of which involves physical suffering, but his selection of these rights lacks international and intercivilizational grounds.[42]

Prioritization of rights is an enormously difficult task. Experts are far from agreement with each other. However, we can at least point out some perspectives that must be taken into consideration when dealing with this problem. First, we must look into the existing international instruments on human rights and identify the significance of a right in question from the following perspectives: how many states are parties to the instruments that provide for the right in question; whether states that are parties to the conventions are allowed to derogate from the protection of the right; whether the right is construed to be a peremptory norm; and whether the violation of the right is characterized as an international crime.[43] Second, we must consider transnational

---

41. See Goldstein, "The Limitations of Using Quantitative Data in Studying Human Rights Abuses," pp. 40–4.
42. Humana, *World Human Rights Guide*, pp. 5–6.
43. Regarding the question of how to prioritize rights, see T. Meron, "On a Hierarchy of International Human Rights," *American Journal of International Law* vol. 80 (1986), pp. 1–23.

and intercivilizational perspectives: whether major NGOs and leading media (both North and South) regard a particular right as being more important than other rights; whether a right in question is prescribed, endorsed, or at least construed to be compatible with the precepts of major religions; and whether we can find an equivalent norm among major legal systems or social ethics transcending civilizational boundaries.

Humana does not bother himself with these subtleties and ramifications, but simply relies on what he "regards as a straightforward exercise of common sense" in selecting prioritized rights.[44] There might be a global agreement on giving extra weight to the rights whose violation involves physical suffering. However, it is highly doubtful whether the entire international community would agree to the seven items that Humana actually lists. This is particularly the case with the "freedom from capital punishment." As of December 1996, only 29 out of some 190 states are parties to the Second Optional Protocol to the ICCPR, aiming at the abolition of the death penalty. The prohibition of the death penalty does not constitute a contemporary norm of general international law. From an intercivilizational perspective, how one judges the death penalty is a fundamental question of one's philosophical and religious views. Debates on these matters will continue for years to come. Whatever Humana's view may be, the "freedom from capital punishment" cannot be an objective, even less a weighted, criterion to assess contemporary human rights conditions around the world.

The need for an international and intercivilizational perspective on human rights that encompasses civil and political rights as well as economic, social, and cultural rights should now be evident. Let us now suggest, in the limited space available, what such a framework might look like.

AN INTERCIVILIZATIONAL PERSPECTIVE ON HUMAN RIGHTS

The Term "Civilization"

We must have a perspective that enables us to evaluate human rights in the long history of humanity, to judge its proper range and applicability, and to compare it with other mechanisms pursuing spiritual and material well-being of humanity.[45] We may call this perspective an intercivilizational

---

44. Humana, *World Human Rights Guide*, p. 6.
45. As to my view of human rights as a specific formulation of a universal pursuit for spiritual and material well-being, see Onuma Yasuaki, "In Quest of Intercivilizational Human Rights," esp. pp. 8–9, 14 n. 4, and 15 ns. 54 and 55.

approach to human rights. This approach requires us to see the mechanism of human rights not merely within the West-centric modern civilization where it was born and raised, but from other civilizational perspectives as well.

Of course, the term "civilization" is an ambiguous notion with hundreds of definitions.[46] There is also the danger of abusing and overusing the notion of civilization in dealing with global affairs.[47] Thus, it may be better to avoid this term and instead to adopt the term "culture" as a comprehensive analytical concept, defined as a prevailing way of thinking and behavior in society. There have actually been remarkable studies in the area of human rights utilizing the notion of "cross-cultural perspectives" in recent years.[48] These studies share perspectives with the intercivilizational approach in many respects.

However, there are problems in using the term "culture" as a comprehensive analytical concept. First, in the field of human rights, the term has not been used as a comprehensive notion designating a prevailing way of thinking and behavior in general. Rather, it is used as a narrower concept, not including economic, social, civil, and political fields. All international instruments on human rights follow this narrower terminology. Thus, it is difficult to avoid confusion if one uses "culture" as a comprehensive concept. It would be better to use the term "civilization" as a comprehensive concept.

Second, there are factors that influence ways of thinking and behavior of certain people whose existence transcends national boundaries, but without covering the entire globe. We may call such a sphere a "region." However, this sphere of peoples has both a geographical and a *historical* dimension. It may last long with substantial changes in its characteristic features. Such a sphere of people can be most appropriately termed a "civilization." Religions, languages, ethics, and customs that influence the thoughts and behavior of people transcending national boundaries are all part of a "civilization." Although the term "international" will continue to be the most important concept to understand various phenomena interrelating or transcending nations, the term "intercivilizational" will be most useful to supplement perspectives on human rights and other global issues.[49]

46. See, for example, L. Febvre et al., *Civilisation: le mot et l'idée* (Paris: Le renaissance du livre, 1930).
47. Samuel Huntington, in his alarming article "The Clash of Civilizations," *Foreign Affairs* (August 1993), pp. 22–49, apparently made the mistake of overestimating the role of civilizations in international relations. His recent book, *The Clash of Civilizations and the Remaking of World Order* (New York: Simon & Schuster, 1996), basically retains the themes and characteristic features of the article.
48. See Abdullahi An-Na'im, ed., *Human Rights in Cross-Cultural Perspectives: A Quest for Consensus* (Philadelphia: University of Pennsylvania Press, 1992); see also Chapter 6 in this volume.
49. See my remarks in "Promoting Training and Awareness – The Tasks of Education in International Law," *Proceedings of the 75th Anniversary Convocation of the American Society of International Law, April 23–25, 1981* (1983), pp. 163–7.

The Need for Dialogue

A major reason why non-Western nations, especially East Asian nations, have criticized West-centric universalism is political, or even emotional, opposition to the self-righteous human rights diplomacy of the West. As such, the political controversies over the universality versus relativity of human rights have been rather futile from a theoretical perspective. Yet, they have played a significant role. They have provided the opportunity to a large number of people both in the East and the West to realize that sincere intercivilizational dialogues are needed if ever human rights are to be truly globalized. The chapters in Part II of this book attest to the fact that there has been an increasing amount of research dealing with diverse religions, cultures, and social customs in relation to human rights: cross-cultural perspectives on human rights, non-Western cultural, religious, or ethical components of human rights, and so on. Intercivilizational frameworks of human rights may well be established in the process of such endeavors. In order to make these endeavors more theoretically solid, it is submitted that we must take into consideration the following points.

First, previous studies dealing with tensions between religions or cultures on the one hand, and human rights on the other, have tended to focus on non-Western religions or cultures. They have sought to find out the "cultural or religious bases" of human rights in non-Western cultures, or "enlightened interpretations" of such non-Western religions, so that they can be construed as compatible with the existing standards of human rights.[50] Given the fact that predominant religions and cultures in many developing countries have been used to rationalize serious human rights violations including cruel punishment, inhuman treatment, and discriminatory practices, this is understandable. However, from an intercivilizational perspective, this kind of project has a problem: It assumes that only non-Western religions or cultures must be reinterpreted to ground human rights. In other words, it is implicitly assumed that Western cultures or religions have no problem in grounding human rights.

That is obviously not the case if we note the prevalent understanding of human rights in some Western nations, such as the reluctance to accept the international recognized notion of social and economic rights in the United States. Cultural or religious factors such as American individualism and/or American exceptionalism may help to explain this opposition to social and

---

50. See An-Na'im, ed., *Human Rights in Cross-Cultural Perspectives,* especially An-Na'im, "Toward a Cross-Cultural Approach to Defining International Standards of Human Rights," and the chapters by W. Alford on China, J. Zion on North American Indians, A. McChesney on Canadian Aborigines, H. Fruhling on Latin America, and M. Carneiro da Cunha on Brazilian Indians.

economic rights.[51] This suggests that scrutiny of the tension between predominant local cultures, ethics, or religions, with the aim to provide "enlightened interpretations" compatible with international human rights standards, is needed in developed countries as well.[52]

Second, when one seeks to ground human rights in local cultures or religions, one should not explore merely traditional cultures or religions, or original teachings. Cultures and religions change over time, particularly in this age of increasing globalization. Although Confucian values are still important factors in explaining ways of thinking and behavior of the Chinese, Koreans, and Japanese, they are different from each other and from the original teachings of Confucius. One must explore cultures or religions that are actually "living" in peoples' ordinary lives.

On the other hand, one can find some ideas or expressions similar to those of human rights in almost all religious teachings or traditional cultures. Merely pointing out particular teachings or particular forms of culture as "compatible with," "similar to," or even "an origin of" particular human rights makes little sense. Such sporadic or ad hoc references do not base human rights as a whole. We must explore the specific status and functions of such "similar" or "equivalent" norms in the comprehensive normative and societal settings. As Panikkar put it, a perspective of the homeomorphic, or existential, functional equivalent to the concept of human rights is important.[53]

We must also seek to identify sources and methods in exploring local cultures, religions, and ethics to ground human rights. In the contemporary world, there are thousands of cultures and religions, ranging from world religions to cults shared by a small number of believers. What criteria do we use to choose "important" or "relevant" cultures, religions, or ethical systems? By what procedures? Is the notion Charles Taylor develops in the following chapter of an unforced consensus, or the principle of retribution tied to proportionality advocated by Alison Renteln,[54] a useful tool for this purpose? Is the notion of a civilization, shared by several nations within a region for a certain period of time, a useful tool to limit the number of cultural, religious, or ethical systems to be selected? These questions must be explored and answered.

---

51. See hostile opinions based on individualism and civil and political rights cited in Philip Alston, ed., *The United Nations and Human Rights* (New York: Oxford University Press, 1992), pp. 373–4, 378, 381–4.

52. Leary rightly interprets An-Na'im's view that internal discourse within particular cultural traditions should include the one in Western cultures. V. Leary, "Postliberal Strands in Western Human Rights Theory," in An-Na'im, *Human Rights in Cross-Cultural Perspectives,* p. 107. However, in this and in other studies, the overall emphasis is on discovering the cultural or religious bases of human rights in the non-Western world.

53. R. Panikkar, "Is the Notion of Human Rights a Western Concept?" *Diogenes* vol. 120 (1982), pp. 77–8.

54. Alison Renteln, *International Human Rights* (Newbury Park: Sage, 1990), pp. 14, 88–137.

Rereading the Major Instruments on Human Rights

In order to identify a major source of globally legitimate standards of human rights, it is important to rely on international instruments on human rights, but with certain reservations. A clue about identifying intercivilizational human rights can be found in the provisions of the major international instruments on human rights to which the overwhelming majority of nations are committed. The most important among these are the so-called International Bill of Rights, that is, the Universal Declaration, the ICESCR, and the ICCPR. The Vienna Declaration of 1993 is also an important instrument for the expression of an interstate consensus on human rights at the end of the twentieth century.

From the perspective of international law, the multilateral human rights conventions are more important than the declarations or resolutions, because the former formally binds the contracting parties whereas the latter generally have only recommendatory force. However, an increasing number of international lawyers hold that at least some provisions of the Universal Declaration embody norms of general international law, or even of *jus cogens*.[55] Still, it cannot be denied that the Universal Declaration is relatively West-centric, reflecting the international power structures existing in 1948, when many Afro-Asian nations were still under colonial rule. The Vienna Declaration, in contrast, was a product of elaborate negotiations accommodating not only differences in terms of foreign policies, but also conflicts involving diverse religious, cultural, and ethical views held by almost all nations composing the international society. Its intercivilizational legitimacy is strengthened relative to the Universal Declaration.

Thus, taken as a whole, international human rights instruments can no longer be characterized as products of the West. They are the products of long discussions, controversies, and negotiations among various nations with diverse civilizational backgrounds. The Universal Declaration has been explicitly accepted or implicitly acquiesced to by an overwhelming majority of nations since its inception. Whatever political motivations governments had in ratifying, voting for, or acquiescing, these instruments represent common normative standards based on the widest attainable consensus among nations with diverse perspectives. No other instruments, whether they be U.S. or Chinese government's statements, claims of leading human rights

---

55. See, for example, Oscar Schachter, *International Law in Theory and Practice* (Dordrecht: Martinus Nijhoff, 1985), p. 338. Although Professor Shachter is critical of hasty characterizations of provisions of the UDHR as norms of customary international law, he argues that some basic rights such as freedom from slavery, torture, mass murder, prolonged arbitrary imprisonment, and systematic racial discrimination constitute part of customary international law.

NGOs, or views of leading scholars (not to mention Humana's "common sense"), can claim to represent the global consensus more legitimately.

If that is the case, we must operationalize these instruments in assessing human rights conditions as today's universal standards. If these instruments provide a comprehensive notion of human rights comprising economic, social, cultural, civil, and political rights, then the standard of assessment must reflect it. This will liberate us from West-centrism in the form of civil rights–centrism. At the same time, this will help to persuade both developing and developed countries to accept international judgments on human rights conditions in their countries.

Still, the existing international human rights instruments are no more than a starting point for identifying globally legitimate, intercivilizational human rights. They are essentially political products, taking the form of normative consensus. Thus, scrutiny of these instruments from critical perspectives as well as the search for other clues to intercivilizational human rights are needed. Views of experts, human rights NGOs, and the insights that emerge from cross-cultural dialogues on human rights can naturally provide some of these clues.

Finally, it is important to emphasize that the intercivilizational approach characterizes human rights as a means – an extremely important means – of realizing the spiritual and material well-being of humanity. It does not regard them as the end. Accordingly, it is critical of the absolutism or fetishism of human rights sometimes seen in human rights activists, and even in academics. Human rights should only be appreciated as long as their merits outweigh their demerits. As things stand now, there is no better alternative for promoting the spiritual and material well-being of humanity, which is why I think human rights should be universally adopted.[56] The usefulness and flaws of human rights must be constantly scrutinized, however, and their role must be complemented and substituted whenever it is necessary.

56. See my essay "In Quest of Intercivilizational Human Rights," p. 9.

CHAPTER 5

CONDITIONS OF AN UNFORCED
CONSENSUS ON HUMAN RIGHTS

CHARLES TAYLOR

INTRODUCTION

What would it mean to come to a genuine, unforced international consensus on human rights? I suppose it would be something like what Rawls describes in his *Political Liberalism* as an "overlapping consensus."[1] That is, different groups, countries, religious communities, and civilizations, although holding incompatible fundamental views on theology, metaphysics, human nature, and so on, would come to an agreement on certain norms that ought to govern human behavior. Each would have its own way of justifying this from out of its profound background conception. We would agree on the norms while disagreeing on why they were the right norms, and we would be content to live in this consensus, undisturbed by the differences of profound underlying belief.

The idea was already expressed in 1949 by Jacques Maritain: "I am quite certain that my way of justifying belief in the rights of man and the ideal of liberty, equality, fraternity is the only way with a firm foundation in truth. This does not prevent me from being in agreement on these practical convictions with people who are certain that their way of justifying them, entirely different from mine or opposed to mine, . . . , is equally the only way founded upon truth."[2]

Is this kind of consensus possible? Perhaps because of my optimistic nature, I believe that it is. But we have to confess at the outset that it is not

---

1. John Rawls, *Political Liberalism* (New York: Columbia University Press, 1993), lecture IV.
2. From the Introduction to UNESCO, *Human Rights: Comments and Interpretations* (London: Allan Wingate, 1949), pp. 10–11; cited in Abdullahi An-Na'im, "Towards a Cross-Cultural Approach to Defining International Standards of Human Rights: The Meaning of Cruel, Inhuman, or Degrading Treatment or Punishment," in Abdullahi Ahmed An-Na'im, ed., *Human Rights in Cross-Cultural Perspectives* (Philadelphia: University of Pennsylvania Press, 1992), pp. 28–9.

entirely clear around what the consensus would form, and we are only beginning to discern the obstacles we would have to overcome on the way there. I
want to talk a little about both these issues here.

First, what would the consensus be on? One might have thought this was
obvious: on human rights. That's what our original question was about, but
there is an immediate obstacle that has often been pointed out. Rights talk is
something that has roots in Western culture. Certain features of this talk have
roots in Western history, and there only. This is not to say that something
very like the underlying norms expressed in schedules of rights don't turn up
elsewhere, but they are not expressed in this language. We can't assume without further examination that a future unforced world consensus could be formulated to the satisfaction of everyone in the language of rights. Maybe yes,
maybe no. Or maybe partially yes, partially no, as we come to distinguish
among the things that have been associated in the Western package.

This is not to say that we already have some adequate term for whatever
universals we think we may discern between different cultures. Jack Donnelly speaks of "human dignity" as a universal value.[3] Onuma Yasuaki criticizes this term, pointing out that "dignity" has itself been a favorite term in
the Western philosophical stream that has elaborated human rights. He
prefers to speak of the "pursuit of spiritual and material well-being" as the
universal.[4] Where "dignity" might be too precise and culture-bound a term,
"well-being" might be too vague and general. Perhaps we are incapable at
this stage of formulating the universal values in play here. Perhaps we shall
always be incapable of this. This wouldn't matter, because what we need to
formulate for an overlapping consensus are certain norms of conduct. There
does seem to be some basis for hoping that we can achieve at least some
agreement on these norms. One can presumably find in all cultures condem-
nations of genocide, murder, torture, and slavery, as well as of, say, "disap-
pearances" and the shooting of innocent demonstrators.[5] The deep underlying values supporting these common conclusions will, in the nature of the
case, belong to the alternative, mutually incompatible justifications.

I have been distinguishing between norms of conduct and their underlying justification. The Western rights tradition in fact exists at both of these
levels. On one plane, it is a legal tradition, legitimating certain kinds of legal
actions and empowering certain kinds of people to make them. We could,
and people sometimes do, consider this legal culture as the proper candidate

---

3. Jack Donnelly, *Universal Human Rights in Theory and Practice* (Ithaca: Cornell University Press, 1989),
   pp. 28–37.
4. See Chapter 4.
5. See Sidney Jones, "The Impact of Asian Economic Growth on Human Rights," *Asia Project Working
   Paper Series* (New York: Council on Foreign Relations, January 1995), p. 9.

for universalization, arguing that its adoption can be justified in more than one way. Then a legal culture entrenching rights would define the norms around which world consensus would supposedly crystallize.

Some people already have trouble with this, such as Lee Kwan Yew and those in East Asia who sympathize with him. They see something danger-ously individualistic, fragmenting, dissolvent of community in this Western legal culture. (Of course, they have particularly in mind – or in their sights – the United States.[6]) In their criticism of Western procedures, they also seem to be attacking the underlying philosophy, which allegedly gives primacy to the individual, whereas supposedly a "Confucian" outlook would have a larger place for the community and the complex web of human relations in which each person stands.

The Western rights tradition also contains certain views on human nature, society, and the human good and carries some elements of an underlying jus-tification. It might help the discussion to distinguish these two levels, at least analytically, so that we can develop a more fine-grained picture of what our options are. Perhaps in fact, the legal culture could "travel" better, if it could be separated from some of its underlying justifications. Or perhaps the reverse is true, that the underlying picture of human life might look less frightening if it could find expression in a different legal culture. Or maybe neither of these simple solutions will work (this is my hunch), but modifica-tions need to be made to both; however, distinguishing the levels still helps, because the modifications are different on each level.

In any case, a good place to start the discussion would be to give a rapid portrait of the language of rights that has developed in the West and of the surrounding notions of human agency and the good. We could then proceed to identify certain centers of disagreement across cultures, and we might then see what if anything could be done to bridge these differences.

THE LANGUAGE OF RIGHTS

Many societies have held that it is good to ensure certain immunities or lib-erties to their members – or sometimes even to outsiders (think of the strin-gent laws of hospitality that hold in many traditional cultures). Everywhere

---

6. "I find parts of [the American system] totally unacceptable: guns, drugs, violent crime, vagrancy, unbecoming behaviour in public – in sum, the breakdown of civil society. The expansion of the right of the individual to behave or misbehave as he pleases has come at the expense of orderly society. In the East the main object is to have a well-ordered society so that everybody can have maximum enjoyment of his freedoms. This freedom can only exist in an ordered state and not in a natural state of con-tention." Fareed Zakaria, "Culture Is Destiny: A Conversation with Lee Kuan Yew," *Foreign Affairs* (March/April 1994), p. 111.

it is wrong to take human life, at least under certain circumstances and for certain categories of persons. Wrong is the opposite of right, so this is relevant to our discussion.

A quite different sense of the word is invoked when we start to use the definite or indefinite articles, or to put it in the plural, and speak of "a right" or "rights," or when we start to attribute these to persons, and speak of "your rights" or "my rights." This is to introduce what has been called "subjective rights." Instead of saying that it is wrong to kill me, we begin to say that I have a right to life. The two formulations are not equivalent in all respects, because in the latter case the immunity or liberty is considered as it were the property of someone. It is no longer just an element of the law that stands over and between all of us equally. That I have a right to life says more than that you shouldn't kill me. It gives me some control over this immunity. A right is something that in principle I can waive.[7] It is also something which I have a role in enforcing.

Some element of subjective right exists in all legal systems. The peculiarity of the West is that, first, the concept played a bigger role in European medieval societies than elsewhere in history, and, second, it was the basis of the rewriting of Natural Law theory that marked the seventeenth century. The older notion that human society stands under a Law of Nature, whose origin is the Creator, and that is thus beyond human will, became transposed. The fundamental law was reconceived as consisting of natural rights, attributed to individuals prior to society. At the origin of society stands a Contract, which takes people out of a State of Nature, and puts them under political authority, as a result of an act of consent on their part.

Subjective rights are not only crucial to the Western tradition; even more significant is the fact that they were projected onto Nature and formed the basis of a philosophical view of humans and their society, one that greatly privileges individuals' freedom and their right to consent to the arrangements under which they live. This view has become an important strand in Western democratic theory of the last three centuries.

The notion of (subjective) rights both serves to define certain legal powers and also provides the master image for a philosophy of human nature, of individuals and their societies. It operates both as legal norm and as underlying justification. Moreover, these two levels are not unconnected. The force of the underlying philosophy has brought about a steady promotion of the legal norm in our politicolegal systems so that it now occupies pride of place

---

7. Which is why Locke had to introduce a restrictive adjective to block this option of waiver, when he spoke of "inalienable rights." The notion of inalienability had no place in earlier natural right discourse, because this had no option of waiver.

in a number of contemporary polities. Charters of rights are now entrenched in the constitutions of a number of countries, and also of the European Union. These are the bases of judicial review, whereby the ordinary legislation of different levels of government can be invalidated on the grounds of conflict with these fundamental rights.

The modern Western discourse of rights involves, on one hand, a set of legal forms by which immunities and liberties are inscribed as rights, with certain consequences for the possibility of waiver and for the ways in which they can be secured – whether these immunities and liberties are among those from time to time granted by duly constituted authority or among those that are entrenched in fundamental law. On the other hand, it involves a philosophy of the person and of society, attributing great importance to the individual and making significant matters turn on his or her power of consent. In both these regards, it contrasts with many other cultures, including the premodern West, not because some of the same protections and immunities were not present, but because they had a quite different basis.[8]

When people protest against the Western rights model, they seem to have this whole package in their sights. We can therefore see how resistance to the Western discourse of rights might occur on more than one level. Some governments might resist the enforcement of even widely accepted norms because they have an agenda that involves their violation (for example, the contemporary Peoples Republic of China). Others, however, are certainly ready, even eager to espouse some universal norms, but they are made uneasy by the underlying philosophy of the human person in society. This seems to give pride of place to autonomous individuals, determined to demand their rights, even (indeed especially) in the face of widespread social consensus. How does this fit with the Confucian emphasis on close personal relationships, not only as highly valued in themselves, but as a model for the wider society? (See Chapter 9.) Can people who imbibe the full Western human rights ethos, which reaches its highest expression in the lone courageous individual fighting against all the forces of social conformity for her rights,

---

8. According to Louis Henkin, "The Human Rights Idea in Contemporary China: A Comparative Perspective," in R. Randle Edwards, Louis Henkin, and Andrew J. Nathan, *Human Rights in Contemporary China* (New York: Columbia University Press, 1986), p. 21:

> In the Chinese tradition the individual was not central, and no conception of individual rights existed in the sense known to the United States. The individual's participation in society was not voluntary, and the legitimacy of government did not depend on his consent or the consent of the whole people of individuals. . . .
>
> In traditional China, the idea was not individual liberty or equality but order and harmony, not individual independence but selflessness and cooperation, not freedom of individual conscience but conformity to orthodox truth. . . . . The purpose of society was not to preserve and promote individual liberty but to maintain the harmony of the hierarchical order and to see to it that truth prevailed.

ever be good members of a "Confucian" society? How does this ethic of demanding what is due to us fit with the Theravada Buddhist search for self-lessness, for self-giving and *dana* (generosity)?[9]

Taking the rights package as a whole is not necessarily wrong, because the philosophy is plainly part of what has motivated the great promotion enjoyed by this legal form. But the kinds of misgivings expressed in the previous paragraph, which cannot be easily dismissed, show the potential advantages of distinguishing the elements and loosening the connection between a legal culture of rights enforcement and the philosophical conceptions of human life that originally nourished it.

It might help to structure our thinking if we made a tripartite distinction. What we are looking for, in the end, is a world consensus on certain norms of conduct enforceable on governments. To be accepted in any given society, these would in each case have to repose on some widely acknowledged philosophical justification, and to be enforced, they would have to find expression in legal mechanisms. One way of putting our central question might be this: What variations can we imagine in philosophical justifications or in legal forms that would still be compatible with a meaningful universal consensus on what really matters to us, the enforceable norms?

Following this line of thinking, it might help to understand better just what exactly we might want to converge on in the world society of the future, as well as to measure our chances of getting there, if we imagine variations separately on the two levels. What I propose to do is look at a number of instances in which there seem to be obvious conflicts between the present language of human rights and one or more major contemporary cultures. The goal will be to try to imagine ways in which the conflict might be resolved and the essential norms involved in the human rights claim preserved, and this through some modification either of legal forms or of philosophy.

ALTERNATIVE LEGAL FORMS

I would like to look at four kinds of conflict. The first could be resolved by legal innovation, and I will briefly discuss this possibility, but it can best be tackled on the philosophical level. The other three involve the basic justification of human rights claims. In developing these, I will have to spell out much further the justificatory basis for Western thinking and practice about

9. See Sulak Sivaraksa, "Buddhism and Human Rights in Siam" (unpublished paper presented at Bangkok Workshop of the Human Rights Initiative, Carnegie Council on Ethics and International Affairs, March 1996), pp. 4–5. Sulak wonders whether the Western concept of freedom, closely allied with that of right, "has reached an end point in environmental degradation."

rights than I have in my rather sparse remarks about Natural Rights theory. I shall return to this later.

Let us take the kind of objection that I mentioned at the outset, that someone like Lee Kwan Yew might raise about Western rights practice and its alleged unsuitability for other societies, in particular East Asian ones. The basic notion is that this practice, obviously nourished by the underlying philosophy I described in the previous section, supposes that individuals are the possessors of rights and encourages them to act, to go out and aggressively seek to make good their rights. But this has a number of bad consequences. First of all, it focuses people on their rights, on what they can claim from society and others, rather than on their responsibilities, what they owe to the whole community or to its members. It encourages people to be self-regarding and leads to an atrophied sense of belonging. This in turn leads to a higher degree of social conflict, more and more many-sided, tending ultimately to a war of all against all. Social solidarity weakens, and the threat of violence increases.

This scenario seems rather overdrawn to some. However, it seems to have elements of truth to others, including to people within Western societies, which perhaps might make us doubt that we are on to a difference *between* civilizations here. In fact, there is a long tradition in the West warning against pure rights talk outside a context in which the political community has a strong positive value. This "communitarian" theorizing has taken on a new urgency today because of the experience of conflict and alienation and the fraying of solidarity in many Western democracies, notably but not only the United States. Does this mean that Lee Kwan Yew's formula might offer a solution to present-day America?

The absurdity of this suggestion brings us back to the genuine differences of culture that exist today. But if we follow through on the logic of the "communitarian" critique in the West we can perhaps find a framework in which to consider these differences.

One of the key points in the critique of a too exclusive focus on rights is that this neglects the crucial importance of political trust. Dictatorships, as Tocqueville pointed out, try to destroy trust between citizens,[10] but free societies vitally depend on it. The price of freedom is a strong common commitment to the political formula that binds us, because without the commit-

---

10. "L'égalité place les hommes à côté les uns des autres, sans rien commun qui les retienne. Le despotisme élève des barrières entre eux et les sépare. Elle les dispose ne point songer à leurs semblables et il leur fait une sorte de vertu publique de l'indifférance." [Equality places people next to each other, without a common link that really keeps them together. Despotism elevates barriers between people and keeps them apart. It predisposes individuals not to think of their compatriots and makes a kind of public virtue out of their indifference.] *La Démocratie en Amérique,* vol. 2, IIe partie, chapitre IV (Paris: Édition Garnier-Flammarion, 1981), vol. 2, p. 131.

ment the formula would have to be aggressively enforced and this threatens freedom. What will very quickly dissolve the commitment for each and every one of us is the sense that others no longer share it or are willing to act on it. The common allegiance is nourished on trust.

This goes for a political regime centered on the retrieval of rights as much as for any other. The condition of our being able to go out and seek to enforce our own rights is that the system within which this is carried out retains the respect and allegiance of everybody. Once rights retrieval begins to eat into this, once it begins to create a sense of embattled grievance pitting group against group, undermining the sense of common allegiance and solidarity, the whole system of freewheeling rights enforcement is in danger.

The issue is not "individualism" as such. There are many forms of this, and some have grown up together with modern, democratic forms of political society. The danger is in any form of either individualism or group identity that undercuts or undermines the trust that we share a common allegiance as citizens of this polity.

I don't want to pursue here the conditions of political trust in Western democracies, at least not for its own sake,[11] but I want to use this requirement as a heuristic tool, in search of a point of consensus on human rights. One way of considering a claim, similar to that of Lee Kwan Yew's, that the Western rights focus does not fit a certain cultural tradition would be to ask how certain fundamental liberties and immunities could be guaranteed in the society in question, consistent with the maintenance of political trust. This means, of course, that one will not consider satisfactory any solution that does not preserve these liberties and immunities while accepting whatever modifications in legal form one needs to generate a sense of common acceptance of the guaranteeing process in the society concerned.

In the concrete case of Lee Kwan Yew's Singapore, this would mean that his claim in its present form is hardly receivable. There is too much evidence of the stifling of dissent and of the cramping (to say the least) of the democratic political process in Singapore. However, this kind of claim should lead us to reflect further on how immunities of the kinds we seek in human rights declarations can best be preserved in "Confucian" societies.

Turning back to Western societies, we note that judges and the judicial process enjoy in general a great deal of prestige and respect.[12] In some countries, this respect is based on a long tradition in which some notion of funda-

---

11. I have talked about substantially similar issues in somewhat different terms in the last chapter of *The Malaise of Modernity* (Toronto: Anansi Press, 1991), and in "Liberalism and the Public Sphere," *Philosophical Arguments* (Cambridge, MA: Harvard University Press, 1995), chapter 13.
12. That is what is so dangerous to public order in cases like the 1995 O. J. Simpson trial, which both show up and further entrench a deep lack of respect for and trust in the judicial process.

mental law played an important part, and hence in which its guardians had a special place. Is there a way of connecting rights retrieval in other societies to offices and institutions that enjoy the highest moral prestige there?

Adverting to another tradition, we note that in Thailand at certain crucial junctures the immense moral prestige of the monarchy has been used to confer legitimacy on moves to end military violence and repression and return to constitutional rule. This was the case following the student demonstrations in October 1973, and again in the wake of the popular reactions against the seizure of power by General Suchinda Kraprayoon in May 1992. In both cases, a military junta responded with violence, only to find its position unsustainable and to be forced to give way to a civilian regime and renewed elections. In both these cases, King Bhumibhol played a critical role.[13] The king was able to play this role because of elements in the traditions that have contributed to the Thai conception of monarchy, some of which go way back. For example, the conception of the king as *dharmaraja,* in the tradition of Ashoka,[14] sees the ruler as charged with establishing dharma in the world.

It was perhaps crucial to the upheavals of 1973 and 1992 that a king with this kind of status played the part he did. The trouble is that the power of the royal office can also be used in the other direction, as happened in 1976 when right-wing groups used the slogan "Nation, King and Religion" as a rallying cry in order to attack democratic and radical leaders. The movement of reaction culminated in the October 1976 coup, which relegated the democratic constitution once again to the wastebasket.[15]

The issue arising from all this is the following: Can the immense power to create trust and consensus that resides in the Thai monarchy be in some way stabilized, regularized, and channeled in support of constitutional rule and the defense of certain human rights, such as those concerned with the security of the person? In Weberian terms, could the charisma here be "routinized" enough to impart a stable direction to it without being lost altogether? If a way could be found to draw on this royal charisma, together with the legitimacy enjoyed by certain individuals of proven "merit" who are invested with moral authority as in the Thai tradition, to enhance support for a democratic order respectful of those immunities and liberties we gener-

---

13. There is a Western analogue in the positive part played by Juan Carlos during the coup in Madrid in 1974.
14. See Stanley Tambiah, *World Conqueror and World Renouncer* (New York: Cambridge University Press, 1976).
15. See the discussion in John Girling, *Thailand: Society and Politics* (Ithaca: Cornell University Press, 1981), pp. 154–7. Frank Reynolds in his "Legitimation and Rebellion: Thailand's Civic Religion and the Student Uprising of October, 1973," in Bardwell L. Smith, ed., *Religion and Legitimation of Power in Thailand, Laos, and Burma* (Chambersburg, PA: Anima Books, 1978), discusses the use by the student demonstrators of the symbols of "Nation, Religion, Monarchy."

ally describe as human rights, the fact that it might deviate from the standard Western model of judicial review initiated by individuals should be accorded less importance than the fact that it protects human beings from violence and oppression. We would have in fact achieved convergence on the substance of human rights, in spite of differences in form.

ALTERNATIVE FOUNDATIONS

Suppose we take the "communitarian" arguments against Western rights discourse emanating from other societies at another level, not questioning so much the legal forms but expressing disagreement with the underlying philosophical justification. My example is again drawn from Thailand. This society has seen in the last century a number of attempts to formulate reformed interpretations of the majority religion, Theravada Buddhism. Some of these have sought a basis in this form of Buddhism for democracy and human rights. This raises a somewhat broader issue than the one I'm focusing on because it concerns an alternative foundation for both democracy and human rights. The job of attaining a consensus on human rights in today's world will probably be simplified, however, if we don't try – at least at first – to come to agreement about forms of government, but concentrate solely on human rights standards. I believe that the developments in Thai thinking described here illustrate what is involved in coming to an "overlapping consensus" on the narrower basis as well.

One main stream of reform consists of movements that (as they see it) attempt to purify Buddhism, to turn it away from a focus on ritual, on gaining merit and even worldly success through blessings and acts of piety, and to focus more on (what they see as) the original goal of Enlightenment. The late Phutthathat (Buddhadasa) has been a major figure in this regard. This stream tries to return to what (it sees as) the original core of Buddhist teaching, about the unavoidability of suffering, the illusion of the self, and the goal of Nibbana. It attacks the "superstition" of those who seek potent amulets, the blessings of monks, and the like; it wants to separate the search for enlightenment from the seeking of merit through ritual; and it is very critical of the whole metaphysical structure of belief that has developed in mainstream Buddhism about heavens, hell, gods, and demons, which plays a large part in popular belief. It has been described by the Sri Lankan anthropologist, Gananath Obeyesekere, as a "protestant Buddhism."[16]

This stream seems to be producing new reflections on Buddhism as a basis

---

16. Richard Gombrich and Gananath Obeyesekere, *Buddhism Transformed: Religious Change in Sri Lanka* (Princeton, NJ: Princeton University Press, 1988), chapters 6 and 7.

for democratic society and human rights. Sulak Sivaraksa and Saneh Chamarik are among the leading figures whose writings reflect this. They and others in their milieu are highly active in social justice advocacy. They are concerned with alternative models of development, which would be more ecologically sound, concerned to put limits to growth, critical of "consumerism," and conducive to social equality. The Buddhist commitment lies behind all these goals. As Sulak explains it, the Buddhist commitment to nonviolence entails a nonpredatory stance toward the environment and calls also for the limitation of greed, one of the sources of anger and conflict.[17]

We can see here an agenda of universal well-being, but what specifically pushes to democracy, to ensuring that people take charge of their own lives rather than simply being the beneficiaries of benevolent rule? Two things seem to come together in this outlook to underpin a strong democratic commitment. The first is the notion, central to Buddhism, that ultimately each individual must take responsibility for his or her own Enlightenment. The second is a new application of the doctrine of nonviolence, which is now seen to call for a respect for the autonomy of each person, demanding in effect a minimal use of coercion in human affairs. This carries us far from the politics of imposed order, decreed by the wise minority, which has long been the traditional background to various forms and phases of nondemocratic rule. It is also evident that this underpinning for democracy offers a strong support for human rights legislation, and that, indeed, is how it is understood by thinkers like Sulak.[18]

There is an outlook here that converges on a policy of defense of human rights and democratic development but that is rather different from the standard Western justifications of these. It isn't grounded on a doctrine of the dignity of human beings as something commanding respect. The injunction to respect comes rather as a consequence of the fundamental value of nonviolence, which also generates a whole host of other consequences (including the requirement for an ecologically responsible development and the need to set limits to growth). Human rights don't stand out, as they often do in the West, as a claim on their own, independent from the rest of our moral commitments, even sometimes in potential conflict with them.

This Buddhist conception provides an alternative way of linking together the agenda of human rights and that of democratic development. Whereas in the Western framework, these go together because they are both seen as corequirements of human dignity, and indeed, as two facets of liberty, a connection of a somewhat different kind is visible among Thai Buddhists of this

17. See Sulak Sivaraksa, *Seeds of Peace: A Buddhist Vision for Renewing Society* (Berkeley and Bangkok: Parallax Press, 1992), chapter 9.
18. See Sulak Sivaraksa, *Seeds of Peace,* especially Part Two.

reform persuasion. Their commitment to people-centered and ecologically sensitive development makes them strong allies of those communities of villagers who are resisting encroachment by the state and big business, fighting to defend their lands and forests. This means that they are heavily into what has been recognized as a crucial part of the agenda of democratization in Thailand – decentralization, and in particular the recovery of local community control over natural resources.[19] They form a significant part of the NGO community committed to this agenda. A rather different route has been traveled to a similar goal.

Other differences stand out. Because of its roots in a certain justice agenda, the politics of establishing rights in the West has often been surrounded with anger, indignation, the imperative to punish historic wrongdoing. From this Buddhist perspective comes a caution against the politics of anger, itself the potential source of new forms of violence. My aim here is not to judge between these approaches but to point to these differences as the source of a potentially fruitful exchange within a (hopefully) emerging world consensus on the practice of human rights and democracy.

We can in fact see a convergence here on certain norms of action, however they may be entrenched in law. What is unfamiliar to the Western observer is the entire philosophical basis and its appropriate reference points, as well as the rhetorical source of its appeal. In the West, both democracy and human rights have been furthered by the steady advance of a kind of humanism that stressed that humans stood out from the rest of the cosmos, had a higher status and dignity than anything else. This has its origins in Christianity and certain strands of ancient thought, but the distance is greatly exacerbated by what Weber describes as the disenchantment of the world, the rejection of a view of the cosmos as a meaningful order. The human agent stands out even more starkly from a mechanistic universe. For Pascal, the human being is a mere reed, but of incomparably greater significance than what threatens to crush it, because it is a thinking reed. Kant echoes some of the same reflections in his discussion of the sublime in the third critique[20] and also defines human dignity in terms of the incomparably greater worth of human beings compared to the rest of the contents of the universe.[21]

The human rights doctrine based on this humanism stresses the incomparable importance of the human agent. It centers everything on him or her,

19. See the discussion in Vitit Muntarbhorn and Charles Taylor, *Roads to Democracy: Human Rights and Democratic Development in Thailand, Bangkok and Montréal* (International Centre for Human Rights and Democratic Development, July 1994), part 3.

20. *Kants Werke*, vol. 6: *Kritik der Urteilskraft* (Berlin: Walter de Gruyter, 1964), first part, second book, sections 28–9.

21. *Grundlegung zur Metaphysik der Sitten*, Berlin Academy edition (Berlin: Walter de Gruyter, 1968), vol. 4, p. 434.

makes his or her freedom and self-control a major value, something to be maximized. Consequently, in the Western mind, the defense of human rights seems indissolubly linked with this exaltation of human agency. It is because humans justifiably command all this respect and attention, at least in comparison to anything else, that their rights must be defended.

The Buddhist philosophy that I have been describing starts from a quite different place, the demand of *ahimsa* (nonviolence), and yet seems to ground many of the same norms. (Of course, there will also be differences in the norms grounded, which raises its own problems, but for the moment I just want to note the substantial overlap.) The gamut of Western philosophical emotions, the exaltation at human dignity, the emphasis on freedom as the highest value, the drama of age-old wrongs righted in valor, all the things that move us in seeing *Fidelio* well performed, seem out of place in this alternative setting. So do the models of heroism. The heroes of *ahimsa* are not forceful revolutionaries, not Cola di Rienzi or Garibaldi, and with the philosophy and the models, a whole rhetoric loses its basis.

This perhaps gives us an idea of what an unforced world consensus on human rights might look like. Agreement on norms, yes, but a profound sense of difference, of unfamiliarity, in the ideals, the notions of human excellence, the rhetorical tropes and reference points by which these norms become objects of deep commitment for us. To the extent that we can only acknowledge agreement with people who share the whole package and are moved by the same heroes, the consensus will either never come or must be forced.

This is the situation at the outset, in any case, when consensus on some aspect of human rights has just been attained. Later a process can follow of mutual learning, moving toward a "fusion of horizons" in Gadamer's term, in which the moral universe of the other becomes less strange. Out of this will come further borrowings and the creation of new hybrid forms.

After all, something of this has already occurred with another stream of the philosophy of *ahimsa,* that of Gandhi. Gandhi's practices of nonviolent resistance have been borrowed and adapted in the West, for example, in the American Civil Rights Movement under Martin Luther King. Beyond that, they have become part of a world repertory of political practices, invoked in Manila in 1988 and in Prague in 1989, to name just two examples.

Also worthy of remark is one other facet of this case that may be generalizable as well. An important part of the Western consciousness of human rights lies in the awareness of an historic achievement. Human rights define norms of respect for human beings, more radical and more exigent than have ever existed in the past. They offer in principle greater freedom, greater security from violence, from arbitrary treatment, from discrimination and oppression than humans have enjoyed at least in most major civilizations in history. In a sense they involve taking the exceptional treatment accorded to privileged people in the past, and extending it to everyone. That is why so many of the landmarks of the historical development of rights were in their day instruments of elite privilege, starting with Magna Carta.

There is a curious convergence in this respect with the strand of Reform Buddhism I have been describing. Here too there is the awareness that very exigent demands are being made that go way beyond what the majority of ordinary believers recognize as required practice. Reform Buddhism is practiced by an elite, as has been the case with most of its analogues in history. But here too, in developing a doctrine of democracy and human rights, Reform Buddhists are proposing to extend what has hitherto been a minority practice and entrench it in society as a whole. Here again there is a consciousness of the universalization of the highest of traditional minority practice.

It is as though in spite of the difference in philosophy this universalization of an exigent standard, which human rights practice at its best involves, was recognized as a valid move and re-created within a different cultural, philosophical, and religious world. The hope for a world consensus is that this kind of move will be made repeatedly.

HIERARCHY AND IDENTITY

This example drawn from Thailand provides one model for what the path to world consensus might look like – a convergence on certain norms from out of very different philosophical and spiritual backgrounds. The consensus at first doesn't need to be based on any deep mutual understanding of these respective backgrounds. Each may seem strange to the other, even though both recognize and value the practical agreement attained. Of course, this is not to say that there is no borrowing involved at all. Plainly, democracy and human rights practices originated somewhere and are now being creatively recaptured (perhaps in a significantly different variant) elsewhere, but a mutual understanding and appreciation of each other's spiritual basis for signing on to the common norms may be close to nonexistent.

This, however, is not a satisfactory end point. Some attempt at deeper understanding must follow or the gains in agreement will remain fragile, for at least two closely connected reasons. The first is that the agreement is never complete. We already saw that what we can call the *ahimsa* basis for rights connects to ecological concerns differently from the Western humanist basis, in that the place of anger, indignation, righteous condemnation, and punishment is different in the two outlooks. All this must lead to differences of practice, of the detailed schedule of rights, or at least of the priority ordering among them. In practice, these differences may not emerge in variant schedules of rights. They may be reflected in the way a given schedule is interpreted and applied in different societies. After all, entrenched charters have to be applied by courts, and the courts make their interpretations within the framework of the moral views prevalent in their society. Some, like the Canadian charter, specifically provide for this adaptive interpretation by calling on the courts to interpret the charter in the light of social requirements, including those of a democratic society.[22] The demands of a world consensus will often include our squaring these differences in practical contexts, our accommodating or coming to some compromise version that both sides can live with. These negotiations will be inordinately difficult unless each side can come to some more fine-grained understanding of what moves the other.

The second reason follows on from the first and is in a sense just another facet of it. The continued coexistence in a broad consensus that continually generates particular disagreements, which have in turn to be negotiated to renewed consensus, is impossible without mutual respect. If the sense is strong on each side that the spiritual basis of the other is ridiculous, false, inferior, unworthy, these attitudes cannot but sap the will to agree of those who hold these views while engendering anger and resentment among those who are thus depreciated. The only cure for contempt here is understanding. This alone can replace the too-facile depreciatory stories about others with which groups often tend to shore up their own sense of rightness and superiority. Consequently, the bare consensus must strive to go on towards a fusion of horizons.

In this discussion I have analytically distinguished consensus from mutual understanding and have imagined that they occur sequentially as successive phases. This is certainly a schematic oversimplification, but perhaps not totally wrong in the Thai case I was examining. However, in other situations some degree of mutual understanding is an essential condition of getting to consensus. The two cannot simply occur successively, because the path to agreement lies through some degree of sympathetic mutual comprehension.

I want to look now at another difference that seems to be of this latter type. To lay it out here, I will have to describe more fully another facet of the Western philosophical background of rights, which can hit a wall of incomprehension once one crosses the boundary to other cultures. This is the Western concern for equality, in the form of nondiscrimination. Existing charters of rights in the Western world are no longer concerned only with ensuring certain liberties and immunities to individuals. To an important degree, they also serve to counter various forms of discrimination. This represents a shift in the center of gravity of rights talk over the last centuries. One could argue that the central importance of nondiscrimination enters American judicial review with the Fourteenth Amendment, in the aftermath of the Civil War.

22. See the discussion in Joseph Chan, "The Asian Challenge to Universal Human Rights: A Philosophical Appraisal," in James T. H. Tang, ed., *Human Rights and International Relations in the Asia-Pacific Region* (London: Pinter, 1995).

Since then nondiscrimination provisions have been an important and growing part of schedules of rights both in the United States and elsewhere.

This connection is perhaps not surprising, although it took a long time to
come to fruition. In a sense, the notion of equality was closely linked from
the beginning to that of Natural Right, in contradistinction to the place of
subjective rights in medieval systems of law, which were also those of certain
estates or privileged individuals. Once right inheres in nature, then it is hard
in the long run to deny it to anyone. The connection to equality is the
stronger because of the thrust of modern humanism mentioned earlier, which
defines itself against the view that we are embedded in a meaningful cosmic
order. This latter has been a background against which various forms of
human differentiation could appear natural, unchallengeable – be they social,
racial, or sexual. The differences in human society, or gender roles, could be
understood to reflect differentiations in the order of things and to correspond
to differences in the cosmos, as with Plato's myth of the metals. This has
been a very common form of thinking in almost all human societies.[23]

The destruction of this order has allowed for a process of unmasking existing
social and gender differences as merely socially constructed, as without basis in
the nature of things, as revocable and hence ultimately without justification.
The process of working this out has been long, and we are not yet at the end,
but it has been hard to resist in Western civilization in the last two centuries.

This aspect of Western rights talk is often very hard to export because it
encounters societies in which certain social differences are still considered
very meaningful, and they are seen in turn as intrinsically linked to certain
practices that in Western societies are now regarded as discriminatory. However hard these sticking points may be for a Westerner to grasp in detail, it is
not difficult to understand the general shape of the conflict, particularly
because we in the West are far from having worked out how to combine gender equality with our conflicted ideas of gender difference.

To take this issue of gender equality as our example, we can readily understand that a certain way of framing the difference, however oppressive it may
be in practice, also serves as the reference point for deeply felt human identities. The rejection of the framework can be felt as the utter denial of the basis
of identity, and this not just for the favored gender, but also for the oppressed
one. The gender definitions of a culture are interwoven with, among other
things, its love stories, both those people tell and those they live.[24] Throwing

23. A good example is Pierre Bourdieu's description of the "correspondences" between the male–female
difference and different colors, cardinal points, and oppositions like wet–dry, up–down, etc. See his
Outline of a Theory of Practice (Cambridge: Cambridge University Press, 1977), chapter 3.
24. See, for example, Sudhir Kakar, *The Inner World* (Delhi: Oxford University Press, 1978), who claims
that Hindu culture foregrounds a love story of the young married couple, already with children, as
against the prevalent Western tale of the love intrigue that leads to marriage.

off a traditional identity can be an act of liberation, but more than just liberation is involved here; without an alternative sense of identity, the loss of the traditional one is disorienting and potentially unbearable.

The whole shape of the change that could allow for an unforced consensus on human rights here includes a redefinition of identity, perhaps building on transformed traditional reference points in such a way as to allow for a recognition of an operative equality between the sexes. This can be a tall order, something we should have no trouble appreciating in the West because we have yet to complete our own redefinitions in this regard. This identity redefinition will be the easier to effect the more it can be presented as being in continuity with the most important traditions and reference points, properly understood. Correspondingly, it gets maximally difficult when it comes across as a brutal break with the past involving a condemnation and rejection of it. To some extent, which of these two scenarios gets enacted depends on developments internal to the society, but the relation with the outside world, and particularly the West, can also be determining.

The more the outside portrayal, or attempt at influence, comes across as a blanket condemnation of or contempt for the tradition, the more the dynamic of a "fundamentalist" resistance to all redefinition tends to get in train, and the harder it will be to find unforced consensus. This is a self-reinforcing dynamic, in which perceived external condemnation helps to feed extreme reaction, which calls down further condemnation, and hence further reaction, in a vicious spiral. The world is already drearily familiar with this dynamic in the unhealthy relation between the West and great parts of the Islamic world in our time.

In a sense, therefore, the road to consensus in relation to this difference is the opposite from the one mentioned earlier. There, the convergence on norms between Western humanism and reform Buddhism might be seen as preceding a phase in which they come better to understand and appreciate and learn from each other. In the field of gender discrimination, it may well be that the order would be better reversed, that is, that the path to consensus passes through greater sympathetic understanding of the situation of each party by the other. In this respect, the West with its own hugely unresolved issues about equality and difference is often more of a menace than a help.

THE POLYVALENCE OF TRADITION

Before concluding, I want to look at another difference, which resembles in different respects both of the preceding. That is, it is certainly one in which the dynamic of mutual miscomprehension and condemnation is driving us away from consensus, but it also has potentialities like the Thai case, in that we can see how a quite different spiritual or theological basis might be found for a convergence on norms. I am thinking of the difference between international human rights standards and certain facets of the *Shari'a,* recently discussed in so illuminating a fashion by Abdullahi Ahmed An-Na'im.[25] Certain punishments prescribed by the *Shari'a,* such as amputation of the hand for theft or stoning for adultery, appear excessive and cruel in the light of standards prevalent in other countries.

It is worthwhile developing here, as I have in the other cases, the facet of Western philosophical thought and sensibility which has given particular force to this condemnation. This can best be shown through an example. When we read the opening pages of Michel Foucault's *Surveiller et Punir* we are struck by its riveting description of the torture, execution, and dismemberment of Damien, the attempted assassin of Louis XV in the mid-eighteenth century.[26] We cannot but be aware of the cultural change that we have gone through since the Enlightenment.[27] We are much more concerned about pain and suffering than our forebears; we shrink more from the infliction of gratuitous suffering. It would be hard to imagine people today taking their children to such a spectacle, at least openly and without some sense of unease and shame.

What has changed? We can distinguish two factors, one positive and one negative. On the positive side, we see pain and suffering and gratuitously inflicted death in a new light because of the immense cultural revolution that has been taking place in modernity, which I called elsewhere "the affirmation of ordinary life."[28] What I was trying to gesture at with this term is the momentous cultural and spiritual change of the early modern period, which dethroned the supposedly higher activities of contemplation and the citizen life, and put the center of gravity of goodness in ordinary living, production, and the family. It belongs to this spiritual outlook that our first concern ought to be to increase life, relieve suffering, foster prosperity. Concern above all for the "good life" smacked of pride, of self-absorption. Beyond that, it was inherently inegalitarian, because the alleged "higher" activities could only be carried out by an elite minority, whereas leading rightly one's ordinary life was open to everyone. This is a moral temper to which it seems obvious that our major concern must be our dealings with others, in justice and benevolence, and these dealings must be on a level of equality. This affirmation, which constitutes a

---

25. See his "Towards a Cross-Cultural Approach to Defining International Standards of Human Rights," chapter 1; also see Chapter 6 in this volume.
26. Foucault, *Surveiller et Punir* (Paris: Gallimard, 1976).
27. Tocqueville was already aware of the change when he commented on a passage from Mme. de Sévigny in *La Démocratie en Amérique.*
28. See Charles Taylor, *Sources of the Self* (Cambridge, MA: Harvard University Press, 1989), chapter 13.

major component of our modern ethical outlook, was originally inspired by a mode of Christian piety. It exalted practical agape, and was polemically directed against the pride, elitism, and one might say self-absorption of those who believed in "higher" activities or spiritualities.

We can easily see how much this development is interwoven with the rise of the humanism that stands behind the Western discourse of human rights. They converge on the concern for equality, and also for the security of the person against burdens, dangers, and suffering imposed from outside.

But this is not the whole story. There is also a negative change; something has been cast off. It is not as though our ancestors would have simply thought the level of pain irrelevant, providing no reason at all to desist from some course of action involving torture and wounds. For us, the relief of suffering has become a supreme value, but it was always an important consideration. It is rather that, in cases like that of Damien, the negative significance of pain was subordinated to other, weightier considerations. If it is necessary that punishment in a sense undo the evil of the crime, restore the balance – what is implicit in the whole notion of the criminal making *amende honorable* – then the very horror of regicide calls for a kind of theatre of the horrible as the medium in which this undoing can take place. In this context, pain takes on a different significance; there has to be lots of it to do the trick. A principle of minimizing pain is trumped.

Thus, we relate doubly to our forebears of two centuries ago. We have new reasons to minimize suffering, but we also lack a reason to override the minimizing of suffering. We no longer have the whole outlook – linked as it was to the cosmos as meaningful order – that made sense of the necessity of undoing the crime, restoring the breached order of things, in and through the punishment of the criminal.

In general, contemporaries in the West are so little aware of the positive change they have gone through – they tend anachronistically to think that people must always have felt this way – that they generally believe that the negative change is the crucial one that explains our difference from our predecessors. With this in mind, they look at the *Shari'a* punishments as the simple result of premodern illusions, in the same category in which they now place the ancien régime execution scenarios. With this dismissive condemnation, the stage is set for the dynamic I described earlier, in which contemptuous denunciation leads to "fundamentalist" reaffirmations, which in turn provoke even more strident denunciations, and so on.

What gets lost in this struggle is what An-Na'im shows so clearly, the possibilities of reinterpretation and reappropriation that the tradition itself contains. What also becomes invisible is what could be the motor of this change, analogous to the role played by the cultural revolution affirming ordinary life in the West. What this or these could be is not easy for an out-sider to determine, but the striking Islamic theme of the mercy and compas-sion of God, reinvoked at the beginning of almost every sura of the *Qur'an,* might be the locus of a creative theological development. This might help toward a convergence in this domain, in which case we might see a consensus among those of very different spiritual backgrounds, analogous to the Thai Buddhist views I discussed earlier.

CONCLUSION

I started this chapter with the basic notion that an unforced world consensus on human rights would be something like a Rawlsian "overlapping consen-sus," in which convergent norms would be justified in very different under-lying spiritual and philosophical outlooks. I then argued that these norms have to be distinguished and analytically separated not just from the back-ground justifications, but also from the legal forms that give them force. These two could vary with good reason from society to society, even though the norms we crucially want to preserve remain constant. We need, in other words, a threefold distinction: norms, legal forms, and background justifica-tions, which each have to be distinguished from the others.

I then looked at four examples of differences. These by no means exhaust the field, though each is important in the present international exchange on human rights. One of these dealt with the issue of variations in legal forms. In the other three, I tried to discuss issues around the convergence on norms out of different philosophical and spiritual backgrounds.

Two important facets of these convergences emerged. In one way, they involve the meeting of very different minds, worlds apart in their premises, uniting only in the immediate practical conclusions. From another side, it is clear that consensus requires that this extreme distance be closed, that we come better to understand each other in our differences, that we learn to rec-ognize what is great and admirable in our different spiritual traditions. In some cases, this kind of mutual understanding can come after convergence, but in others it seems almost to be a condition of it.

An obstacle in the path to this mutual understanding comes from the inability of many Westerners to see their culture as one among many. An example of this difficulty was visible in the last difference discussed. To an extent, Westerners see their human rights doctrine as arising simply out of the falling away of previous countervailing ideas – such as the punishment scenarios of the ancien régime – that have now been discredited to leave the field free for the preoccupations with human life, freedom, the avoidance of suffering. To this extent they will tend to think that the path to convergence requires that others too cast off their traditional ideas, that they even reject their religious heritage, and become "unmarked" moderns like us. Only if we in the West can recapture a more adequate view of our own history, can we learn to understand better the spiritual ideas that have been interwoven in our development and hence be prepared to understand sympathetically the spiritual paths of others toward the converging goal.[29] Contrary to what many people think, world convergence will not come through a loss or denial of traditions all around, but rather by creative reimmersions of different groups, each in their own spiritual heritage, traveling different routes to the same goal.

29. I have discussed at greater length the two opposed understandings of the rise of modernity that are invoked here in "Modernity and the Rise of the Public Sphere," Grethe B. Peterson, ed., *The Tanner Lectures on Human Values* (Salt Lake City: University of Utah Press, 1993).

PART III

CULTURE AND
HUMAN RIGHTS

CHAPTER 6

THE CULTURAL MEDIATION OF HUMAN RIGHTS: THE AL-ARQAM CASE IN MALAYSIA

ABDULLAHI A. AN-NA'IM

INTRODUCTION

On Friday September 2, 1994, Thai police accompanied by Malaysian security agents trailed Ashaari Muhammad, the Malaysian founder and leader of the Al-Arqam Islamic group, and his entourage, who were on their way to Chiang Mai, and forced their two vehicles off the road.[1] Ashaari and ten of his followers were then taken into custody and handed over to Malaysian Special Branch intelligence officials. This arrest and "deportation," followed by detention without charge or trial in Malaysia, was part of a systematic campaign by the Malaysian government to eliminate the Al-Arqam group and ban its written, audio, and visual publications of any sort, in accordance with a ruling from the "National Fatwa Council" and decree by the Ministry of Home Affairs, both in August 1994. Malaysian Muslims were thereby prevented from joining Al-Arqam or participating in any of its activities. As soon as Ashaari "repented" and "retracted" his views, and complied with the banning of Al-Arqam, he and his associates were released without charge or trial.

I will use this case here to discuss what might be called the cultural mediation of human rights: Because cultural context is integral to the formulation and implementation of all state policies, including those that have clear human rights consequences, detailed and credible knowledge of local culture is essential for the effective promotion and protection of human rights in any society. Consequently, I will argue, human rights advocates must not only understand the role of cultural factors in the motivation and dynamics of

---

1. *Far Eastern Economic Review,* August 11, 1994, pp. 25–6, 28. There was much controversy in Thailand about the legality and propriety of the actions of the Thai police, but that is beyond the scope of this paper.

official behavior and its consequences, they must also integrate and deploy that understanding in their strategies of response. As elaborated later, this view neither takes culture to be monolithic or static, nor overlooks the role of state and nonstate actors in defining culture and manipulating its legitimizing potential at any given point in time. On the contrary, I take the pluralistic, interactive, and constantly evolving nature of cultural perspectives within all societies, however homogeneous they may seem or are claimed to be, as a valuable resource in challenging and contesting official and unofficial authoritarian claims and hegemonic tendencies. Though this chapter explores this thesis with particular reference to Southeast Asia, in accordance with the theme of this volume, I believe that its underlying premise and rationale can apply to other regions of the world.[2]

Human rights are always violated or respected at the local and immediate level by official decisions and action impacting on individuals or groups. Whether it is a matter of freedom from arbitrary detention without charge or trial, freedom from torture, freedom of expression or association, right to education, right to health care, or any other human right, it is always the result of deliberate action or omission by officials of the state. In the normal course of human affairs, such official actions and omissions would necessarily be prompted or rationalized by certain political, economic, social, and cultural or other considerations and calculations. Similarly, the perceptions and reactions of the victim and other individuals and groups, including local and international organizations and foreign governments, would also be prompted or rationalized by their respective considerations and calculations.

It would therefore seem clear that human rights advocates must understand the precise nature and dynamics of official behavior on its own terms and in its local and wider context if they are to devise and implement effective strategies of response. Without in any way accepting official claims at face value, human rights advocates should ask: How do politicians and officials think and behave with regard to rights issues in general? In what ways, if any, is the specific human rights violation presented as incidental to or necessary for what they claim or perceive to be the pursuit of "legitimate" objectives? How is the story told, and what images and symbols are invoked in the process to justify the action or promote the outcome, and why? How are the official story and that of the victim received and reacted to by different constituencies at home and abroad? What is the role of timing, for political or other reasons, on the calculations of official actors of the likely response

---

2. This thesis is explained and applied to various parts of the world in Abdullahi Ahmed An-Na'im and Francis M. Deng, eds, *Human Rights in Africa: Cross-Cultural Perspectives* (Washington, DC: Brookings Institution, 1990); and Abdullahi Ahmed An-Na'im, ed., *Human Rights in Cross-Cultural Perspectives: Quest for Consensus* (Philadelphia: University of Pennsylvania Press, 1992).

of other significant actors? How do other contextual factors influence the behavior of the official actors and the perceptions and responses of others? One needs to fully understand what happened, how and why the momentum and dynamics of the situation developed in that specific way, to decide what sort of intervention to seek at any given point in time. One should also reflect, in light of all these considerations, on who should intervene and how, against which officials or element of their behavior.

Human rights advocates should also practice what they preach by examining their own perceptions of the situation as a whole and their motives and responses to the case in question: What considerations, including the nature and behavior of the victim, influenced or conditioned their view of the official action? How did they see a given case from a human rights point of view, what priority did it receive in their agenda, and why? What limitations or inhibitions affected their responses, or lack thereof, to the particular case?

The cultural mediation of human rights means that, instead of denying or underestimating the vital role of cultural context, human rights advocates should seek to claim for their own cause by questioning how and by whom social values are defined and prioritized in practice and to what conclusions. To effectively challenge claims of cultural justification of human rights violations on their own premise, one should ask: Who determines the standards of conformity with cultural values and national objectives? What are the realistic possibilities and consequences of contesting prevailing perceptions of cultural values and priorities, and their human rights implications? By raising such questions, human rights advocates would be contesting the ability of ruling elites to manipulate supposedly spontaneous social and political processes in support of their actions at home and in coopting regional and international actors.

The aforementioned case of the Al-Arqam group in Malaysia, as explained later, presents a useful illustration of the possibilities as well as the limitations of this approach precisely because it seems to raise a difficult dilemma for human rights advocates and official authorities alike. For human rights advocates, the ideological position and long-standing practices of this group are clearly problematic from a human rights perspective. As East Asia is being propelled by internal and external forces into an era of economic growth, modernization, and integration into global systems and regimes, ruling elites in the region are tempted to discard and disavow what they deem to be "regressive" religious and cultural relics like Al-Arqam. Moreover, the plight of such marginalized and unattractive victims are unlikely to generate opposition from modern sectors of civil society, who are the usual constituency of human rights advocacy.

In my view, in failing to uphold the principle of protecting the rights of their opponents as much as their own, these modern sectors are betraying the essence of the universality of human rights as rights due to all human beings by virtue of their humanity. Given the realities of differential power relations in human societies, the principle of universality is most urgently needed for the protection of those who hold marginal and "problematic" views because they are more likely to be attacked and less able to protect themselves than are those who are conforming to prevailing orthodoxies. In the process, modern sectors of society would be undermining the interdependence of human rights and legitimizing the ideology and mechanisms of their own persecution in the future. Because none of the charges made in justification of the suppression of Al-Arqam was ever tested or substantiated in court of law, the extrajudicial mechanisms legitimized in the process can easily be used in the future against other supposedly "undesirable" elements, as and when ruling elites deem it expedient to do so.

Although human rights factors may have also been considered by the government of Malaysia,[3] a more pressing concern was probably the alleged political ambitions of Al-Arqam and the group's real or assumed connections to militant Islamic activists in Middle Eastern/North African Islamic countries. In the process of suppressing this group, however, Malaysian authorities used an alleged Islamic principle of combating "deviationism," a profoundly problematic concept even by traditional Islamic standards, as explained later. Moreover, the purported rationalization of the suppression of Al-Arqam explicitly used religious institutions and processes under the guise of securing the "separation" of religion from politics, thereby in fact enhancing the "unity" of the two with greater possibilities of abuse.

Although I appreciate such concerns of human rights advocates and governments, I am concerned with the possibility of a constructive solution to such difficult cases from a pragmatic, yet principled, human rights point of view. In terms of the theme of this volume, I propose to address the implications of the Al-Arqam case for the possibilities and limitations of looking for cultural sources of human rights in Southeast Asia. For example, I wish to explore whether, and to what extent, differences in the prioritization of social values justify differences in interpretation of which rights are universal.[4]

---

3. It is important not only to give credit to political leaders for the commitment they express to human rights and humane values in government, but also to appreciate the delicate line they need to negotiate between principled position and political pragmatism. See, for example, the speech Prime Minister Mahathir Mohamad gave at the International Seminar on the Administration of Islamic Laws, *New Straits Times*, July 24, 1996, pp. 14 and 16–17. That does not mean, of course, that these leaders always live up to their rhetoric, but holding them to what they say is part of the process of implementation.

4. Joseph Chan, "The Asian Challenge to Human Rights: A Philosophical Appraisal," in James T. H. Tang, ed., *Human Rights and International Relations in the Asia-Pacific Region* (New York: St. Martin's Press, 1995). Without attempting a full discussion of Chan's thesis, I will raise some questions to clarify its utility as a promising approach for our purposes here.

How can that view be reconciled with the contention that some human rights are "undeniably universal," and how are the spheres of universality and cultural specificity to be negotiated in practice? Ultimately, I am concerned not only with defining the scopes of the universal and culturally specific in human rights regimes, and the relationship between the two, but also with the processes of ensuring the validity and efficacy of human rights regimes in achieving their presumably shared objectives of safeguarding and enhancing individual and communal life, liberty, and dignity. If human rights are to be firmly founded on local cultural sources, as they should in my view, the question is how to do so in ways that enhance, rather than detract from, the universality of human rights.

TAKING THE UNIVERSALITY "PROJECT" SERIOUSLY

In view of the aforementioned immediate and local nature of every instance of violation or protection of human rights, I believe that accepting and working with the notion of the cultural mediation of these rights is essential for the realization of their genuine and lasting universality. Like all normative systems, human rights regimes must necessarily be premised on a particular cultural framework (including philosophical and religious perspectives as well as material circumstances) of specific human societies in their respective historical context. In other words, the issue is not simply how to find local cultural sources for a "given and culturally neutral" human rights regime. Rather, it is that since all and every conceivable regime of rights necessarily and by definition derives from some cultural sources, what are (or ought to be) the sources of a regime of "universal" human rights? In this regard, it is necessary to consider the apparent paradox in the quest for universality of any human rights regime: Because on the one hand rights are organically linked to culture, and on the other hand human cultures are so different, how can one establish a universally valid and universally applicable set of specific human rights and enforcement mechanisms?

My approach to what I call the project of constructing a universal human rights regime begins with the acknowledgment that, historically speaking, the present system of international human rights has clearly evolved from Western cultural perspectives that were "universalized" through colonial and postcolonial hegemonic processes that were inconsistent with the fundamental collective human right to self-determination.[5] Nevertheless, this system should be taken as a very useful, though not necessarily definitive, framework

---

5. As now enshrined in common Article 1 of the International Covenant on Economic, Social and Cultural Rights and the International Covenant on Civil and Political Rights, both of 1966, and other international instruments

for genuine and lasting universality of human rights for several reasons. First, this system has evolved in response to certain political, economic, social, and legal national and international conditions of Western societies, which have also been "universalized" through the same colonial and postcolonial hegemonic processes. As Yash Ghai has shown, neither are East Asian societies immune from the sort of economic, political, and social phenomena and serious dislocation of traditional values and institutions addressed by human rights norms in the West, nor do "official" claims of religious and cultural distinctiveness justify the relativistic priorities asserted by government.[6]

Second, I am in agreement with scholars who maintain that the lack of such individual human rights as freedom of expression and association in fact diminishes the existence of the community in whose name authoritarian regimes rule.[7] I also accept the view that fundamental improvements in the sort of economic efficacy and security sought by East Asian states require greater, not less, adherence to constitutionalism, the rule of law, and protection of civil and political human rights.[8] These arguments, it seems to me, reinforce the commonly accepted view of the interdependence of all human rights – civil and political as well as economic, social, and cultural rights, individual and collective alike.

In this light, I maintain that despite its Western origins, the present regime of international human rights is not only appropriate for conditions that are currently prevalent in many non-Western societies, it also appears to be necessary for creating the political and social "space" for effective participation in the cultural mediation of human rights at both the national and international levels. Thus, even the most extreme cultural relativist would need protection of his or her freedom of expression and association in order to argue for greater respect for local cultural traditions in the formulation and implementation of human rights norms.

Third, I would emphasize the fact that there has already been a significant degree of non-Western contribution to the formulation and implementation of the present international regime of human rights, not only through the work of various organs of the United Nations, but also at the nongovernmental level. Despite its problems and limitations as an intergovernmental

---

6. Yash Ghai, "Human Rights and Governance: The Asia Debate," *Occasional Paper No. 4* (The Asia Foundation's Center for Asian Pacific Affairs, November 1994), especially pp. 10–12.
7. Daniel A. Bell, "A Communitarian Critique of Authoritarianism," *Society* (July/August 1995), pp. 39–43.
8. See, for example, Jon Elster, "The Impact of Constitutions on Economic Performance" (unpublished paper prepared for the World Bank's Annual Bank Conference on Development Economics, April 28–9, 1994); and Sidney Jones, "The Impact of Asian Economic Growth on Human Rights," *Asia Project Working Paper Series* (New York: Council on Foreign Relations, January 1995).

"diplomatic" process,[9] the adoption of international human rights has in fact produced a greater degree of cross-cultural legitimacy for these rights and enhanced their relevance to concrete social and economic conditions throughout the world. Whatever may have been the vision and intention of the members of the United Nations who adopted the Universal Declaration of Human Rights in 1948, that founding document and subsequent treaties have since been adopted, adapted, expanded, and deployed by peoples throughout the world in pursuit of their own locally defined objectives. Much needs to be done to promote more effective popular appropriation and operationalization of international human rights, but it cannot seriously be argued that these rights are still the exclusive product of Western societies.

To these arguments, I would also add the practical and tactical point that it is better to try to improve an existing regime, if only as a point of departure and framework for critique, than to seek to dismantle and replace it with a new system. Given its original legitimacy in Western societies and its growing familiarity and relevance in non-Western settings, the present international regime is the best possible candidate for the proposed universality of human rights. From this perspective, I call for the deployment of a deliberate strategy of internal discourse and cross-cultural dialogue to deepen and broaden consensus on the cultural foundations of human rights. The more the concept and content of a human rights regime is accepted through internal discourse as valid within the frame of reference of each culture, the more it is likely to be implemented in that society, especially in light of its similar acceptance by other cultures.[10] In this way, I suggest, the prima facie universality of the present international human rights regime would be gradually founded on a jointly constructed cultural foundation that will progressively diminish the aforementioned apparent paradox of the organic link between rights and culture on the one hand, and the reality and permanence of global cultural diversity on the other.

This project is unlikely to succeed, however, unless it is taken seriously by all the peoples of the world as relevant and applicable to their own cultures, and not only as something non-Western cultures need to do in order to subscribe to an established "club" of European and North American countries. Each society can easily find problems with its own conceptions of human rights when compared to current international formulations – whether it is

9. See my chapter "Problems of Universal Cultural Legitimacy for Human Rights," in An-Na'im and Deng, eds., *Human Rights in Africa: Cross-Cultural Perspectives*, pp. 345–55.

10. For an example of a theological and legal argument for internal cultural legitimation in an Islamic context see, generally, Abdullahi Ahmed An-Na'im, *Toward an Islamic Reformation: Civil Liberties, Human Rights and International Law* (Syracuse, NY: Syracuse University Press, 1990).

in relation to economic, social, and cultural rights or notions of collective rights in the case of Western societies, the rights of women and religious minorities in the case of Islamic societies, or of lower-caste peoples in Hindu cultures, and so forth. To take the universality of human rights seriously, each society needs to examine its own difficulties with the theory and practice of the international regime in order to establish moral authority to demand the same from other societies. Moreover, as I will argue in the final section of this chapter, the project of universality must also be pursued with an open mind and willingness to examine and renegotiate any presumed "prioritization of social values," rather than as a means of endorsing and legitimating the existing scheme of political, economic, social, and/or religious power relations and hierarchies. Engaging in this process will be extremely instructive, I submit, not only in appreciating the difficulties and dynamics of self-criticism, especially when we are confronted with the possibility of having to abandon a view that we assume to be self-evident from our own ethnocentric perspective, but also in gaining insights about how to persuade others to do the same.

To further clarify this thesis, I will now relate it to the following suggested typology of arguments for a culturally sensitive approach to human rights in relation to East Asia:[11]

1. That situation-specific justifications for the temporary curtailment of particular human rights can only be countered through the acquisition of substantial local knowledge from which one can show that such a claim is unwarranted in the actual case.
2. That East Asian cultural traditions can provide sufficient resources for justifying and increasing local commitment to values and practices that in the West are typically realized through a human rights regime.
3. That given the limits of Western liberal universalism, especially from an East Asian communitarian perspective, it may be necessary to consider alternative frameworks that are more sensitive to legitimate needs for governmental protection and promotion of particularistic conceptions of "vital human interests."

In commenting on these arguments, I would first note that alleged justifications of human rights violations are often made, or "appropriated," by ruling elites who are seeking to justify their repressive policies with little or no regard to genuine human rights issues and concerns. In my view, this sad reality does not necessarily negate the validity and relevance these arguments

11. See Daniel A. Bell, "The East Asian Challenge to Human Rights: Reflections on an East–West Dialogue," *Human Rights Quarterly* vol. 18 (1996), pp. 643–5.

may have in genuine debate among serious-minded human rights advocates and scholars. In fact, ruling elites attempt such opportunistic use of these arguments precisely because they believe them to have resonance and credibility with popular constituencies they are seeking to influence. That does not necessarily mean that official authorities should never be heard to make such arguments, but they should be required to demonstrate their good faith through the general policies and actions of their government. No East Asian or other government can be taken seriously in claiming the mantle of protecting culture and community against the "cultural imperialism" of Western conceptions of human rights when the policies and practice of such a government undermine and repudiate the same culture and community in whose name it claims to speak.

It should also be noted that these three types of arguments for a culturally sensitive approach are not necessarily mutually exclusive, because they may overlap in their objectives and reasoning, depending on one's view of their scope and implications. For example, to the extent that the second argument is seen as a justification of human rights as internationally recognized today, rather than proposing an alternative regime premised on indigenous "pro-toideas," it would share with the first argument an acceptance of the present formulation of these rights. Should the second argument be seen as proposing an alternative paradigm, rather than alternative justification of international human rights, then it would be closer to the third argument. However, even to the extent that the second and third arguments are seen as seeking to either limit or expand the scope of Western conceptions of human rights in accordance with East Asian perceptions of vital human interests, they may still remain open to human rights norms as expression of a "minimal universal moral code" that East Asia shares with Western and other societies.

The first type of argument is more in the nature of a strategy of human rights activism that can be deployed in any part of the world, and it would involve a local cultural dimension only to the extent that culture is supposed to be part of the alleged justification of a limited human rights violation that is admitted by the violator as such. That is, it simply seeks to dispute the justificatory claim through the mobilization of local knowledge of indigenous culture, which is used to support a limited short-term curtailment of a particular human right to achieve a specific public or national objective, without disputing the validity of the specific human right as such. In addition to disputing the claim that local culture justifies the "temporary" violation, one can also raise doubts about the possibility of identifying the limits of the time frame of justification and the ability to resist the violation at some point. Assuming that there is good reason for a temporary violation of certain human rights, how can one tell when the violation is no longer justified, and what assurance can one have that state security forces will actually refrain from further violations at that time?

Where culture as such is used to justify, for example, discrimination against women or the use of corporal punishment against children as consistent with a local conception of the "best interest of the child,"[12] the claim of cultural particularity would be much more radical and indefinite. Such a claim goes to the essence of the human right in question and permanently, rather than merely being an alleged justification of the curtailment of an accepted right for a limited period of time. In this case, a different type of response is required, one that would seek to challenge the validity of the claim that there is no human right at all because indigenous culture requires such treatment of women or children. That is, a different type of response is needed when local culture is used as the basis for rejecting the existence of a human right permanently, as distinguished from simply seeking to justify the temporary violation of an acknowledged right.

A cultural response to such a radical claim can be developed under the rubric of the second type of argument mentioned earlier by showing that the culture in question in fact supports, rather than repudiates, equality for women or rejects the use of corporal punishment against children. However, to be useful in response to a claim of cultural rejection of a human right, this type of argument needs to be supplemented by developing a coherent and comprehensive methodology of internal cultural discourse that is capable of challenging prevailing conceptions of indigenous culture in favor of the proposed human rights norm. As they are commonly expressed at present, claims that indigenous cultures should be used as a resource to justify and increase local commitment to human rights norms not only fall short of supporting the full range of international standards of human rights, they are highly selective in the choice of the human rights norms they choose to found on local culture and fail to address the problem of those human rights norms that the local culture is commonly believed to reject.

For instance, references to Islam as a source of human rights are usually confined to a few rights, and fail to acknowledge the fact that even these rights under currently accepted *Shari'a* (traditional formulations of Islamic law and ethics) are inherently premised on distinctions on grounds of sex and religion, rather than being provided for as inalienable rights of all human beings by virtue of their humanity. Thus, it is misleading to speak

---

12. See, for example, Abdullahi A. An-Na'im, "Cultural Transformation and Normative Consensus on the Best Interest of the Child," *International Journal of Law and the Family* vol. 8 (1994), pp. 62–81; also published in Philip Alston, ed., *The Best Interest of the Child: Reconciling Culture and Human Rights* (Oxford: Clarendon Press, 1994), pp. 62–81.

of freedom to found a family under *Shari'a* without accounting for the prohibition of marriage between Muslims and non-Muslims on grounds of religion.[13] It is also misleading to speak of freedom of religion in view of not
only the inferior status of non-Muslims under *Shari'a,* but also the imposition of the death penalty on a Muslim who repudiates his faith in Islam,
whether or not he adopts another religion.[14] In my view, these limitations of
Shari'a as a foundation of human rights can be redressed through the modern reformulation Islamic law, but that is not yet the prevailing view in
Islamic societies today. In other words, radical Islamic reform is likely to
face cultural resistance similar to that presently encountered by the concept
of universal human rights itself. Such resistance should be expected whenever the interests of the guardians of the status quo are threatened, whether
by cultural challenge (as through Islamic reform) or advocacy of human
rights, especially when the former seeks to support the latter, but there is no
alternative to developing a coherent and comprehensive methodology of
internal cultural discourse if prevailing conceptions of indigenous culture
are to be challenged and modified in favor of the proposed human rights
regime.

A reading of the second type of argument in the preceding typology that
suggests that human rights were already recognized and respected in traditional needs to be qualified as follows: The present concept of human rights
arose in opposition to particular forms of oppression and abuse of powers
associated with those in control of the apparatus of the modern nation-state.
Because the nation-state is now a global reality, despite its European origins
and development, human rights are needed everywhere to protect people
against oppression and abuse of power by those in control of the state. The
fact that many traditional cultures have had "functional equivalents" for pre-
nation-state societies neither negates the need for human rights in the modern context nor means that human rights in this modern sense are automatically accepted and supported because they had premodern antecedents in the
local culture. Moreover, because of their selective and ad hoc nature, existing
tentative efforts to found human rights on premodern cultural norms and
institutions are unlikely to support a comprehensive regime that can fully
respond to the present realities of the centralized state, social dislocations of
massive urbanization, and economic consequences of globalized free-market

---

13. According to Islamic *Shari'a* law, as accepted and practiced throughout the Muslim world, a Muslim
woman cannot marry any non-Muslim man, whereas a Muslim man can marry a woman from "the
People of the Book" (mainly Christians and Jews), but not an unbeliever by *Shari'a* criteria. Asaf A.
A. Fyzee, *Outlines of Muhammadan Law,* 4th ed. (Delhi: Oxford University Press, 1974), pp. 96–9.
14. Mohamed S. El-Awa, *Punishment in Islamic Law* (Indianapolis: American Trust Publications, 1982),
pp. 40–56.

economies. Traditional Chinese procedural safeguards, for example, are unlikely to work as the basis of a modern system of criminal justice in today's overpopulated and increasingly urbanized China. Traditional Islamic notions of the rule of law through the supremacy of *Shari'a* over political expediency require effective enforcement mechanisms, which have always been weak in *Shari'a* as a regime designed for small traditional communities radically different from the impersonal urban centers of present Islamic societies.

It is useful and important to identify traditional cultural support for the values and institutions of human rights, but more must be done to make the connection. A possible way of doing so, it seems to me, is to argue that traditional norms and mechanisms of protection against the abuse of power or the attainment of some "human rights good," such as realization of economic or social rights to food and shelter, indicate the need to adopt and support internationally recognized human rights as the more appropriate response to those needs in the present context of the nation state and its global environment. To make that argument persuasively, however, one must have the methodology for addressing those aspects of traditional culture that are negative from a modern human rights point of view, as well as supporting the transformation of what is positive in traditional cultures to make it appropriate for present-day conditions.

Finally, if the third type of argument in the aforementioned typology means a total rejection of the human rights paradigm and its replacement with an indigenous "vital human interests" model, then the question would be whether the latter is a good substitute for the former in effectively responding to the challenges of life in a modern nation-state and its global environment. The rejection of the present human rights paradigm may be for some people something of an article of faith, rather than a matter for rational debate. This view is usually associated with some religious fundamentalist groups (whether Christian, Jewish, Islamic, or Hindu), but it can also fit or be claimed by some nationalists and adherents of an "ideology of economic development." The fundamental difficulty I have with this approach is simply to ask: How are "vital human interests" to be identified, and by whom? How can a presently dominant "prioritization of social values" ever be challenged and rearranged unless the regime of vital human interests itself includes the sort of freedoms of expression and association envisaged by the human rights paradigm? Without these freedoms, how can the proponents of this view know that the alternative conceptions of vital human interests presented in the name of their culture are valid and current?

Therefore, in concluding this section, I say that those who seek to base the universality of human rights on cultural foundations must be willing and able to challenge, as and when necessary, prevailing conceptions of the culture in question. As I have argued elsewhere,[15] all cultures have a certain degree of ambivalence that allows for contesting prevailing perceptions and seeking to replace them with new or formerly suppressed conceptions through an internal discourse within the terms of reference of the particular culture and in accordance with its own criteria of legitimacy. For the subject of this chapter in particular, an Islamic alternative to historical formulations of *Shari'a* can be developed by present-day Muslim scholars on the basis of a reinterpretation of the *Qur'an* and *Sunna* of the Prophet, as *Shari'a* itself was constructed by early Muslim scholars a thousand years ago on the basis of their interpretation of those sources.[16]

THE ANATOMY OF PERSECUTION
IN THE AL-ARQAM CASE

A minimal "factual" account of the suppression of the Al-Arqam group in Malaysia will probably be accepted by all sides to the issue in this case, but only if other elements and factors they believe to be "true and relevant" are added to the story. It is over these other elements and factors that strong disagreement is bound to arise. In reality, every account of a story, even at the most elementary and supposedly factual level that all sides would tentatively accept, will always be influenced by the perspectives and motives of those who tell it, hence the questions raised early in this paper about who is telling the story and what images and symbols are thereby invoked in an attempt to justify specific actions or promote a certain outcome. The language and tone of a narrative can also make a significant difference in how a story is received by its intended audience. However, one must begin with some account of "what happened," even if it is to be revised through analysis of the context, sequence, and dialectic of events, as well as knowledge of the political, economic, and other factors influencing the behavior of key personalities, and so forth.

A generally accepted account would indicate that Ashaari Muhammad, a former school teacher who was a member of Party Islam (or Pas, Malaysia's main Islamic opposition party) in the 1960s, established Al-Arqam in 1968,[17] advocating the rejection of the secular way of life practiced by Western societies, and the creation of "an Islamic way of life, which has its own systems of education and economics."[18] Over the years, the organization developed

15. See sources cited in notes 9 and 12.

16. See An-Na'im, *Toward an Islamic Reformation,* especially chapters 3 and 7.

17. To note the symbolism in the name, "Dar Al-Arqam" is the house the Prophet and his early few and persecuted followers used in Mecca, before they migrated to Medina in 622.

18. *Far Eastern Economic Review,* August 11, 1994, p. 28. For the following account, see pp. 25–6; and *Far Eastern Economic Review,* September 15, 1994, pp. 14–15.

sophisticated methods of propagating its views, combined with an extensive system of business enterprises in several mostly Muslim countries and communities in Southeast Asia. By the time of its suppression in August 1994, Al-Arqam ran 48 communes within Malaysia alone, complete with their own schools and medical clinics, and had an estimated $115 million in worldwide assets. It also claimed around 100,000 in membership throughout Southeast Asia and beyond, many among the educated and professional middle class.[19]

Another aspect of a minimal generally accepted account would include the mechanism and sequence of suppression, without speculating about its motivation or justification/rationalization. The immediate sequence can be taken to have begun with the August 5, 1994, ruling of Pusat Islam (the National Fatwa Council) that the teachings and beliefs of Al-Arqam contravene Islamic practice and tenets, and could lead Muslims astray. On August 25, the Ministry of Home Affairs declared Al-Arqam unlawful under the Societies Act of 1966, but arrests of scores of members had already begun by then. Following his arrest in Thailand on September 2 and handing over to Malaysian security officials, Ashaari himself was detained in Malaysia under the Internal Security Act. This Act allows detention at the pleasure of the Home Minister for up to two years to begin with, which can be extended to an unlimited number of subsequent periods of up two years at a time, without charge or trial at any time.[20] In other words, a person can be detained under this Act indefinitely without ever having the opportunity to challenge the reasons for his or her detention before a court of law, as long as the detention order is renewed every two years.[21] Ashaari was released, subject to restrictions on his movements, on October 28, 1994, after he, his wife and six others recanted their "deviationist" views on national television on October 20, as "interpretations contrary to the teachings of Islam."[22]

I would also note here that Zainal Abidin Abdul Kadir, director-general of Pusat Islam, was reported to have declared at the same time that Malaysia will start a tough five-year plan in 1995 to wipe out all Muslim movements in the country that are "deemed to be deviant." The director said that at least 47 deviant groups had been identified, of which 17 were active. Describing these Muslim sects as a cancer, he prescribed that the only way to curb them

19. Reuters, Kuala Lumpur, October 28 and 31, 1994.
20. See section 8 of the Internal Security Act 1960 (Act 82) current as of March 15, 1995 (published by International Law Book Services, Kuala Lumpur).
21. Section 8B (1) reads: "There shall be no judicial review in any court of, and no court shall have or exercise any jurisdiction in respect of, any act done or decision made by the Yang di-Pertuan Agong [the Constitutional monarch or head of state] or the Minister in the exercise of their discretionary power in accordance with this Act, save in regard to any question on compliance with any procedural requirement in this Act governing such act or decision."
22. Reuters, Kuala Lumpur, October 28, 1994; Associated Press, Kuala Lumpur, October 21, 1994.

was to carry out a "full treatment"; "the new programme will check the activities of these deviant groups before they have a chance to spread."[23] He also indicated that Malaysia's Islamic authority will send a team to Indonesia in November (1994) to convince religious groups in that country that Al-Arqam's teachings were deviant.

The controversial part of the story would relate to the validity of claims made by various government officials in justification of the campaign against Al-Arqam, different or additional political or other "explanations" suggested by independent observers, and responses by the group and other critics of the government's behavior. Moreover, I would emphasize that evaluations of the perspectives of all sides to the issues should take into account such contextual factors as the timing of the government's action just before general elections were to be held, especially in view of the long-standing competition between United Malays National Organization (UMNO; the government's party) and Pas (the main opposition Islamic party) over the Islamic orientation of Malaysia. Another factor that might be added is the ambivalence among some elements within Umno about Islamization in contrast to the professional training and ideological inclination of Pusat and other key actors within the Prime Minister's office who are closer to Pas than to Umno on these issues.

For the purposes of my analysis here, I will focus on the case from the official perspective without accepting it at face value or discounting counterperspective(s). For example, the following claims by high government officials were reported by the media.[24] Prime Minister Mahathir Mohamad said: "If we do not take action, we are at fault as Al-Arqam has deviated from Islam's teachings." It is interesting to note that at that point (in July 1994, when some 41 Al-Arqam members were arrested for handing out leaflets, an activity that police said violated publishing laws) the Prime Minister also indicated that the government would wait for a ruling from religious scholars before taking further measures against Al-Arqam. Deputy Prime Minister Anwar Ibrahim maintained: "We don't have a choice, we have a responsibility. This is precisely what we've been fighting all our lives to clear . . . this extreme, intolerant, anti-modern view of Islam." Foreign Minister Abdullah Badawi said: "We have to stop it. . . . It has developed into a cult." Defense Minister Najib Tun Razak claimed: "It is a very dangerous form of teaching, which, if left unchecked, would cause a severe dislocation in Malaysian society." "Obviously they [Al-Arqam leaders] have a political agenda, kept secret all this while, to gain political power." Datuk Islmail Ibrahim, director-gen-

---

23. Reuters, Kuala Lumpur, October 22, 1994.
24. The statements and views are quoted here as reported in *Far Eastern Economic Review*, August 11, 1994, pp. 25–6; and September 15, 1994, p. 15; and in *The Nation*, September 22, 1994.

eral of the progovernment Institute of Islamic Understanding Malaysia chimed in: "Al-Arqam is outside the current teaching of Islam. . . . This is one thing that can divide Muslims."

Furthermore, the government alleged that Ashaari Muhammad has trained and armed a 313-man "death squad" in Thailand,[25] a charge denied by both Ashaari and Thai officials. The serious implications of this charge can be appreciated by recalling Malaysia's history of violence associated with religious sects in the 1970s and 1980s, especially the bloody confrontation between security forces and followers of Ibrahim Libya in November 1985, when 18 people died and 29 were injured.[26] It should be noted, however, that Al-Arqam maintained a completely peaceful stance throughout this period of official persecution[27] and fully complied with the banning order after the release of Ashaari.

An immediate precursor to the persecution is also said to have been the arrest of 19 Malaysian women students members of Al-Arqam in Cairo in March 1994 and their release after questioning about associating with Islamic extremist groups in Egypt. Some observers mention direct and indirect political and personal connections between Al-Arqam and political parties, factions, and leading personalities as relevant to understanding the timing and manner of the government's behavior. Negative perceptions of Al-Arqam's ideology and rhetoric as an obstacle to modernization and progress,[28] and apprehensions of the group's "hidden political agenda," may have also played a role not only in the government's decision to ban the group, but also in the muted response of other forces in Malaysian society, including nongovernmental human rights organizations. One newspaper editorial, for example, not only dismissed protests against the banning of Al-Arqam as a human rights violation, but actually applauded the actions of the government of Malaysia as "a principled bid to keep religion out of politics. The objective: to maintain the fairness and harmony that such a separation brings to a multi-racial, multi-religious country."[29]

There were some protests in the region, such as that by the Union of Civil Liberties (based in Bangkok), and some by Amnesty International, but little in

25. To note the symbolism, 313 is the traditionally reported number of Muslim fighters at the battle of "Badr," where the Prophet and his followers won their first decisive victory against the unbelievers of Mecca in 624, soon after their flight to Medina from persecution in Mecca.

26. *Far Eastern Economic Review,* August 11, 1994, p. 28.

27. *The Asian Wall Street Journal Weekly,* September 19, 1994, pp. 8, 11; Reuters, Kuala Lumpur, October 31, 1994.

28. Such as the group's very active advocacy and practice of polygamy, and Ashaari's claims to have regular dialogue with the Prophet of Islam predicting political developments in Malaysia, and that he is the messenger of Imam Mahdi, the leader who will rouse Islam's true believers in an apocalyptic struggle against the infidels.

29. An editorial from *Asiaweek,* Hong Kong, published in *The Nation,* October 14, 1994.

Malaysia itself. Inside Malaysia, the only publicly known protest I could find was that led by Suaram (the Voice of the Malaysian People), joined by a few others, including AWAM, the Malay Social Science Association, and Sisters in Islam. Even if there were some less-known instances of protest, my point is that there were not of the level and persistence required by the occasion.

Turning now to the possibilities of cultural mediation suggested earlier, I would first note that an Islamic and a human rights points of view would both raise similar objections and come to similar conclusions about the behavior of the government of Malaysia in this case. The essential questions to be raised from an Islamic as well as a human rights point of view include these: On what basis does the government assume the mantle of the guardian of the beliefs of its citizens to adjudicate who is a "deviationist" and who is a "conformist"? Granted that the state is responsible for maintaining national security and public safety, how can it purport to do so on the basis of vague accusations and unsubstantiated claims? If it does have the evidence to support its allegations, why not present that before the courts in accordance with the rule of law? What is the meaning of constitutional civil liberties and fundamental human rights if the state can be the exclusive judge in its own cause as to whether these safeguards are complied with under conditions of discretionary indefinite detention without charge or trail or judicial review?

To briefly elaborate on Islamic objections to the suppression of Al-Arqam, I would first note that the concept of "deviationism" as such is unknown to any orthodox formulation of *Shari'a* and has no clear basis in the present legal system of Malaysia. It seems that official justifications for the persecution of Al-Arqam made vague references to the *Shari'a* notion of apostasy (*ridda,* a Muslim repudiating his faith in Islam), which is punishable by death if the apostate refuses to repent and reembrace Islam. I am personally opposed to the concept of apostasy and its punishment from an Islamic point of view, and do not in the least want to endorse its application today anywhere in the Muslim world,[30] but if the government of Malaysia wishes to uphold this regressive principle of *Shari'a,* it should have explicitly enacted an "offense" of apostasy in its penal code and prosecuted Ashaari and his followers accordingly. By failing to apply even the notion of apostasy with its own legal safeguards under traditional formulations of Islamic law, the government of Malaysia has given itself license to penalize and persecute Ashaari and his followers without conforming to the demands of the principle of legality and rule of law under *Shari'a* itself.

30. See An-Na'im, *Toward an Islamic Reformation,* pp. 183–4, and "The Islamic Law of Apostasy and Its Modern Applicability: A Case from Sudan," *Religion* vol. 16 (1986), pp. 197–223. For a commentary on apostasy in modern Muslim thinking and practice in general, see Ann E. Mayer, *Islam and Human Rights: Tradition and Politics,* 2nd ed. (Boulder, CO: Westview Press, 1995), pp. 141–7.

When the state claimed the power to judge the beliefs and views of Muslims in the past, outstanding scholars (like Abu Hanifa, Ibn Hanbal, and Ibn Taymiyya) have all been persecuted – some tortured, imprisoned, and even executed – for views now accepted by the vast majority of Muslims, including those of Malaysia today. For the state to assume this power now is for Sunni rulers to condemn Shi'a Muslims as heretics and for Shi'a rulers to condemn Sunni Muslims as heretics. Because in every case, those in control of the state could be judged by some other Muslims as "deviationists," the outcome depends on who is in political power, not who is the most knowledgeable and conforming to the "true teachings and principles of Islam." In any case, who is authorized to speak for all Muslims on these teachings and principles?

I am not in the least favorably comparing Ashaari to leading Muslim jurists of the past or suggesting that Al-Arqam was advocating "correct" or valid views about the teachings of Islam. In fact, I strongly disagree with what I know of Al-Arqam views.[31] Rather, my purpose is to uphold and defend their *right to be wrong or mistaken* about the meaning and implications of Islam in their own societies. It is precisely those who hold controversial views that are rejected by the established theological or political order, or by the public at large, who need and deserve the protection of their freedoms of belief, association, and expression. Those who speak for orthodoxy already have more than ample opportunities to organize and propagate their views. By protecting the right of holders of marginal and unpopular views to be heard, all Muslims will have the opportunity to debate, agree or disagree with every shade of opinion, and make their own mind about the validity or invalidity of one interpretation or the other.

The state and its officials should be the guardians of that public space for all to participate, and not a self-appointed judge of who is right and who is wrong. As guardian of the public space of debate and deliberation, the state has the right and duty to uphold the rule of law. If and when any individual or group violates the rights of others or seeks to undermine the principles of the rule of law, official authorities would be entitled, indeed required, to investigate and, when appropriate, prosecute before the regular courts in public and fair trial. For those in control of the state to abuse their formidable powers by arbitrarily suppressing views they disagree with is a most flagrant violation of the rule of law, by Islamic as well as human rights standards. I am not suggesting that *Shari'a* and human rights perspectives always agree, but in this case they do, albeit through different conceptual frameworks and terminology.

31. For example, Ashaari is reported to have written in Al-Arqam's publication, *This is Our Way* (1994): "After Satan . . . our enemies are unbelievers [communists, Jews, Zoroastrians and Christians] and hypocrites." I find this view totally unacceptable, from a traditional Islamic *Shari'a* point of view, let alone the modernist perspective I argue for in *Toward an Islamic Reformation*, chapters 4, 6, 7.

Both Islamic and human rights perspectives would be particularly concerned about well-grounded suspicion of the use or advocacy of violence by an individual or group of persons. If and to the extent that Al-Arqam is responsible for the use or advocacy of the use of violence, it should be held accountable under the law. Officials of the state are obliged to always protect the safety and rights of all persons and of society at large, but only in accordance with the rule of law and not through vague and unsubstantiated allegations and arbitrary exercise of power to detain persons, restrict freedom of expression, confiscate property, and/or ban organizations. To the extent that Al-Arqam's ideology and propaganda tend to undermine a culture of toleration and respect for the human dignity of all human beings, without distinction, that should certainly be challenged and discredited in public debates.

As to the view that the action of the government of Malaysia "is a principled bid to keep religion out of politics," the exact opposite is the case. This is a case of official abuse of religion for political ends by denying a group of citizens their freedoms of belief, expression, and association, and detaining them without charge or trial on the basis of a ruling from a government-appointed council of "religious scholars" (Pusat Islam) that those citizens are "guilty" of holding "deviationist" views. Why does the government refer matters of private belief to this council and refuse to consult it on its economic, penal, social, or foreign policy? Would the government accept a ruling of Pusat Islam that any aspect of these official policies deviates from the teachings of Islam, as they are understood by that Council?

In concluding this section, I wish to emphasize that my analysis does not claim that any of the human rights violated by the government of Malaysia in Al-Arqam case is absolute or to suggest that no group can ever be legitimately banned from an Islamic or a human rights point of view. Both normative systems acknowledge the need for balancing individuals' and groups' rights against the rights of others and the interests of society and the state at large. Thus, a group can be banned and its leaders and members prosecuted if it is proven in accordance with the rule of law that they are advocating the use of force to overthrow the constitutionally constituted authorities of the state or are otherwise implicated in criminal activities. In my view, the state not only failed to comply with the rule of law in Al-Arqam case, it also actively violated the human rights of members of this group by the use of arbitrary power.

CULTURAL MEDIATION AND THE
UNIVERSALITY OF HUMAN RIGHTS

In calling upon human rights advocates to understand and deploy the cultural legitimation argument suggested earlier in pursuing their objective through the processes the of cultural mediation of human rights, I invite them to ask: How and by whom are social values defined and prioritized in practice and to what ends? Taking the relativist perspective at its own premise, who determines the standards of conformity with cultural values and "national" objectives? What are the realistic possibilities and consequences of contesting prevailing perceptions of social values and priorities and their human rights implications? More specifically, what can human rights advocates do about the ability of ruling elites to manipulate supposedly spontaneous processes of social conciseness in legitimizing their behavior to the public at home, and in coopting regional and international actors, as clearly illustrated by Al-Arqam case.

Although I support efforts to identify and enhance local cultural sources for human rights, I believe that human rights advocates must be prepared to challenge negative perceptions and manipulations of cultural norms and institutions of the culture in question. In the Al-Arqam case, for example, the government's propaganda campaign skillfully combined playing on both traditional concerns with upholding "the teachings of Islam" and modernist demands for the protection of the human rights of women and promoting the education of children. Appeal was also made to public apprehensions about an "extreme, intolerant, anti-modern view" of Islam taking hold of the minds and hearts of young people, the middle classes, and professionals. In response to such a strategy for the legitimation of oppression, those who wish to defend the human rights of Al-Arqam members as a matter of principle, regardless of one's evaluation of the views of the group as such, must engage in a similar multifaceted and culturally sensitive response.

It seems clear to me, however, that the common formulations of the three arguments discussed earlier may not provide an effective strategy of response unless supplemented in the ways I have suggested earlier. If the government is claiming that there will never be freedom to believe in or to associate for the purpose of propagating Al-Arqam views in Malaysia, then the first type of argument for a culturally sensitive approach would not be helpful. In this case, the government claim goes to the essence of the human right in question, rather than as justification of temporary curtailment while still acknowledging the binding force of these rights under "normal circumstances." Should the claim be one of limited suspension of these rights, then local knowledge of the culture and its dynamics may indeed be part of a challenge to the alleged justification of temporary curtailment of human rights in the Al-Arqam case.

Looking for local cultural sources for human rights under the second type of argument or claiming a "vital human interest" under the third type may require a challenge to certain elements of the prevailing perceptions of

Malay/Muslim culture, which might condone the persecution of Al-Arqam in the interest of the state and society at large. That is, although it is important to work within the framework of the culture in question, a clear defense of human rights may not be readily available under prevailing conceptions of cultural norms and institutions. Human rights advocates may therefore have to challenge such claims of cultural legitimacy for violations by proposing and substantiating alternative conceptions of cultural norms and institutions that are supportive of human rights.

In the Al-Arqam case, for example, human rights advocates should not only insist on the procedural safeguards of due process indicated earlier, they should also seek to address the underlying issues of tolerance of diversity and dissent. In particular, they must challenge the notion of apostasy as totally inconsistent with freedoms of conscience and belief from an Islamic point of view and/or a Malaysian cultural perspective as well as being in violation of universal human rights to freedoms of belief and expression.[32] To make the case for these freedoms from Islamic and Malaysian cultural perspectives, human rights advocates may need to dispute traditional interpretations of Islam and perceptions of Malay culture as proclaimed by ruling elites. More fundamentally, they must challenge the claim of the government, or any segment of the established order for that matter, to monopolize the right to speak for either Islam or Malay culture. For the cultural mediation of human rights to work at all, there must be the widest possible multiplicity of voices and perspectives on the meaning and implications of cultural norms and institutions. Otherwise, ruling elites and their allies will control and manipulate the relationship between culture and human rights, and thereby claim cultural justification for their violations of human rights instead of securing the cultural foundation of these rights.

Genuine and lasting global consensus on the principle and content of the universality of human rights can be constructed through an acknowledgment of permanent cultural diversity of an increasingly globalized world. I would further suggest that, in view of the inescapable local and cultural context of the practical protection of human rights, such an approach to developing and sustaining an overlapping consensus on a human set of social values as the basis of agreement on a concept and content of human rights is the only viable way to achieve universality. Those who subscribe to this view must of course realize that this process is neither risk-free nor secure against reversal. Engaging in the processes of the cultural mediation of human rights involves

32. For an example of how this argument can be made from an Islamic point of view, see Abdullahi A. An-Na'im, "Islamic Foundations for Religious Human Rights," in John Witte, Jr., and Johan van der Vyver, eds., *Religious Human Rights in Global Perspectives: Religious Perspectives* (Dordrecht: Martinus Nijhoff, 1966), pp. 337–60.

the risk of having to accept a prioritization, or reprioritization, of social values that one believes to be contrary to universal human rights. For example, this process may endorse the death penalty or corporal punishment, though some human rights advocates see these as cruel, inhuman, or degrading treatment or punishment. Provided opportunities for contestation remain open for all seeking to change public opinion on these matters, such outcomes must be "accepted" as legitimate manifestations of cultural mediation. That is, this approach is premised on openness of the process to challenge and reprioritization that will enable human rights advocates to "rectify" the situation in favor of their perspective. However, it would be misleading to claim that this will be easy to achieve initially or that past achievements in this regard are guaranteed for eternity.

In conclusion, I would emphasize that the search for local cultural sources must continue in East Asia and throughout the world, despite its risks and uncertainties. In my view, it is not a matter of choice between cultural mediation and other approaches to the universality of human rights. Rather, it is simply that there is no alternative to the cultural mediation approach if genuine and lasting universality of human rights is to be achieved.

CHAPTER 7

GROUNDING HUMAN RIGHTS ARGUMENTS IN NON-WESTERN CULTURE: *SHARI'A* AND THE CITIZENSHIP RIGHTS OF WOMEN IN A MODERN ISLAMIC STATE

NORANI OTHMAN

INTRODUCTION

The argument that Western notions of human rights may be culturally and civilizationally contingent, not universal, challenges all human rights activists – and especially those from non-Western contexts – to consider whether it is the Western tradition alone that has historically formed an explicit concern with the rights of people as individuals, as citizens within a political community, and as members of important social groupings. Does only Western discourse have the capacity to generate such a conception of human rights? Or can an affirmation of human rights be effectively and autonomously generated from within other, non-Western cultural traditions, philosophical idioms, and religious and civilizational frameworks? Are such intellectual resources available in other, non-Western contexts and traditions?

This chapter considers these questions through an exploration of women's rights in an Islamic context, particularly present-day Malaysia and Indonesia. Internationally, so far as human rights issues are concerned, Islam frequently gets very bad press, sometimes unfairly, but all too often deservedly. Yet actions taken in the name of Islam are often not based on true Islamic principles or their animating concepts. The following discussion will explore the potential and realities of, as well as the entrenched resistance to, the generation and elaboration of an effective non-Western discourse on human rights in Islamic societies. I argue that although Islam may be as culturally contingent as its Western counterpart, it nevertheless has the capacity to yield a notion of universal human rights: the idea that by virtue of their intrinsic humanity, transcending all culturally and historically conditioned differences, people share certain essential entitlements.

ISLAMIC REASSERTION VERSUS REASSERTING HUMAN RIGHTS ON ISLAMIC GROUNDS

In the West the development of the modern nation-state is generally equated with secularization. But in East Asia, the development of the modern nation-state over the past three decades has demonstrated that often the influence of religion has grown as the consolidation of the nation-state takes place. A striking example of this is Islamic resurgence. The postcolonial development of most Muslim countries saw increasing tension between the adopted social and political order and the renewed efforts of many of their citizens to define and strengthen their Islamic identity.

In the course of the difficult modernization process, traditional societies all over the Muslim world – South and Southeast Asia as well as the Middle East – have been undergoing transformations that have affected both those societies and their Islamic institutions and cultural heritage. Even as the economic and political systems of these societies modernize, Islam retains great influence over the general populace, so the confrontation of modernity on the social level has also become a confrontation of Islam and modernity on the theological and ideological levels.[1]

This confrontation has accelerated various forms of "Islamic" discourse about human rights. Contemporary Muslims, like followers of the other two great Abrahamic religious traditions, Christians and Jews, have shown a notable concern for human rights that is not grounded in any borrowed "Western model." Instead they have attempted to demonstrate that a human rights culture comes from the *Qur'an* and the teachings of the Prophet Muhammad. This drive to reclaim for Islam a vision of human beings and a practice of law and politics that sustains an Islamic version of human rights has resulted in extensive writings by contemporary Muslims on the relation-

---

1. There are many analyses of this problem. Among others see Fazlur Rahman, *Islam and Modernity* (Chicago: University of Chicago Press, 1982); Malek Bennabi, *Islam in History and Society*, trans. Asthma Rashid (Kuala Lumpur: Berita Publishing, 1991; orig. *Vocation de l'Islam*, 1949); Bassam Tibi, *The Crisis of Modern Islam: A Preindustrial Culture in the Scientific Technological Age*, trans. Judith von Sivers (Salt Lake City: University of Utah Press, 1988), and *Islam and the Cultural Accommodation of Social Change*, trans. Clare Krojzl (Boulder, CO: Westview Press, 1990); Mohammed Arkoun, *Rethinking Islam: Common Questions, Uncommon Answers*, trans. and ed. Robert D. Lee (Boulder, CO: Westview Press, 1994; orig. *Ouvertures sur l'Islam*, 1989).

ship of Islam and human rights.[2] Yet the vast social changes that span the time between the establishment of the first Islamic community and the emergence of the contemporary world order require a creative and historically sensitive interpretation of that model that is not often reflected in the literature. Most Islamic writings are dominated by two problematic positions, which are in fact not so far apart in terms of their implications for contemporary human rights principles.

On one side are Muslims who maintain that Islam embraces human rights standards similar to Western-derived international human rights standards. They advocate integrating Islamic rules and concepts with internationally recognized rights to bring them to conformity with Islamic standards – the rules of *Shari'a*. However, close scrutiny of this approach reveals various levels of ambivalence about the concept of rights. It is fraught with reservations and restrictions on a range of rights and freedoms, especially as they pertain to women and non-Muslims. At the other extreme are those Muslims who claim outright that current human rights concepts and standards (especially those incorporated within prevailing international human rights documents) are completely alien to Islam and incompatible with Islamic law as they interpret it.[3]

Between these poles lies a precarious middle ground – a space within which some of the most creative and inclusive Islamic sociolegal thought is now being created. However, like courageous and innovative thinking elsewhere, such sociolegal modernism is far from dominant within the Islamic world, especially in its Middle East heartlands. It is a discourse propagated in the main by Muslim intellectuals, many of whom are now forced to live in exile in the West for advocating their ideas.[4] Although their positions may vary to

---

2. See Ann Elizabeth Mayer, *Islam and Human Rights: Tradition and Politics* (Boulder, CO: Westview Press, 1991). Mayer provides a careful study and a critical assessment of various human rights ideas and documents from both Islamic traditions – the Sunni and Shi'i. Foremost among them are the 1981 Universal Islamic Declaration of Human Rights (UIDHR) presented to UNESCO in Paris and the pamphlet by Sultanhussein Tabandeh, *A Muslim Commentary on the Universal Declaration of Human Rights* (1970, orig. in Persian, 1966).

3. See Mayer, *Islam and Human Rights,* chapter 2.

4. Among these Muslim scholars and their works, see Fathi Osman, *Jihad: A Legitimate Struggle for Human Rights, The Muslim World: Issues and Challenges* (1992), and *Shari'a in Contemporary Society: The Dynamics of Change in Islamic Law* (Los Angeles, CA: Multimedia Vera International, 1994); Abdullahi A. An-Na'im, *Toward an Islamic Reformation: Civil Liberties, Human Rights and International Law* (Syracuse, NY: Syracuse University Press, 1990). Another scholar is the Egyptian Nasr Hamid Abu Zayd, who with his hermeneutic approach to textual analyses has opened the *Qur'an* to new interpretations; this approach has led him to voice trenchant criticisms of the position of some of the Islamists figures such as Shaykh Muhammad al-Ghazali, Shaykh Mohamed Metwali al-Sha'arawi, and Yussef al-Qaradawi. He has recently been forced to flee Cairo. See Mona Abaza, "Civil Society and Islam in Egypt: The Case of Nasr Hamid Abu Zayd," *Journal of Arabic Islamic and Middle Eastern Studies* vol. 2, no. 2 (1995), pp. 29–42. Mohammed Arkoun in many of his writings has also advocated similar positions, that is, a new reading of the text based on his claim that the highest religious teachings and even the revelation itself of the three monotheistic religions (Judaism, Christianity, and Islam) are subject to historicity. See also Arkoun, *Lectures du Qur'an* (Paris: Alf, Les Editions de la Méditerranée, 1990).

some extent, the common thread among these intellectuals is that they advocate a critical reexamination of exegetical and jurisprudential texts as well as, wherever possible or pertinent, a reinterpretation of Islam's foundational religious texts. Muslims advocating equal rights for women have emphasized in their discussion the problematics of interpretation of texts and, from those interpretations, of the contemporary codification of Muslim laws on the rights of women. The call for a review of the long-accepted juridical opinions and interpretations established during the classical age of Islam also characterizes many contemporary movements promoting the rights of women and of non-Muslims coexisting in a predominantly Muslim country.

Religious doctrines as first principles are conditioned by the sociocultural reality within which they are actualized. The life history and social action of the Prophet Muhammad himself attests to this fact. Herein lies the contradictory relationship between religion as text and religion as practice. A disregard for the historical context within which the *Shari'a* was constructed, and for the historical character of the *Shari'a* itself as it was developed and applied within early and classical Islamic civilization, has permitted fundamentalists to perpetuate in our own times a premodern antagonism against women.

The sociocultural bias built into the interpretive process and the exclusively male composition of its permitted exponents among the experts of interpretive legal reasoning (*fuqaha*) and religious scholars (*ulama*) have worked to disqualify, and even suppress, not simply new interpretations, but also any endeavor to broaden interpretive practices and processes. The current debate in countries such as Malaysia and Indonesia on *hadith,* the remarks attributed to the prophet, is a case in point. The relevant issue is not the rejection of *hadith* by some modern Muslims, but rather the real need to reexamine their classical interpretations.[5] Tied up with this debate is the yet unrealized need to review or provide a critique of the conventional theory of the Prophetic *Sunna,* the normative practice of the Prophet Mohammed. Together, the *hadith* and the *Sunna* form the tradition that guides Muslim conduct.

This problem of consensus on interpretation of texts in Islam and among contemporary Muslims all over the world is ironically a mirror image of the "cultural relativist/cultural legitimacy" debates challenging Western conceptions of universal human rights. Muslims today must confront the claim by

5. The debate on *hadith* is particularly relevant to the project of Muslim women's groups, which endeavor to promote a more egalitarian interpretation of gender statuses and rights. Much of the gender bias in historical *Shari'a* and conventional theological views derives from traditionalists' interpretation of *hadith* texts. (See the explanation in "Reconciling Local Culture and the International Human Rights Regime" in this chapter.) See also Fathi Osman, *Muslim Women in the Family and Society* (Kuala Lumpur: SIS Forum Publications, 1996); Barbara F. Stowasser, *Women in the Qur'an, Traditions, and Interpretations* (New York: Oxford University Press, 1992); and Fatima Mernissi, *Women and Islam: An Historical and Theological Enquiry* (Oxford: Blackwell, 1991).

militant resurgent Islamist forces that only their interpretation of Islam, of its values and its view of human rights and women's rights, is the "universal" and legitimate view for all Muslims at all times. As with Western conceptions of universal human rights, this claim of universality needs to be negotiated and challenged within the internal discourse of contemporary Muslim societies.

This challenge should be mounted according to An-Na'im's proposal for cultural mediation (see Chapter 6): The idea that human equality is pervasive in all religious ideals, with no exceptions for gender or other differences, must be subject to debate within the worldwide Muslim community, or *umma*. Muslim men and women must make the choice to undertake that debate, commit themselves to principled participation in challenging the narrowness of traditionalist and neotraditionalist views of human rights in Islam, and thereby enlarge the contemporary Islamic discourse on rights.

HUMAN RIGHTS AS A UNIVERSAL CONCEPT IN ISLAM

Muslims need to consider how they can apply their own distinctive perspective to existing international human rights. Two main issues confront modern Muslims. The first is prevailing *Shari'a* definitions of human and citizenship rights. Consideration of the position of any special category or subset of human beings can only follow from, and exist within the parameters of, an acceptance of the rights of humans simply by being humans. This awareness is by no means alien to Islam. It is grounded in the *Qur'an*ic notion of a common human ontology (*fitna*) and couched in an Islamic idiom of moral universalism that predates much of the Western discourses about human rights. It is thus doctrinally a part of the *Qur'an*ic worldview itself. The challenge to contemporary Islam and to Muslims, especially the new traditionalist ideologues, is to revive and embrace that which is their own. It is nothing more than a challenge to begin to see humans, all humans, in the way that their faith insists God/Allah sees them.

Second, Muslims need to contribute to the human rights discourse their own modern and Islamically appropriate conceptions of equal social relations between men and women. Here again, *Qur'an*ic conceptions of the rights and duties of men and women – in the family, to own and manage property, and to participate in public life and hold public office, for example – provide the basis for a far more enlightened and egalitarian view of gender relations than the regressive ideas that are currently offered, misleadingly in the name of Islam, by fundamentalist Islamists the world over.

Until these two main issues are clearly defined, human rights instruments and their moral foundations, derivatively Western in their origins and history, can be neither embraced wholesale nor summarily rejected by modern

Muslims. Only after a critical reevaluation of their Islamic heritage and the acceptance of an underlying common humanity can progressive Muslims decide in what ways and to what extent they should accept, reject, modify, or renegotiate the stock of concepts and ideas that are now offered as the basis for a universal concept of human rights.

CITIZENSHIP RIGHTS AND THE POSITION
OF MUSLIM WOMEN

{W}ith respect to the status of Muslim women: although it is true that they have full legal capacity under Shari'a *in relation to civil law and commercial law matters, in the sense that they have the requisite legal personality to hold and dispose of property and otherwise acquire or lose civil liabilities in their own independent right, Muslim women do not enjoy human rights on an equal footing with Muslim men under* Shari'a.

Abdullahi A. An-Na'im[6]

According to An-Na'im, most of the published expositions of human rights in Islam by contemporary Muslim scholars are not helpful because they overlook the problems of slavery and discrimination against women and non-Muslims. Muslim women scholars, on the other hand, have mainly highlighted those verses of the *Qur'an* that are consistent with human rights standards. But a major problem still remains: Some crucial verses exist that are inconsistent with or even contradictory to universal human rights conceptions.[7] An-Na'im has suggested that the only effective way to achieve sufficient reform of *Shari'a* in relation to universal human rights is "to cite sources in the *Qur'an* and *Sunna* which are inconsistent with universal human rights and explain them in historical context, while citing those sources which are supportive of human rights as the basis of the legally applicable principles and rules of Islamic law today."[8]

A major, often ignored, problem with respect to rights is that the "*Shari'a*-minded," "traditionalist," or "fundamentalist" recodification of modern state laws redefining people's rights, especially women's rights, affects democratic participation and citizenship rights as well as personal rights. Yet this proposed *Shari'a*-based recodification is promoted by and also borrowed and imitated from countries, especially in the Middle East, that typically lack any articulated notion of citizenship rights. They are states with regimes, but without

---

6. An-Na'im, *Toward an Islamic Reformation*, p. 171.
7. See, for example, Riffat Hassan, "On Human Rights and the Qur'anic Perspectives," *Journal of Ecumenical Studies* vol. 19 (1982), p. 12 [cited by An-Na'im, *Toward an Islamic Reformation*, p. 171].
8. An'Na'im, *Toward an Islamic Reformation*, p. 171.

citizens or "civil society." They invoke and uphold the adequacy of conventional Islamic views of the purely personal status rights of women and non-Muslims. By this maneuver, intentionally or by oversight, they set aside or rule out any consideration of the broader social, civic, and political rights and full legal standing of women and non-Muslims as equal citizens of the state.

No wonder that the Islamist ideologues promoting this *Shari'a*-based recodification can blithely dismiss the disquiet voiced by modernist Muslim critics with empty assurances that "all will be well" under the new Islamist legislation. Denying women's citizenship rights is not problematic for Islamic ideologues because they have no modern experience of citizenship: Such moral and intellectual foundations are well beyond the reach of the ideologues' sociolegal consciousness. This draws into question how appropriate their ideas and agenda are, arising from their own limiting circumstances, as a basis for modern social policy and legal reform under different, less restricted conditions. Why should countries like Malaysia, which are already launched on a trajectory toward modernity, with modern notions of the nation as a community of people sharing citizenship rights, accept the elaboration of modern notions of citizens' rights from religious ideologues and developmentally deadlocked nations that lack any modern understanding of citizenship?

That such "Islamist" ideas, with their yearning for an unrealized utopian ideal, should be able to exert a powerful appeal among social groups that see themselves as excluded from or victims of development is not surprising. But it remains troubling to modern Muslims sensitive to the centrality and resonance of the issue of rights in both Western and Islamic historical consciousness and civilization. What especially concerns modernist Malaysians is the apparent readiness of some of their national leaders, who at the overtly political level directly oppose the "Islamist" agenda and the parties advocating it, to accommodate these tendencies and capitulate piecemeal to demands in such areas as the recodification of modern state law, especially in areas most affecting women.

In many Islamic societies today there is a tendency to define the rights and obligations of citizens on the basis of gender and faith. This mind-set reflects the popular view that the typical citizen is a Muslim male. What is missing from this view is a recognition of the rights of human beings simply as human beings, which, as stated earlier, is a *Qur'an*ic notion.[9] This gap between the ethical principles of the *Qur'an* concerning gender equality and the kinds of retrogressive and male-centered interpretations that have been

9. Part of this section is drawn from Norani Othman, "Islam, *Shari'a* and Women in Contemporary Muslim Societies" (unpublished paper presented at a panel discussion, Women and Law, Muslim Politics Study Group series, Pluralism in the Muslim World: The Changing Roles of Women, Council on Foreign Relations, New York, January 12, 1996), pp. 7–10.

codified into *Shari'a* law provides a challenge for modern Muslim women's pursuit of equality and respect for their rights.[10]

THE CONCEPT OF CHANGE IN ISLAMIC SOCIETY

As today's Muslim nations modernize, the socioeconomic circumstances of the majority of Muslim women will inevitably change.[11] Many Muslim scholars assert that the way to move forward is for Muslims to develop (or recover) the imaginative ability to grasp such fundamental change. I say "recover" because from the inception of the history of Islam, Muslims have always held, at least theoretically, that change (change in people and in society) is possible, part of the human condition itself. But while the Muslim worldview has encompassed this possibility as a matter of principle, most Muslims themselves have lost the practical ability to face, understand, and master change.

There are many examples of *Qur'an*ic foundation of the concept of change: the *Qur'an,* in taking humankind beyond the age of ignorance (*jahiliyya*), oriented human thinking toward the possibility of change. Early Islam also incorporates the idea of change through migration or *hijra:* a movement not simply from one place to another (Mecca to Medina, in the paradigmatic instance) but from one social and moral plane to a higher one. Muslims have evolved from being one community, a part of the city-state Medina, to become part of an empire, a political identity that extended well beyond a state by the time of the Abassid Empire. From a state with a central authority in Damascus or Baghdad emerged a polity with many autonomous governments and distinct political entities. In other words, change has been a constant of Muslim existence.

Islamic law itself has evolved along with changing circumstances, in part through the operation of *ijtihad,* or informed critical reason, which applies Islam's broad legal principles to emerging social and historical realities. Yet despite these possibilities for flexibility and dynamism, Islam has become stagnant.

Many Muslims in Malaysia and elsewhere are always ready to blame colonialism for this cultural stagnation. Whether it is colonialism itself that is at

10. See Fatima Mernissi, *Women and Islam* [The American edition is titled *The Veil and the Male Elite: A Feminist Interpretation of Women's Rights in Islam* (Reading, MA: Addison-Wesley, 1991)]. Also Margot Badran and Miriam Cooke, eds., *Opening the Gates: One Hundred Years of Arab Feminist Writings* (London: Virago Press, 1990); and Stowasser, *Women in the Qur'an, Traditions, and Interpretations.*

11. This section draws on the Sisters in Islam [registered name: SIS Forum (Malaysia)] Study Group's discussions with Prof. Fathi Osman, August–September 1994 and October–November 1995, and also on its series of public lectures on *Shari'a* and Modernity in 1995. Based on these intensive discussions, SIS Forum hopes to publish pamphlets on "Islam, *Shari'a* and Modernity" and "Islam, Human Rights and Democracy" as a continuation of its booklet series on the theme of a renewal of Islamic thought.

fault or, as Malek Bennabi suggests, the readiness to accept colonialism (or its twin phenomenon – *colonisibilité* – the domination of the mind by alien ideas, and a habituation to passivity toward alien cultural domination) is another debate.[12] In any case, Muslims are now heirs to a history of stagnation that must be overcome and Muslims need to regain a belief in change and in the ability to manage it intelligently, to pursue independent agendas rather than capitulate to those of others. In this context, modern Muslims, especially in countries such as Malaysia that lie outside the culturally Arabic heartlands of Islam, need to be wary of acquiescence to a new colonization, one carried out by traditionalistic Islam misunderstood as the transhistorically essential Islam. What is required is a calm and reasonable debate on the issue of historicity and change in the Islamic heritage of contemporary Muslims. This in turn requires modern Muslims to act upon a basis that is historically informed and feasible, not historically and religiously confused.

A necessary part of this discussion turns upon understanding what is divine in the *Shari'a* and what, in the scholarly tradition interpreting it, is of human origin. What is divine is the *nass* of the *Qur'an* or the "word of Allah," the text and all its intentions and purposes. The act of interpreting the text and deriving its meaning and intended purposes is human, especially the methodology of interpretation devised by the experts of interpretive legal reasoning, the *fuqaha*s. This means that various methods of interpreting the text through the use of critical reason (*ijtihad*), analogy (*qiyas*), and consensus (*ijma'*) can be reassessed and reevaluated.[13] Modern Muslims are entitled to further develop those corpora of interpreted material. The choice is between futility and creativity: between attempting to impose archaic and limited legal understandings upon the present and seeking to understand the history of Islamic civilization in its entirety so that modern believers, members of an interdependent humankind, may act authentically as well as realistically and effectively as Muslims upon the stage of global history.

EXAMPLES OF WOMEN'S RIGHTS STRUGGLES IN MALAYSIA

Muslims past and present, from all juristic schools (*madhhab*) and political persuasions, orthodox conservatives as well as modernists, acknowledge that Islam was the earliest religion to emancipate women, giving them rights

---

12. Malek Bennabi, *Islam in History and Society,* Asthma Rashid, trans. (Kuala Lumpur: Berita Publishing, 1991; orig. *Vocation de l'Islam,* 1949).
13. An-Na'im provided the basis of this argument in chapters 2 and 3 of *Toward an Islamic Reformation.*

unknown to any other society at the time. They agree that the *Qur'an* introduced various positive reforms for women, including a woman's right to contract marriage, to divorce, and to inherit and dispose of her property as she pleases. Early *Qur'an*ic injunctions also called for the outlawing of female infanticide and enforcing the payment of male dowry (*mahr*) to the bride herself, rather than to the bride's father or guardian. Although progressive in tendency, these early ideas of the rights and status of women did not develop further, nor did they sustain any emancipating or egalitarian impetus within the interpretation of *Shari'a* by later generations of Muslims.

What is at present accepted as a body of Islamic tenets and laws concerning women does not rest solely on the *Qur'an* or on direct interpretation of its text, but includes inferences and interpretations drawn from the so-called traditions (*hadith* and *Sunna* of the Prophet), as well as the accumulated interpretations (*tafsir*) of the classical Islamic scholars and exegetes. The Islamic paradigm of the ideal role, status, and duties of Muslim women was largely derived from the *tafsir* of male jurists and scholars, particularly those of the classical age of Islamic civilization.

This heritage has now become a bone of contention, providing a challenge for contemporary Muslim women as they do daily battle to reclaim their rights and assert their equal status with men in their own societies. For Muslim women in Malaysia and Indonesia, the struggle is doubly problematic. It not only involves the clash between traditionalist and modernist understandings of the Islamic social ethic and legal heritage but a conflict between certain Malay cultural traditions and those traditions derived from Middle Eastern Islam. In Malay society, as in other Southeast Asian systems, cultural traditions or customs, known as *adat,* define and affirm women's role and their public contribution or participation, often in positive, nonhierarchical ways.[14] The tension between Southeast Asian cultural definitions of women's gender roles and rights and traditionalistic Islamic formulations is most prominent in the rule of *hijab,* which entails not just the covering of a woman's face, but more fundamentally female seclusion and segregation of social space – a separation that characterizes gender relations throughout much of the Middle East but that is not a cultural characteristic of the "Malay world" or *Nusantara.*

Other rules codified into Muslim law that are detrimental to women's rights include the right of Muslim men to practice polygamy and the *Shari'a* principle limiting a female's inheritance right to the value of half of whatever

---

14. See M. B. Hooker, *Adat Laws in Modern Malaya: Land Tenure, Traditional Government and Religion* (Kuala Lumpur/New York: Oxford University Press, 1972); Wazir J. Karim, *Women and Culture: Between Malay Adat and Islam* (Boulder, CO: Westview Press, 1992).

her male siblings inherit. These have become controversial issues, particularly for Muslim women in Southeast Asia, because they often go against local *adat,* especially the matrilineal *adat perpateh* rules of kinship and inheritance long practiced in areas such as Negeri Sembilan in Malaysia and in Minangkabau and parts of Acheh in Indonesia. It is noteworthy that despite their emphasis on female property rights and women's unfettered social participation, these *adat perpateh* areas have been known historically as regional centers of Islamic activism and renewal.

Family Law and the Promotion of Polygamy

The issue of polygamy is at present extremely contentious in Malaysia. Since the second half of the 1980s and throughout the 1990s there have been many attempts by local *ulama* and other Muslim authorities in several of the thirteen Malaysian states' Islamic Affairs Departments to allow and even encourage the practice of polygamy among Malaysian Muslims as a matter of principle and to ignore (in recent months to remove) many of the restrictions and conditions contained in the existing *Shari'a* enactments. As recently as October 1996, two of the states (Selangor and Perlis) sought to amend the state *Shari'a* enactments in order to make polygamy easier by removing the condition requiring consent of the first wife and/or existing wives.[15] Spurred into action, many women's groups questioned the wisdom and religious basis for such a move. In a meeting between a group of more than 50 women representing various Muslim women's associations and NGOs with the Chief Minister of the State of Selangor and several of its top religious officials – namely, the Selangor State Mufti, the Selangor Religious Department Director, the Petaling Jaya Syariah Court Judge, the State Muslim Marriage Registrar, and the Selangor State Legal Adviser – the focus of discussion was not the interpretation of Islamic foundational texts. Rather, the overriding issue was the *Qur'an*ic legitimacy of the proposed amendment removing those restrictions.[16]

The challenge by Muslim women since the mid-1980s to the religious authorities' interpretation of polygamy has been partially successful insofar as

---

15. When the Selangor Islamic Affairs department announced its proposal to drop a legal requirement that husbands obtain the permission of their first wives before taking others, it claimed that this move was aimed at allowing men to "obtain their God-given right and to reduce adultery." Other *ulama* in the state also added that this will help to reduce the alarmingly high percentage of single/unmarried professional Muslim women in the economically booming Klang Valley surrounding Kuala Lumpur (a social statistic often quoted by male *ulama* since the 1990s whenever they bemoan the so-called lack of social morality and the breakdown of family values among urban Muslim population).

16. See *The Sunday Star,* November 3, 1996, special article, "Focus: Facing Up a Touchy Issue."

the view that "polygamy is a right enshrined in the *Qur'an*" is no longer considered valid. Efforts by women's groups and other Muslim modernist groups have made some headway in questioning entrenched traditionalist views, in opening up debate over some traditional interpretations of text, and in challenging the codification of religious laws by the state Islamic authorities. The modernist argument that such codifications are anachronistic rests on the "historicity critique," which argues that, even in classical times, the way that *Shari'a* has been interpreted and promulgated into law has always been shaped by local conditions. It should be noted that opposition to instituting anachronistic understandings of *Shari'a* is not unique to contemporary Malaysian Muslims, but has been an ongoing discourse among Muslims in many Middle Eastern countries since the late nineteenth century, particularly in Egypt and Syria.

The debate over polygamy in modern Muslim countries is just one illustration of the many issues that are involved in the internal and cultural contestation for the assertion and establishment of women's rights in Islam. Polygamy is an important rights issue for women's groups in Malaysia; they argue that acknowledging polygamy as the inalienable right of a Muslim male nullifies the Islamic notion of a woman's rights in a marriage. Because in Islam a woman cannot be forced into a marriage without her consent, how can there be a law that gives a Muslim husband the right to unilaterally change the circumstances of the marriage contract without her prior knowledge or consent? Making polygamy the unquestionable right of a Muslim male also contradicts the general principle of equality between Muslim male and female. Many Malaysian Muslim women's groups consider that making laws or regulations concerning polygamy on the basis that it is "an inalienable right of a Muslim male" contradicts the *Qur'an*ic view of polygamy and at the same time entails a great injustice toward women in marriage, both the existing wife and the prospective one.

This case exemplifies the difficulties of implementing legal reforms in Islam in the face of the current resurgent Islamization movements.[17] Even though the state has successfully mandated a more open and egalitarian reading of religious texts through its legal codification, the actual implementation of its progressive stance remains obstructed. This is especially so because male Muslims with decidedly traditionalistic and regressive doctrinal inclinations predominate among the decision-makers within the various departments of administration of Islamic affairs and the administration of the *Shari'a* court system.

The power dimension further underscores the urgency of an argument for

---

17. See Norani Othman, ed., *Shari'a Law and the Modern Nation-State: A Malaysian Symposium* (Kuala Lumpur: SIS Forum (M) Berhad, 1994), chapters 9, 13, and especially 14 for an elaboration of what is meant by "retraditionalizing" Islam – an anachronistic approach of Islamization that seeks to reaffirm and reimpose in the present the understandings of *Qur'an*ic ethical imperatives of early formative Islam.

the citizenship rights of Muslim women in their own respective countries. No simple internal reform of the *Shari'a* court and administrative system will suffice to remedy these problems. Redress lies not within the narrow confines of the system of Islamic religious administration, but in assuring and advancing the citizenship rights of Muslim women on a broad social front.

Gender Equality and Qur'anic Islam

The Muslim traditionalist position on women's rights rests heavily on the argument that Islam recognizes no notion of gender equality. This assertion is based on two theological claims: first, that because at the time of Creation the female was created from a man's rib, she is therefore in her origins derivative and thus men are inherently superior to women, who exist for men's use. The second claim is that men are *qawwamun* ("have responsibility") over women, a claim based on the traditionalists' preferred interpretation of a key *Qur'anic* verse (*Al-Nisa'*, 4:34). Thus it is the woman's role to provide for the man's needs and continued reproduction through loyal service in the domestic realm. This claim finds its expression in the interpretation and emphasis given by traditionalists to the *Qur'anic* injunction that "your women are a tilth for you to cultivate so go to your tilth as you will."[18]

The theological foundations for this imposition of female subordination have been critically and effectively challenged in recent years. For example, Fatima Mernissi of Morocco and other Muslim scholars from Egypt, India, Pakistan, and the Sudan have provided cogent arguments that in principle and intention Islam actually promotes gender equality.[19] The common assertion of Muslim modernist scholars is that Islam is a liberating religion that uplifted the status of women and gave them rights considered revolutionary 1,400 years ago. Their arguments rest on the shared assertion that none of the *Qur'anic* verses that speak of human creation makes any mention of woman as an inferior or derivative being. "There is absolutely no difference

18. See Muhammad Assad's rendering as "your wives are your tilth; go, then, unto your tilth as you may desire, but first provide something for your souls and remain conscious of God," to which he adds the footnote "in other words, a spiritual relationship between men and women is postulated as the indispensable basis of sexual relations." In its context the injunction to individuals swept up in the dynamics of a pastoral military or derivatively tribal society, that they should go to their tillage can only be understood as a call to adopt a settled, stable, orderly, and socially responsible form of life. It is not an injunction or authorization to men to treat women simply as the vessels of their personal gratification and of the social reproduction of their patriarchal clan groups. See Muhammad Assad, *The Message of the Qur'an* (Gibraltar: Dar-ul Andalus, 1980), p. 49.

19. See Fatima Mernissi, *Women and Islam,* and her *The Forgotten Queens of Islam* (Cambridge: Polity Press, 1993); Leila Ahmed, *Women and Gender in Islam* (New Haven: Yale University Press, 1992); Asghar Ali Engineer, *The Rights of Women in Islam* (London: C. Hurst and Company, 1992); Aftab Hussain, *Status of Women in Islam* (Lahore, Pakistan: Law Publishing Co.); and An-Na'im, *Toward an Islamic Reformation.*

in the value given to the creation of woman and the creation of man. Biological differences do not mean that women and men are not of equal value."[20] Riffat Hassan, for example, has shown that "the story of the rib" was derived from the Old Testament, which was later absorbed in *hadith* literature.[21]

The ethical outlook of the *Qur'an*, which humankind is urged to adopt as its own, is uncompromisingly universalistic and inclusive. It acknowledges no categorical precedence of men over women or Arabs over non-Arabs but instead insists that, regardless of particular identity, "the noblest in the sight of Allah are those who are most devoutly conscious" of Allah's omnipresent reality (*Al-Hujurat*, 49:13). Because the equal status of women and men in spiritual matters is not only recognized but insisted upon in the *Qur'an*, can the Islamic insistence upon the equal rights and obligations of women and men be any less in daily matters?[22]

The assertions of the modernists and contemporary Muslim women scholars are based on thoughtful, principled, and contextualized reexamination of texts, which reach beyond the kinds of narrow literalist interpretations offered by traditionalist scholars and ideologues. They do not simply reject the adverse views of women's status that have held sway throughout much of Islamic history, they seek to account historically for them. The modernists explain women's inegalitarian status as arising from the persistent tendency of traditionalist exegetes to decontextualize *Qur'an*ic verses concerning women and gender relations, thereby inappropriately transforming the specific meaning (*matna*) into a universal rule. The obligations of family economic responsibility that are placed on men in *Surat Al-Nisa'* (4:34) are thereby misunderstood by traditionalist religious scholars (*ulama*) as endowing men with general authority over women.

The economic responsibility for women that is mandated here must be related to "the occasion of revelation" of that verse, the need to secure the economic welfare of women. This included especially widows and divorced women of the clan-based patriarchal society of the Prophet Muhammad's time, when women lacked full autonomous economic participation and enjoyed only half of the inheritance rights of men. But this verse, the modernists argue, cannot be understood as instituting a general subordination of women because the *Qur'an* and *Sunna* at the same time recognized women's equal capacity to fulfill other roles – social, intellectual, and spiritual.[23]

---

20. See Sisters in Islam, *Are Women and Men Equal Before Allah?* Booklet Series (Kuala Lumpur: SIS Forum (M) Berhad, 1991), pp. 3–12.
21. See Riffat Hassan, "Made from Adam's Rib: The Woman's Creation Question," in *Al-Mushir Theological Journal of the Christian Study Centre* (Rawalpindi, Pakistan, Autumn 1985).
22. See also Sisters in Islam, *Are Women and Men Equal Before Allah?*
23. In fact, during the Prophet's lifetime Muslim women were engaged as nurses and volunteers in all the Muslim battles and military campaigns against their Meccan enemies.

A common feature of the counterarguments provided by these critical scholars is their persistent questioning of the historical bases of the standard male-supremacist and orthodox interpretations. They demonstrate that what was generally enshrined within and elaborated through the evolving Islamic legal culture failed to distinguish clearly between conservative Islamic social tradition and the normative Islamic legal principles expressed in the foundational texts.

Muslim Women and the Holding of Public Office

Another area in which the traditionalists and modernists diverge is over the traditionalist belief that only men can be leaders. Proponents of women's equal rights regard this as a fallacy. They maintain that neither the *Qur'an* nor the remarks attributed to the Prophet (*hadith*) espouse that a woman cannot be a leader or hold public office. There is no clear *Qur'an*ic injunction (*nass*) either allowing or forbidding women to lead or to be appointed judges. However, under juristic interpretations that prevail in Southeast Asian as well as Middle Eastern Islam, the criteria of eligibility for judicial appointment are as follows: that a person be a Muslim, of majority in age, a free person, mature, just and with integrity, possessing a sense of hearing and sight, a proficient interpreter (*mujtahid*), and male.[24]

Despite this, Indonesia today has approximately one hundred women judges (known as *Ibu Hakim*) in the *Shari'a* court or Peradilan Agama. Their appointment came with the enactment of the Indonesian Marriage Law of 1974 (No. 1 of 1974).[25] In the face of gender constraints in the traditionalist interpretation of *hadith*, the appointment of women *Shari'a* court judges in Indonesia is justified by modernist Muslim *ulama* and scholars on several grounds.[26]

First, the *hadith* statement that "a nation can never prosper if it is ruled by

---

24. A *mujtahid* is one who is proficient in all fields of Islamic jurisprudence (knowledge of the textual sources, methodology of arriving at a legal ruling, the differences of opinion among jurists, and all branches of law). Where no such person is available, the best-qualified person on these matters would suffice. See Mahmud Saedon A. Othman, *Kadi: perlantikan, perlucutan dan bidang kuasa* [Qadi: Appointment, Dismissal and Powers of Jurisdiction] (Kuala Lumpur: Dewan Bahasa dan Pustaka, 1980).

25. See Salbiah Ahmad, "The Judiciary and the Appointment of Women Judges in the Shari'a Courts of Malaysia," in Sisters in Islam, ed., *Islam, Gender and Women's Rights: An Alternative View* (Kuala Lumpur: SIS Forum (M) Publication, 1993), pp. 46–54. For an analysis of the origins and operation of the Indonesian Marriage Law 1974, see Nakamura Hidako, *Divorce in Java* (Yogyakarta: Gadjah Mada University Press, 1983).

26. The following passage is taken from Ibu Hakim Dra. Faizah Manshur, "Kedudukan hakim wanita dan perannya di Lingkungan Peradilan Agama [The Status and Role of Women Judges in the Indonesian Shari'a Court]" (unpublished, Yogyakarta, 1987), pp. 12–17. Ibu Hakim Dra. Faizah Manshur is a judge of the Peradilan Agama Rembang [Religious Court of Rembang]. Her paper was prepared for discussion at a special meeting of Surakarta women judges in Yogyakarta where Salbiah Ahmad, a member of Sisters in Islam, was an observer.

a woman" is not a direct prohibition on female political leadership. It does not reject the appointment of women as military or executive leaders, still less as judges. Second, according to the views of the *Hanafi* school, women may be appointed under *Shariʿa* to sit on civil but not criminal cases. Because in Indonesia the jurisdiction of the Islamic courts covers only civil matters, it is reasoned on *Hanafi* grounds that women may serve as *Shariʿa* court judges. Quite independent of this *siyasah Shariʿa* reasoning, women may also be appointed as judges in Indonesia's criminal court system. However, when a woman judge hears criminal cases, she operates under Indonesian state law – not as an agent of, and beyond any restrictions emanating from, Islamic law. This rationale may seem casuistic, but it does provide a pragmatic way for women to be appointed as judges as long as Islamic traditionalist resistance seeks to prevent such appointments.

Third, their appointment is consistent with the fact that both men and women are enjoined to do good and prevent evil (*Al-ʿImran,* 3:104). Fourth, because it is inconceivable that all women are morally and intellectually incapacitated, any categorical exclusion of women from eligibility to serve would be unjustifiable. Fifth, contrary to traditionalist and neotraditionalist assertions, the interaction of women and men in public does not necessarily bring about a corruption of morality (*fitna*). Sixth, the fact that the rightly guided caliphs (the Prophet Muhammad's four immediate successors as political leader of the *umma*) did not appoint women as judges does not indicate any prohibition against their appointment. It is explicable in terms of the circumstances of the time. The *Qurʾan* has left to humans the appointment of arbiters (male or female) who, according to prevailing circumstances, can fulfill the requirements of the task of judging.

Judges must meet certain requirements if their appointment is to be legitimate, but modernists argue that there is no a priori reason why women should not fulfill those requirements, especially under modern social conditions. These modernist arguments serve to demonstrate that classical juristic opinions are not immutable. As An-Naʾim has argued:

> Once it can be understood that juristic opinion or historical *Shariʿa* is a construction by founding jurists, it should become possible to think about reconstructing certain aspects of (historical) *Shariʿa,* provided that such reconstruction is based on the same fundamental (revealed) sources of Islam and is fully consistent with its essential moral and religious precepts."[27]

This again highlights the insufficiently recognized fact of the historicity of all human interpretations of the *Qurʾanic* revelations.

---

27. See An-Naʾim, *Toward an Islamic Reformation,* p. xiv.

The Case of the Kelantan Hudud Law

Hudud in its legal sense means a punishment prescribed by God in the revealed text of the *Qur'an* or the *Sunna* (of the Prophet), the application of which is in the right of God (*haqq Allah*). Meaning literally "limits," the *hudud* in their original legal sense and intent were instituted as a set of maximum, and in effect mandatory, punishments for various major categories of crimes.[28]

At the November 1993 sitting of the Kelantan State Legislative Assembly, the Syariah Criminal Code (II) of the State of Kelantan was introduced. This act became the first piece of legislation seeking to institute the *hudud* and *qisas,* or retaliatory, provisions of Muslim criminal law as state law in modern Malaysia. The *hudud* punishments, the most contentious part of the law's provisions, require that those found guilty of certain offenses (for example, adultery, armed robbery and apostasy) be subjected in public to such punishments as flogging, mutilation of limbs by amputation, stoning to death, and crucifixion. The legislation also has other extremely troubling features, including the grounds for the presumption of illicit sex (*zina*) by women in clause 46(2); the inadmissibility of women as eyewitnesses in clause 41(1); the termination of a marriage by a husband's accusation (*al-li'an*), whether proven or not, of *zina* against his wife in clauses 14 and 15; and the implied endorsement in clause 2(I) of the view that *diyat* or compensation for death or injury to a woman should be half that for a man.

An important breakthrough took place in December 1993, when the Malaysian women's rights organization Sisters in Islam[29] submitted a memorandum to the Prime Minister of Malaysia (Datuk Seri Dr. Mahathir Mohamad) urging the federal parliament not to endorse the Kelantan *hudud* law. Though passed by the Kelantan's state legislature, the law cannot be implemented unless the federal parliament endorses it. To pass such an amendment by the federal parliament would require the support of the prime minister's ruling party, which held a massive majority in the federal legislature. The passing of the enactments by the Kelantan legislature and their impending referral to the federal legislature for approval produced a tense stand-off in Malaysian politics: Did Dr. Mahathir and his party dare to approve Kelantan's *hudud* law legislation or did they dare to reject it? Either way the political implications were profound.

In a high-profile public campaign in 1993 and throughout 1994, Sisters in Islam sought to provide a principled and intellectually coherent case against

---

28. See Rose Ismail, *Hudud in Malaysia: The Issues at Stake* (Kuala Lumpur: SIS Forum (M) Berhad Publications, 1995), pp. 1–50.
29. This author is an active member of Sisters in Islam.

the endorsement of the Kelantan enactments, a case grounded in modernist Islam that, by invoking the modernist "historicity critique," rejected the crude equation of *hudud* with *Shari'a,* and *Shari'a* with Islam, upon which the support of the Kelantan enactments was urged by the traditionalist Islamists.

The federal parliament has stated that it will not pass the Kelantan *hudud* code, and to this day it has not been implemented. Moreover, the federal parliament has said it would block any move by PAS or other conservative opposition members to amend the federal constitution in order to implement the *hudud* laws. The reason given is that the country is "not ready" to implement such criminal laws. Here, the sisters-in-Islam campaign deserves much of the credit for creating awareness among some of the more powerful modernist Muslim politicians that there is a valid Islamic argument to suspend the implementation of *hudud* laws in the contemporary context.

Consistently arguing on religious (Islamic), legal, political, and human rights grounds against the endorsement of the Kelantan *hudud* law, the campaign waged by Sisters in Islam demonstrates again the need for a human rights activism grounded in non-Western terms. Where religious orthodoxy is an influential source of the political impetus to impose laws that transgress contemporary notions of rights and freedom, internal cultural and religiously informed contestation is pertinent and urgent.

Shari'a-*based Opposition to Protecting Women from Domestic Violence*

Efforts to have legislation on domestic violence passed by the Malaysian parliament in 1995 are instructive of contemporary debates over the religious bases for public policy. The Domestic Violence Act of 1995 had been drafted following multilateral consultation among Islamic religious authorities and organizations as well as women's groups in the country. The much revised final draft of the act was approved by all of those consulted before it was presented to parliament.

Then, at the final hour, some influential figures in the federal government's Islamic Affairs Department opposed the legislation. Their opposition was not only to some of its details, but – in the name of the *Shari'a* whose guardians they claimed to be – to its entire jurisprudential foundations. Now, after all the details had been patiently negotiated, they argued that the Domestic Violence Act contradicted the *Shari'a* and undermined its supremacy in its designated domain, for it would enable Muslim women to invoke the application of a law other than the *Shari'a* against their husbands. This would compromise the Islamists' contention that the existing *Shari'a* enactments should have exclusive application to family or domestic matters among Malaysian Muslims, and that only through recourse to the *Shari'a* court system should Muslim victims of domestic violence be permitted to seek protection and redress.

Islamists who opposed the Domestic Violence Act in effect argued that Muslim women should not have the right to any effective protection against violence perpetrated in the domestic realm. The insistence that they employ only the existing Muslim family laws would often leave a woman unprotected because the *Shari'a* courts are generally more concerned with persuading both partners to preserve a failing marriage than with ensuring a woman's rights and personal security within it. Until they reluctantly agree that divorce is inevitable, the *Shari'a* courts will require a victimized woman to return to her conjugal home and reconcile with her husband, whatever his "imperfections," even if his violence toward her is the cause for her situation having come to the court's attention.

These arguments disregard the fact that the Domestic Violence Act is part of the national Penal Code and in no way, in intention or implementation, would replace the application of any existing Muslim family law in matters of marriage and the family. The existing Muslim family laws do not, in fact, provide any effective legal procedures for the protection of, or legal redress for, Muslim women who become victims of domestic violence. Because the Domestic Violence Act deals with matters that lie outside of the concerns of the *Shari'a* law system and its legislation, it cannot be said to encroach upon their jurisdiction.

By opposing the Domestic Violence Act and in blindly upholding the sanctity of *Shari'a* over the legal rights of Muslims, these Malaysian Islamists have shown themselves incapable of addressing contemporary social problems. They are prepared to tolerate widespread abuse and violence against women in marriage and the family as the price for maintaining the principle of the supremacy of *Shari'a,* as they anachronistically understand it, and as the bulwark for their own political interests. In the end, thanks to the efforts of women's groups in Malaysia, the Domestic Violence Act was finally passed just before the Malaysian general elections in April 1995. The problem that women's groups in Malaysia confronted in their campaign for an early enactment of this act is indicative of the kind of challenge that they also faced later in campaigning for the ratification of the International Convention on Women's Rights.

RECONCILING LOCAL CULTURE AND THE INTERNATIONAL HUMAN RIGHTS REGIME

Acceptance of the *International Convention for the Elimination of All Forms of Discrimination Against Women* – the United Nations Organization's Women's

Convention (CEDAW) – has been problematic in countries in which Muslim law is applied.[30] Certain influential Muslims resist CEDAW purportedly on *Shari'a* grounds, and their critique must be addressed at a fundamental level.[31]

Several important factors must be taken into account to understand how *Shari'a* law, as implemented in most contemporary Muslim countries, may pose problems for states in their decision to accede to CEDAW. Foremost among them is the difference between *Shari'a* in the *Qur'an* and *fiqh,* or the interpretation and codification of the *Qur'anic Shari'a* precepts, as discussed earlier.[32] As an instrument for women's rights, CEDAW will naturally have to confront these issues. CEDAW is particularly vulnerable on two grounds: (1) that women's enjoyment of the rights and of the autonomy from male control that these instruments promise can be depicted on purportedly religious grounds as being "shameless," and (2) inasmuch as these international instruments are experienced as outside interference, they can be represented as an affront on nationalist, cultural, or religious grounds.

There are simply no short-cuts around these obstacles. In the long run, before instruments such as CEDAW (or even recent domestic laws that provide for rights of women) can have a positive impact in these societies, women and women's movements will have to ensure, first of all, that the sources of all the various forms of subordination that arise from cultural and religious traditions are identified. Only then can they be differentiated from what Islam enjoins and can they be exposed to thoroughgoing criticism, leading to their rejection and abolition, precisely on the grounds of what Islam enjoins.[33]

This seems to be the most effective strategy for ending women's subordination within their own local and national cultures. Having in this way promoted the emergence of locally acceptable cultural and moral systems favoring recognition of women's rights, women and women's movements will then be in a position to advocate equality in ways that are locally persuasive. They then will be able to argue that women's emancipation, as required by international human rights instrument such as CEDAW, is consistent with

30. See Norani Othman, "Shari'a Law and the Rights of Modern Muslim Women: An Overview of the Implementation of CEDAW in Muslim Societies, with Special Reference to Current Developments in Malaysia" (unpublished paper presented at the International Women's Rights Watch (IWRAW), a Round Table Meeting on Women, Islam, and CEDAW, New York, January 14, 1995).

31. See also Aihwa Ong, "Globalization and Women's Rights: The Asian Debate on Citizenship and Communitarianism" (unpublished paper presented at a Symposium on Feminism and Globalization, September 1996); also L. Amede Obiora, "Feminism, Globalization and Culture: After Beijing" (unpublished manuscript presented at the same symposium in response to Aihwa Ong's paper).

32. For arguments and explanation for the need of an internal Islamic renewal approach in contemporary Muslim societies, see Asghar Ali Engineer, *The Rights of Women in Islam* (London: C. Hurst and Co., 1992), pp. 154–71; Othman, ed., *Shari'a Law and the Modern Nation-State,* pp. 147–53; Stowasser, *Women in the Qur'an, Traditions, and Interpretations;* and Fatima Mernissi, *Islam and the Fear of Democracy* (London: Virago Press, 1993).

33. See, for example, the popular presentation of these issues in the two booklets issued in 1991 by Sisters in Islam on gender equality and the unacceptability in Islam of domestic violence described earlier.

local and national values. In this way, they will avoid placing themselves, or being placed by others, in a position in which their challenge to women's subordination and their support for women's full enjoyment of human rights are seen as merely an imposition of outside Western cultural ideals.

The examples in the previous section demonstrate the need for a sensitive internal cultural discourse that is capable of challenging existing dogma. Ultimately, the primary project for Muslim women's groups in their struggle for women's rights is not the recognition of CEDAW per se. More important is the need for consensus within their own culture that the kinds of women's rights they are advocating are indeed acceptable on the grounds of a public ethic derived from their own cultural and religious sources.

THE *QUR'AN* AND THE UNIVERSAL RIGHTS OF HUMANKIND

There is no question for the urgency of a "reconsolidation" of Islam's religious heritage (*turath*). The initiation of change, a shift in the Islamic paradigm, is consistent with the *Qur'an*ic foundations of the faith. This emphasis on a *Qur'an*ic receptivity toward change is also consistent with the lessons customarily drawn by Muslims from the life and practice of the Prophet Muhammad himself. A readiness to accept, embrace, and even consciously shape change is a cultural "*sunnatic*" lesson. Throughout his life the Prophet Muhammad's work clearly demonstrated "an emancipatory impetus." Islam developed in the time of the Prophet Muhammad as a democratic religion, a morally energetic religion of committed participatory activism that was open to all who believed in Allah, the one God, and were ready to share in the divinely ordained pursuit of justice, fairness, and virtue.

This underlying notion of rights and freedom open to all faithful believers, and to all who may yet come to recognize the supremacy of Allah (that is, all of humankind), is not dissimilar to modern notions. According to the *Qur'an*, a Muslim person who suffers oppression and does not do anything about it is a sinner. Such a person is encouraged to migrate elsewhere if he or she is unable to fight against an oppressive system. The *Qur'an*ic term *ibn al-sabil* refers to someone who is forced to move from place to place in order to seek a more peaceful life free from oppression.[34] That is, to endure oppression involves a double violation of divinely ordained human nature and autonomy: by the oppressor and by the victim. Implied in this is a profound affirmation of human freedom, dignity, and autonomy – and of the human as a rights-bearing being.

---

34. See also Fathi Osman, *Concepts of the Qur'an: A Topical Reading* (Kuala Lumpur: Angkatan Belia Islam Malaysia [ABIM], 1997), p. 122.

Apart from the concept of *fitna,* which refers to humankind as an undifferentiated whole, the *Qur'an* also speaks of human dignity. The *Qur'anic* term "descendants of Adam" does not refer just to Muslims, or to a particular group of people, but to all humankind: "We have conferred dignity on the descendants of Adam" (*Al-Isra',* 17:70). There is also the notion of diversity in the one humankind. On the basis of their differences, humans are to come together not just in a superficial way, but in profound human and cultural contact. The notion of *umma* refers to humankind in its entirety and diversity, and human beings are given the right of religious conscience, an entitlement to their respective religious views and commitments. This is the capacity for spirituality that all humans share. It is not a Muslim monopoly, but is immanent in every human heart and mind according to the *Qur'an.* As humans we not only enjoy a generic equality but also an ontological common ground.[35]

In their social relations humans are urged to respect freedom of expression. The *Qur'an* also supports the principle that no hurt should be meted out to a person on account of her or his testimony. In *Surat Yunus,* the *Qur'an* emphasizes that differences between humans are God's will. Difference is a part of the human condition and therefore there is to be no compulsion of faith.[36] Religious freedom as affirmed by the *Qur'an* is the basis of human rights.

The cultivation of an internal discourse within Islamic civilization about the meaning and interpretation of Islamic texts, as with all other texts, is fraught with problems. For Muslims the *Qur'an* is the word of God, revealed to the Prophet Muhammad as a guide to all people. Contemporary Muslims have to acknowledge that there are problems with interpreting that message. The *Qur'an* is for all time, but its immediate concern is with the Arabs of Muhammad's time.

The society in which Islam was first revealed was qualitatively different from Muslim societies today. When interpreting how rules were devised and changed, Muslims need to bear in mind that the *Qur'an* is not organized chronologically but topically. This makes it difficult for modern-day Muslims to establish the exact chronology of the revelation of the verses. Language is another problem. The medium is in the form of classical Arabic poetry with a long story, a form that is not easily accessible. Its literary structure is based on the Arab environment and experience.

Once the divine manifested itself among humans, in the form of the

---

35. See the *Qur'an, Al-Baqarah* 2:283, which says "Conceal not evidence; for whoever conceals it – his heart is tainted"; see the *Qur'an* 2:282 which urges that "neither scribe nor witness suffer harm. If ye do (such harm), it would be wickedness in you." See Abdullah Yusuf Ali, *The Holy Qur'an: Text, Translation and Commentary* (Brentwood: Amana Corporation, revised edition, 1989).

36. *Yunus* 10:99; also see the commentary for this verse in Muhammad Assad, *The Message of the Qur'an* (Gibraltar: Dar Al-Andalus, 1980), p. 308.

*Qur'an*ic word, and was launched by the Prophet as the bearer and messenger of that word into human history, everything that followed in Islam is undeniably historical. There can be very few literal interpretations or interpretations of enduring, immutable validity. Muslims have to be clear on general principles and have to work out for themselves the two levels of the text – the transitory or contingent and the permanent. The transitory and contingent texts enunciate specific guidelines for Muslims during the Prophet's lifetime – according to modernists like An-Na'im and his mentor Ustaz Mahmud Taha, particularly for the Muslim community in Medina. The permanent texts refer to those verses revealed in Mecca or outside Medina that happen also to be general principles about equality, morality, virtue, and social justice.

Some modernists see the permanent texts as having primary relevance today and suggest that modern Muslims put aside many of the Medinan verses, or at least not refer to them at all in the codification of modern Islamic public law. But such a position is regarded as heretical by traditionalists, who believe that the earlier Meccan verses were abrogated by the later Medinan verses. In fact, because many of the Medinan verses were specific elaborations of matters pertaining to the social institutions of family, community, and society, and also to women, women's status in marriage and society, and gender relations in general, traditionalists feel these rules should be followed in all their detail.

Other modernist thinkers are located between these two views, believing that the Medinan verses are transitory and contingent, but not going so far as to say they are irrelevant to modern Muslims and totally abrogated by the Meccan verses. Although it may be inappropriate to follow the Medinan verses absolutely in modern Islamic societies, some useful analogies can be derived from their context. This position abides by the rule that the sanctity and unity of the *Qur'an*'s divine message must be maintained. Ultimately, all interpretation relies upon the human practice of *ijtihad,* critical reason. It is this urgent need for *ijtihad* that can give modern Muslims the potential to devise a useful debate among themselves that will enable them to effectively participate in the cultural mediation of human rights with others.

CONCLUSION

The struggle for human rights, especially women's rights, in Muslim countries is complex. It involves the validity and hegemony of certain religious interpretations over others, gender bias, patriarchy, and the politics of identity. The often heard criticism that Western conceptions of women's rights and gender equality contradict Islamic principles of gender relations can no longer be accepted at face value.

Yet because of the pervasive influence of the literalist Islamic resurgent movements in many Muslim countries, women and women's groups struggling for recognition of their rights, both personal and public, have to make common cause with whatever modernist religious impulses are to be found in their own societies. By doing so they not only enhance the Islamic legitimacy of their cause, they also thereby ensure that their endeavors are recognized as an integral part of the overriding question facing contemporary Islam: the attainment, based on the cultural and ethical foundations of Islam, of modernity. Negotiating space for public debate of the many issues relating to women's rights and freedom is a task that Muslim women can most readily achieve not through a solitary, separatist struggle, but in concert with other Islamic modernists and human rights activists who recognize their cause as an inescapably public concern for twenty-first-century Islam.

The view of some human rights activists that women's rights movements are better served by utilizing the "secular" approach – one that bases its arguments in the supposedly universal rule of law and democratization – is not at all pragmatic, nor as easily implemented as its proponents claim. The experience of many women's groups operating in Muslim countries these past two decades demonstrates that in their daily battles a great deal more progress is achieved by working within their religious and cultural paradigm. This gives Muslim women's movements a distinctive character when compared to Western women's movements. Muslim women's rights activists have to employ a wide variety of approaches in their project to advance the status and rights of Muslim women. Their ideas, conceptions, and recommendations for rights and social emancipation must be religiously and culturally informed as they confront the challenge from their own religious, political, and community leaders, male or female. A common thread between Western and non-Western women's movements is found only within a social fabric or against the background of persistent gender bias in the assertion of modern-day patriarchal ideologies.

CHAPTER 8

LOOKING TO BUDDHISM TO TURN BACK PROSTITUTION IN THAILAND

Suwanna Satha-Anand*

By the power of my merit, may I be reborn as a male.
A Sukhodaya Queen

Let the one among you who is guiltless be the first to throw a stone at her.
John 8:8

INTRODUCTION

Accusing fingers have been pointing to Buddhism as one of the guilty parties in the tragedy of Thai prostitution. A favorite question is: How is it possible that a Buddhist society like Thailand allows so many prostitutes in its
streets? Of course, one could also ask: How is it possible that so many Christian nations export arms to Third World countries? The point here is not to
identify as many guilty parties as possible, but instead to underline a simple
fact: It is not possible to ascribe a single cause to such complex phenomena as
arms exportation or prostitution. According to Buddhism,[1] causality is best
expressed in terms of a complex process of multiple factors operating simultaneously. This chapter is written in this spirit.

Even if the logic of the question is untenable, it should not be dismissed

---

*Although I could not participate in the Seoul workshop, I did have the opportunity to listen to the taped discussions of a draft of this chapter, which were of great help for its revision. These discussions indicate to me the true meaning of "critical, fair, and constructive" comments. My sincere thanks to Joanne Bauer, who has done a truly marvelous job.
1. When I use the term "Buddhism" in this chapter I do not mean the Thai Sangha Buddhist institution; rather I mean the contested readings of Buddhist texts.

out of hand. Although Buddhism may not be an active party to the crime, we must still ask whether it has done enough to prevent some of the cases from happening. The reason I single out Buddhism in the prostitution question is because I strongly believe that Buddhism *can* and *should* do something to help remedy the situation. Although some Buddhist scholars are adamant that Buddhist ethics do not inherently involve any conception of human rights, others argue that the *Benja-sila,* the Five Precepts for all Buddhists, are themselves a protection of rights.[2] It lies beyond the scope of this paper to present the philosophical arguments behind these two positions; rather I offer some feminist readings of certain Buddhist passages and introduce a feminist analysis of the most popular *jataka* tales (stories about former births of the Buddha) in Thai traditions. This is done to illustrate some of the possibilities for finding new meanings in Buddhism, which has been the most important cultural framework for Thai life.[3]

This paper is divided into four sections. The first deals with the economic conditions in Thailand. Particular attention is given to the global economic imbalance that is repeated at the national level. The second section deals with the historical–cultural conditioning of male–female relationships, which are the wider context for the practice of prostitution in Thai society. The third section explores the facts and figures of prostitution in Thailand, which, unfortunately, has become one of the capitals for the flesh trade in the past decades. And the fourth offers feminist reinterpretations of some key Buddhist passages, together with a feminist analysis of the *Vessantara jataka* tale. In conclusion, I argue that the cultural empowering of women is crucial to creating more awareness of this problem as a salient rights issue in a society where economic, legal, historical, and cultural conditioning are working *against* the recognition of women's human rights.

THAILAND'S ECONOMIC ENVIRONMENT

There is no need to repeat here how certain authoritarian regimes in Asia have – too conveniently in the past – been violating the civil and political rights of their citizens. This image of some Asian rulers as ruthless violators of human rights has been well covered in the international media. In the past

2. Take, for example, Boontham Poonsab, "Ethics and Human Rights in Theravada Buddhist Philosophy" (M.A. thesis, Graduate School, Chulalongkorn University, BE 2533). Boontham does not find any conception of human rights in Buddhist ethics. Another Buddhist scholar, Somparn Promta, argues that the Five Precepts are essentially human rights protections. In the latter's opinion, the first precept of nonkilling is but another expression of the right to life. See more detail in Somparn Promta, "Rights in Buddhism," *Journal of Buddhist Studies* vol. 1, no. 1 (January–April, BE 2537), pp. 44–64.
3. Prostitution of young boys is also a severe problem in Thailand, but lies outside the scope of this chapter.

few years, however, some Asian intellectuals have tried to fill out the picture by pointing out the missing aspect of the international discourse on human rights: economic injustice. One such attempt is made by Chandra Muzaffar, founder of the Malaysia-based Just World Trust, who uses statistics from the *UNDP Human Development Report* of 1992, and argues:

> Between 1960 and 1989, the countries with the richest 20 percent of the world population increased their share of global GNP from 70.2 percent to 82.7 percent. The countries with the poorest 20 percent of the world population saw their share fall from 2.3 percent to 1.4 percent. The consequences for income inequalities have been dramatic. In 1960, the top 20 percent received 30 times more than the bottom 20 percent, but by 1989 they were receiving 60 times more. These disparities become even starker when one examines real consumption levels. The North, with about one fourth of the world's population, consumes 70 percent of the world's energy, 75 percent of its metals, 85 percent of its wood and 60 percent of its food. Contrast this with the situation in the South. Over one billion people are mired in absolute poverty. One and a half billion people are deprived of primary health care. About one billion adults are illiterate. What this shows is that a huge portion of the population in the South do not enjoy the most basic economic and social rights.[4]

It should also be noted that in Asia, over 700 million people live in absolute poverty. Over 600 million Asians, two thirds of them women, cannot read or write.[5] Although many people in the South, most of whom are women, still "do not enjoy the most basic economic and social rights," their neighbors in the North seem to be enjoying an easy existence. According to one Thai social worker, "Because of surplus from the South, people in the North now have more time and more money to travel around, as consumption patterns become more and more complicated. Leisure time activity no longer means sports or traveling; it also includes exotic sexual consumption as well."[6]

---

4. Chandra Muzaffar, *Human Rights and the New World Order* (Penang: Just World Trust, 1994), p. 19. Muzaffar uses statistics from the United Nations Development Programme (UNDP), *Human Development Report* (New York: Oxford University Press, 1992).

5. These statistics are cited in Sanitsuda Ekachai, "A Report of Global Proportions," *The Bangkok Post,* Outlook Section, June 29, 1994.

6. Sinit Sitthirak, "Prostitution in Thailand," *Thai Development Newsletter* no. 27–28 (1995), p. 65. Sinit also uses data from Maria Mies, "Consumption Patterns of the North – The Cause of Environmental Destruction and Poverty in the South" (unpublished paper presented at the UNCED symposium Women and Children First, Geneva, Switzerland, May 27–30, 1991). An interesting point is made here that private consumption in the North has not only increased dramatically during the past few decades, but its pattern has also changed. According to Mies, "Whereas around 1950 almost half of household expenses were spent on food, this proportion was only 23 percent in 1987. A much greater part of the income of private households could be now spent on leisure time activities and luxury items."

What is so disheartening about these global statistics is that the pattern appears to be repeated at the local level. In Thailand, in 1962–3 the richest 20 percent enjoyed 49.8 percent of national income; the poorest 20 percent received 7.9 percent. After some thirty years of rapid but obviously imbalanced economic development, in 1989 – 90 the richest 20 percent enjoyed 55 percent; the poorest 20 percent received 4.51 percent. This means the poorest are getting a smaller share of the income increase, that is, from 7.90 percent to only 4.51 percent.[7]

In the 1960s when Thailand, with the help of the World Bank and the International Monetary Fund, decided to "industrialize" rather than develop a viable national industrialization plan or maintain an agriculture-based economy, it resorted to a number of tactics to earn foreign currency, one of which was the sale of "nature" and "culture." It seems plausible that images of docility, submissiveness, and the exotic play into the appeal of Thai prostitutes to foreign men and their pocketbooks. In October 1980, the "Year of Tourism" in Thailand, then deputy prime minister Boonchu Rojanasathien declared to the national meeting of governors:

> Within the next two years, we have a need of money. Therefore, I ask of all governors to consider the natural scenery in your provinces, together with some forms of entertainment that some of you might consider disgusting and shameful because they are forms of sexual entertainment that attract tourists. Such forms of entertainment should *not* be prohibited if only because you are morally fastidious. Yet explicit obscenities that may lead to damaging moral consequences should be avoided, within a reasonable limit. We must do this because we have to consider the jobs that will be created for the people.[8]

It seems all too clear from Mr. Boonchu's statement that the economic incentive as a *conscious* choice of action operating at the national level is used to *justify* the practice of "forms of sexual entertainment that attract tourists." The same economic incentive is echoed in the lives of millions of women involved in the lucrative sex trade in Thailand and beyond. Amid the

---

7. NSO, Socioeconomic Surveys, as cited in Chalongpob Susssangkarn, *Towards Balanced Development: Sectoral, Spatial and Other Dimensions, the 1992 Year-End Conference,* TDRI (December 12, 1992), p. 34, table 3.6. Also quoted in Akin Rabibhadana, "The State and the People," *Thai Development Newsletter* no. 27–28 (1995), p. 30.

   Some people might argue that this statistical gap should not cause too much concern because, objectively speaking, the poor are also better off. My question is, does this argument justify an enormous income disparity between the rich and the poor? Also, does it reflect a desire to brush aside the question of socioeconomic justice?

8. Quoted in Sukanya Hantrakul, "Prostitution in Thailand," in Victoria Clayton, ed., *Displacement: Women in Southeast Asia* (Centre for Southeast Asian Studies, Monash University, 1988), pp. 130–1. There is a rare and interesting study that examines the "demand" side of prostitution in Jeremy Seabrook, *Travels in the Skin Trade: Tourism and the Sex Industry* (London and Chicago: Pluto Press, 1996).

1997–8 financial crisis in Asia, some people in Thailand are again speaking of the flesh trade as a means to bring in highly valued U.S. dollars.

HISTORICAL AND CULTURAL CONDITIONS

According to noted Thai historian Thanes Apornsuwan, there was never a concept of human rights in traditional Thai culture. There were only concepts of rights relative to a person's sociopolitical status, not rights as universal claims for each individual as a human being.[9] With respect to the male–female relationship, it seems quite clear that "in most respects women in traditional Siamese society were subordinate to men."[10] And this subordination was sanctioned by religion. In the words of Craig J. Reynolds, a prominent scholar of Thai history:

> Buddhism structured the world in such a way that *karma* – the physical, verbal, and cognitive actions of past lives – and the accrual or loss of merit in consequence of those actions conditioned the differences between any two individuals in social status, talent, wealth, and power. *Karma* also conditioned gender. To be a woman and not a man meant that the individual had inadequate store of merit, and the only way to remedy this situation was for a woman to make merit through acts of religious devotion. . . . In this worldview differences in gender reflected inequalities of accumulated merit, and Buddhism by explaining differences in this way thereby ratified them as inequalities.[11]

Once this line of reasoning is accepted, it follows that women occupy an inferior status in this life. Being female is not permanent to a person's nature, it applies only in the individual's current life. There are always opportunities to change one's sexual fate. What one can do is to "make and store" merit in this life to be reborn a male in the next. The fact that one's sexuality is not

---

9. Thanes Apornsuwan, "The Rights of Thais in the Thai State," in Chaiwat Satha-Anand, ed., *New Paradigms in Thai Studies in the Year 2000* (Bangkok: Thailand Research Fund, BE 2539), pp. 192–3.

10. Craig J. Reynolds, "A Nineteenth Century Thai Buddhist Defense of Polygamy and Some Remarks on the Social History of Women in Thailand" (unpublished paper prepared for the Seventh Conference, International Association of Historians of Asia, Bangkok, August 22–26, 1977), p. 2.

11. Reynolds, "A Nineteenth Century Thai Buddhist Defense of Polygamy," p. 3. The theory of karma explained here indicates the Thai cultural understanding of this doctrine, which does not necessarily correspond with the original philosophical message of the Buddha. It can be argued that for the Buddha, karma was explained as an equality principle, that is, one is what one is and where one is by one's own actions, and not by birth as in the case of the Hindu caste system. However, this is a very complex issue that is still the focus of many debates among Buddhist scholars. Take, for example, Phra Rajavoramuni, a highly respected Buddhist monk-scholar in Thailand, who argues that in Buddhism no one is born equal (because of past karma), but it is everyone's right to struggle for equality in this life. For more detailed arguments, see Saneh Chamarik, *Buddhism and Human Rights* (Bangkok: Thai Khadi Research Institute, 1982). Another recently published book on the topic that deserves attention is Damien V. Keown, Charles S. Prebish, and Wayne R. Husted, eds., *Buddhism and Human Rights* (Surrey: Curzon Press, 1997).

permanent reinforces the power of the Buddhistic belief in women's inferiority. Because Buddhism has offered a way out within the system, women in effect are strengthening the belief of their inferiority by working that way out. If sexuality were seen as fixed, women might have been more willing to revolt against the system.

The Three Worlds, a Buddhist cosmography text of the fourteenth century, depicts a picture of an ideal marriage relationship between the Universal Monarch and his Queen:

> When the Universal Monarch comes to visit his precious wife she does not remain seated where she was but gets up to greet him; taking a golden fan, she sits down next to him and fans him. Then she massages him, pressing on him with her hands and feet, and then she seats herself lower than him. This precious wife never lies down on the bejewelled bed before the Universal Monarch and never gets off the bed after him. If she wants to do something she always greets the Universal Monarch and tells him so that he may be informed. When the Universal Monarch gives an order she executes it. She never disobeys her husband, and in the smallest action and in her slightest words she pleases him. Only a Universal Monarch can be her husband; there is no other man who can become her spouse. (Her heart is bound to that of the Universal Monarch) and she absolutely cannot break away from him.[12]

Although this ideal of absolute devotion may not be common, the message is clear: A woman's role is to serve her husband.

And she cannot break away from him. Traditionally, the queen is one of the seven gems, the possession of which designates the ruler as a Universal Monarch. This idea that women are the possessions of men was legalized in Siamese laws. The Three Seals Code, promulgated in 1805, reinforced the subordinate position of women in the way it allocated property rights in the event of the death of a spouse or the dissolution of the marriage. Fundamental to the family law in the 1805 code was the conjugal power of the husband, which meant that he managed the property held jointly by the spouses, that he could sell his wife or give her away, and that he could even administer bodily punishment to her, provided the degree of punishment was in proportion to the misdeed. A woman was also obliged to obtain the consent of her parents to marry, though her parents could not compel her to marry. Before marriage, the man presented his future parents-in-law with the sum of silver deemed to be compensation for the expenses they incurred in raising their daughter. By this exchange, the parents transferred the custody of their daughter to the man. A woman was not a free agent and had to be

---

12. Quoted in Reynolds, "A Nineteenth Century Thai Buddhist Defense of Polygamy," p. 5.

placed under someone's else's protection. Bondage may be too strong a word to describe this dependency, but as late as 1857 a royal decree gave husbands above a certain noble rank (*sakdina* 3000) the right to government assistance in pursuing a wife who had fled the household.[13]

The Three Seals Code of 1805 reissued a fourteenth-century law, which divided wives into three categories: the principal wife (*mia klang muang*), whose parents consented to her marriage; the secondary wife (*mia klang nok*); and the slave wife (*mia klang thasi*), who was acquired through purchase (for example, by a man redeeming a woman from debt-bondage). This ranking determined a wife's rights with respect to property. The slave wife had no claim on any part of her husband's estate, but the secondary wife had some inheritance rights.[14] The husband managed the conjugal property, but in the event of divorce by mutual consent, each spouse was compensated for prenuptial property disposed of in the course of the marriage. As for post-nuptial property, the husband received two thirds and the wife one third. An adulterous wife lost all right to prenuptial and postnuptial property. Yet if a husband abandoned a wife he could recover his prenuptial property as well as his share of the postnuptial property.[15]

The family law promulgated in 1935 adopted monogamy as the only basis for a legal marriage contract, but it still countenanced polygamy by recog-nizing all children conceived by a man, irrespective of the mother, if he chose to register them.[16] Women do not enjoy the same right – Thai mothers need a legal husband to have legal children, but Thai husbands do not need a legal wife in order to have children by law.

In the eyes of religion, women are subordinate through inferior birth due to an inadequate store of merit, and in the eyes of the law women are subordi-nate because they are not considered free agents. Their ultimate role, cultur-ally defined, is that of a devoted wife. Moreover, when one looks at the lives of Thai villagers, one finds that women are expected to sustain and provide a substantial financial contribution to the family. According to Thomas Kirsch:

> It seems clear that the Thai-dominated part of the private sector of the premodern economy was in the hands of women. Private interregional trade tended to fall into non-Thai hands. . . . No class of women traders arose to take control of the

---

13. See historical treatment of this issue in Reynolds, "A Nineteenth Century Thai Buddhist Defense of Polygamy," pp. 6–7.

14. Quoted in Reynolds, "A Nineteenth Century Thai Buddhist Defense of Polygamy," p. 7.

15. Reynolds, "A Nineteenth Century Thai Buddhist Defense of Polygamy," p. 8.

16. Thai prime minister Chuan Leekpai made good use of this provision of the family law by registering a son born to a not-so-well-reputed woman. He chose not to marry her legally. Although legally Thai-land has adopted monogamy, in practice a husband taking a minor wife (*mia noi* – literally small wife) is common among all classes of Thai society.

marketing system of the entire kingdom. Instead, the role of women in the Thai economy remained petty and localized, in part because they remained oriented to Buddhist goals. Women might still attempt to enhance their merit status in future existence, but such attempts were tied to being a wife and a mother.[17]

Another noted anthropologist, Charles Keyes, although disagreeing with Kirsch on some points, does confirm the fact that the woman as mother is expected to enhance the well-being of the family. In Keyes's words,

> Petty trading, unlike operating a full-time shop or store, is viewed by women and men alike as a dimension of the domestic economy and thus most appropriately undertaken by women. . . . In short, I do not find any deep religious significance to the fact that women play roles as market women. Rather, these roles can be seen as in keeping with the ideal of woman as mother, since they serve to enhance the well-being of the family.[18]

Statistics on migrant workers compiled by independent scholars and the National Statistical Office provide further evidence of the financial providing role played by women in their families. Since the mid-1970s women migrants have come to outnumber men. In 1978, for example, 64 percent of all migrants from northeastern villages to Bangkok were female.[19] This trend continued into the 1980s and revealed a very interesting picture of how many women are actually in the work force. According to Pasuk Phongpaichit, who conducted a pioneering research on the female presence in the labor force, although on average only 44.4 percent of the city's women over the age of eleven participated in the labor force, the rate of participation by migrant women from the north was 54.5 percent, and among migrant women from the northeast it had soared up to 80.8 percent.[20]

These studies and statistics all reveal the extent to which Thai women are heavily burdened with their families' financial responsibilities, but at the same time lack the legal protection or religious–cultural support that men enjoy. Thus, the tragic story of prostitution in Thailand, which has been one of the best-known destinations for the flesh trade, should not surprise anyone.

---

17. Thomas Kirsch, "Buddhism, Sex Roles and the Thai Economy," in Penny Van Esterik, ed., *Women of Southeast Asia Occasional Papers No. 9* (Chicago: Center for Southeast Studies, Northern Illinois University, 1982), p. 29. This depiction does not exclude the fact that there are quite a few successful Thai women in big business in urban areas. These two seemingly contrasting realities seem to reinforce the fact that Thai women and economic responsibility go hand in hand. It seems that less economic expectation is imposed on the Sino-Thai women.

18. Charles F. Keyes, "Mother or Mistress but Never a Monk: Buddhist Notions of Female Gender in Rural Thailand," *American Ethnologist* vol. 11, no. 2 (May 1984), p. 229.

19. Keyes, "Mother or Mistress but Never a Monk," p. 235.

20. Pasuk Phongpaichit, *From Peasant Girls to Bangkok Masseuses* (Geneva: International Labor Office, 1982), pp. 32–5.

THE TRAGIC STORY OF THAI PROSTITUTION

As stated in the introduction to this chapter, the situation of prostitution in Thailand is a complex process, simultaneously conditioned by many factors. The most important "pull factor" in the chain of conditions explaining Thai prostitution is economics.[21] How can a woman stay in her rural village when she knows that by going to Bangkok she can work in a factory and earn as much as twenty-five times more than she could at home? Better yet, if she goes into the sex trade, a couple of years of "work" will enable her to build a house for her family, a house of a size and quality that very few people in the countryside could hope to attain over a lifetime of earnings.[22] The answer to this question is clear from the evidence: As of the early 1980s prostitution accounted for by far the largest percentage of women employed in any occupation outside of farm work.[23]

At this point, some figures on prostitution may be useful.[24] With a total population of 60 million, Thailand has an estimated 200,000–700,000 prostitutes, of which 30,000–35,000 are child prostitutes, according to most NGOs. One NGO, the Centre for the Protection of Children's Rights, puts the figure as high as 2.8 million prostitutes, of which 800,000 are thought to be child prostitutes. This contrasts with the official figures of 86,494 prostitutes. Compared to a minimum wage of roughly 4680 baht or U.S.$120 per month, a prostitute can expect to earn 20 thousand baht, or U.S.$1,000. The aggregate income received by all Thai prostitutes in 1990 has been estimated at 14 billion baht, or U.S.$350–400 million per month. And in terms of sex service operators, the NGO estimate is roughly 60,000, whereas the official figure is 6,160 for female prostitutes and 58 for male prostitutes.

In comparison to the minimum wage of 156 baht a Thai worker gets for a day's work, these figures suggest there is an enormous economic incentive for prostitution. A conservative estimate of the income prostitutes made in the year 1993–4, amounts to more than four times that made from narcotics and three times that made from illegal arms sale, and is equal to 60 percent of

21. I wish to thank Charles Taylor for utilizing the term "pull factor" in commenting on my paper at the Seoul Workshop to indicate the economic incentive that pulls many Southeast Asian women into prostitution. He uses the term "push factor" to indicate the cultural forces that almost "push" Thai women from their home into prostitution. Cultural "push factors" will be discussed later in this chapter.
22. Phongpaichit, *From Peasant Girls to Bangkok Masseuses*, p. 74.
23. Quoted in Keyes, "Mother or Mistress but Never a Monk," p. 235. Unfortunately, there is no data available for the 1990s.
24. These figures are for 1990 and are found in Sinit Sitthirak, "Prostitution in Thailand," p. 68. The U.S. dollar values quoted in this publication are prior to the depreciation of the baht. To account for the depreciation, I have used the dollar values here. For example, the aggregate income figure of U.S. $700 million which Sinit cites is now closer to U.S.$350 to 400 million.

the annual budget of the Thai government.[25] Much of this money is being sent home. The postmaster in Do Khan Tai district in the northern province of Payao (an area most famous for its beautiful girls going "south" to work in Bangkok) observed that the remittances swell during the months of March to June and November to January. These are the months of greatest activity in the agricultural calendar, and the girls increase their remittances home to cover the costs of wage labor hired to sustain agricultural operations.[26]

Another fascinating aspect of Thai prostitution is the fact that it does not remain "Thai." On the one hand, Thailand is exporting some 200,000 "sex workers" to other countries, the favorite destinations being Germany, Japan, and the United States. On the other hand, Thailand is importing sex workers from other neighboring countries, like China, Burma, Laos, and Cambodia. In some parts of red light districts in Bangkok, preferred girls are those with blonde hair, most of whom are from the former Soviet Union and Eastern Europe. It is estimated that there are some 40,000–50,000 Thai sex workers in Japan, and some 50,000 Burmese and some 1,500 Chinese sex workers in Thailand.[27]

Though on a somewhat less dramatic scale, prostitution in the neighboring countries of Burma, Laos, and Cambodia is also mushrooming. Since the late 1980s, after the SLORC took power in Burma and after the UN peacekeeping force arrived in Cambodia, the demand for sex services has been increasing. According to data provided by the Organization Against the Trafficking of Women, many ethnic women from the Shan state "chose" to leave Burma to become sex workers in Thailand.[28] In an interview, an ethnic Shan woman said that she left Burma to work as a sex worker in Thailand because even in her native village in Shan state, she expected to be raped by SLORC soldiers sooner or later. She said that many of her friends had been raped by SLORC soldiers, and she was waiting for her turn. Her friends who had been raped felt hopeless about their future because they had lost their virginity, which is highly valued in Burmese society. As long as military operations continue in their villages, she said, there will be incidents of rape, sexual coercion, forced portering, and torture. The story of Shan women preferring to leave for Thailand to work in the sex industry for payment rather

25. Pasuk Phongpaichit, "Overall Picture of Illegal Economy in Thailand," *Research Digest* no. 6 (March 1996), p. 11.
26. Phongpaichit, *From Peasant Girls to Bangkok Masseuses*, p. 69.
27. See fascinating studies of the international trafficking of Thai women in Pasuk Phongpaichit, "International Migrant Workers in Thailand" (unpublished paper presented at the seminar on Illegal Economy and Public Policy in Thailand, Centre for Political Economy Studies, Faculty of Economics, Chulalongkorn University, 1995), pp. 11, 15. Another intriguing study on Chinese prostitution in Thailand can be found in Worasak Mahatthanobol, *Chinese Prostitution in Thailand: A Case Study of Young Girls from Yunnan* (Bangkok: Institute of Asian Studies, Chulalongkorn University, BE 2539).
28. "Burmese Women Sex-Workers in Thailand" (unpublished paper made available to this author by the Friends of Women Foundation, Bangkok).

than serving SLORC soldiers without payment is common throughout Shan state and other ethnic states in Burma. Like their Thai sisters, these Shan women regularly send money home to help their family members escape from forced labor and portering by the SLORC.[29]

In Cambodia since 1989 there has been a dramatic increase in prostitution, including child prostitution, and in the trafficking of women and children. Sophisticated operations of abduction and trafficking in women have been established by Cambodian and foreign business interests seeking to exploit an underdeveloped legal infrastructure, poor law enforcement, and poverty. Other contributing factors include the opening up of Cambodia after twenty years of isolation, economic liberalization, the relaxing of border controls, increased tourism, and the presence of 22,000 UN peacekeeping personnel. The Ministry of Health estimates that more than 17,000 women sex workers are employed in brothels, bars, and nightclubs in Cambodia. According to a survey carried out by the Cambodian Women's Development Association in 1993–4, 47 percent of the sex workers interviewed reported that they had been sold into the sex industry, usually by parents, friends, neighbors, or relatives. Sixty-three percent reported that they had been abused by clients or brothel owners. Thirty-four percent said that they had no alternative but to become sex workers because of poverty and lack of alternative employment opportunities.[30]

According to the same survey, about 35 percent of the sex workers in Cambodia are Khmer and the remaining 65 percent are Vietnamese, Chinese, and Filipino. In addition to their illegal status, these foreign sex workers face problems of racism and language difficulty, which increase their vulnerability to coercion, extortion, exploitation, and abuse. This survey also confirmed the economic exploitation of sex workers by brothel owners, with 82 percent of women reporting that they received only 50 percent of their earnings and 13 percent receiving no income for their labor.[31] The demand for young girl virgins has also resulted in women being forced to undergo unhygienic vaginal operations to increase their "market value." These operations have greatly increased the risk of HIV infection.

Perhaps there is no other trade that better characterizes the systematic viola-

---

29. "Burmese Women Sex-Workers in Thailand."
30. These statistics are taken from Cambodian Women's Development Association, "The Prostitution Trafficking of Women" (unpublished paper made available to this author by the Friends of Women Foundation, Bangkok).
31. Cambodian Women's Development Association, "The Prostitution Trafficking of Women." This paper, together with "Prostitution and Sex Trafficking: A Growing Threat to the Human Rights of Women and Children in Cambodia," prepared by Human Rights Task Force Cambodia, were made available to this author by the Friends of Women Foundation, Bangkok. I would like to express my deep appreciation to Siriporn Skrobanek and Barbara Limanowska for being so generous with their data.

tions of human rights than the flesh trade. In these extreme cases of human exploitation in Burma and Cambodia, we can see that the right to freedom from slavery and servitude, the right to work and free choice of employment, the right to just remuneration ensuring an existence worthy of human dignity, and the right to a standard of living adequate for health and well-being are being violated on a regular basis.

CULTURAL EMPOWERING OF WOMEN

Some people hold that we should get rid of the exploitative nature of prostitution, not prostitution itself. The arguments seem to be that if prostitution is an act of free choice between consenting adults, then it should not be judged. Another rationale is that prostitution, if practiced without exploitation, makes a lot of money for a lot of people and harms no one. But prostitution as it is currently practiced in these countries is hardly a matter of "free choice" and causes much suffering to a lot of people. Given the severity of the prostitution situation in Thailand and in its neighboring countries, the proper question is: What are the appropriate strategies to remedy the situation?

In the cases of neighboring countries, "cultural empowering" might need to be designed differently; immediate and drastic legal measures are necessary to stop or reduce trafficking of women. In Thailand, an attempt to reduce the problem requires at least two approaches. First is the structural approach: Concerted efforts have to be made to redirect or reorient economic development policy to make it more conducive to human development, particularly the development of women. This approach includes changing unfair family laws and providing better law enforcement, as well as rereading and reinterpreting certain elements in traditional and religious cultures that have subordinated women for so long. Second is the situational approach: Providing programs of action that would remedy the ills of the sex workers involved. This latter approach has been attempted by many national and international NGOs in the past decades. Programs of action include, for example, giving women skills so that alternative employment is a real possibility, extending literacy and human rights and law education to women, and improving and reinforcing laws that punish traffickers.[32]

As previously stated, economic incentives are the major "pull factor" in

---

32. In Thailand, many NGOs are providing help to sex workers in the forms of training, providing a temporary sanctuary, and offering legal and other services. A very prominent feminist lawyer has also provided guidelines to reform the Thai family laws to better protect women's rights. See, for example, Sudarat Suppipat and Malee Prekpongsavalee, *Human Rights and Sexual Exploitation of Thai Women and Women and Thai Law* (Bangkok: Thammasat University Press, 1984).

Thai prostitution; however, the economic factor is only part of the story. There are simultaneously "push factors" operating in the form of historical and religio-cultural conditioning that are compelling women to leave their villages for the city. Although recognizing the importance of the economic incentive, in this section I will concentrate on the issue of cultural empowerment of women. I argue that, because the problem of prostitution is so complex, neither cultural empowerment nor economic policy reform alone can resolve it; both approaches are necessary but neither is sufficient. In the case of coerced prostitution, cultural empowerment is obviously not the solution, and those engaged in kidnapping and trafficking must be dealt with through legal mechanisms. However, at the base of any problem plaguing a society lies its cultural traditions, and in these cases they are Buddhist traditions. I propose to search for the cultural elements that can be renegotiated so that women in Thai, Burmese, and Cambodian societies will be better equipped to fight exploitation.

I will take the "structural" approach to this issue by injecting feminist perspectives into key passages of the Buddhist *Tripitaka,* which carry direct bearings on women's issues, and by introducing a feminist analysis of the *Vessantara jataka* tale. This story of Prince Vessantara, the Bodhisattva who perfects the virtue of giving so that he can be reborn as the Buddha in his next life, is transmitted in sermons, related as myth, expressed as ritual and drama, and in recent times portrayed in film. Throughout Thai history, this tale has arguably served as the most important narrative of Thai cultural life. Several versions in Siamese of this *jataka* tale have been recorded since the beginning of the nation of Siam in the fourteenth century. The *Vessantara jataka* tale has not only been the most popular but has also been constructed as the Thai "national" *jataka.* It is widely believed that anyone who listens to the full sermon on this tale in the space of one day will gain a great deal of merit. Given the importance of this tale, any alternative, rights-sensitive interpretation would carry wide-ranging implications for the understanding of religion, Thai culture, and male–female relations in Thai society.[33]

In the story, Prince Vessantara's extreme generosity leads him to give away the elephant that is the talisman of his father's kingdom, thus resulting in his expulsion. Before he leaves he gives away all his wealth and goes to live in the forest as a hermit with his wife and children. But finally he gives away his two children to an old greedy Brahmin by the name of Jujaka. He also gives away his wife, Queen Madsi, to another Brahmin who is actually a god

33. For an authoritative discussion of the importance of the *Vessantara jataka* tale in Thai culture and politics, see Sombat Chantornvongse, "The Political Meanings of Royal Mahachat," in Sombat Chantornvongse and Chai-anan Smudhavanijja, *Thai Political Thoughts* (Bangkok: Thai Khadhi Research Institute, BE 2523), pp. 106–24.

incarnate. Having done so, however, at the end of the story all is restored to him as a "reward" for his generosity.

I believe it is time to transform the way Buddhism is transmitted to members of society through means such as this tale, so that a more equitable relationship between men and women can be developed. The hope is that this kind of cultural empowering would, in the long run, provide a condition wherein women's self-formation process will be more conducive to female dignity. As a consequence of negotiating more space for feminist concerns in the Thai Buddhistic culture, more openness to and awareness of women's rights can develop in society.

The Buddha was a reformist in his bold attempts to fight against many elements of the Hindu caste system prevalent in his time. For example, he refused to accept the Hindu myth about the divine origin of the superior Brahmin caste. His religion was for all to practice. He was the first religious founder who established an order of female monks. He recognized the full potential of women to become enlightened. In spite of the Buddha's egalitarian perspective, however, in the *Tripitaka* itself one finds passages that carry negative messages about women. For example:

> Women easily lose their temper, they are jealous, narrow-minded and of low intelligence. Therefore they cannot participate in an assembly to administer a country, nor can they uphold big responsibility, neither can they travel to engage in a foreign trade. (*Anguttara nikaya* II, 80)
>
> Women are an enemy to the path of purity. (*Samyutta nikaya* I, 37)
>
> Women cannot become a Buddha. (*Anguttara nikaya* XX, 164)

In the past decade, Thai feminist thinkers have offered some illuminating explanations of these passages. The statement "Women cannot become a Buddha" originated from a Hindu belief in the thirty-two auspicious bodily signs of an enlightened one; one of the signs is the "concealed genital." (It is believed that the sexual organ of an enlightened one does not appear obvious as in the case of an ordinary person.) This statement has been understood in traditional Thai Buddhism to mean that a woman cannot become a Buddha because she does not have the male sexual organ in the first place, thus making it impossible to have a "concealed" one. However, some feminist thinkers have pointed out that this statement should not be taken in the literal sense. The intended message is rather that the Buddha is someone who is beyond sexual passion, hence, the "concealed genital."[34] The absence of this would therefore not automatically exclude a woman from being a Buddha.

---

34. See, for example, Chatsumarn Kabilsingh, "Understanding the Tripitaka from Feminist Perspectives," in *Proceedings of the International Conference on Buddhist Women* (Pathumthanee: Thammasat University, 1991), pp. 9–10.

In any ascetic tradition the opposite sex is considered a potential hindrance to one's spiritual path. Buddhism is no exception. The statement "Women are an enemy to the path of purity," which implies that women are bad for the Buddhist religion, should not be taken in isolation. It is followed by another statement saying, "Men are an enemy to the path of purity (for women)." Since the disappearance of the Bikkhuni order (the Buddhist female monk order established by the Buddha and later transmitted to Sri Lanka during the reign of King Ashoka) in Sri Lanka in the twelfth century A.D., the latter part of this statement is not usually quoted. Because there are no longer female monks in Thailand, it has become irrelevant. Placed in historical context, this statement would not sound so biased as is generally understood.

Of the three statements, the first, critiquing women's temperment, is most problematic for feminists. Some Buddhist scholars argue that this statement was an insertion made by later commentators and not the words of the Buddha himself. The difficulty of this position is that it is not always easy to determine which statements were actually the words of the Buddha and which were not. Another line of reasoning is that the Buddha as a man was only human, which means he could not help but accept certain judgments of his time, some of which include the prevailing attitudes toward women. The problem with this explanation is that if the Buddha was truly enlightened, why did his enlightenment not extend to gender equality?

I am not fully satisfied with any explanation, but an attempt by Somparn Promta, a young Buddhist scholar, sounds sensible. According to him, all statements made by the Buddha can be put into one of two categories: "ultimate statement" and "temporal statement."[35] Ultimate statements include those that deal directly with the question of sufferings and the cessation of sufferings. These statements by Buddha are beyond sexual differentiation. For example, the teachings on the Four Noble Truths and the Noble Eightfold Paths do not indicate any sexual preference. They address the human condition in general, and they carry the ultimate truth of Buddhism. In contrast, statements about historical–cultural conditions of the time are considered temporal. They do not speak about the ultimate truth in Buddhism. A statement such as "Women are jealous, narrow-minded and of low intelligence," should not be understood as carrying the same weight as those in the

---

35. Somparn Promta,"Women in Buddhism," *Journal of Buddhist Studies* vol. 1, no. 3 (September–December, BE 2537), pp. 38–52. The translation of *Kho-khuam uttara* into "ultimate statement" and *Khokhuam prachak* into "temporal statement" are made by this author, although Dr. Somparn chooses to use "transcendental statement" and "empirical statement" for the two types of statements. I made this change because I feel that the term "transcendental" might connote a sense of theism in Western philosophy of religion, and the term "temporal" better conveys a sense of something limited to a particular time frame, which does not indicate ultimate validity.

first category because when the existential condition of women changes over time, the statement may no longer hold. And the changing truths of these temporal statements do not in any way dilute or invalidate the ultimate truth of Buddhism.

PRINCE VESSANTARA AND MODELS
OF THE IDEAL IN BUDDHISM

Although Theravada Buddhism has always prided itself as a religion of wisdom and not of faith, the importance of faith for the masses cannot be denied in any Theravada Buddhist country. According to noted Buddhist scholar Gunapala Dharmasiri:

> The *Bodhisatva* concept is the ultimate fruition of Buddhist ethics. It is the *Jataka* book, rather than the other highly doctrinal texts, that has affected and shaped the lives of the Buddhist villagers for centuries. . . . The *Jatakas* are the divine song of the Bodhisatva ideal in a form which speaks directly to the human heart and which, therefore, is not only understandable to the wise but even to the simplest mind. . . . Up to the present day the *Jatakas* have not lost their human appeal and continue to exert a deep influence upon the religious life in all Buddhist countries. In Ceylon, Burma, Siam and Cambodia, crowds of people listen with rapt attention for hours when Bhikkhus, during the full-moon nights, recite the stories of the Buddha's former lives.[36]

It is beyond controversy that of all the *jatakas,* the *Vessantara* tale has been the most popular in Siam throughout history. In this story Queen Madsi is the ideal woman because she sacrifices all, including her children, to advance the religious goal of her husband. However, a contrasting image of woman is also found in the story. She is Amittada, the wife of Jujaka, the villain beggar who asks for Vessantara's children to work as Amittada's slaves. Amittada was given as a young woman to the old Jujaka as payment for a debt her parents had incurred to him. She had no reason to be pleased with this marriage arrangement and thought of herself as a "slave, never taking it to heart that she was a young woman being married to an old man. She only thought that it was her parents' *karma,* and she just submitted herself to that *karma.* She cooks every morning and every night, always performing her wifely duties, always taking good care of the old man."[37] Indeed she is so perfect that other Brahmins begin to upbraid their wives for not being like her. The wives then vent their anger at Amittada at the village well where they meet daily. Amittada one day decides she cannot take it any longer, so she threatens to leave

---

36. Gunapala Dharmasiri, *Fundamentals of Buddhist Ethics* (Singapore: The Buddhist Research Society, 1986), p. 113.
37. *The Vessantara Jataka* (Bangkok: Dharmabannakarn, 1978), p. 110.

her husband unless he finds her slaves to help with the household. She tells her husband to go and ask for Prince Vessantara's children, providing another extreme occasion for Vessantara to perform his giving.

It is interesting to note here that Amittada's fate is not that much different from present-day Thai prostitutes, who in many cases resign themselves to the fate of their family's karma. Amittada has to enter into a sexual relationship with a man and "finds herself constrained to barter for sexual favors for some material gain from a man she does not love."[38] As a result, she is considered a "bad woman" (ying-choa), a label commonly ascribed to prostitutes in the Thai language. What seems so tragic about this situation is the fact that the decision of the parents, the economic situation of the village, and the decision of Amittada herself are not perceived as a systematic violation of human rights. Amittada only "thought of herself as a slave," the jataka tale tells us. The issue of the rights to her own life and liberty is conveniently concealed in the virtue discourse of "gratitude" toward one's parents. One final note is that Amittada demands her own "slaves" after being put under pressure by other village wives. The vicious cycle continues. Feminist cultural empowerment of Thai women would highlight the issue of women's rights in this situation by arguing that Amittada was denied the right to build her own family, as she was given away in exchange for debts accrued by her parents to Jujaka. Her parents' "bad karma" actually led to violations of her rights.

At the royal level, Queen Madsi, as the ideal wife, sacrifices the comfort of palace life, insisting on following her husband into the forest. She also decides to take the two children with her. She actually begs her husband to let her go with him. She reasons, "Wherever you have to go, I shall follow you. I shall devote my life to you until the day I die. The thought of leaving my husband is impossible, even if it means living in a pathetic condition. I shall endure all hardships to serve you. If I have to die, I will devote my life as golden shoes to protect your royal feet." Toward the end of the story, after realizing that her husband had given away their children to Jujaka, Madsi submits to her husband's "great wish to perfect the virtue of alms-giving." She overcomes her personal sorrow, puts her heart to joy, and praises her husband for what he did. At the end of the chapter on "Madsi," the tale celebrates her in the following words,

> Queen Madsi, daughter of great royal blood, holds a dignified face, then presses her two palms together, and bows her head in celebration of the great charity. Her heart is full of pure joy. When all the gods in heaven see this, they clap their hands in unison, singing glory to this grace of giving. Then God Indra, the greatest

---

38. Keyes, "Mother or Mistress but Never a Monk," p. 233.

among the gods, lets a flow of golden flowers and crystal leaves through the clouds, as sign of praise to Queen Madsi, as she has submitted to her husband's great wish to perfect the virtue of alms-giving.[39]

In the conventional understanding of the story, the ultimate virtue of a woman is her absolute and total devotion to her husband. This devotion transcends the love of her own life and the love of her own children. Instead, she celebrates her husband's wish with "pure joy." In doing so, she is praised and celebrated even by the gods in heaven. It is interesting to note that God Indra gives as the reason for praising Queen Madsi that "she has submitted to her husband's great wish to perfect the virtue of alms-giving." What is totally absent in all this is the question of whether Queen Madsi, who has given away everything she holds dear, herself deserves to be a Bodhisattva. The only plausible answer seems to be that she does not actually belong to herself and neither do the children belong to her. She and the children belong to her husband. Therefore, the credit of giving belongs to him. If Queen Madsi should be praised by the gods, it should be because of her great wish to provide charity, not her submission to her husband's wish. There are two important messages here. First, the virtue possible for a woman is defined by her commitment to her husband. Second, because she does not "belong" to herself, the question of her rights does not arise. In the final analysis, the only possible condition under which Prince Vessantara would not be violating the rights of his queen and his children would be for them to be praised as Boddhisattvas as well. But this is not what the tale tells us.

There are two possible interpretations for a human rights advocate with a feminist perspective to offer. The first is to follow the logic of the story in its praise of Madsi for her sacrifice. This is done by adding another dimension to the story: namely, asking why Madsi, who does as much as she possibly can for others, is not considered a Bodhisattva. This would imply "equal" status of women, especially in the aspect of spiritual attainment. The second interpretation is to "liberate" Madsi from the conventional logic of the story by criticizing the alms-giving efforts of Prince Vessantara as a violation of the rights to liberty and security of person of his own family members. I suspect that the first interpretation might be more palatable to Thais. This choice would not antagonize the male's spiritual effort, which holds the highest value in Thai culture, but it would give value to the female's effort in an important way. As a consequence, this feminist rereading of the story would put an end to the monopoly male members of Thai society hold on the attainment of the highest level of spirituality.

39. Dharmasiri, *Fundamentals of Buddhist Ethics*, pp. 266–7.

A feminist rereading would diminish the religious justification that men belong to a higher social status because they have a higher spiritual potential. This kind of rereading of the tale could help elevate women's religious roles and thereby their social status. When our male-centered sociopolitical world is overturned by the cultural empowerment of women, then women's self-understanding through Thai Buddhistic culture will be transformed to include a more equal relationship with men, with increased possibilities for rights awareness.

CONCLUSION

Human rights cannot exist or prosper in the absence of laws or favorable economic conditions. Nor can they exist without an awareness of a legitimate claim to reasonable control and determination of one's own life, in one's own cultural milieu. Even in present day Thailand, the frequenting of prostitutes is considered "natural" for men, and prostitutes are actually preferred by wives when faced with the alternative of minor wives[40] because prostitutes are less of a threat to the family, the household income, and the major wife's social face. However, the spread of AIDS poses a frightening threat and may be leading to a change in this attitude. Why is it the case that male sexual "rights" can extend and overrule the rights to a decent life of so many women? The astronomical economic "success" of prostitution, national and international, testifies to this tragic truth.

The strategies needed to remedy the violations of human and women's rights in Thai society are as complex as the phenomenon of prostitution itself. The "situational approach" adopted by many NGOs needs to be coordinated with a "structural approach." The missing link in this process is the self-formation of women. As long as the male–female relationship in Thai society is not redirected, it seems unlikely that the tragedy of prostitution will end of itself. One of the ways to alleviate the situation is to develop "rights awareness" within the cultural transmission of traditional values. This strategy should help redress the "push factor," the inexorable pressure placed on young females by families that, on the one hand, tend to put less value on their daughters and, on the other, expect such an economic contribution from them. I strongly believe that the process of cultural empowerment of Thai women will not only reduce the traditional readiness to turn to prostitution in the face of economic need, but will also lead to a more active pursuit of women's rights in this society.

---

40. According to a recent study by Mahidol University, many wives "prefer" their husbands to visit prostitutes rather than have minor wives.

CHAPTER 9

A CONFUCIAN PERSPECTIVE
ON HUMAN RIGHTS
FOR CONTEMPORARY CHINA

JOSEPH CHAN*

WHY CONFUCIANISM?

There are at least two main intellectual approaches to justifying universal human rights. The first, and more traditional, approach is to show that there are universal values and moral principles that can justify human rights to all reasonable persons.[1] The second approach tries to seek consensus on human rights from within cultural perspectives. It encourages different cultures to justify human rights in their own terms and perspectives, in the hope that an "overlapping consensus" on the norms of human rights may emerge from self-searching exercises as well as common dialogue. I shall call the first approach the "fundamentalist" approach and the second "ecumenical." The ecumenical approach has some advantages. If successful, it would ground human rights on less alien sources, and would make them more receptive to the cultures that originally lacked the idea of human rights. However, it is possible that this approach might create as much conflict as common ground for consensus: The deeper one digs into cultural perspectives, the more apparent might be the gap among them. In this chapter, I will test the feasibility of this approach by examining the case of Confucianism as a cultural perspective.

* This chapter has greatly benefited from the criticisms and constructive comments of many people. I want to thank the participants at the Bangkok workshop: Joanne Bauer, Daniel A. Bell, Simon Caney, Chan Keung-Lap, Chan Sin-Yee, Albert Chen, Ci Jiwei, Lusina Ho, Kuan Hsin-Chi, Lan Zhiyong, Joe Lau, Leung Man-To, Kevin May, Shih Yuan-Kang, Sing Ming, Dorothy Solinger, Tu Weiming, Robert Weatherley, and Martin Wilkinson. They have raised more objections than I can answer within the limited space of this chapter. The chapter was completed too soon for me to take account of Wm. Theodore de Bary and Tu Weiming, eds., *Confucianism and Human Rights* (New York: Columbia University Press, 1997).
1. A notable example is Alan Gewirth, *Human Rights: Essays on Justification and Applications* (Chicago: University of Chicago Press, 1982).

To begin with, let me make two preliminary remarks. The first one is on the meaning and scope of Confucianism; the second, its contemporary significance. Like "liberalism," the word "Confucianism" can be used at several levels: philosophical thought, political ideology, actual state policies and practices, or way of life. In this chapter, I take it to mean a tradition of philosophical thought rather than a state ideology or actual political practices. Confucianism as a state ideology or practices was more a kind of product of time and historical circumstances, whereas Confucianism as a philosophical thought, founded by Confucius, has survived the test of time and remains today a lively source of ideas for Chinese. Moreover, separating the historical, institutional expression of a tradition of thought from its philosophical expression can create a space for people to critically evaluate, appropriate, and further develop that tradition of thought. Just as Marxists often turned to Marx's own words to denounce the political practices in communist states and develop new Marxian thinking on contemporary issues, we can likewise turn to the philosophical masters of Confucianism to do similar things. In discussing Confucianism as a tradition of philosophical thought, I shall further limit myself to the thoughts of early Confucianism, namely those of Confucius and Mencius. Despite the flourishing developments of Confucian thought in the later stages of the Chinese history, the thought of Confucius, represented by *The Analects* and further expounded by Mencius, has continued to serve as the paradigm and basis for further critical reflections. Because of this limited scope, the Confucian perspective on human rights that I reconstruct here is only *one* perspective in Confucianism. Confucianism is a long and complex tradition that certainly allows for more than one view of the subject.

But to what extent does Confucian thought constitute a lively cultural tradition in China today? To what extent can this philosophical thought be regarded as a *cultural* perspective, that is, a perspective that is generally endorsed by the Chinese and embodied in their way of life and practices? Confucianism was severely criticized and denounced in the 1960s and 1970s in Socialist China. Is there any hope that it will become an influential cultural perspective again? There are, I think, a few reasons for believing that Confucianism, perhaps in a modernized and reconstructed form, has the potential to become a main source for values and cultural regeneration, if not an influential cultural perspective as such. First, the ideology of Marxism has been discredited after the fall of the Soviet Union and the communist bloc in Eastern Europe. Today, although China remains officially committed to Marxism, it has become no more than lip service. China is in a moral and ideological crisis, and Confucianism as a cultural perspective seems most natural to fill the vacuum.

Second, with the end of the Cold War, nationalism has been on the rise. With Marxism being discredited in the international scene, China has seized nationalism as a strategy to reshape its image in the international scene and to rally for internal political and moral cohesion. Recourse to cultural traditions is considered necessary to build up a national identity. In this regard, some high-level Chinese officials have openly acknowledged the need to learn from the past – the cultural and moral traditions of China.[2] In addition, recently there have also been some major academic conferences organized by semigovernmental bodies on the revival of Chinese traditional ethical thought, Confucianism in particular.[3] Moreover, by the early 1990s a significant part of the Confucian ethic was already incorporated into the curriculum and the "behavior guidelines" for secondary and primary school students.[4]

This interest in Confucianism is not confined to a small group of politicians and academics in Beijing. At the provincial level, academics are even more enthusiastic than officials in promoting the study of Chinese history, traditional cultures, and philosophies. Numerous works have been published on traditional ethical thought. This phenomenon is present not only in a few provinces, but throughout the whole of China.

Finally, precisely because Confucianism is a potentially viable perspective but not yet a living tradition, and hence both its meaning and its concrete institutional content remain to be constructed, there is room for state officials to manipulate Confucianism for political purposes. Serious and open discussion on, for example, the relationship between Confucianism and human rights would help prevent politicians from hijacking Confucianism.

For these reasons, then, it is important to look at the relationship between Confucianism and human rights. Is Confucianism capable of embracing the modern idea of human rights, thus making it more familiar for Chinese culture? Or is Confucianism an obstacle for the promotion of human rights in China because its doctrines are inherently incompatible with the idea of human rights?

I attempt to answer these questions in the second and third sections. In the second section, "Four Alleged Confucian Reasons for Rejecting the Idea of

2. For example, Li Lanqing, vice premier and member of the Political Bureau in China, said that in developing Chinese ethics for the nation today, we ought to learn from the valuable ethical traditions developed in the last 5,000 years in China. Guojie Lou and Qizhi Zhang, eds., *Dongfang lunli daode yu qinshaonian jiaoyu* [Eastern Ethics and Education for the Youth] (Shanghai: Shanghai Education Publishers [in Chinese], 1994), pp. 1–2.

3. For example, an international conference on the theme of Eastern Ethical Traditions and Contemporary Youth Education, organized by some major educational bodies in China, was held in Beijing in 1993. Confucian ethics was the main focus in the conference.

4. For useful descriptions of this phenomenon, see the articles collected in Lou and Zhang, eds., *Dongfang lunli daode yu qinshaonian jiaoyu* [Eastern Ethics and Education for the Youth], pp. 324–31, 339–46, 347–58.

Human Rights," I argue that the central doctrines of Confucianism, as represented by the thought of Confucius and Mencius, are compatible with the idea of human rights. In the third section, I argue that Confucianism may provide a justification for human rights, but this justification differs from the dominant strand in Western liberalism. One implication of this is that Confucianism would define the function and scope of some major human rights differently. In other words, although an overlapping consensus among the Confucian and other cultural perspectives might emerge through examination and dialogue on the existence of human rights, there will remain serious disputes over the justification and scope of those rights.[5] In the final section, I draw together several points made in the earlier sections to form a Confucian perspective of human rights. I then illustrate its implications and significance with some concrete human rights issues. Let me emphasize, however, that in exploring the possibility of a Confucian perspective on human rights, I do not intend to claim that such a perspective is philosophically superior to other alternatives, such as liberalism.[6] What I do wish to defend is a weaker claim – that such a Confucian perspective is philosophically plausible, and that because it is plausible, the Chinese may have a practical reason to prefer it to perspectives that are equally plausible but alien to their culture.

FOUR ALLEGED CONFUCIAN REASONS FOR REJECTING THE IDEA OF HUMAN RIGHTS

It has been a common view that Confucianism is incompatible with human rights. The view is not only that one cannot find the idea of human rights in Confucianism, but that any endorsement of the idea would go deeply against the Confucian view of human nature, ethics, and society. I concur with the first half of the statement, but I disagree with much of what has been said to support the second half. In this section, I argue that many key elements in Confucianism are indeed compatible with the idea of human rights. In arguing for this point, I shall cite and evaluate some common arguments to the effect that there are clear "Confucian" reasons for rejecting human rights. I have identified four of them and shall discuss these one by one.

---

5. For an illuminating discussion on the possibility of an overlapping consensus of different traditions on human rights – despite disagreement on the justification and scope of those rights–see Charles Taylor's contribution to this book (Chapter 5).
6. This position reflects the spirit of an ecumenical approach. In fact, I believe that the general nature of human rights allows a plurality of interpretations of the basis, scope, and ranking of rights. For detailed arguments on this point, see Joseph Chan, "The Asian Challenge to Universal Human Rights: A Philosophical Appraisal," in James Tang, ed., *Human Rights and International Relations in the Asia Pacific* (London: Pinter, 1995); and Joseph Chan, "Hong Kong, Singapore, and 'Asian Values': An Alternative View," *Journal of Democracy* vol. 8 (1997).

Contextual Individuals and Role-Based Ethics in Confucianism

Some scholars of Confucianism think that any assertion of human rights must presuppose that human beings are *asocial* beings and have rights independent of culture and society. They argue that this presupposition goes against the Confucian view that human beings must live in society to become really human and to lead flourishing lives. For example, Henry Rosemont, Jr., claims that because human beings have rights regardless of personal character- istics such as cultural background, they can live independently of culture, and this clearly goes against the Confucian view of humanity. In any case it is extremely difficult from a Confucian perspective to imagine these bearers of rights, because there are no culturally independent human beings.[7] Similarly, R. P. Peerenboom writes that because human rights are rights to which humans are entitled *from birth,* human beings must be thought of as beings "*qua* members of a biological species" and not "*qua* social beings," a view deeply incompatible with the Confucian one.[8] Roger Ames also argues that Confucianism cannot accept human rights because they protect human inter- ests, which are "independent of and prior to society."[9]

The problem with these arguments lies in their understanding of human rights and their presuppositions. Human rights are rights that people have solely by virtue of being human, irrespective of sex, race, culture, religion, nationality, or social position. But this concept of human rights does not pre- suppose or imply that human beings can be thought of as having none of these attributes. What it asserts is rather a *normative* claim: one's sex, race, or culture is morally irrelevant insofar as one's entitlement to basic human rights is concerned. Similarly, the concept of human rights does not imply that humans are asocial beings with interests independent of and prior to society, quite the contrary. The international charters of human rights include rights that protect those interests of an individual that are social in nature: Freedom of expression protects an individual's interest in communi- cating with others, especially in the public sphere; freedom of religion pro- tects one's interests in joining religious associations. These rights show pre- cisely that the concept of human rights presupposes the fact that human beings are social and cultural animals. We must not confuse the basis of indi- vidual rights with the content of those rights. It is the *individual's* interest,

---

7. See Henry Rosemont, Jr., "Why Take Rights Seriously? A Confucian Critique," in Leroy Rouner, ed., *Human Rights and the World's Religions* (Notre Dame: University of Notre Dame Press, 1988), p. 167.
8. See R. P. Peerenboom, "What's Wrong with Chinese Rights? Toward a Theory of Rights with Chinese Characteristics," *Harvard Human Rights Journal* vol. 6 (1993), p. 40.
9. See Roger T. Ames, "Rites as Rights: The Confucian Alternative" in Rouner, ed., *Human Rights and the World's Religions,* p. 205.

not *society's* interest, that justifies a human right, although the content of the individual's interest may be *social*.[10]

Critics may argue that the concept of human rights does imply that people have rights irrespective of their social roles, and this goes against the notion of contextual individuals and the role-based ethics in Confucianism. For them, Confucianism subscribes to a view of morality which precludes the ascription of duties (or rights, if any) to human individuals as such. We may call this view a *pure role-based view of morality*. According to this view, moral duties or rights arise solely from social relationships, such as familial relationships, friendship, and political associations. For example, most of the Confucian teachings are about how we should behave in the five basic social relationships (*lun*): father–son, husband–wife, elder brother–younger brother, ruler–ruled, and friend–friend. Indeed, many scholars go so far as to claim that in the Confucian morality, the very identity of human persons is constituted by nothing but a web of social relationships.[11] In this vein, Rosemont writes,

> For the early Confucians there can be no *me* in isolation, to be considered abstractly; I am the totality of roles I live in relation to specific others. I do not *play* or *perform* these roles; I *am* these roles. When they have all been specified I have been defined uniquely, fully, and altogether, with no remainder with which to piece together a free, autonomous self.[12]

This understanding of human personhood and morality is endorsed by a number of scholars and is used as a reason to reject human rights. By their interpretation, because (1) human persons consist of a web of roles in personal relationships, and (2) the duties or rights human persons owe to one another are exhausted by their role-based duties, there is no room for any duties or rights that belong to human persons *simpliciter*, independent of their roles.[13]

I agree that Confucianism does place great emphasis on particularistic social relationships, but it is a mistake to view Confucianism as a *pure* role-based or relation-based view of human person and morality. The Confucian view is that human persons are first and foremost moral agents capable of realizing *ren*, which means, among other things, a certain ability or disposition to care for and sympathize with others. Although the sites for the realization of

---

10. For more discussion on this point and on the relationship between individual rights and common goods, see Joseph Chan, "Raz on Liberal Rights and Common Goods," *Oxford Journal of Legal Studies* vol. 15 (1995).

11. See Peerenboom, "What's Wrong with Chinese Rights?" pp. 44–5; Lee Seung-hwan, "Was There a Concept of Rights in Confucian Virtue-Based Morality?" *Journal of Chinese Philosophy* vol. 19 (1992), p. 256; and Ames, "Rites as Rights: The Confucian Alternative," p. 208.

12. See Rosemont, "Why Take Rights Seriously? A Confucian Critique," p. 177.

13. For examples of this interpretation, see Peerenboom, "What's Wrong with Chinese Rights?" pp. 44–5; and Lee, "Was There a Concept of Rights in Confucian Virtue-Based Morality?" p. 256.

ren are commonly found in personal relationships such as those of father–son and husband–wife, there are *nonrelational* occasions when moral actions are also required by *ren*. That is to say, not all moral duties in Confucianism arise from social institutions or relationships. There are strong nonrelational elements in the Confucian morality. Consider a few examples:

1. A clear example of the expression of *ren* in a nonrelational or noninstitutional situation is Mencius's example of a child on the verge of falling into a well.[14] For Mencius, a man with *ren* would be moved by compassion to save the child, not because he had personal acquaintance with the child's parents, nor because he wanted to win the praise of his fellow villagers or friends, but simply because of his concern for the suffering of a human person. Mencius's point is that no man is devoid of *ren* – which means, among other things, a sensitivity to the *suffering of others*. These "others" are not confined to those personally known. Rather they may include all people within the "Four Seas" – everywhere in the world.

2. In another place, Mencius says that "a gentleman retains his heart by means of benevolence (*ren*) and the rites (*li*). The benevolent man loves others, and the courteous man respects others."[15] Again, in the passage the "others" are *unspecified*. This same notion of loving others *including all men* can also be found in Book VII of *Mencius,* where Mencius says that "a benevolent man loves everyone, but he devotes himself to close association with good and wise men."[16]

Of course Mencius's notion of the potentially unlimited scope of benevolence was adopted from Confucius. Confucius says clearly that to be benevolent (*ren*) is to "love your fellow men."[17] James Legge's translation better captures the meaning of the phrase, which is "to love *all* men."[18] Confucius also teaches young men to learn to "love the multitude at large."[19]

3. There is another important moral teaching in Confucianism that is applicable not only to close personal relationships but to *everyone:* "Do not impose on others what you yourself do not desire."[20]

It should now be clear that Confucianism does not hold a purely role-based view of morality. There are clearly nonrelational aspects in Confucian ethics. Of course, nothing said thus far shows that Confucianism recognizes

---

14. D. C. Lau, trans., *Mencius* (Harmondsworth: Penguin Books, 1970), book II, part A, chapter 6; referred to hereinafter as *Mencius* IIA:6. Unless otherwise stated, all translations of *The Analects* and *Mencius* are taken from D. C. Lau, trans., *Confucius: The Analects* (Harmondsworth: Penguin Books, 1979), and Lau, trans., *Mencius,* respectively.

15. *Mencius* IVB:28.   16. *Mencius* VIIA:46.

17. *The Analects* XII:22.

18. See James Legge, trans., "Confucian Analects," in Legge, *The Chinese Classics* vol. I (Hong Kong: Hong Kong University Press, 1960), p. 269 (italics in original).

19. *The Analects* I:6.   20. *The Analects* XII:2, XV:24.

that human individuals have rights irrespective of their roles. Rather, it shows that the argument for the charge that Confucianism is *unable to accommodate* universal human rights is unsound, for it is based on a *false* premise, namely, that Confucianism subscribes to a purely role-based view of morality.

The Confucian Ideal of Community

It is commonly thought that the Confucian ideal of society is basically of the family writ large. As pointed out by many scholars, although three of the five basic human relationships belong to the family (father–son, husband–wife, and elder brother–younger brother), the other two (ruler–ruled and friend–friend), though not familial, are modeled after familial relationships.[21] What characterizes the ideal family is mutual love and caring between members. A virtuous son would regard the well-being of his family members as part of his own well-being, and so would a virtuous father. In this ideal of the family, rights talk is inappropriate, for the reason that

> Confucianism emphasizes that a genuine community is not composed of mutually disinterested egoistic individuals, but is composed of virtuous members thinking of shared goals and values over one's own. . . . In this ideal community, the highest moral virtue is *jen* [*ren*] (benevolence) when expressed in an active form; "overcoming one's selfishness" in a passive form.[22]

Accordingly, any assertion of human rights would be premised on the view that human beings are egoistic, a tendency that should be protected rather than curbed. This view, it is argued, runs counter to the Confucian ideal of familial relationships. By extension, human rights would be incompatible with the larger society of which the family is the microcosm.

This argument is, however, based on an erroneous view of human rights. Human rights does not depend on the notion that human beings are egoistic, totally unconcerned with the well-being of others. Human rights protect legitimate interests of individuals. We must distinguish between "*self*-interest" and "*selfish* interests." For example, people have a self-interest in not being tortured or raped, but this interest is obviously not selfish. Unlike what Marx proclaims, human rights need not be the rights of "egoistic men." A person defending his right to not be tortured by others is surely not acting egoistically or selfishly.

For human rights to be asserted, then, only two claims need to be assumed: (1) Every individual has certain legitimate self-interests that he or she ought

21. Lee, "Was There a Concept of Rights in Confucian Virtue-Based Morality?" p. 253.
22. Lee, "Was There a Concept of Rights in Confucian Virtue-Based Morality?" p. 252.

to be allowed to protect, and (2) not all individuals are altruistic enough to sacrifice their own legitimate interests for the sake of others. The first claim makes human rights possible; the second gives them importance.[23] Clearly, these claims do not imply that human beings are egoistic or selfish.

However, one might still suspect that even these two weaker presuppositions of human rights are incongruous with the spirit of the Confucian community. For Confucians, people in close personal relationships should not even think of themselves as subjects possessing rights upon which they make claims against their partners. Rather they should think of themselves as participating in a relationship of reciprocal commitments, or of mutual caring and love. To introduce considerations of rights is inappropriate to this relationship, because this would motivate us to see other members' interests more as limitations on ours than as interests we wish to promote.[24]

I am sympathetic to this view that rights do not play an important role in virtuous relationships. I agree that in a healthy, close relationship parties should best ignore rights and focus on mutual caring and love. But what if the relationship turns sour? Do we need rights to repair it? Probably not, since it would still be best to repair the relationship by refreshing the partners' commitment to the ideal of mutual caring, rather than by invoking rights.[25] If the relationship breaks down to a point of no return, would rights not be relevant and useful to protect the parties' interests? Consider the example of the breakdown of a marriage. If a husband's love for his wife has died and in many ways he has harmed her interests, it would be highly desirable and even necessary for the wife to have formal and legal rights (marriage rights as well as human rights) to fall back on in order to protect her interests.[26]

Thus, there is reason to give rights a role even in familial relationships, and I think Confucianism would endorse rights in this sense. No ethics of benevolence and care would seek to diminish the needs of individuals. After all, when we care for a person, *what* are we supposed to care for if not that person's needs and interests? If an assertion of rights is sometimes necessary to protect important individual interests, then there is no reason why Confu-

---

23. It could perhaps be argued that rights may be necessary even in an altruistic society, because people may have morally divergent or even unacceptable views about what human interests consist of and how they should be promoted. Invasion of a person's legitimate interests can come from blind, obsessive love as well as selfish egoism.

24. See Hugh LaFollette, *Personal Relationships: Love, Identity and Morality* (Oxford: Blackwell, 1996), p. 146.

25. LaFollette, *Personal Relationships*, p. 146.

26. The notion of rights as a fallback apparatus is taken from Jeremy Waldron, "When Justice Replaces Affection: The Need for Rights," in Waldron, *Liberal Rights* (London: Cambridge University Press, 1993), p. 374.

cianism would prohibit it. If familial relationships require rights as a fallback position, all the more reason to support the greater community by maintaining an apparatus of rights. The Confucian community is not a community composed *entirely* of close personal relationships. The relationships between ruler and ruled and between strangers are not personal relationships, for example. In the workplace, the market, the government, the court, and other less personal social spheres, people do not interact according to the norms of close personal relationships. Rights talk need not be destructive of the relationships in these contexts. And ultimately, rights are important instruments for the vulnerable to protect themselves against exploitation and harm.

Nonetheless, a Confucian perspective might not want to give human rights a role greater than that of a fallback apparatus. Rights constitute neither human virtues nor virtuous relationships. This point has important implications for a current, popular trend of rights talk in some Western countries such as the United States. There has been a strong tendency for some Western liberals to adopt an inflated view of rights, and this tendency ought to be resisted. Some liberals argue that even the most valuable forms of mutual caring and love can flourish only in a relationship based on rights.[27] Simon Caney argues that "benevolence as a virtue is more desirable if based on knowledge of one's rights and entitlements. It has a greater degree of intentionality."[28] The claim is contestable, however. It amounts to saying that the life of Mother Theresa would not be as desirable had she no knowledge of rights – a counterintuitive claim. John Tomasi gives the following example to support Caney's general point:

> Imagine a marriage relation in which one spouse is utterly deferential to the other. Consider a "deferential wife" whose most every act toward her husband would be perceived by others as being beyond her reasonable duty, as being – apparently, at least – supererogatory (we could as easily imagine a "husband"). However uncomfortable, she nonetheless always wears clothes she knows he prefers; however much they annoy her, she always invites guests he enjoys; however ill suited for her schedule, she always rises and retires when he does. . . . It seems clear that the deferential wife . . . does not act in a way properly called virtuous. . . . She does not recognize that she is most often in a good position to act otherwise; she has forgotten – and likely would prefer not to be reminded – that she even has rights.[29]

27. Simon Caney, "Sandel's Critique of the Primacy of Justice: A Liberal Rejoinder," *British Journal of Political Science* vol. 21 (1991), p. 517; John Tomasi, "Individual Rights and Community Virtues" *Ethics* vol. 101 (1991), pp. 532–3; and Joel Feinberg, *Freedom and Fulfillment* (Princeton, NJ: Princeton University Press, 1992), p. 238.
28. See Caney, "Sandel's Critique of the Primacy of Justice," p. 517.
29. See Tomasi, "Individual Rights and Community Virtues," p. 533.

One may agree with Tomasi that, in the example, the wife is deficient, lacking self-respect or self-worth. The basis of self-respect, however, need not lie in the fact that she has rights (although she does), but in the belief that she is worthy of care and concern and that her well-being matters. So she has a legitimate basis to complain about her husband, but the basis need not be that the husband ignores her *rights*. A more appropriate basis is the very ideal of mutual caring and love – that the husband is not caring toward her and is not recognizing her needs and aspirations.[30] The wife need not think in terms of rights to assess the relationship. In fact, once she thinks in these terms, she starts distancing herself from the persons on whom she may press her claims. What she ought to do in the first place, in the Confucian view, is rather to reaffirm and remind her husband of the ideal of mutual love and caring.

Hierarchy and Paternalism in Confucianism

For some scholars, the Confucian conception of personal relationships advocates hierarchy and submission. Individuals in the five basic relationships are unequal. "The power to enjoy one's personal and public interests was limited and graded in accordance with his/her social status and relational standing."[31] Consider the example of the duties of children in a father–son relationship. According to some interpretations, the Confucian view of *xiao* (filial piety) preaches submission of children (young or adult) to their parents (the father in particular). A son is expected to follow every instruction of his father, however unreasonable it may be. According to this interpretation, a Confucian view of human relationships would reject human rights even if they are intended as a protective apparatus for family members.

There might be a certain element of truth in this interpretation of Confucianism. But first, it is essential to separate early Confucianism from the later developments of Confucianism on this issue. Most if not all of the teachings on absolute obedience or hierarchy in familial relationships date from the later developments during and after the Han dynasty – for example, the teaching of *san gang,* which preaches the absolute authority of the husband over his wife and children and the absolute authority of the ruler over the

---

30. Some might say that the husband violates the norm of reciprocity, which is one form of fairness. But reciprocity, as I understand it, is a minimum notion embedded in many kinds of ethics. One can say that the ideal of mutual caring and love, and Confucius's notion of *shu* – not to impose on others what we ourselves do not desire, and to establish and enlarge others insofar as one seeks to establish and enlarge oneself – embodies some notion of reciprocity. In any case, reciprocity as a form of "fairness" is still very different from the notion of a right.
31. See Lee, "Was There a Concept of Rights in Confucian Virtue-Based Morality?" p. 251.

ruled. Further, as will be explained later, Confucius's own teaching might appear to imply children's submission to their parents. But even according to Confucius thought, there is reason to reject this kind of teaching. The reason lies in the perspective of *ren* in understanding basic human relationships and their associated virtues. Let us take filial piety as an example. For Confucius, *ren* is the basis of all human virtues. The family is the most natural and important site for the exercise of *ren*. How does *ren* bear on the understanding of filial piety? Several points are in order.

First, *ren* means, among other things, to love people.[32] It requires us to show concern and respect to people. To treat our parents with *ren,* we should not only provide them with food but also treat them with concern and respect. "[E]ven hounds and horses are, in some way, provided with food. If a man shows no reverence [to his parents], where is the difference?"[33] Second, a filial son with *ren* would be concerned with his father's *ren* as well. He would want his father to act according to *ren*. Thus he would not want to obey the unreasonable or immoral instructions of his father, for so doing would reinforce his father's indulgence in vices. Filial piety should not be stressed at the expense of *ren*. Third, *ren* also requires that the parents love their children, to promote their well-being (*ci,* paternal love). *Ren* also implies the principle of reciprocity: We should not impose on others that which we do not desire.[34] If this reciprocity could be applied to a relationship with different roles, then we could say that a virtuous father should not impose on his son what he would not desire if he were in his son's position.

We can now see how Confucius's teaching of filial piety can be criticized from his own perspective of *ren*. According to one interpretation, Confucius says that a son should be obedient to his parents even if his parents are doing wrong and do not pay heed to the son's advice.

> The Master said, "In serving your father and mother you ought to dissuade them from doing wrong in the gentlest way. If you see your advice being ignored, you should not become disobedient but remain reverent. You should not complain even if in so doing you wear yourself out."[35]

The first part of the passage shows that in Confucius's view, children should care about the moral character of their parents. Thus the perspective of *ren* is implicit in this passage. But the second part of the passage does not seem to take the perspective far enough. It makes the mistake of placing reverence above *ren* – asking the son to let or even help his parents act against *ren*.

However, there is a more charitable interpretation of the passage. By this

32. *The Analects* XII:22.   33. *The Analects* II:7.
34. *The Analects* VX:24.   35. *The Analects* IV:18.

interpretation, the key phrase "not disobedient" is not the only possible translation of the Chinese *bu wei*. James Legge notes that *bu wei* may mean "not abandoning his [the son's] purpose of remonstrance," rather than "not daring to go against the mind of his parents."[36] If this interpretation is accepted, then the passage does not support the claim that Confucius advocates absolute obedience. Rather, it supports the *ren* perspective of filial piety.

To conclude the argument thus far, if one subscribes to a *ren*-based view of filial piety, one should rule out absolute obedience as a norm of filial piety.[37] This point holds for other familial relationships. Whatever the specific norms of these relationships, they should be grounded in and constrained by principles of *ren*. In short, *ren* requires mutual love and excludes self-centered or selfish domination of one party over another.

However, critics may still find that this argument thus far does not fully answer the objections. Although one may agree that familial relationships should be grounded in and constrained by *ren,* there are specific norms of these relationships that may be congruent with *ren* but nonetheless violate certain human rights. Take the example of arranged marriage. This practice, widely observed in traditional China, does not seem to violate *ren* but is certainly incompatible with the human right to freely choose a partner in marriage.

How should we respond to this objection? Although *ren* does set some theoretical limits to filial piety, whether its many specific norms are required by *ren* would depend on cultural norms and social contexts. Confucius holds that to be filial is to comply with rites (*li*) in serving one's parents when they are alive and in burying them when they die.[38] Confucius lived in a feudal society in which many norms or *li* placed great demands and limitations on children. For example, according to *li,* a filial son is required to follow his father's footsteps and life ambitions for three years after his father's death.[39] But we need to bear in mind that for Confucius, *li* should come after *ren.*[40] Confucius displays a humanistic attitude toward *li:* "What can a man do with the rites who is not benevolent [*ren*]? What can a man do with music who is not benevolent?"[41] Certain rites may be required by *ren* in certain social or economic situations, but they should be changed when the situation changes in such a way that they no longer help or express *ren.* Confucius also says that a virtuous person, in applying principles, should be able to weigh

36. Legge, trans., "Confucian Analects," pp. 170–1.
37. Notice that the point is not meant to support general equality in the family. From the Confucian perspective, some inequalities in the family may be appropriate. For example, the elderly should be treated with reverence or more respect. They may have greater decision-making power on certain common affairs in the family.
38. *The Analects* II:5.   39. *The Analects* I:11, IV:20.
40. *The Analects* III:8.   41. *The Analects* III:3.

the exigencies of the times and circumstances.[42] This line of thought could be used to analyze the case of arranged marriage in modern society. Rather than pursuing further this particular case, I want to examine the general theoretical question behind the criticism.

The theoretical issue seems to be that although *ren* may rule out selfish domination, it may not rule out paternalism – coercion aimed at improving the well-being of the coerced. A theory with strong paternalistic elements would find it difficult to accept some of the basic liberties that human rights protect. Theoretically, a strong emphasis on care and concern might lead to paternalism. Indeed Confucianism is often criticized as being too paternalistic and not giving enough recognition to individual autonomy. In reply to this objection, I want to make two points. First, as a matter of history, paternalism was widely practiced in ancient China as in other parts of the world in ancient times. But as a matter of theory, to my knowledge I do not find, in *The Analects* at least, any endorsement of any recommendation or principle equivalent to paternalism, except in the controversial passage about filial piety discussed earlier. It is very important to distinguish a theory that has a high propensity to lead to paternalism from a theory that affirms paternalism as a comprehensive policy or principle. Endorsement of human rights contradicts a theory of the latter kind – you cannot inject human rights into that theory without abandoning its paternalistic principles – but I believe Confucianism is closer to the first type and no "surgery" is needed for Confucianism to incorporate human rights. It might be true that Confucianism has a high propensity to lead to paternalism because of its ethic of care and emphasis on the moral life and because of its relatively weak emphasis on individual liberty. But if this is true, it demonstrates that Confucianism has an *internal need* for human rights – if human rights were incorporated, it would be less likely for Confucianism to slide into paternalism. Such incorporation need not involve uprooting or taking away any central value or principle in Confucianism.

What I have said may still not be sufficiently sympathetic to Confucianism, and this is my second point. Confucius not only does not affirm the use of force to promote people's virtues or well-being, he explicitly discourages it. In many kinds of relationships, such as ruler–ruled, father–son, friend–friend, and even the relationship between culturally superior and inferior groups, Confucius does not recommend the use of force in changing or transforming people's lives or in preventing morally bad people from corrupting others. Instead he persistently asks those in a superior position – the ruler, the father,

42. *The Analects* IX:30.

the culturally superior group – to behave themselves and to set a moral example for others:

> Chi Kang Tzu asked, "How can one inculcate in the common people the virtue of reverence, of doing their best and of enthusiasm?" The Master said, "Rule over them with dignity and they will be reverent; treat them with kindness and they will do their best; raise the good and instruct those who are backward and they will be imbued with enthusiasm."[43]

Confucius gives similar advice to rulers who want to rule over the "barbarians," people living far away from the central regions of China and having a low level of cultural and moral achievement: you should cultivate your own moral quality in order to *attract* people to settle in your territory, and once they have come you should make them content.[44] More will be said on the aversion to coercion in Confucianism in the next section. Suffice it to say that while there may be elitism in Confucianism, there is no recommendation for paternalism.

The Nonlitigious Nature of Confucian Society

The fourth "Confucian" reason for rejecting human rights is that the appeal to rights would turn social relationships from harmonious to conflictual or litigious. The Confucian ideal of social harmony emphasizes the virtues of concession and yielding rather than competition and self-assertion. "Anyone who is overly contentious, self-assertive, quarrelsome or litigious is considered contemptible. A virtuous Confucian man is one preoccupied himself with self-overcoming and yielding, not one with claiming and asserting what he is entitled to."[45]

I agree that Confucianism would, if possible, prefer to avoid the use of litigation or rights instruments. Confucius says: "In hearing litigation, I am no different from any other man. But if you insist on a difference, it is, perhaps, that I try to get the parties not to resort to litigation in the first place."[46]

The recourse to rights and litigation often implies that *li* or virtuous relationships have already broken down. Thus, in the case of conflict, we should first try to compromise in a way still faithful to the ideal of mutual caring and love. But in this passage Confucius does not say that litigation should be avoided absolutely or at all costs. As argued earlier, when people no longer act according to virtues or *li* – when they harm others, for example, there is a need for us to fall back on rights to protect our legitimate interests. More

---

43. *The Analects,* II:20; also III:3, 26; XII:19, 23; XIII:4; XV:14.
44. *The Analects* XVI:1.
45. See Lee, "Was There a Concept of Rights in Confucian Virtue-Based Morality?" p. 255.
46. *The Analects* XII:13.

important, Confucius does *not* say that we should always yield to others at all times, even when we are unjustly harmed. There is a passage that may correct this popular misunderstanding of Confucius:

> Someone said, "What do you say concerning the principle that injury should be recompensed with kindness?" The Master said, "With what then will you recompense kindness? Recompense injury with justice [*chih,* or straightness], and recompense kindness with kindness."[47]

When we are wronged, injured, or harmed by others, Confucius says that it would be appropriate to react by recourse to fairness or justice. The preference for mediation, reconciliation, and compromise implies neither that human beings do not have rights nor that they should never use them to protect themselves when harmed. This said, the Confucian preference for nonlegal methods of conflict resolution is worth mentioning in the contemporary discourse of human rights. As Peerenboom writes,

> Although far from perfect, traditional methods [of conflict resolution] such as mediation offer many advantages. Both parties save face, fully participate in the proceeding, and shape the ultimate solution. The process, usually faster and cheaper than more formal methods, allows for a more particularized justice and for the restoration of social harmony, with both sides feeling they have received their due.[48]

In fact, for our purposes the concern for nonlitigation can be understood as an objection not to human rights as such but to the abuse of rights. But in order not to abuse rights, we need a theory of virtues to guide right holders in the exercise of their rights. Confucianism, being a rich theory of virtues, precisely complements a theory of human rights in this regard.[49]

THE GROUNDS AND CONTENT OF HUMAN RIGHTS – A CONFUCIAN PERSPECTIVE

Thus far I have argued that Confucianism as represented by Confucius and Mencius need not reject the idea of human rights. But would Confucianism endorse the specific rights commonly found in contemporary human rights charters? How would it understand the scope and limits of these rights? In

---

47. *The Analects* XIV:36, from Legge, trans., "Confucian Analects."
48. See Peerenboom, "What's Wrong with Chinese Rights?" p. 55.
49. Space does not permit me to elaborate on this point. For more discussion, see Jeremy Waldron, *Nonsense Upon Stilts* (London: Methuen and Co., 1987), p. 194; Michael J. Meyer, "When Not to Claim Your Rights: The Abuse and the Virtuous Use of Rights," *The Journal of Political Philosophy* vol. 5 (1997), pp. 149–62; and especially Lee Seung-hwan, "Liberal Rights or/and Confucian Virtues?" *Philosophy East and West* vol. 46 (1996), pp. 367–79. Regrettably, the last article, which gives a very interesting analysis of the relationship between Confucian virtues and liberal rights, came to my attention only after this chapter was essentially completed.

this section I will show in what ways Confucianism's answers to these questions differ from some typical liberal ones. (Whether the former answers are better than the latter is a different question.)

Freedom to Choose the Good

Would Confucianism endorse modern human rights, such as the right not to be tortured, the right to fair trial, freedom of expression, freedom of religion, freedom of association, and so on? It is understandable why Confucianism would not reject the right not to be tortured and the right to fair trial. As explained earlier, the Confucian perspective would take rights as a fallback auxiliary apparatus that serves to protect basic human interests in case virtues do not obtain or human relationships clearly break down. A man with *ren* would be sensitive to the sufferings of others.

How about those traditional civil liberties that liberals cherish? The Confucian perspective on this question is somewhat more complicated.[50] I want to argue for three points: (1) The Confucian perspective would endorse basic civil liberties or rights such as freedom of expression and religion, (2) but its understanding of the scope of these liberties would be different from some Western, rights-based perspectives, and (3) the two perspectives differ on the justification of civil liberties. To illustrate these points, consider the right to freedom of expression as an example.

Neither Confucius nor Mencius explicitly (or even implicitly) advocated freedom of expression or any equivalent state policy. However, a Confucian perspective would have a reason, albeit an instrumental one, to endorse freedom of expression. Both Confucius and Mencius hold that social and political discussion and criticism are necessary to prevent culture and politics from degenerating. For example, Confucius justifies political speech in terms of its contribution to healthy politics:

> If what [a ruler] says is not good and no one goes against him, then is this not almost a case of a saying leading the state to ruin?[51]

Mencius also finds that ministers have the duty to criticize the ruler for wrongdoing:

> If the prince made serious mistakes, they [ministers] would remonstrate with him.[52]

---

50. In this chapter I do not discuss whether a Confucian perspective would endorse political rights: the right to vote in a free election, political equality, or democracy in general. A serious discussion of this issue requires a separate study.

51. *The Analects* XIII:15; see also XIV:7; XVI:1.

52. *Mencius* VB:9.

One might think that, in these passages, Confucius and Mencius ask only those holding public office (ministers) to perform the task of admonishing the ruler, and so freedom of expression should be confined to them alone, but this is not true. Neither Confucius nor Mencius were state officials, but they were active in speaking publicly to criticize current politics and schools of thought. Mencius was once asked why he was fond of disputation. He replied that he was not but had no alternative, because the schools of Yang and Mo had a perverse effect on people's minds, morality, and politics. He also said that Confucius himself composed the *Spring and Autumn Annals* in order to counsel the sovereign and people of his time.[53]

> If the way of Yang and Mo does not subside and the way of Confucius is not pro-claimed, the people will be deceived by heresies and the path of morality [benevo-lence and righteousness] will be blocked. . . . What arises in mind will interfere with policy, and what shows itself in policy will interfere with practice. . . . I am not found of disputation. I have no alternative. *Whoever can, with words, combat Yang and Mo is a true disciple of the sages.*[54]

In the last sentence, Mencius even invites people to publicly challenge the thoughts of Yang and Mo.

This does not prove that Confucius and Mencius valued *free* speech as such, nor is this my intention. What it shows, rather, is that both of them saw the importance of *speech* in politics and culture. Now if, as an empirical claim, it is true that freedom of speech in the long run helps society to correct wrong ethical beliefs and to prevent rulers from indulging in wrongdoing, then a Confucian perspective would endorse freedom of political speech. In short, if freedom of expression is generally conducive to the flourishing of these prac-tices and hence to the pursuit of *ren,* there is no reason why the Confucian perspective would reject it outright.

Let me add two brief remarks on the nature of this justification of freedom of expression. First, this justification is only indirectly individualistic. The ultimate goal in the Confucian perspective is the attainment of *ren* for each and every individual rather than the glorification of the state or the ruler. In this sense, the justification of freedom of expression is individual oriented. But the immediate justification is its contribution to social, cultural, and political activities, the flourishing of which helps promote *ren.* In this imme-diate sense, the justification appeals to the social good rather than the indi-vidual good.

Second, the justification is a perfectionist one, in the sense that it takes an ethical good to be the goal promoted by the state. Freedom of expression is

53. *Mencius* IIIB:9.   54. *Mencius* IIIB:9 (italics added).

then justified on the ground that it serves, in the long run, to promote that goal. In terms of its structure, this justification is similar to the perfectionist-instrumental justifications of freedom of expression in Western political philosophy.[55] The Confucian justification differs primarily in its specification of the ethical goal – *ren* in this case. But this perfectionist–instrumental justification differs from the rights-based justification proposed by some liberal philosophers. This can be seen from the way these two types of justification differ on the question of "tolerating the bad."

Tolerating the Bad

Although the Confucian perspective does offer some justification for civil liberties or rights, some might criticize this justification as being moralistic and thus seriously limited. According to the Confucian perspective, the criticism goes, we have rights only insofar as we use them to promote the ethical life or *ren*. The Confucian perspective would find it hard to recognize the rights of people who would use them to promote the bad instead of the good. Thus we should not have the right to publish pornography or to express views or lifestyles that are considered morally corrupt or debased, even if they do not harm others. As a well-known Chinese scholar, Hsieh Yu-Wei, wrote on Confucian ethics in 1960s, we have freedom to choose the good or to develop our humanity or one's true self, but this freedom is not extended to choosing the bad: "On condition that we choose within the limits of goodness, we can choose freely. Outside the limits of goodness, one should not be free. . . . Whatever freedom you want, you should not violate this ethical principle of freedom to choose the good."[56]

Many human rights scholars in the West would find this view unacceptable. They think that individuals have the right to express their thoughts whatever the content, as long as the expression does not harm others. For example, Thomas Nagel writes,

> My objection to the censorship of pornography . . . is [that the danger is] quite out of proportion to the actual harm done by such prohibitions. . . . I am aware that life without pornography is perfectly livable. . . . But that is just the point. It is not the consequences, but the idea that state power *may* be legitimately used in

55. See, for example, John Stuart Mill's *On Liberty,* which has a strong perfectionist justification of freedom of expression (though it has some other justifications as well), and T. H. Green's moral and political philosophy. For contemporary perfectionist-instrumental justifications, see Joseph Raz, *The Morality of Freedom* (Oxford: Clarendon Press, 1986), chapter 10; and Robert P. George, *Making Men Moral: Civil Liberties and Public Morality* (Oxford: Clarendon Press, 1993), chapter 7.
56. See Hsieh Yu-wei, "The Status of the Individual in Chinese Ethics," in Charles A. Moore, ed., *The Chinese Mind* (Honolulu: University of Hawaii Press, 1967), p. 313.

such ways that seems grossly wrong. . . . They simply have no right to control people in that way.[57]

Nagel bases his claim on the notion of the moral status of individuals: Each is equal as a moral being and should enjoy substantial *personal independence,* immune from coercion by the will of others."[58] Joel Feinberg, another liberal philosopher defending the right to produce pornography, bases his claim on the idea that individuals are sovereign in their personal affairs. The notion of *"sovereign individuals"* is suggested by "the language of international law in which autonomous nation-states are said to have the sovereign right of self-determination."[59] Just as a sovereign state rules over its territory, onto which no other state can trespass, a sovereign individual rules his or her own life and actions (so long as the actions do not harm others). Notice that, for Feinberg, personal sovereignty, like state sovereignty, is "an all or nothing concept; one is entitled to absolute control of whatever is within one's domain however trivial it may be."[60] This right to personal sovereignty thus forbids external intervention that is *not* based on other-regarding reasons such as the prevention of harm or offense to others.

This is one type of liberal justification of civil rights (which is, arguably, also a politically influential vision of public morality in the United States).[61] Civil rights are not only instrumentally useful, they express the very idea of the moral status of individuals understood in terms of personal independence or individual sovereignty. The scope of civil rights should be very wide, and the only reason for limiting them should be the prevention of harm to others. By this liberal perspective, Confucianism does not take individual rights seriously enough. "To admit the right of the community to restrict the expression of convictions or attitudes on the basis of their content alone is to rob everyone of authority over his own mental life. It makes us all, equally, less free."[62]

Here lies the main difference between the Confucian perspective and this brand of liberal one. The liberal ideal of individual sovereignty or independence seems entirely foreign to Confucianism. Does this therefore indicate that the Confucian perspective is deficient? In my opinion, it is essential to

---

57. See Thomas Nagel, "Personal Rights and Public Space," *Philosophy and Public Affairs* vol. 24 (1995), pp. 95–9.
58. Nagel, "Personal Rights and Public Space," p. 94.
59. See Joel Feinberg, *Harm to Self* (Oxford: Oxford University Press, 1986), p. 47.
60. Feinberg, *Harm to Self,* p. 55.
61. For a detailed account of how this brand of liberalism developed in the United States, see Michael Sandel, *Democracy's Discontent: America in Search of a Public Philosophy* (Cambridge, MA: Harvard University Press, 1996).
62. See Nagel, "Personal Rights and Public Space," p. 99.

distinguish two views: (1) in general, debased acts (which are harmless to others) should not be prohibited by law, and (2) individuals have the moral right to say or do debased things (if they are harmless to others).[63] The liberal, individualist perspective of the kind just discussed justifies (1) by means of (2), whereas the Confucian perspective might be inclined to accept (1), though not (2).

The Confucian perspective would not adopt the strong view of individual moral rights as expressed in (2). As said earlier, this strong view is based on the notion of individual sovereignty or independence. Confucians would find it hard to accept this notion. They might accept the notion of moral autonomy, which means that individuals should be autonomous in moral deliberation and in making moral choices.[64] However, moral autonomy is valuable because it is a constitutive part of the moral life. The moral or ethical life is valuable in itself; moral autonomy, being a constitutive part of the moral life, is also valuable. For the Confucians, then, individual sovereignty would be of no value if it is used in the pursuit of the bad rather than the good.[65] Individuals have civil rights or liberties not because they are grounded in personal sovereignty but because (1) they have important interests in developing their humanity or *ren* in all of its personal, social, cultural, and political dimensions, and (2) these interests can best be served by protecting civil rights or liberties. These rights are not to be intended as an excuse or protection for moral decay. Individuals do not have the basic moral right to moral wrongdoing (in the self-regarding sense).

Some might think that the view that individuals have no basic moral right to moral wrongdoing may easily justify legal suppression of civil liberties, especially when people misuse their liberties to pursue the bad. However, Confucians do not favor the use of legal coercion to foster virtues or prevent people from indulging in the bad or debased. Confucius reckons that legal punishment cannot change one's heart or soul; only rites can. "Guide them by edicts, keep them in line with punishments, and the common people will stay out of trouble but will have no sense of shame. Guide them by virtue, keep them in line with the rites, and they will, besides having a sense of shame, reform themselves."[66]

One cannot be compelled by force to be virtuous. To live a genuinely virtuous life, the agent must see the point of that life – he or she must endorse the virtues and be motivated to live by virtues and to enjoy that life. "One who is

---

63. For a similar distinction, see George, *Making Men Moral,* chapter 4.

64. See also Benjamin Schwartz's discussion of moral autonomy in Confucius's thought, *The World of Thought in Ancient China* (Cambridge, MA: Harvard University Press, 1985), p. 113.

65. This view is not uniquely Confucian. It is shared by Raz, *The Morality of Freedom,* pp. 378–90, and George, *Making Men Moral,* chapters 4 and 5.

66. *The Analects* II:3.

not benevolent cannot remain long in strained circumstances, nor can he remain long in easy circumstances. *The benevolent man is attracted to benevolence because he feels at home in it.*[67] The cultivation of virtue is done through education and practice in rites – it is rites, not physical force, that make people feel at home with virtue. This point bears on personal freedom as absence of coercion. To act virtuously, we must act for the right reason. Avoidance of punishment is not a reason for virtuous action. The law is thus not a good instrument of moral edification. Anyone recognizing this point would want to limit the scope of criminal law. Neither should punishment be used to prevent the bad from influencing the good, for Confucius thinks that the best method is still moral edification by example, and he urges the rulers to set a good example.

> Lord Ji Kang asked Confucius about government, saying: "Suppose I were to kill the bad to help the good: how about that?" Confucius replied: "You are here to govern; what need is there to kill? If you desire what is good, the people will be good. The moral power of the gentleman is wind, the moral power of the common man is grass. Under the wind, the grass must bend."[68]

Confucius puts demanding standards of moral behavior on the rulers and gentlemen, not the common people. This is consistent with the general spirit of tolerance in Confucianism – "to set strict standards for oneself, and make allowances for others."[69] Confucian tolerance is not grounded in liberal values like personal independence or sovereignty or any notion of a moral right to wrongdoing. It is based on sympathy, on the view that coercion is ineffective in promoting *ren,* and on a particular approach to moral edification.

CONTEMPORARY RELEVANCE OF THE CONFUCIAN PERSPECTIVE OF HUMAN RIGHTS

The main elements of the Confucian perspective of human rights can be summarized as follows:

1. There are human rights that protect important interests in *ren* or humanity.
2. Such protection should be seen as a fallback apparatus: Rights are important when virtues fail to obtain or personal relationships break down.
3. Human rights should not be inflated, that is, they should not be considered constitutive of valuable personal relationships or necessary for

---

67. *The Analects* IV:2 (italics added).
68. *The Analects* XII:19, from Simon Leys, trans., *The Analects of Confucius* (New York: W. W. Norton and Company, 1997).
69. *The Analects* XV:15.

the display of virtue and they should not be intended to offer protection for debased acts as well as good ones.

4. Rights instruments should be the last means to resolve conflicts.

With regard to the significance of a Confucian perspective for contemporary human rights issues, one must take into consideration a range of normative, practical, and historical factors before one can judge. I hope to show, albeit briefly, that this perspective does clarify some genuine concerns. I shall consider two issues related to the jurisprudence of human rights, namely, the constitutional protection of freedom of expression and the rights of the elderly.

Jurisprudence of Human Rights: The Case of Freedom of Expression

From a Confucian perspective, human rights do not include the right to say or do immoral things. This view has important implications for the jurisprudence of human rights. Modern bills or charters of rights include the right to free expression, but what forms of speech or expression should be protected by this right? From a liberal, individualist view, many forms of speech should be stringently protected (except those that cause clear and distinct harm to others such as libel). In the case of the United States, freedom of expression receives almost absolute protection in the Constitution. However, Confucians would be reluctant to place certain forms of expression under such protection (obscene or pornographic magazines, for example) because human rights are not properly used to protect people's prurient or debased interests. This has some significant implications. First, judicial review could not be used to strike down laws censoring pornography, although they could be changed by the legislature itself. Second, in assessing the reasonableness of a censorship law, public interest in pornographic expression would carry far less weight than the interest in political, academic, or artistic expression. Of course, whether pornography should be *banned* is another question. As I argued in the last section, Confucians are generally reluctant to use legal punishment for the purpose of moral edification. They aim at transforming peoples' desires rather than suppressing them.[70]

Consider also the case of expression of ideas encouraging racial hatred and discrimination in violation of the rights of others. Such expression should not be protected by the right to free expression guaranteed by human rights charters. Objections to banning these forms of expression argue that it is difficult to differentiate genuine hate speech from less overt discriminatory expression, but if this kind of speech were not banned, it would not be because people have the moral right to express ideas advocating racial hatred.

---

70. This might perhaps partly explain why pornography was tolerated in ancient China.

The Rights of the Elderly

Several Asian countries, including China and Taiwan, have legislation to the effect that parents who are unable to support themselves have the right to be supported by their children who have come of age. In the case of China, this right is guaranteed by Article 49 of the Chinese Constitution. Recently Singapore followed the example of China and Taiwan. Although most Western human rights laws protect the rights of children under the care of parents or adult guardians, no reciprocal rights are granted to parents. It seems that the idea of a parental right is a distinctively Chinese phenomenon. Would the Confucian perspective outlined here endorse this idea of parental right?

This sort of legislation would strike many Western people as unheard of. First, unlike in Chinese culture, I find no clear, widely shared understanding in the West that children have a moral duty to support their parents. The second reason is that most parents in Western economically advanced countries have pensions to support themselves after retirement. There is no need for parents to rely upon their children for support. Neither of these conditions exists in China or Taiwan. In Chinese culture, filial piety, which includes the moral duty to support parents, is still widely shared. Moreover, in the past Chinese parents who were not well-off selflessly spent all their energy and earnings to help their children receive the best education and training; in retirement, they needed and expected support from their children.

What should the solution to this problem be for Chinese societies? A legal parental right to receive support from children or a state/personal pension scheme? What would the Confucian perspective indicate? The Confucian perspective would say that we should first try a more indirect means to both support retired parents and enhance filial piety. For example, it would support the idea of giving a tax exemption to children who live with or support their parents. This has been practiced in Hong Kong for a long time, and it has been well received by the community. (Recently, people supporting their siblings and grandparents can also get a tax deduction.) Moreover, it would support the idea of enlarging the definition of family to include the parents. At present Hong Kong follows the Western idea of the nuclear family, which includes the married couple and their children. Thus the fringe benefits that an employee receives do not cover his or her parents. For example, medical benefits and housing allocations do not allow for the fact that the employee may have to live with and support his or her parents.[71] These policies should be changed.

71. See also Daniel A. Bell, "The East Asian Challenge to Human Rights: Reflections on an East West Dialogue," *Human Rights Quarterly* vol. 18 (1996), pp. 665–6.

If these proposed policies work, and if filial piety is strong in a country, then there is no general need to resort to law to force children to support their parents. However, what are we to do with those exceptional cases where children do not have a strong sense of filial obligation? Or what if the culture of filial piety declines? Should we resort to the legal parental right as a fall-back apparatus to protect the parents? The answer depends on how we conceive of the goals of legal parental right. Let us first consider the marriage case. Recall our previous argument that if a marriage turns sour, it is best to repair it by renewing the partners' commitment to mutual caring and love, rather than by asserting their rights. But if the relationship comes to a point of complete breakdown, then it would not be inappropriate for one party to resort to rights to protect her interests.

Similar points can be made in the elderly rights case. If the aim of an elderly right is to sustain or even repair a parent–child relationship based on filial piety, then rights would not be appropriate. The use of a legal instrument would fail to promote filial piety as a virtue, for it fosters a false motivation for children – supporting their parents out of fear of punishment. But if the aim is not to sustain a parent–child relationship, but to protect the parents' interests when the relationship breaks down, then the use of a legal parental right to protect the parents may not be inappropriate. Consider a 1993 case in China, described by Li Chenyang:

> In Shandong Province a ninety-year-old woman sued her two sons for failing in their filial duty. The woman's husband died young and left her with two sons, one and three years old, respectively. Through countless hardships she brought them both up. Now she had become old and could not work. Neither of her two sons wanted to take care of her. The court intervened in her favor, and the sons agreed to take full responsibility for her living and medical expenses.[72]

Confucians believe that grown children have a moral duty to support their aged parents. In a divorce situation, one party – usually the wife – has the right to financial support by another party who was unfaithful to her. Confucians would consider it equally legitimate for helpless aged parents to resort to a rights instrument to demand financial support from their uncaring grown children. Of course, not all parents would sue their uncaring children. Some might find this a very shameful and painful thing to do. But in situations like the one described in the example, resorting to a legal right seems a necessary means to protect one's interests as a person and one's due as a parent.

72. See Li Chenyang, "Shifting Perspectives: Filial Morality Revisited," *Philosophy East and West* vol. 47 (1997), p. 218. Li's article stated that this case was reported in the August 25, 1995 issue of *People's Daily*.

CONCLUSION

In this chapter I have argued that Confucianism, as represented by the thoughts of Confucius and Mencius, is compatible with the idea of human rights. The central elements in Confucianism – the emphasis on role-based ethics, the Confucian ideal of community, the respect for seniority and the elderly, and the preference for harmony rather than litigation – are all compatible with the idea of human rights. Moreover, the Confucian philosophy of *ren* would endorse human rights as an instrument to protect humanity and important human interests, although such an instrument should be seen as primarily a fallback apparatus. On the Confucian view, we should strive to resolve conflicts first by means of education, mediation, and compromise in order to preserve the spirit of mutual caring and trust, but this should not mislead us to believing that the instrument of human rights is unimportant. Both human rights and virtues are important in the reconstructed Confucian ethics, and they require each other. Virtues may fail at times, and so they are precarious in protecting human interests. On the other hand, virtues are needed to guide the conduct of the right-holders in the exercise of their rights. Virtues help prevent people from misusing their rights.

I have also argued that Confucianism would justify civil liberties – freedom of expression, for example – on instrumental rather than intrinsic grounds. Whereas Western liberals justify freedom of speech on the ground of personal autonomy, Confucians would see this as a means for society to correct wrong ethical beliefs, to ensure that rulers would not indulge in wrongdoing, and to promote valuable arts and cultures in the long run. Confucians would not recognize that individuals have the moral right to debased speech, although Confucianism would not advocate the use of legal punishment to ban it.

What does this examination of Confucianism and human rights reveal about the possibility of an overlapping consensus on human rights? Insofar as Confucianism and Western liberalism are concerned, I think both traditions may converge upon a certain list of human rights, which includes at least some personal rights such as the right against torture and some basic civil liberties such as the freedom of expression, but this consensus does not reach to the level of justification and scope. Of course, both perspectives can be revised and further developed, so a greater degree of consensus might be achieved. The awareness that there are interesting perspectives on human rights other than one's own precisely provides a strong impetus for mutual dialogue and self-progress.

PART IV

ECONOMIC DEVELOPMENT AND HUMAN RIGHTS

CHAPTER 10

RIGHTS, SOCIAL JUSTICE, AND GLOBALIZATION IN EAST ASIA

Yash Ghai*

INTRODUCTION

East Asia provides a particularly good focus for the study of the impact on rights and justice of economic processes that are associated with globalization. Outside the major Western economies, East Asian economies were the first to be integrated into the world economy. They achieved significant levels of economic development. The success of their economies was attributed largely to that integration, which was fostered by their export orientation, the willingness to receive foreign capital and use foreign technology.

A particularly effective prism through which to examine the foundations of rights is provided by the connections between politico-economic systems and rights and justice in East Asia, juxtaposed with the advocacy of Asian values. It helps to shed light on the debate on the relativism of cultures and their links to rights. It has promoted fruitful analysis of cross-cultural perspectives on rights.[1] It can also help us to explore the importance of material conditions for the perception and reality of rights, especially the impact on rights of the material conditions produced in systems dominated by market principles.

My analysis is based on the view that particular values and attitudes toward rights are conditioned primarily by material conditions, although there is frequently a time lag between ideology and reality. Globalization generally, but more particularly in East Asia, is largely concerned with the change in material

*I thank Philip Alston, Jill Cottrell, Dharam Ghai, Louis Henkin, Michael Salvaris, Francis Snyder, David Trubek, and the editors of this volume for comments on earlier drafts of this chapter.
1. Apart from the contributions by Charles Taylor, Abullahi An-Na'im, and Joseph Chan in this volume, see Abdullahi An-Na'im, "Towards a Cross-Cultural Approach to Defining International Standards of Human Rights" in the book he edited, *Human Rights in Cross-Cultural Perspectives* (Philadelphia: University of Pennsylvania, 1991); and Boaventura de Sousa Santos, *Towards a New Common Sense: Law, Science and Politics in the Paradigmatic Transition* (New York: Routledge, 1995).

conditions and is thus likely to have a significant influence on perceptions and realities of rights. I also believe that class or social position determines an individual's or group's perception of rights. There is no necessarily uniform attitude of rights within a state; for example, business executives give priority to rights different from those preferred by trade unionists and minorities may differ from members of the majority community on the importance of particular rights. The convergence of class interests across states also makes less realistic the assumptions of a "national" view of rights. The current economic crisis in East Asia also invites speculation on the future of "Asian values," which is born out of the hubris of economic success.

I begin with an analysis of economic globalization to demonstrate how it has brought about the integration of the world on the basis of global markets. I discuss in particular the social and political tendencies of the market, including the relationship of the market to the state, which constitute a fruitful framework for an analysis of the impact on rights. I next examine the regime of rights and contrast its orientation with the tendencies of the market before turning to an analysis of East Asian economies, especially their integration into the global economy, as a prelude to a discussion of rights in East Asia.

GLOBALIZATION

The effects of globalization on human rights are complex, confusing, and contradictory. This is scarcely surprising, because globalization is itself a complex and contradictory process. The effects of globalization are changing and dynamic; the process is dialectical, so it is important to establish the trajectory of and interaction between the forces underlying it. Already in the last ten years we have seen important shifts in relationships, modes of legitimacy, and bargaining positions, and more recently the economic crisis in East Asia has begun to change perceptions of globalization. Although this leads one to eschew definite conclusions, one can certainly extrapolate from the tendencies, and their contradictions, inherent in economic globalization.

Globalization is a compendium of ideas, practices, institutions, directions of change, and ideologies. Some of these diminish rights, others promote them, and some do both simultaneously: for example, the Internet and the new forms of technology more generally, which provide more opportunities for both freedom of expression and access to information, and open new possibilities of networking; at the same time they greatly increase the influence of corporations and opportunities for hate speech, pornography, and sexual trafficking. That makes it particularly hard to distinguish between the positive and negative consequences of globalization for rights. However, even though they are interconnected, it may be possible to distinguish the economic processes of globalization from the more political and social processes. There is considerable tension between the economic and other processes insofar as rights and justice are concerned.

The economic processes are connected principally with the development of national market economies and their integration globally on market principles. In some states the two processes are occurring simultaneously (as in China, Vietnam, and Cambodia); in others, significant integration followed the rise of national markets – although the markets are now being "perfected" for further integration (as in Malaysia, Korea, and Indonesia). To establish a framework to assess the effects of globalization in East Asia and elsewhere, I examine the social dynamics of market economies.

Dynamics of the Market Economy

The market tends to expand, so its transactions cover ever larger areas of social and political life. Market economies are driven by the fundamental principle of profit. Efforts of business enterprises to maximize their profits involve a complex organization for production and marketing. The market economy is based on exchanges, which are mediated through the common medium of the currency. The market is considered to work more efficiently as more items can be brought within market exchanges. This leads to increasing commoditization, whereby more and more objects become alienable, that is, the subject of sale. The rise of the market economy in the West was marked by the commoditization of land and labor. Since then the scope of commoditization has increased manyfold (extending even, for example, to mother-surrogacy). The more absolute the concept of property in a commodity, the easier is it to alienate it. The market therefore tends to remove restraints or multiple claims on ownership, so a clear and comprehensive relationship is established between an object and its owner.

Commoditization represented a shift from the community to the individual, captured by Maine in his statement that the movement of all "progressive societies" has been from status to contract. As Polyani has demonstrated, commoditization of land and labor changed the very foundations of societies touched by capitalism. Before this form of commoditization,

> man's economy, as a rule, is submerged in his social relationships. He does not act so as to safeguard his individual interest in the possession of material goods; he acts so as to safeguard his social standing, his social claims, his social assets. He values material goods only in so far as they serve this end. Neither the process of

production nor that of distribution is linked to specific economic interests attached to the possession of goods; but every single step in that process is geared to a number of social interests.[2]

The importance of social obligations arises from the salience of the community; "by disregarding the accepted code of honour, or generosity, the individual cuts himself off from the community and becomes an outcast; second, because in the long run, all social obligations are reciprocal, and their fulfilment serves also the individual's give-and-take interests best."[3] Reciprocity and redistribution are essential principles of such societies. The multiple claims in relation to a parcel of land, for example, are a manifestation of this sharing and obligations.[4]

The commoditization of land destroys forms of communal ownership and of labor that sustain the more communally oriented societies. Commoditization sets in motion a process in which, instead of social relationships subsuming the economic, economic relationships and considerations become dominant over social relationships, even close kinship relations. Economic relationships become increasingly abstracted from their communal and social matrix, and there arises the dependence of individuals and families, and in the end of communities, on the market. The cohesion of the community is replaced by the integration of the market.

The process of the destruction or modification of old structures can be socially progressive. The release of the individual from these structures facilitates his or her autonomous development and can free persons and groups from social and economic oppression. But the market creates new social and economic divisions and stratification. It vests enormous economic and political power in the capitalists over the workers. An essential feature of the market economy is the appropriation by capitalists of profits, which are generated in substantial part by labor. This constitutes an inherent exploitation in the capitalist market system. At the same time wage employment becomes necessary for survival.

The growth of the market economy was facilitated by, and in turn supported, the development of technology and more efficient ways of production. The greater use of newer technologies and automation increased margins of profits. This resulted in the growing scale of production, the economies of scale, which built into the market economy the impulse toward its dominance by a few large firms, and eventually toward monopolization.

---

2. Karl Polyani, *The Great Transformation: The Political and Economic Origins of Our Time* (Boston: Beacon Press, 1957), p. 46.
3. Polyani, *The Great Transformation*, p. 46.
4. Max Gluckman, "Property Rights and Economic Activity" in his book, *Politics, Law and Ritual in Tribal Society* (Oxford: Blackwell, 1965).

Dominance and monopolization strike at the underlying assumptions of the efficiency of the system; attempts to deal with them through regulation have rarely been successful. The drive to enlarge the scope of markets, from feudal domains to the national, also led to the search for resources and markets overseas. The expansion of capital overseas led by large firms, the forerunners of the transnational corporations, laid the basis for globalization.

An important aspect of the ideology of the market is its claim to efficiency through self-adjustment and self-regulation. The more autonomous the market, the more the matters of everyday life are brought under its domain, snatched from the domains of the state, the community, and the family. The very greed and selfishness of entrepreneurs and business groups, recognized explicitly by defenders of the market to be the driving force behind the market, are claimed to be beneficial to the community, guaranteeing it efficiency and fairness. However, few states, even the colonial, have found it possible or expedient to let markets unfold in the fullness of their logic, because the consequences of free markets threaten social peace and stability. The market system is essentially exploitative – of workers and consumers as well as of resources. In early capitalism, profits were generated on the backs of workers, who included women and young children. Outside Europe, the effects were even more horrendous: genocide, slavery, expropriation of others' resources, the uprooting and frequently the destruction of communities. Today capitalism also finds other ways of throwing the costs of the market economy upon society – through, for example, redundancies, bankruptcies, and environmental degradation.

The nineteenth century in Europe saw many forms of regulation to moderate the tendencies of the market, leading in the twentieth century to the rise of the welfare state. Although the welfare state took care of those who suffered most acutely from the operation of the market (and so legitimized the market), the rise of organized labor led to the development of workers' rights in the marketplace as well as in politics (for example, the right to organize, strike, and negotiate collective agreements, the amelioration of safety standards, hours of work, and minimum wages as well as the political achievement of the franchise). The juxtaposition of economic with political forces became essential to class settlement in Europe. For these purposes the state became the main framework for struggles and consolidation. In the West a new class balance was achieved through these developments – but not in many other parts of the world, including East Asia, as I seek to demonstrate here.

However, even in the West the balance between the autonomy of the economic processes and their regulation has shifted over centuries. The proponents of a particular school of economists have consistently argued for a

Hayekian autonomous and self-regulating market, on the grounds both that the market has its own internal mechanisms for checking abuse and excesses and that state regulation is inefficient (and a derogation from rights of property and liberty). There is historically little justification for the claim that the market is autonomous. From the days of mercantilism onward, the market has been parasitic upon the state, requiring its intervention in numerous ways to establish the dominance of the market. Recent decades, however, have seen the revival of the appeal of the autonomy of the market and the rolling back of state regulation; it constitutes the ideology of globalization. But, although globalization seems to have a momentum and a market dynamic of its own, it is no more autonomous than in its earlier phases, requiring overt and extensive political support, whether in the form of aid conditionalities, privatization, weakening of labor, and the strengthening of enforcement mechanisms under the hegemony of the United States.

Legal and political developments in the West have in part led to claims that markets promote democracy and rights. The market, it is claimed, disperses power and frees individuals from the bonds of the community and the state. It requires for its operation the power of individuals and groups to make a host of decisions, necessitates the opening up of channels of information and communication, and develops professional and propertied classes with a stake in rights and fair procedures. The market is said to promote a legal–rational system of authority, particularly the Rule of Law, without which neither property nor contracts nor state abstention from the economic affairs of men and women is guaranteed. In the process it promotes certain conceptions of the autonomy of civil society and notions of rights, in particular that of equality (because all persons meet in the market as free and equal individuals).

Although elements of these ideological claims may be true of "mature" capitalism, it is not easy to generalize about the form of the state that emerges out of or promotes capitalism, for capitalism in the West and elsewhere has been associated with different types of political structures. However, this much can be said: Despite forms of apparent decentralization of power, the capitalist state has been a strong state. Historically in the West, it needed to overcome feudalism to provide the spatial and regulatory framework of ever expanding markets. A strong state was also necessary to facilitate the expansion of national capital and markets overseas (even today this constitutes a key function of the state in the United States, for example). It was also needed to ensure the subordination of labor and to cope with the consequent tensions and conflicts in society. But its coercive power was not deployed equally against all social and economic groups. Thus, although there is a strong emphasis on legal equality, unequal economic resources or status means that in practice there is seldom equality.

As for rights, it is indeed true that certain kinds of rights, procedures, and the generality of rules have been necessary for the growth and operation of the market, and they do form an important infrastructure for the claims and enforcement of rights. However, the kinds of rights and procedures associated with the market are narrow, seeking for the most part to strengthen the legal and economic position of capitalists. They are not geared toward social justice or wide political participation. Limited as they are, they are not even essential for all forms of capitalism, as the East Asian experience demonstrates. On the other hand, rights directed toward social justice and democracy have been secured through a struggle against capitalism.[5]

The Global Economy

Globalization has been facilitated by the remarkable dismantling of barriers to trade through the abolition of quotas and the reduction of duties. It has also been consolidated through: the liberalization of currency regimes; the opportunities for trading of national stocks on world exchange markets; the proliferation of public and private securities; the general removal of barriers to the movement of capital, goods, and increasingly services; the privatization of state-owned companies; the removal of discrimination against foreign capital; the elimination of state subsidies to industry or for social services; and clearer definition and increased protection of property and contractual rights. Along with technologies that are highly mobile, universally protected, and for the most part freely available commercially, these developments have enabled the organization of production on a global basis. Transnational corporations are able to bring together capital, technology, raw materials, marketing skills, and labor to organize production where costs are low and opportunities for profits are high.

The process of globalization has old roots. Nevertheless, for various reasons the present phase of globalization is distinctive and needs to be addressed on its own terms. For one, it seems to be a truly global project, with the active support of most governments. The tremendous development in the means of communication and transport makes for almost a qualitative change in interstate and interpeople relationships, and in economic exchanges. The possibility of the rapid transmission of money, in an effective twenty-four-hour exchange system, provides for a global monetary system. The ideological basis of globalization appears to be more secure. There has been a striking growth in institutions and regulations that cater to globalization, the development of

---

5. See Samuel Bowles and Herbert Gintis, *Democracy and Capitalism: Property, Community, and the Contradictions of Modern Social Thought* (New York: Basic Books, 1986).

an international superstructure of laws, tribunals, and sanctions for a global economy. Even if in strict quantitative terms the nineteenth century may have been more globalized than our own times, the present phase of globalization is more central to economic decision making, international security considerations, the location of power, the compression and the consciousness of the world, and a rapidly emerging transnational culture.

The conditions for modern globalization have not arisen spontaneously through autonomous processes. To a significant extent, they are the price that, under pressure from international capital, world powers have exacted from states that have fallen into debt or other forms of dependence (such as Indonesia or Thailand), or are seeking greater engagement with the international economy (such as China, Vietnam, and even India). At one stage foreign capital was content to collaborate with local political elites or entrepreneurs. Now it demands that the very conditions of production and trade be changed to provide for a direct and dominant role for international capital. Whether it is the World Bank–inspired structural adjustments in Africa or the International Monetary Fund–sponsored "bailouts" in East Asia, they follow a similar pattern. States are increasingly compelled to submit to the dictates of "globalization" and to change their economic and legal systems accordingly.

THE REGIME OF RIGHTS

With the destruction of the old communal economy, people's life chances, values, and expectations were increasingly shaped by the matrix of the market and the state. The modern concept of rights is a device to cope with the rise to eminence of state power within the integuments of a market economy, and later, in a different form, of the inegalitarian tendencies of the market. The provenance of rights is the state and the market economy, and with the eclipse of the protective mechanisms of the community, rights have become increasingly important. The subordination of the community by the state is typified in the shift of language as regards obligations from duties to rights.[6]

The national and international movement of rights is itself a product of globalization. The concept of "human rights" (as the term is used in contemporary debates) developed in national jurisdictions, though even then there was an international exchange of ideas of rights. There was a rapid spread of regimes of rights to national jurisdictions through independence constitutions of newly established states with the post–World War II decolonization (following to some extent the metropolitan model). Since then international organizations (under the general auspices of the United Nations) have

---

6. This is one of the themes of Norberto Bobbio in his book *The Age of Rights* (Cambridge: Polity Press, 1996).

assumed the primary responsibility for the further elaboration of human rights, resulting in a large number of legally or morally binding instruments. The earlier international instruments were informed by a firm, philosophical view – largely the liberal democratic, but subsequent instruments have sought to accommodate a diversity of interests and views. The earlier emphasis on the individual and on civil rights has been supplemented by a recognition of groups and communities (such as women, children, minorities, indigenous peoples, and migrant workers) as well as the imperative of economic and cultural rights, and social justice in general, as in the instruments dealing with the rights of these groups. The regime of rights is much better balanced now than is acknowledged by its critics among Asian governments.[7]

The enterprise of enunciating new norms of rights has become truly global, in the double sense of interests protected and of the parties who participate in it (which include not only states from different regions of the world, but also nonstate groups, as with the instruments on indigenous peoples or minorities). It is now generally recognized that the protection by a state of rights within its jurisdiction is also its international responsibility. To that extent the regime of rights has qualified state sovereignty, although in a more legalistic and formal sense than the more material sanctions with which the economic processes of globalization have qualified state sovereignty. There exists machinery at the international level, however minimal and ineffective, for the supervision of the guarantees of rights; the machinery is more effective in some regional arrangements.

Rights are increasingly seen as empowering weaker sections of communities and as the basis for social and political mobilization. They have facilitated the rise of NGOs and social movements, and networking across the world, with human rights providing their agenda and legitimacy. There is now a general acceptance of the legitimacy of human rights, reflected in the demands by the privileged and the disadvantaged alike that their rights be respected, in conditionalities, and in the discourse of international relations. The big moral issues of our times are cast in terms of rights and their violations. There are attempts to secure more and more international regulation through "rights" (e.g., social welfare, social justice, environment, and North– South relations as in the Right to Development). "Rights" are performing (or more accurately, are seeking to perform) more and more the functions of legislation and regulation at the

---

7. It is important to make the distinction between the formal inclusion of social, economic, and cultural rights and the significance attached to them by governments, multilateral agencies, and international NGOs. It is in the latter sense that Onuma may be correct when he complains of an imbalance between different kinds of rights (see Chapter 4). Even here I would partially disagree with him, for the work of multilateral institutions such as the UNDP, WHO, ILO, FAO, HABITAT, and the aid agencies of many Western states is largely concerned with social and economic rights, although not perceived as such. Also the work of several NGOs, such as Oxfam, deals with economic rights and basic needs of people.

international level, reflecting perhaps the absence of a global political authority. In that sense rights are preceding political authority.

The regime of rights provides the nearest thing to a coherent challenge to economic globalization. It emphasizes the importance of human dignity, the right to work in just conditions and in return for fair wages, the right to welfare, the care of children, the equality of women, the respect for the cultural and economic rights of indigenous peoples, the protection of the environment, the exercise of popular sovereignty through democratic constitutional orders, and the accountability of holders of power. It seeks to conserve natural resources for future generations while aiming to distribute the fruits of their contemporary exploitation on a more equitable principle, returning in some cases to the concept of communal ownership on a global basis, redefining the concept of property – the commons of the world. It promotes cosmopolitanism and respect for diversity. It has produced a greater consciousness of rights and provides an important foundation for networking (of individuals, groups, and NGOs) around rights and against the dehumanizing effects of globalization. Contemporary economic globalization is self-evidently inconsistent with these objectives.

Although the regime of rights challenges globalization at conceptual and rhetorical levels, its capacity to translate the challenge into concrete forms of opposition is severely limited due to the dominance of capital in world politics. Few of the international or regional institutions for the promotion of human rights even remotely approach the power of international economic institutions to discipline states and corporations that deviate from the emerging norms of globalization.

GLOBALIZATION AND RIGHTS IN EAST ASIA

The connections between globalization and rights can be best examined through the effects of markets and the structure of the state. The outlines of that framework have already been presented in the second section of this chapter, "Globalization." Here I point to some features that have a major impact on rights.

The first is the strengthening of market practices and their ideology, which has discredited the concepts of social welfare and social justice. Globalization is intolerant of state regulation of the economy (except when it suits the interests of international capital, as in the pivotal role of the state in economic restructuring). It tends increasingly to turn key issues of intra- and interstate policies into trade or trade-related issues and to move their resolution from more democratically constituted forums, such as the United Nations and the UN Conference on Trade and Development, to those in which private international economic interests dominate, such as the World Trade Organization (WTO) or the World Intellectual Property Organization (WIPO).

Closely connected is the emergence of transnational corporations as the principal sites of economic and political power. They deploy enormous resources, and the income of the larger among them exceeds that of several states. They make the primary decisions on the location of production and increasingly of prices, with a major impact on workers and consumers. The removal of barriers to trade and the movement of capital has given them enormous flexibility in the organization of production and has made them "footloose," able to exploit economic opportunities around the world. The privatization of state enterprises has increased the scope of activities of transnational corporations. Other factors have increased the power of corporations: the increasing protection in international law of their property and other interests; international institutions, which regulate trade and other global economic issues in which the corporations play an influential, sometimes decisive, role (dispensing with the reliance on state mechanisms that marked earlier phases of globalization); and the increasingly monopolistic position of these corporations.

The third feature is a particular asymmetry in economic globalization. Of the major factors of production, labor alone is not mobile (except for highly skilled labor, in which there is a global market). This produces an imbalance between capital and labor, which has a significant effect on the consequences of globalization. Labor finds itself in a weak position because of sharper fragmentation between knowledge workers and manual workers, and the inability of labor to organize transnationally, which is reinforced by both law and economics.[8] The consequent superior position of capital gives it a negotiating power over both state and labor, and privileges those rights and institutions that it favors at the expense of those that favor labor.

Finally, following from these is the changing relationship between states and markets. Opinion is deeply divided over whether globalization has weakened states vis à vis the market. However, there is considerable evidence to suggest that the powers of most states have been eroded by globalization, principally by the conditions of international economic competition. Since capital can move freely, states, anxious to woo capital have lost control (or are less willing to exercise it) over many aspects of economic policy. As capital and skilled labor can move freely from high-tax to low-tax countries, a state's room to set tax rates higher than elsewhere is constrained.[9] If states are unable to raise revenues in amounts they would wish, they are forced to cut down on public expenditures and accordingly to curtail welfare policies. Governments may also reduce labor costs by cutting down on pension and

8. Gary Teeple, *Globalization and the Decline of Social Reform* (Atlantic Highlands, NJ: Humanities Press, 1995), p. 116.
9. See *The Economist,* May 13, 1997, for an account of the constraints on the capacity of states to tax.

other labor rights, control strikes, reduce minimum wages, promote more flexible employment policies, and eliminate or reduce the scope of regulatory schemes (although it has been argued that economies that set high standards in these matters benefit from them).[10] A government's ability to determine the form of national markets has diminished.

Even one of the most traditional functions of the state, law making, closely connected to its sovereignty, has increasingly been appropriated by corporations or international economic organizations acting at their behest. This is made manifest in the new *"lex mercatoria,"* whereby rules and regulations governing trade and commerce are now established either by corporations (as in joint ventures in China) or through their influence over organizations like the WTO or WIPO.[11] States are losing control not only over the value of their currency, but over its very form.

It has been argued that the state remains the principal site of political activity and to some extent policy making, but my earlier analysis suggests that the state is increasingly subordinated to international capital and that policy making is dictated by the exigencies of that capital. Nor is there an effective international political organization able to act as a restraining influence on international capital. Consequently, at the moment there is no political balance to the economic power of the market, and the kind of compromises that national capitals were forced into in the late nineteenth and most of the twentieth century are unlikely to be effected on a global and even national basis today. We are rapidly moving to what looks like a Hayekian autonomous market over the globe. National politics are played out within a framework that offers little prospects of change. Combined with the state's exaggerated protection of property and other imperatives of globalization, it threatens the very project of democracy.

EAST ASIAN ECONOMIES

My analysis proceeds on the assumption that the material forces represented by the state and the economy are decisive for the ideology and practice of rights. It is necessary to recognize that East Asian economies are quite diverse and that they have reached their present status through different trajectories. Some states are important capital-exporting economies, particularly Japan, but in recent years Taiwan, Singapore, and Hong Kong as well. Others, with

10. See John Braithwaite, "Global Business Regulation and the Sovereignty of Citizens," *Social Sciences Research Centre Occasional Paper 19* (Hong Kong: University of Hong Kong, 1995); and Michael Porter, *The Competitive Advantage of Nations* (London: Macmillan, 1990).

11. See Braithwaite, "Global Business Regulation and the Sovereignty of Citizens."

the partial exception of South Korea, are principally capital importing. Some like Taiwan, South Korea, Hong Kong, and Singapore have become highly industrial, whereas there are significant sectors of rural and agricultural economies in the Philippines, Indonesia, and Malaysia. The state has played a more important role in economic development in Japan, South Korea, Singapore, and Taiwan than in the other states.

However, subject to the necessary qualifications, it is possible to find some commonalities. They are market economies (or in the case of China, Cambodia, and Vietnam, are rapidly becoming so). Second, they are not, or have not been until recently, liberal market economies. There has been a high degree of protection in some of them of local products and restrictions on foreign investments. Moreover, there has been a close connection between the government and the business elite in most countries, a considerable amount of it illicit.

East Asian economies have undergone fundamental social and structural changes since the Second World War. Before the war they were largely agricultural economies, in which there were significant differences in the amount of land held by different groups. They were in many respects "traditional societies," rural, peasant based, and hierarchical, with the consequent dominance of an ideology that justified hierarchy and obedience to rulers, and emphasized the primacy of the family and the community. They are now mostly industrial, exposed to new and sophisticated technologies, the factory workplace replacing the rural work environment. This has been achieved by rapid shifts of population from the rural to urban areas and from subsistence to wage employment. The dominant social relations – family, kinship, and the community – have been replaced by those of waged employment, which dictates the location and nature of work and produces dependence on the market for survival.[12] Even those who subsist in the few

---

12. It is sometimes argued that "Asian" capitalism strengthens the family and the community because businesses are family based and rely on community trust. It is true that those who are well off, at least among overseas Chinese, use family connections to promote their businesses. There is a rapidly growing literature on this. See, for example, Gary Hamilton, "The Organisational Foundations of Western and Chinese Commerce: A Historical and Comparative Analysis," in Hamilton, *Business Networks and Economic Development in East and Southeast Asia* (Hong Kong: Oxford University Press, 1991); Gordon Redding, *The Spirit of Chinese Capitalism* (Berlin: Walter de Gruyter Press, 1990); Robert Tricker, "Corporate Governance: A Ripple on the Cultural Reflections," in S. R. Clegg and Gordon Redding, eds., *Capitalism in Contrasting Cultures* (Berlin: Walter de Gruyter Press, 1990); and Wong Siu-lun "Chinese Entrepreneurs and Business Trust," in Hamilton, *Business Networks and Economic Development in East and Southeast Asia*.

However, the situation for working–class families is obverse – both spouses have to work; children are neglected; grandparents can no longer live with or rely on children. Similarly the reliance on community resources frequently amounts to exploiting the labor of kin and discouraging unionization. Ammar Sianwalla explains the heavy gearing of Thai companies, a direct cause of the crisis in that country, in his J. Douglas Gibson Lecture, "Can a Developing Democracy Manage Its Macroeconomy? The Case of Thailand" (delivered at Queen's University, Ontario, October 15, 1997).

remaining precapitalist formations are increasingly subordinated to and dependent on the national or international economy. In these circumstances the relationship of individuals and groups to the market and the state becomes crucial – a relationship which is regulated by rights or by unregulated authority.

I have already argued that markets in Asia have not been liberal and frequently have not been capitalist. They were particularistic, often family or ethnically oriented, in which opportunities for participation in the economy were limited. Nor did these markets necessarily promote entrepreneurship or business creativity, because they relied so heavily on state patronage for cheap loans, licensing, and government contracts – a species of crony capitalism. Political imperatives overrode the rationality of markets. The market did not generate a notion of rights, for as Robison says: "It is the contest of power and the formation of coalitions and alliances, rather than systems of rules and procedures about contracts, property, exchange and procurement that determine the market."[13]

The close connection between the business elite and governments tended to blur distinctions between private and public spheres of the economy, particularly in the Philippines under Marcos or Indonesia under Suharto, and elsewhere in East Asia as well. More fundamentally, this meant that there was little control over the way business elites used and abused the market. This not only allowed numerous forms of corruption, it produced predatory practices entailing gross exploitation of labor, resources, and the environment.

THE STATE IN EAST ASIA

Political systems in East Asia have varied from place to place and over time, but except for Japan's, few have been democratic for long. A special role of the state has been the fostering of nationalism, principally through the subordination of minority groups and the undermining of cultures other than that of the majority community. The state has also fostered, as argued earlier, particular kinds of markets, as vehicles for integration with the international economy and to manage international relations, but also through official control to influence domestic social and political processes. It has provided an essential framework and apparatus for personal and group accumulation through nepotism and other forms of corruption. There has been limited accountability of government and its agencies. Government leaders have elaborated various forms of ideologies, particularly "Asian values," to justify

---

13. Richard Robison in Rodan, Hewison, and Robison, eds., *The Political Economy of South-East Asia* (Melbourne: Oxford University Press, 1997), p. 57.

the structure of the state and official policies. "Asian values" were advanced to challenge the concept and content of human rights, which were characterized as "Western." The suppression of rights was justified in terms of stability and competitiveness. The success of their economies enabled governments to offer an alternative vision of the organization of political society. So we had a nice paradox here, that the Western and Eastern states most integrated into the world market attributed their economic success to different political philosophies.

This conjunction of state and market provided the framework for globalization in East Asia. It is not my argument that these features were indispensible to the global integration of their economies, but that they played a key role in that process and that their examination sheds light on the processes and consequences of globalization. Some key features are discussed next.

Political Authoritarianism

The economic development of East Asian countries has been achieved through policies that have favored capital, especially foreign capital. The attraction of East Asia to foreign investment has lain in cheap natural resources, a skilled and at the same time disciplined work force, low wages, and low taxes. Two dominant, interconnected features have been political authoritarianism, intended to assure foreign and domestic investors of political stability, and the availability of cheap labor.

Even countries like Japan, Singapore, and Malaysia, which had the outward trappings of democracy, were run under the hegemony of one-party or coalition rule that severely restricted or neutralized open political competition. Except for Japan, all of these countries had draconian legislation that permitted state authorities to detain persons they did not like for long periods without trial and to ban political or social organizations. All of them rewarded friends and punished enemies through state interventions in the economy. Taiwan, Korea, Thailand, and the Philippines were governed by the military for long periods, and the government of Indonesia is still dominated by the armed forces. Hong Kong was a colony until June 30, 1997, without a whiff of democracy; in that respect the situation is scarcely better now.

There has been a gradual move to democracy and more accountable government in the region. However, whether it was necessary or not, economic development for much of the postwar period was accompanied by authoritarian governance, and indeed to a considerable extent economic success was offered as the justification for that type of governance.

The Regime of Labor

Authoritarianism was manifested most clearly in the restrictions on labor.[14] The regime of labor was very closely connected with the dynamics of globalization. Economic growth in Japan, South Korea, Taiwan, and Singapore was spurred by the low cost of labor. As labor costs escalated in these countries, their capital looked for cheaper sources of labor and found them in Malaysia, Thailand, and Indonesia, to which Western capital had also found its way for similar reasons. It has been said that the effect of international competition in the age of globalization is the tendency toward the reduction of labor costs, triggering a downward spiral. The integration of East Asian economies testifies to this hypothesis.

The subordination of labor was not achieved through a uniform labor regime in the region. In Singapore, labor was quickly coopted by Lee Kwan Yew's government through a corporatist strategy and the demise of an independent labor movement. In Japan, the labor movement was weakened by the legal difficulties of forming industrywide unions. Unions were enterprise based, assimilated into the "family" traditions of large enterprises, and thus rendered innocuous; there was little unionization in smaller firms. In Hong Kong and Taiwan, control over labor was exercised by the employers, principally through employment practices that favored kin and others from the employer's home region. Further, particularly in Hong Kong, the small size of enterprises makes unionization problematic. Only in South Korea was labor well organized, with robust trade unions with a tradition of tough collective bargaining. In general, nowhere in East Asia has a political party based its support on labor, in marked contrast to a similar period of industrialization in the West.

The repression of labor was also facilitated by the actual structure of the laws as well as the nature of economies. Few of the states have implemented the full range of labor rights outlined in the International Labor Organization conventions. Hong Kong, which by the 1970s had made the most progress in this respect, continued to record remarkably low rates of unionization, an active discouragement of union activity, and even now has no provision for collective bargaining. The weakness of labor was also brought about by the political fragmentation of unions between pro-PRC and pro-Taiwan forces.

A weak labor movement was both the cause and consequence of low wages and other employment policies. Employers were in most cases content with a

---

14. For my account of labor laws and conditions, I have drawn on Frederick Deyo, *Beneath the Miracle: Labor Subordination in the New Asian Industrialism* (Berkeley: University of California Press, 1989); and Anthony Woodiwiss, *Globalization, Human Rights and Labour in Pacific Asia* (Cambridge: Cambridge University Press, 1998). I am grateful to Dr. Woodiwiss for making a copy of his book manuscript available to me prior to its publication.

labor force that was transient, given the nature of work. The growth of migrant labor due to uneven development within the region, often with an unclear legal status, further weakened the labor movement (Dorothy Solinger discusses this trend in Chapter 12). During the period of economic growth in Korea and Taiwan under authoritarian regimes, the success of their import-substitution policies was to a large extent accounted for by policies that excluded labor from decision making and allowed the general exploitation of workers, particularly women.[15] Governments did intervene when labor stability was important, but for much of industry it was not important. When intervention was necessary to ensure labor stability, as in Singapore, or to curb the powers of unions, as in South Korea, the government did not hesitate to move in.

A longtime scholar of labor relations in East Asia has summarized the results of his research as follows. Writing in 1989, Frederic Deyo said East Asian development centered on rapid growth in light, labor-intensive export manufacturing:

> The attraction of young, low skilled, and often female workers to employment characterised by low pay, tedium, minimal job security, and lack of career mobility encourages low job commitment, high levels of turnover, and lack of attachment to work groups or firms. These circumstances impede independent unionization efforts among workers in light export industries, the pace setters for early export-oriented industrialization (EOI). In contrast, more skilled and secure male workers in the less dominant, heavy industries such as shipbuilding and automobile manufacturing (especially in South Korea) are able to challenge elite policies from a position of greater strength. . . . The greater the oppositional potential of workers, the greater the likelihood of elite intervention in industrial relations in order to repress or control labor dissent. The relatively intrusive role of the state in South Korea and Singapore stems in part from the greater structural capacity of workers there to challenge employers and state. Conversely, the continued vitality of employment controls in Hong Kong and Taiwan, and the lesser oppositional potential of workers there, invokes less direct state intervention in labor affairs.[16]

Welfare Provisions

The vulnerability of labor was emphasized by the lack of an adequate public welfare system. East Asian states did not develop the kind of "class compromise" that is generally credited with producing a form of social democracy in Europe, in which capitalism is moderated by extensive welfare provisions

15. Roger Goodman and Ito Peng, "The East Asian Welfare States: Peripatetic Learning, Adaptative Change, and Nation-Building," in Gosta Esping-Anderson, *Welfare States in Transition: National Adaptations in Global Economies* (London: Sage Publications, 1996), p. 202.
16. Deyo, *Beneath the Miracle: Labor Subordination in the New Asian Industrialism,* pp. 8–9.

covering unemployment and other benefits for those seriously disadvantaged by the market. Here again the position is far from uniform. Singapore is an outstanding example of a state that offers various public services, particularly in housing, education, and health, and since the 1960s Hong Kong has provided subsidized public housing to families below a prescribed income level. Nonetheless, these policies in Singapore are closely connected with economic and political controls over the public,[17] and in Hong Kong they provide industries with a disguised subsidy by encouraging people to move to new industrial sites and by enabling employers to provide lower wages. In general, East Asian states have not assumed responsibility for social welfare as such, leaving the distribution of resources to rather managed markets.

Two scholars well familiar with welfare policies in East Asia have summarized the position as follows:

> Very broadly speaking, welfare policy has been dominated by economic rather than social considerations supported by some underlying ideas of anti-welfarism and, especially, by resistance to the provision of government-guaranteed social welfare. The ruling elites have generally only accepted the institutional concept of social welfare when confronting political crisis; when this is overcome they return to the residual concept of social welfare . . . by drawing on "Confucian" cultural ideologies.[18]

Beginning in the mid 1970s there was concern in Japan that expenditures on social welfare would make it an unattractive place for investment in an increasingly competitive economy. Even the large corporations are unable to continue "welfare" policies of life employment and other benefits, which are now being phased out.[19]

CONCLUSION

It is evident that human rights have not fared well by economic globalization in East Asia. Undoubtedly economic growth has raised standards of education, health, and nutrition. However, these benefits have not accrued to all, certainly not to all equally. The market has created large disparities of income and wealth. In the midst of incredible affluence, there is appalling poverty. The effects of marketization are vividly demonstrated in China, where there is little doubt that a large number of people live in harsher eco-

17. Christopher Tremewan, *The Political Economy of Social Control in Singapore* (Basingstoke: Macmillan, 1994).
18. Goodman and Peng, "The East Asian Welfare States," p. 198.
19. See Dani Rodrik, "Sense and Nonsense in the Globalization Debate," *Foreign Policy* (Summer 1997), pp. 19–36.

nomic circumstances than when the state still practiced socialist policies. Their access to health, education, and housing has suffered under the application of the market principles to the provision of these services.[20] Equality is not favored even in formal terms.

Nor did East Asian economies, with the partial exception of Hong Kong, produce market-oriented rights, forms of governance that ensure predictability and openness, and the Rule of Law, for reasons that have been indicated. Capitalism in Asia has managed with rather truncated forms of legality, relying more on executive favors and interventions than judicial adjudications. The market has not generated an ideology of equality or rights. On the contrary, governments have needed to nurture ideologies that are antithetical to rights, conscious that rights are inconsistent with their economic and political agenda.

This dilemma is very evident in China, where there was hardly any regime of law when it began on its modernization policies in the 1980s. It was recognized early that an extensive set of laws and the strengthening of legal institutions were necessary for foreign investment and internal marketization. The regime of law did not lead to more rights, although Chinese academics were able to use Western legal theory to argue that the market is a "commodity economy" that is based on notions of rights and legality, and the widening of the market did result in freer access to information, growing private media, and alternative sites of influence.[21]

The dislocations in traditional structures have for the most part not produced liberation from oppression. Frequently the oppression of the market has been added to older social discriminations, for example, of women and children

---

20. See Chapter 12. See also Ann Kent, *Between Freedom and Subsistence: China and Human Rights* (Hong Kong: Oxford University Press, 1993), especially pp. 160–66.

21. For an account of academic debates on the rights-based nature of the market economy, see Albert Chen, "The Developing Theory of Law and Market Economy in Contemporary China," in Wang Guigo and Wei Zhenying, eds., *Legal Development in China: Market Economy and Law* (Hong Kong: Sweet and Maxwell, 1996). However, the limits of this approach and its potential for the rule of law are illustrated by the following remarks in the speech of President Jiang Zemin to the 15th Congress of the Chinese Communist Party: "The deepening of the reform of the economic structure . . . requires that, under the pre-condition of adhering to the Four Cardinal Principles, we should continue to press ahead with the reform of the political structure, further extend the scope of socialist democracy and improve the socialist legal system, governing the country according to law and making it a socialist country ruled by law." He goes on to explain that he does not have in mind "western models" of democracy, but a Leninist one (overlooking the Western provenance of the latter), while his vision of the rule by law (which he described as the "objective demand of a socialist market economy") is captured in his statement: "In ruling the country by law, we can unify the adherence to Party leadership, development of people's democracy, and doing things in strict accordance with the law, thus ensuring, institutionally and legally, that the Party's basic line and basic policies are carried out without fail, and the Party plays the role of the core of leadership at all times, commanding the whole situation and coordinating the efforts of all quarters." Quoted from the Internet source, http://www.chinadaily.net/cndy\history/15/fulltext.html. The quotations appear on pages 15 and 16.

(although, on the other hand, it should be noted that ethnic discrimination in Japan is harder to square with the theory or practice of the market, and in India the "untouchables" who have left their traditional habitats by moving to urban centers are much less the victims of social oppression). As for the professional and middle classes, despite their spectacular rise they have not been a force for freedom or democratization, in large part because of their dependence on state patronage. The East Asian experience shows that states can effectively "humanize" markets only if they are democratic. On the other hand, the ideology of rights has been an effective means for the mobilization of disadvantaged people. Rights are the common currency of all sorts of NGOs, women, journalists, trade unions, and indigenous peoples, although governments have sought to blunt the edge of human rights ideology through appeals to "tradition" and spurious claims of ethnic resistance and "foreign plots."

The shrinking arena for human rights has been aggravated by the growing role and activities of transnational and large national corporations, which play such a dominant role in East Asia. International and national regimes of human rights typically exclude private individuals or groups from their application, restricting redress for violation of rights to actions against public authorities. As the power of many states declines and that of corporations rises, the capacity of the latter to violate the rights of others, or to create conditions in which rights become harder to exercise or protect, has increased vastly. Freedom of expression is now largely in the hands of corporations, which effectively determine what is published. They have enormous powers of censorship. In pursuit of profitable ventures, they are prepared to make deals or establish understandings with states as to what kind of television programs they will not show or books they would not publish (as publisher Rupert Murdoch has done with China, and many foreign publishers with Singapore[22]).

Through their employment practices, corporations are in a position to negate norms of equal opportunity and nondiscrimination. Their employment practices may have more impact on people's health and sense of security than policies of governments. Overseas Chinese capitalism is particularly oppressive, with low standards of industrial safety resulting in an appalling degree of industrial injuries and deaths, and extreme exploitation of labor. Many Asian corporations have wreaked extraordinary damage on the environment within as well as outside the region through their predatory practices, such as in forestry. They have successfully prevented attempts to introduce legislation or have evaded the implementation of legislation that would regulate their conduct in these areas.

The economic and financial crisis currently affecting East Asian states pro-

---

22. See Chapter 11 for a discussion of state censorship of foreign publishers in Singapore.

vides further insights into the nature of globalization and its effect on human rights. I deal first with some immediate consequences. The response to the crisis has demonstrated the ability of international capital to discipline states that fall out of line with the imperatives of globalization. Despite their anger at this intervention, Malaysian Prime Minister Mahathir Mohamad and other Asian officials have been powerless in its face. Far from capital being accountable to the state, the state has now become accountable to capital. Nowhere is this more strikingly evident than in the reversal of policies of the new president of South Korea, Kim Dae-jung, a lifetime champion of democracy and people's rights, who, in his first official act, surrendered state policies to the dictates of the International Monetary Fund (IMF).

The terms on which the IMF has provided the "bailout" requires that these states repeal the remaining barriers to their full integration in the world economy and introduce "strong fiscal policies." Typically, the governments have to (1) liberalize investments by foreign capital and establish "level playing fields," (2) introduce transparency of economic transactions and tougher financial regulations, (3) privatize and deregulate trade and the economy, (4) introduce "international" accounting standards to be supervised by global accountancy firms, (5) provide for the independence of central banks, (6) "liberalize and stabilize labor markets" (meaning remove legal protection for workers and trade unions), and (7) reduce government expenditures (thus further curtailing welfare provisions). In these ways the dynamics of globalization are accelerated.

Second, the response shows the decisive shift of power to the major economic powers and the international economic institutions that they have promoted. The measures undertaken by them have not only obscured their responsibility for the crisis, they were designed to rescue transnational banks and financial institutions from the consequences of their cupidity and imprudence in advancing huge loans to these states (which lie at the core of the crisis). A key element in the crisis is the competition between Asian national bourgeoisies and Western capitalists. The IMF and the World Bank (acting on behalf of international capital) have arrogated to themselves the responsibility to exact accountability from these states and their national bourgeoisies, through periodic reviews and conditionalities. So much for level playing fields!

Third, I turn to some specific consequences of the crisis and remedial measures. The more obvious is the weakening of the position of workers and trade unions. In South Korea agreement has been reached on the reduction of job security and other union rights that were the subject of massive and successful union action at the end of 1996. Elsewhere, where there is less to protect, workers' rights have come under renewed pressure. Large numbers of jobs have disappeared and redundancies have increased. The workers hit hardest are migrants, now a significant number in the region. Migrant workers enjoy few rights under regional or national laws. Many are without any formal permission or documents, and their informal status is tolerated because they, in part owing to their legal status, accept low wages and miserable working conditions. The first victims of recession, they are forced to return to their state of nationality, where they face grim prospects. The situation of redundant workers or returned migrants is aggravated by the lack of welfare provisions.

These and other factors threatening social security have intensified the controversy regarding the causes of the crisis. One of two extreme positions, hitherto unfashionable, is that it was brought on by undemocratic and unaccountable political systems in which the close relationship between political and business elites gave rise to favoritism and corruption. The authority of political leaders is called into question with the decline of the economic performance that formerly provided legitimacy for authoritarian rule and inegalitarian economic development. This development is likely to sharpen a new ideological consciousness regarding politics and market economic relations that has hitherto been retarded by the persistence of older ideologies whose origins lie in a more communally oriented society – reflecting the time gap between ideology and changed material conditions.

On the other hand, the proponents of "Asian values" have been quick to argue that the more democratic countries like South Korea have been as prone to the crisis as the less democratic like Indonesia. They ascribe responsibility for the crisis to the nefarious activities of international speculators and the design of the West to undermine Asia's economic and political success. They have also challenged some assumptions of world markets. Mahathir Mohamad went so far as to attack the legitimacy of the markets his government could not control when he said, "Markets corrupt, and absolute markets corrupt absolutely."

It is clear that "Asian values" will be one casualty of the crisis. In the 1980s and 1990s "Asian values" seemed to fit in with the imperatives of globalization, with their emphasis on minimal state welfare, limited trade union rights, reliance on family, and restricted political participation. In a similar fashion the present crisis has shown their negative aspects, dynastic politics, nepotism, cronyism, the lack of transparency and accountability, the absence of or failure to enforce regulations – and the general disregard of rights of people. The alacrity with which the West has blamed the crisis on these malpractices has further dented "Asian values." The ability of governments to fashion national ideologies has suffered a major setback and will continue to atrophy in the face of new information technologies, which promote more openness and encouraging pluralism.

However, it is hard to predict how the crisis will affect political development in the region. That it will bring about some social instability (including "ethnic" conflict) and challenges to established regimes is obvious. In some states in which democratic movements and practices have developed in recent years, the crisis may lead to political reform, new forms of participation and accountability, and the recognition of the importance of rights (as in Thailand, where a reform-oriented constitution could not have been adopted without the crisis). States like Indonesia with stronger traditions of military rule and the frequent resort to repression are less likely candidates for democracy and rights. There the result may be greater use of state violence to deal with social unrest. In Malaysia, for example, there is now considerable repression against migrant workers, including a threat by the head of the police to use the harsh Internal Security Act against them.[23]

Whether the response to the crisis is a shift to greater democracy and rights will depend ultimately on domestic forces. Global finances and the economic institutions that support them, and that seem currently in the driver's seat, have shown little predilection for democracy, as they are preoccupied with opening up markets further and strengthening conditions for globalization. They are attempting to use the state to underwrite the process of globalization in the face of social and political unrest. In a globalized world, progressive states may have greater ability but, influenced by trade considerations, less inclination to influence the human rights practices of other states. If my general analysis of the negative effects of globalization on rights and social justice is correct, the contemporary economic crisis in East Asia will merely accentuate them.

CHAPTER 11

ECONOMIC DEVELOPMENT, LEGAL REFORM, AND RIGHTS IN SINGAPORE AND TAIWAN

KEVIN Y. L. TAN

INTRODUCTION

In 1959 political scientist Seymour Martin Lipset wrote a now-famous article in which he argued that greater economic growth increases the likelihood that stable democratic forms of politics will emerge.[1] In the twenty-first century, East and Southeast Asia will likely, despite the current currency crisis and economic meltdown, continue to develop at a rapid pace.[2] Does Lipset's argument hold true with respect to human rights in the region? Will rapid social and economic change result in conceptions of human rights being transformed? Indeed, will increased economic growth encourage the development of a more rigorous human rights regime in these countries? Of course, many factors impede the full realization of human rights in East Asia, and it is impossible to deal with them all in an article of this length. I shall concern myself primarily with just one facet of this general question: the question of law, legal culture, and legal reform.

In this chapter, I consider what aspects of the legal culture are likely to change with increasing economic development and what aspects are not. I also examine the reasons why these aspects of legal culture are either conducive or resistant to change. Case studies and examples from two countries – Singapore and Taiwan – are used to illustrate the points raised. I have chosen these two countries for several reasons. They provide a useful comparison

1. See Seymour Martin Lipset, *Political Man* (Baltimore: Johns Hopkins University Press, 1980).
2. Thus far, despite some devaluation in the currencies of Taiwan and Singapore, these two countries have not been directly affected by the currency crisis sweeping throughout Asia in terms of any loss of confidence in their economies. Nonetheless, the fallout from the other economies – Thailand, Indonesia, Malaysia, and Korea – has cast a cloud of gloom over the region generally.

because they are similar in four important respects, but differ in regime type. First, both Singapore and Taiwan are island states that were created under less than propitious circumstances. Second, both territories have large Sinic populations. Singapore's population is largely made up of ethnic Chinese (78 percent), and Taiwan is essentially a Chinese society. In that sense, many of their citizens draw their cultural waters from the same well – China. Third, neither country is party to either the International Covenant on Civil and Political Rights (ICCPR) or the International Covenant on Social, Economic and Cultural Rights (ICSECR).[3] Fourth, both have achieved remarkable economic growth in the last two decades and have been touted (along with Korea and Hong Kong) as "Asian tigers";[4] they have thus succeeded in carving a niche for themselves in the international arena through rapid growth and development.

Nonetheless, these two states differ in that political commentators have often described Singapore as a nonliberal regime and Taiwan as being more liberal and democratic. The evolution of Singapore's legal system ensured a stable environment for international commerce and finance. From a nation-building viewpoint, the ruling party leadership ensured that the material needs and aspirations of the people were met through its successful housing program and the provision of the economic infrastructure. The government's preoccupation (even obsession) with the need to ensure Singapore's survival – both politically and economically – perpetuated the crisis mentality that continues to afflict the Singaporean society. In such a scenario, civil and political rights have taken a back seat.

Taiwan's extraordinary economic performance was similarly achieved by its political stability, which provided a conducive environment in which economic growth could take place; its rapid growth would therefore appear to support Lee Kuan Yew's "development first" thesis. But in the case of Taiwan, the ruling party was determined to make it a showcase of noncommunist development. As a nation-building strategy, this stands in marked contrast to the Singaporean government's emphasis on dissipating potential internal conflict by building an egalitarian society based on multiculturalism, general prosperity, and public projects such as a successful housing program. These strategies led to very different outcomes in terms of political development.

3. It is important to note that Taiwan is not a party to either of the covenants because it is no longer a member of the United Nations. But even when it was a member up through 1979 it did not become a signatory.
4. Singapore's 1995 GDP per capita was U.S. $14,990 while that of Taiwan was U.S. $10,055. For comparison, the GDP per capita of the United States is U.S. $23,474 and that of Great Britain U.S. $15,974.

I argue that the remarkable rate of economic development in Singapore and Taiwan was predicated on the establishment of rule of law in the sense of adherence to a predictable, rationalized system of commercial and investment laws. Government promotion of economic and social rights, such as the right to housing and an equitable distribution of land, was also fundamental to development. However, as has been observed elsewhere, the very legal reforms enacted to promote economic growth and redistribution of wealth at the societal level were often at the expense of individual civil and political rights. A comparison of these two states reveals a less intuitive conclusion: Whereas in Singapore the authoritarian leadership structure that brought about rapid development has not yielded to more liberal forms of government, Taiwan's political system is undergoing a transition to a more "Western" liberal representative democracy and respect for civil and political rights. I argue that the different outcomes in terms of political regime are the result of nation-building decisions made by these countries' leaders in response to perceived threats. In Singapore, the internal threat of ethnic division and exploitation of communal rivalry by the Malayan Communist Party caused the government to promote an idea of nation based on economic prosperity and racial harmony. The apparent result of this, in terms of cultural norms, is that the majority of Singapore's citizens place a higher value on economic growth than on respect for individual rights. The Taiwanese government responded to the security threat posed by mainland China by counterposing Taiwan as a bastion of democratic values in the face of mainland authoritarianism.

In the case studies to follow, I will examine some of the problems in the area of civil and political rights, and examine the trends that seem to have emerged in these two countries. In the conclusion I will return to the question of whether greater economic development is likely to promote the development of a strong human rights regime.

THE SINGAPORE CASE

Singapore inherited a common law legal system from the British, who occupied the island from 1819 to 1958. From the end of World War II until the late 1960s, Singapore was constantly plagued by two problems – the threat of a communist takeover, and communal and ethnic divisions, which pitted Singapore's majority Chinese population against the minority Malays. These problems were compounded by the fact that Singapore was essentially a Chinese state in a Malay–Muslim region, with Malaysia to the north and Indonesia to the south, and the fact that communism and communalism were in fact reinforcing cleavages, with many Chinese supporting the outlawed Malayan Communist Party. To deal with the communist insurgency, the British proclaimed a state of emergency throughout the whole of Malaya and Singapore in 1948, and enacted the Internal Security Act, which empowered the executive to detain without trial persons suspected of being subversives. Singapore inherited the Internal Security Act from this period even after its expulsion from Malaysia. At the time of Singapore's independence in 1965, key national values had already been clearly identified by the ruling People's Action Party (PAP) and disseminated both through statements of the ruling party's values and through state documents.[5] They may be summarized as following two general principles: first, the idea of building a nation based on multiracialism, and second, the belief that a more just and equal society could only be achieved if there were social and economic stability in a Singapore governed by law and order. To this end, the entire government machinery was used to mobilize the nation, whose existence depended almost wholly on its ability to organize itself to compete in the international economy. An examination of the government's development strategy reveals consistent attention to a set of social and economic imperatives founded on three basics: first, establishing predictability in the legal system; second, securing economic development and industrialization; and third, inculcating a sense of nationhood among the populace.

The continued application of English law augments Singapore's role as an international financial center: international transactions are undertaken there against a legal backdrop common to other financial centers, such as Hong Kong and London. Although the maintenance of English commercial and property rights law enabled Singapore to become a leading financial center in Asia, the government also utilized the legal and constitutional apparatus to increasingly strengthen its hold on power and to discourage the growth of a viable political opposition.

Among developing countries, Singapore's human rights record can be considered average.[6] There are no extrajudicial killings or indiscriminate imprisonment of political dissidents – in short, no gross violations of human rights principles – which occur in some Asian countries, such as China or Myanmar. Nevertheless, there are problems, most of which reside in the realm of civil and political rights. In the following analysis, I will first examine the

---

5. See the following documents: "PAP Manifesto," as reprinted in Fong Sip Chee, *The PAP Story – The Pioneering Years* (Singapore: Times Periodicals for Chai Chee Branch of the People's Action Party, 1979), p. 23; "The Proclamation of Singapore," in *Independence of Singapore Agreement* (Government Gazette Notification No. 1824, August 9, 1965); and the debate on multiracialism in Singapore in Singapore Parliamentary Debates Official Reports, 22 December 1965, at columns 429–30.

6. Even the much-criticized Charles Humana index on human rights gave Singapore a 61 percent rating in 1984 and a 60 percent rating in 1991. See Charles Humana, *World Human Rights Guide*, 3rd ed. (New York: Oxford University Press, 1992), pp. 5–8. See Chapter 5 for a critique of the Humana *Guide*.

extent to which selected economic, social, and cultural rights have been promoted. Next, I will deal with two problems in civil and political rights: preventive detention and freedom of speech and the press.

Nation Building and Economic Rights

One consistent theme that has dominated the political discourse and shaped the destiny of Singapore since decolonization discussions began in 1945 is its economic viability. Self-government for Singapore and eventual independence were to have been realized through merger with Malaysia. No one thought that Singapore could survive economically on its own. The main strategy for economic development was massive industrialization, attraction of foreign direct investment, and diversification of the country's economic portfolio. To do this, the ruling People's Action Party (PAP) considered it essential to centralize all the state's resources and power in the hands of the government through legislation.

The constitutional right to own property and to receive fair compensation for state acquisition of such property, embodied in Article 13(1) of the Malaysian Federal Constitution as it applied to Singapore, was deliberately left out of the postindependence Constitution. The overall national interest, which required that vast tracts of land be reclaimed and developed for industrial use, was given priority in the passage of the Land Acquisition Act. Two key objectives were secured through the powers accorded under this act, since it allowed the government to acquire land for both industrial development and public housing.

The PAP public housing scheme has generally been acknowledged to be the most successful social engineering program in Singapore, and it utilizes the law through legislation as its basic operating platform.[7] The Housing and Development Act of 1959 created an agency charged with the duty of building homes for the rapidly growing population. This massive task was undertaken by the government not as a profitable enterprise but as one that underscored the need to give the citizens, whose forbears had been itinerant immigrants, a stake in the country. This was necessary in order to create a sense of belonging and to allow the people to sink their roots into the Singaporean soil. The failure of the Singapore Improvement Trust (SIT) – the

---

7. For a highly critical assessment of Singapore's housing policy and program, see Christopher Tremewan, "Public Housing: The Working-Class Barracks," in Christopher Tremewan, *The Political Economy of Social Control in Singapore* (London: Macmillan, 1994), chapter 3. A more balanced view is found in Chua Beng Huat, "Not Depoliticized but Ideologically Successful: The Public Housing Programme," in Chua Beng Huat, *Communitarian Ideology and Democracy in Singapore* (London: Routledge, 1995), chapter 6.

Housing and Development Board's (HDB's) predecessor statutory board – to provide sufficient low-cost housing for the public left Singapore's post-independence government with a crippling housing shortage. Indeed, between 1928 and 1959, the SIT was only able to build just over 23,000 units, or about 716 units a year.[8] Through its Five Year Plans from 1960 to 1980 the HDB was able to build a total of 372,000 units of low-cost public housing and, by 1981, almost 70 percent of Singaporeans were living in HDB flats.[9] In addition, by keeping the cost low and loan repayments flexible, almost 90 percent of Singaporeans were able to own their own homes. This impressive feat was facilitated to a large extent by a system of enforced savings through the Central Provident Fund contributions levied on all workers and employers. The system of compulsory savings through provident funds, already in existence at independence, was developed further with the passing of the Central Provident Fund Act, giving the people an even greater stake in Singapore.

The success of Singapore's public housing program has contributed immeasurably to the PAP's legitimacy to govern and has vindicated its approach to national development. The HDB was, after all, the first statutory board created by the PAP when it came to power in 1959. At the same time, the housing program successfully desegregated former ethnic enclaves.[10]

Although public housing could be considered the PAP's greatest claim to legitimacy, it is also its nemesis. In the recent general elections of January 1997, the issue of upgrading public housing became a highly contested political issue. In its bid to make the people more "accountable" for their votes, the PAP MPs and their stalwarts linked voting to upgrading programs that would enhance the value of public housing properties. Prime Minister Goh Chok Tong went so far as to say that opposition wards would turn into slums if the people did not vote carefully. Although the PAP won the elections

8. See Cedric Pugh, "The Political Economy of Public Housing," in Kernial Singh Sandhu and Paul Wheatley, eds., *The Management of Success: The Moulding of Modern Singapore* (Singapore: Institute of Southeast Asian Studies, 1989), pp. 833–59; Chua Beng Huat, *Communitarian Ideology and Democracy in Singapore*, pp. 124–46; Tremewan, *The Political Economy of Social Control in Singapore*, pp. 45–73; Jon S. T. Quah, "Public Housing," in Jon S. T. Quah, Chan Heng Chee, and Seah Chee Meow, eds., *The Government and Politics of Singapore* (Singapore: Oxford University Press, 1985), pp. 234–5.

9. This figure is now closer to 95 percent.

10. As sociologist Riaz Hassan noted several decades ago, public housing is playing an important role in the desegregation of these ethnic enclaves. The conditions of obtaining a public flat are citizenship, income, and family size, not ethnic or racial affiliation. The public housing estates are thus desegregated communities where Chinese, Malays, Indians-Pakistanis, and Eurasians live side by side, in many instances for the first time. See Riaz Hassan, "Some Sociological Implications of Public Housing in Singapore," *Southeast Asian Journal of Sociology* vol. 2 (1969), p. 24.

handsomely, there was much unhappiness with the PAP's use of this tactic and in the politicization of public housing.

Civil and Political Rights: Preventive Detention

The main problems and violations under this category stem from the continued enforcement of statutes such as the Internal Security Act (ISA) and the Criminal Law Temporary Provisions Act (CLTPA). The ISA has been invoked several times in the last twenty years to deal with political "subversives." The most recent and highly publicized instances were the 1987 detentions of 22 alleged Marxist conspirators and the 1988 rearrests of some of these 22 detainees. This included political dissident and former Solicitor-General Francis Seow, who was arrested for allegedly conspiring with an American diplomat "to manipulate and instigate Singaporeans, in order to bring about a particular political outcome." Likewise, the CLTPA, originally a temporary measure to deal with the scourge of gangsterism and secret societies, has been invoked to deal with suspected drug traffickers.

The power to preventively detain suspects without trial, be they subversives or drug traffickers, opens the floodgates for potential abuse by politicians who are ruthless enough to invoke them for political purposes. The nub of the problem is found in Section 8 of the Internal Security Act, which provides that if "the President is satisfied with respect to any person that, with a view to preventing that person from acting in any manner prejudicial to the security of Singapore or any part thereof or to the maintenance of public order or essential services therein, it is necessary to do so, the minister shall make an order" to detain this person for a period not exceeding two years.[11] Such detention may be extended for a further period or periods not exceeding two years each. Singapore's longest serving detainee, Chia Thye Poh, a former university don and member of the opposition Barisan Sosialis, was detained under the ISA for more than twenty-two years without being brought to trial.

The idea that a person might be detained without trial, without recourse to the judicial system, and without the need for the executive to produce substantial evidence against the detainees violates rules of natural justice. Again, the approach taken by the Singaporean political leadership is based

---

11. The President's "satisfaction" was held to be reviewable by the groundbreaking Court of Appeal decision in Chng Suan Tze v. Minister for Home Affairs & Ors [1989] 1 Malayan Law Journal 69. However, Parliament immediately sought to nullify the effect of this decision by amending both the Constitution and the Internal Security Act. The constitutionality of these changes is very much in doubt. See the Constitution of the Republic of Singapore (Amendment) Act (1989), which inserted a new Article 149(3), and the Internal Security (Amendment) Act (No. 2 of 1989).

on "efficiency." Lee has repeatedly pointed out that he would not hesitate to use the ISA if he thought it would be better for Singapore's political stability and harmony. In a press conference in 1989, he said:

> It is not a practice, nor will I allow subversives to get away by insisting that I've got to prove everything against them in a court of law or [produce] evidence that will stand up to the strict rules of evidence of a court of law.[12]

The price that the people of Singapore have paid for stability and efficiency is the curtailment of some of the most fundamental human freedoms and rights in the Universal Declaration of Human Rights. For the government, the fall of communism and socialist governments around the world has done little to weaken the case for the continued existence of these laws since the fear of communal or ethnic division continues to loom large. In the General Elections of January 1997, the ruling People's Action Party (PAP) accused Workers' Party candidate Tang Liang Hong of being a Chinese chauvinist and labeled him a threat to racial harmony. Tang subsequently lost a defamation lawsuit brought by the PAP leaders and was ordered to pay S $8 million in damages.[13] With respect to the ISA, the perception among the general population is that the government has acted in good faith in recent years, although elites see this somewhat differently.[14] This does not change the fact that a less scrupulous government will be left free to exploit its almost untrammeled power in relation to preventive detentions.

Civil and Political Rights: Freedom of the Press and Freedom of Speech

Singapore has had its fair share of bad press, especially in foreign newspapers and magazines such as the *Far Eastern Economic Review*, the *Asian Wall Street Journal, Time, Asiaweek,* and most recently, the *International Herald Tribune*.[15]

---

12. See *Straits Times* (June 5, 1987).

13. See *Straits Times* (May 30, 1997), p. 1. Tang was declared bankrupt in February 1998 when he failed to pay about S $700,000 of his damages.

14. It has been a good ten years since the controversial arrests of the alleged proponents of what the government has called the "pro-Marxist conspiracy" in 1987–8. These arrests shocked the Singaporean public. Many local and foreign onlookers remain unconvinced of the government's case for detaining these individuals. For a personal account of this episode, see Francis T. Seow, *To Catch a Tartar: A Dissident in Lee Kuan Yew's Prison* (New Haven: Yale Southeast Asia Studies Monograph No. 42, 1994).

15. The editor and a writer of the *International Herald Tribune* were sued by Senior Minister Lee Kuan Yew, Deputy Prime Ministers B. G. Lee and Hsien Loong, and Prime Minister Goh Chok Tong for defamation in connection with an article published in the paper titled "The Claims About Asian Values Don't Usually Bear Scrutiny." The High Court found a passage of the article to be defamatory to the plaintiffs and awarded the senior minister S $350,000 in damages, and the prime minister and B. G. Lee received S $300,000 each. See Lee Kuan Yew & Anor v. Vinocur & Ors, [1993] 3 Singapore Law Reports 477.

Freedom of speech and expression, the right to assemble peaceably and without arms, and the right to form associations may all be restricted by ordinary legislation if Parliament considers it necessary or expedient.

Singapore has long had restrictive legislation limiting the media.[16] Most of these restrictions are aimed at preventing the mass media from being used as a political weapon to destabilize the government or to foment communist or communalist trouble. In the 1970s and 1980s, Singapore had a lively media scene, with independent newspapers such as the *Eastern Sun,* the *Singapore Herald,* the *Singapore Monitor,* and even the *New Nation* vying for public readership. One by one, these newspapers have been closed down by the government under the Newspapers and Printing Presses Act (NPPA) of 1974 on the grounds that they were funded by foreign sources with a hidden agenda, that it was in the public interest to do so, or that it was a waste of resources to have so many competing papers.[17]

By 1984, the government created a massive conglomerate, Singapore Press Holdings Ltd., which controls all the English-language and Chinese-language dailies in Singapore. This was made possible by the wide discretion afforded the government by the Newspapers and Printing Presses Act; through the Act's licensing mechanism, the government is able to control the press. The NPPA also enables the government to exert control over the structure of a newspaper company by requiring that all directors be citizens of Singapore and that no person either directly or indirectly hold more than 3 percent of the ordinary shares of such a company.

With the local press firmly under its control, the government amended the NPPA in 1986 to empower the Minister for Information and the Arts "declare any newspaper published outside Singapore to be a newspaper engaging in the domestic politics of Singapore." Under this amendment, the minister may restrict the sale or distribution of any foreign newspaper. Since the passing of these amendments, various foreign newspapers and magazines have had their circulation restricted by the Singapore government. The first was *Time* in October 1986, followed by the *Asian Wall Street Journal* in December that same year (and again in 1990), the *Far Eastern Economic Review* in 1987, and, in 1995, the *International Herald Tribune.* Most of these newspapers and magazines had their circulations restricted either because they failed to correct "factual" errors in their reporting on Singapore matters or

16. See, for example, the Sedition Act of 1964, the Undesirable Publications Act of 1967, and the Newspapers and Printing Presses Act of 1974.

17. For a racy but factually accurate account of the government's relations with the press since 1959, see T. S. Selvan, *Singapore, The Ultimate Island: Lee Kuan Yew's Untold Story* (Victoria, Australia: Freeway Books, 1990), pp. 105–28.

because they refused to publish in full the government's reply to what it perceived to be erroneous, malicious, or misleading stories. In addition to curbing their circulation, the government has also prosecuted the newspapers for defamation or contempt.[18]

Trends in Legal Reform

In the last twenty years, legal reforms in Singapore have largely been in the areas of commercial and investment law, changes that have been prompted by the need to maintain Singapore's economic viability and competitive edge. Alas, there have been no corresponding progressive reforms in the area of civil and political rights. The ISA remains in the statute books, and the CLTPA is constantly renewed. In areas such as labor rights, the National Trades Union Congress (NTUC), which is the umbrella body of most of the other unions in Singapore, pursues a tripartite partnership with the government and employers. The secretary-general of the NTUC is also a "minister without portfolio" in the PAP cabinet. Elections have been fair, with no reports of vote buying or election fraud, although the practice of putting serial numbers on ballot papers has been much criticized because this may have a chilling effect on the electorate. Also, from an institutional viewpoint, the short notice required to be given for elections and the minimum campaign period of nine days may hinder the democratic process.[19]

True to the PAP's position that it is not their job to nurture the opposition but to win votes, political opponents have been the prime target of government ire. The PAP government has been willing to use all the legal weapons in its arsenal to expose politicians whom it considers to be unscrupulous, morally questionable, or dangerous to racial harmony in Singapore. Despite the odds, the opposition parties have managed to make dents in the PAP armor: In the 1991 general elections, four opposition members were voted into Singapore's 81-seat Parliament, and in the 1997

18. See, for example, Dow Jones Publishing Co. (Asia) v. Attorney-General of Singapore [1989] 2 Malayan Law Journal 385; and on appeal at [1989] 3 Malayan Law Journal 321; and Attorney-General v. Barry J Wain & Ors [1991] 2 Malayan Law Journal 310; Attorney-General v. Christopher Lingle & Ors [1995] 1 Singapore Law Reports 696. For an excellent account of the role of the press in Singapore, see Roger Mitton, "What Role for the Press: Singapore Answers," *Asiaweek* vol. 25 (September 1992), pp. 44–55.

19. In practical terms, this is not a major problem given that signs of impending elections – pay raises and bonuses for civil servants, school holidays (to enable teachers to help in vote counting and poll station management), the predictable history of election periods (usually four years) – are often there for all to see, and surprises are few and far between. That said, however, Prime Minister Goh Chok Tong has surprised many commentators and observers by scheduling the 1991 general elections just slightly more than three years into the term of Parliament and allowing Parliament to run almost the full term before calling the next general elections in January 1997.

general elections, two opposition members were returned to their seats. Singapore is far from developing an effective two-party system as envisaged in its Westminster constitutional structure, but these developments are encouraging.

The only significant development that offers some measure of checks and balances on the executive's power with respect to its ISA preventive detention powers is the creation of the elected presidency in 1991. Previously, Singapore's president was a ceremonial head of state wielding no real power. However, with the passage of the Republic of Singapore Constitution (Amendment) Act of 1991, the president is elected in a nationwide ballot and is granted wider powers.[20] Of particular relevance to our discussion is the new Article 151(4), which provides that no person shall be detained or continue to be detained under the ISA if the Advisory Board recommends his or her release unless the president concurs with the executive's decision to reject the board's recommendations in favor of further detention.

Institutional changes are, however, only half the story. State-driven change is often slow and tends to operate in favor of the state's interests as perceived by Singapore's rulers rather than by perceptions on the ground. This is where a caveat to Lipset's argument must be made. Singapore's phenomenally successful economic and social transformation has brought about few changes in its civil and political rights arena. This is so despite the fact that, according to a recent comparative survey among Singaporeans and Westerners, Singaporeans' hierarchies of rights are not very different from those of their Western counterparts, save in some areas such as respect for authority and freedom of speech.[21] This situation can be contrasted with state-led changes in Taiwan, where, I argue, the nation-building process has led to development of a national identity based on democratic government rather than on economic prosperity per se.

THE TAIWAN CASE

Since 1948, the island of Taiwan has been controlled by General Chiang Kai-shek's Kuomintang (KMT) army and its successor governments. The Western-style constitution of the Republic of China (1946) was replaced by "Temporary Provisions Effective During the Period of Communist Rebellion" in May 1948 and remained in force until the Temporary Provisions were abolished in 1991.

20. Although the president is elected on a nationwide ballot, the qualifications demanded of presidential candidates are extremely stringent and favor a largely pro-establishment individual, such as a former cabinet minister or high court judge.
21. See Rosalind Ng, "Culture and Human Rights in Singapore: An Empirical Study" (directed research dissertation, National University of Singapore, Faculty of Law, 1996/7).

From 1948 to 1977, while the KMT was consolidating its position by outlawing all forms of political opposition, it was also successfully reforming Taiwan's economy. The KMT's sustained political legitimacy was maintained by the success of its economic and reform programs. Indeed, notwithstanding the liberalization of Taiwanese politics in the 1990s, the rise of alternative choices, and the lowering of the KMT's majorities, it remains a powerful force to be reckoned with. The first section to follow will discuss how Taiwanese social and economic rights benefited from KMT rule.

The main human rights problems in Taiwan, like Singapore, historically are to be found in the realm of civil and political rights. KMT domination of the political scene through repression of dissident factions and of nationalists arguing for greater native participation in policy making and political leadership has led to many human rights abuses. I will outline two categories of civil and political rights reforms: the lifting of martial law and the ban on opposition parties and the instituting of regular elections, and conditions for fundamental liberties.

Social and Economic Rights and Development

Immediately following its occupation of Taiwan in 1949, Chiang's military government launched a series of economic programs to rehabilitate and restore Taiwan's agricultural and industrial production as well as to stabilize prices.[22] Chiang's priority was clear. In 1950, he said:

> To build a prosperous Taiwan is the basic pre-condition for the success of our anti-Communist and anti-Russian campaign. . . . What we should be worried about is whether we can build up a truly prosperous Taiwan to serve as a prototype for the recovered mainland. . . . We are confident that we can transform Taiwan into a model province, founded on Dr. Sun Yat-sen's Three Principles of the People. It is by so doing that we can lay a solid foundation for the reconstruction of the recovered mainland.[23]

The most important of these reforms was the three-step "land-to-the-tiller" reform program, which sought to redistribute land and to reduce the gap between the rich and poor of the island. The first step, commencing in 1949, reduced farm rent and increased tenant farmers' share in crop yields. This increased productivity by encouraging farmers to work harder. Step two was launched in 1951, and this involved the sale of land to tenant farmers. The

---

22. See Tsai Wen-hui, *In Making China Modernized: Comparative Modernization Between Mainland China and Taiwan* (College Park, MD: University of Maryland School of Law, Occasional Papers Reprints Series in Contemporary Asia, No. 4, 1993), p. 103.
23. See Furuya Kaiji, *Chiang Kai-shek: His Life and Times,* trans. Chang Chung-ming (New York: St. John's University Press, 1989), p. 914.

price of land was fixed by the government, and over a 10-year period about 156,000 tenant families acquired land through this land-sale program. The third step, which was probably the most radical, began in 1953 and required landowners to sell their lands to tenant families. Landowners were allowed only to keep 3 *chia* (about 6.9 acres) of medium-grade paddy field or 6 *chia* of dry land. The government purchased all excess land from the landlords and resold it to the tenant farmers who were tilling the land.[24] The main reason this program was successful was that members of the poor Taiwanese landowning class were not part of the KMT ruling elite. By 1988, 85 percent of farmers were full owners of the land they tilled and the number of tenants had declined from 36 percent of the rural population in 1952 to 4 percent.[25]

Many economists agree that Taiwan's land reforms were instrumental "in promoting rural equity and providing an economic stimulus for subsequent industrialization."[26] In the 30 years following the KMT takeover, standards of living rose considerably. Between 1950 and 1988, the literacy rate jumped from 56.0 percent to 92.6 percent, infant mortality declined from 35.16 to 5.34 deaths per 1,000 live births, and average life expectancy increased from 55.57 to 73.51 years.

In material terms, the Taiwanese were certainly better off than in the 1950s.[27] Health care for Taiwanese citizens also improved dramatically between 1961 and 1990. The number of physicians per 10,000 population increased from 6.0 to 11.0 while dentists increased from 0.7 to 2.7, pharmacists from 0.9 to 8.8, and nurses from 1.5 to 8.9. The number of hospital beds increased from 3.70 in 1961 to 43.8 in 1990, and health-related expenditures increased from U.S. $1.07 million in 1961 to U.S. $250 million in 1988.[28]

One significant social change during this period of rapid economic growth has been the change in the status of women in Taiwan. Industrialization has led to the increased participation of women in the workforce and to their greater economic independence. In real terms, this has led to a trend away

---

24. See Tsai, *In Making China Modernized*, p. 104.

25. See Steve Chan and Cal Clark, *Flexibility, Foresight and Fortuna in Taiwan's Development: Navigating Between Scylla and Charybdis* (London: Routledge, 1992), p. 41.

26. Chan and Clark, *Flexibility, Foresight and Fortuna*. See also Samuel P. S. Ho, *Economic Development in Taiwan, 1860–1970* (New Haven: Yale University Press, 1978); S. W. Y. Kuo, *The Taiwan Economy in Transition* (Boulder, CO: Westview, 1983); and E. Thorbecke, "Agricultural Development," in W. Galenson, ed., *Economic Growth and Structural Change in Taiwan: The Postwar Experience of the Republic of China* (Ithaca: Cornell University Press, 1979).

27. For a comprehensive overview and measurement, see Charles H. C. Kao and Liu Ben-cheih, "Socio-economic Development in Taiwan: An Analysis of Its Quality of Life Advancement," in Li Kwoh-ting and Yu Tzong-shian, eds., *Experiences and Lessons of Economic Development in Taiwan* (Taipei: Academia Sinica, 1982), pp. 445–76.

28. See Tsai, *In Making China Modernized*, p. 134.

from arranged marriages and toward later marriages, nuclear families, and higher divorce rates.[29]

Welfare spending is an indication that the distributional effects of economic growth have been equitable. Social welfare spending rose from U.S. $28 million in 1962 to U.S. $2.46 billion in 1986. Two major social insurance programs were implemented: Government Employees' Insurance and the Labor Insurance Scheme, both of which include coverage for retirement and medical expenses. The government also provides free medical treatment and care for the needy, poor, and disabled. Between 1970 and 1981, four major welfare bills were passed: the Welfare Law for Children (1973), the Welfare Law for the Aged (1980), the Welfare Law for the Disabled (1980), and the Social Assistance Law (1980). Of particular note is legislation concerning the aged. Currently, services for senior citizens include retirement pensions, medical care, monthly allowances for low-income elderly, free and half-priced transportation, continuing education, senior centers, social insurance and supplementary income for the aged, free physical checkups, and homemaker services.

Civil and Political Rights: Lifting Martial Law and the Ban on Opposition Parties and Instituting Regular Elections

Martial law, which had been imposed since 1948, was deemed necessary because the Chinese Communist government had adopted a policy of using force to "liberate Taiwan." The creation of the Supplementary Elections in 1972 was the first step in normalizing the political process and structures; this was tied to the increasingly unlikely prospect of KMT forces recapturing the mainland. The death of Chiang Kai-shek in 1975 and the election of his son Chiang Ching-kuo to the presidency in 1978 heralded an era of great political change. The ascent of Dr. Lee Teng-hui – a native-born Taiwanese, who had been Chiang's vice-president – to the country's top leadership post following the younger Chiang's death in 1988 marked a major political milestone and paved the way for implementation of many reforms that had been initiated by Chiang shortly before his death.

On July 15, 1987, President Chiang Ching-kuo lifted martial law and ended the ban on organizing new political parties. With the lifting of martial law, many of the draconian measures that had been used to deal with sedition and political protest were abandoned. Martial law gave the military extraconstitutional powers, and the Taiwan Garrison Command was created to enforce martial law provisions. This Garrison Command was subsequently authorized

---

29. Tsai, *In Making China Modernized,* pp. 135–6.

to control travel abroad, monitor entry into Taiwan; approve meetings, parades, and rallies; and review and censor newspapers, magazines, books, movies, and other forms of communications.[30] These measures were often seen as KMT instruments of repression. Over the years, changes to martial law whittled away the military's influence over many issues, although they maintained their strong role in press censorship throughout the 1980s.

Although political parties had been banned since 1948, in the 1970s opposition politicians began organizing themselves into various campaign organizations, which were amalgamated into a quasi-party called the *dangwai* (outside the KMT) group.[31] After several futile attempts to dissolve this group, the government chose to tolerate its existence despite its illegal status. In September 1986, 112 *dangwai* leaders met and founded the Democratic Progressive Party (DPP), the first genuine opposition party in Taiwan, and won 12 out of the 288 seats in the Legislative Yuan. When martial law was lifted in July 1987, new political parties mushroomed. By March 1988, there were nine new political parties, with at least three others in the process of being organized.[32] The Civil Organization Law, which authorizes the formation of political parties, was amended in 1992 to vest the power to dissolve political parties in the Judicial Yuan rather than the Executive Yuan, which had previously possessed this authority. Since January 1, 1992, all members of the National Assembly, the Legislative Yuan, and the Control Yuan have been subject to periodic elections.

In December 1992 Taiwanese voters went to the polls to elect members to the Legislative Yuan in what has been described as "the most democratic election in the history of any Chinese society."[33] For the first time since 1948, the entire membership of the Legislative Yuan was being elected by the people of Taiwan. The political system was further liberalized in the landmark presidential elections of March 1996. For the first time in Taiwan's history, its people were directly electing their own head of state.

---

30. See John F. Copper, *Taiwan's Recent Elections: Fulfilling the Democratic Promise* (College Park, MD: University of Maryland School of Law, Occasional Papers/Reprints Series in Contemporary Asian Studies, 1990), p. 11. See also John F. Copper, "Ending Martial Law in Taiwan: Problems and Prospects," *Journal of Northeast Asian Studies* vol. 3 (1988).
31. See Lu Ya-li, "Political Developments in the Republic of China," in Thomas W. Robinson, ed., *Democracy and Development in East Asia: Taiwan, South Korea and the Philippines* (Washington, DC: The American Enterprise Institute Press, 1991), p. 37.
32. See Copper, *Taiwan's Recent Elections*, p. 21. The nine new parties were the China Liberty Party, the Democratic Liberty Party, the Labour Party, the China Democratic Justice Party, the China People's Party, the Neo-Socialist Party, the United Democratic Party, the Chinese Republican Party, and the China Unification Party. The three other parties being formed were the China Patriotic Party, the Women's Party, and the Farmer's Party.
33. This election was an important political milestone. The KMT won 60.5 percent of the vote and 103 of the 161 seats, and the opposition Democratic Progressive Party (DPP) won 31.9 percent of the vote and 50 seats. Minor parties and independents won 7.6 percent of the vote and 8 seats. See Andrew J. Nathan, 'The Legislative Yuan Elections in Taiwan,' XXXIII (1993) at p. 424.

Civil and Political Rights: Fundamental Liberties

With the lifting of martial law in 1987, censorship was drastically reduced and previously sensitive topics – such as the Chiang family, Taiwan–mainland relations, self-determination for Taiwan residents, and even Taiwanese independence – began to be more openly discussed. In December 1987 the thirty-six-year ban on the establishment of new newspapers was also lifted. The U.S. State Department reported that in 1994, there were no reported cases of censorship of print media on political grounds, although the police conducted raids to seize pornographic materials and illegal pro-DPP radio stations, including the antiestablishment Voice of Taiwan (VOT), continued to be the subject of official crackdown.[34]

In January 1988 the Legislative Yuan passed a law guaranteeing the right to assemble and demonstrate peacefully, and there have been few reports of political dissidents being imprisoned in recent years. In April 1988, 6,000 political prisoners were released as part of one of the largest amnesty programs ever. This is not to say that security measures would not be invoked should political violence erupt. Martial law was replaced by the National Security Law During the Period of National Mobilization for Suppression of the Communist Rebellion passed by the Legislative Yuan on June 23, 1987, which gave the police widespread powers to "safeguard national security and maintain social stability during the period of national mobilization and suppression of the communist rebellion."[35] Article 2 of the National Security Law restricts freedom of assembly and association with the requirement that no person is to "violate the Constitution or advocate Communism or the division of national territory in the exercise of the people's freedoms of assembly and association." In 1992, amendments were made to the Parade and Assembly Law, which permits peaceful demonstrations provided that they do not promote communism or advocate Taiwan's separation from mainland China, and that protest organizers first obtain a license from the authorities.[36] The 1992 amendments increased the penalties for violating orders to disperse. The authorities have tended to order dispersal of illegal demonstrations rather than prosecute offenders if demonstrations are peaceful. The sedition statutes were also revised in 1992, and the purview of the Sedition Law was restricted to cases involving threats of violence. Following

34. See generally U.S. Department of State, *Taiwan Human Rights Practices, 1994* (Washington, DC: Government Printing Office, March 1995).

35. Article 1. For an English version of this text, see John F. Copper, *A Quiet Revolution: Political Development in the Republic of China* (Washington, DC: Ethics and Public Policy Center, 1988), Appendix B, pp. 49–51.

36. According to the U.S. State Department, these prohibitions are, in practice, hardly ever enforced. See U.S. Department of State, *Taiwan Report on Human Rights Practices for 1996* at http://www.usis. usemb.se/human/taiwan/html.

this, all prisoners convicted of sedition charges were released and all pending cases involving sedition dismissed.

Up until 1987, the KMT-controlled unions had captured only a quarter of the over five million industrial workers in Taiwan. These unions did not afford any opportunities for labor to articulate common interests or grievances, and this resulted in a number of industrial disputes and strikes. With the lifting of martial law, independent trade unions have been established in the various industrial regions of Taiwan. The formation of the Labor Party in December 1987 gave the union movement a much-needed boost, although factionalization led to the formation of a splinter Worker's Party in 1988. In 1994, twelve unions in state-run enterprises threatened to leave the only Taiwan-wide labor federation, the Chinese Federation of Labor, to form a national federation of independent unions.[37] Their application as well as the appeal against its rejection were, however, turned down by the Council of Labor Affairs, and they remain in the CFL. The impetus for independent trade unions has waned in the meantime due to the low unemployment situation in Taiwan. With the 1997–8 currency crisis, a new wave of enthusiasm for independent trade unions could emerge if employers begin laying off workers.

Trends in Legal Reform

The lifting of martial law in 1987 was only the most dramatic of the changes that had begun in the mid-1970s with Chiang Ching-kuo's appointment as Taiwan's Prime Minister. Chiang's role in the democratization of Taiwan and the reform of its political system has been pivotal. Taiwan's spectacular economic growth also contributed to the financial security of its people and brought with it rising expectations in all areas of life, including participation in the political arena and greater respect for civil and political rights. The rise of native Taiwanese to positions of economic and social leadership led to increasing demands for greater Taiwanese political leadership as well. Taiwan has come a long way since the 1970s, when political repression was still widely practiced and when talk of forming an alternative to the KMT government was still heresy. Left to its own, Taiwan would probably liberalize further and emerge as perhaps the first truly democratic Chinese society in history. However, as long as there is a threat of a mainland takeover, communist or otherwise, it remains unlikely that emergency powers such as the National Security Law will be repealed. Whether these laws are invoked

---

37. See Hung-mao Tien, "Transformation of an Authoritarian Party State: Taiwan's Development Experience," in Tun-jin Cheng and Stephen Haggard, *Political Change in Taiwan* (Boulder, CO: Lynne Rienner Publishers, 1992), p. 48.

against Taiwanese citizens is immaterial, for their very presence is sufficient to discourage full participation in the political arena and opens up the possibility that these measures may be used to curb personal rights and liberties without recourse to legal remedy.

One of the emerging problems facing political liberalization has been the need to foster an acceptable civic and political culture among the Taiwanese.[38] Violent and disruptive behavior in the Legislative Yuan has been on the increase in recent years, and widespread violence could threaten the stability of such a fragile democracy and encourage hard-liners in the KMT to use National Security laws to clamp down on the public again. Another problem seems to be corruption in the judiciary. The United States Department of State reported in 1996 that there were "a number of indictments of judges for accepting bribes in exchange for favorable judgments."[39]

The democratization of Taiwan and its move toward a greater recognition of and respect for political and civil liberties has to a large extent been state led. I argued earlier that in Singapore, grassroots perceptions and human rights aspirations among Singaporeans are little different from those of their counterparts in the West; the same can be said of Taiwan. Where the two cases differ is in the fact that Taiwan's move toward greater democracy was spearheaded by the government, starting from President Chiang Ching-kuo's initiatives in the 1970s. His successor, Lee Teng-hui, not only carried on this trend but made tremendous inroads as well. The difference in approach between Singapore and Taiwan is that Singapore's leaders have chosen to define the Singaporean identity through its economic success and efficient and clean form of government, whereas the Taiwanese government has chosen to define Taiwan as a beacon of Chinese democracy. As with Hong Kong, the threat of the PRC and its impact on the lifestyle and liberties of the Taiwanese people have made them more conscious of the rights they would likely lose in case of unification with the mainland. Thus they have thrust human rights issues to the forefront. President Lee's democratization moves and pro–human rights speeches seem to be aimed directly at countering possible alternative realities offered by Beijing and provide a self-defining vehicle for Taiwan.

CONCLUSION

Let us return to the question posed at the beginning of this chapter. Will the dramatic economic development in Taiwan and Singapore provide greater impetus for adherence to the rule of law and to human rights? Economic development and modernization have clearly brought about massive changes

38. See Lu Ya-Li, "Political Developments in the Republic of China," pp. 43–4.
39. See U.S. Department of State, *Taiwan Report on Human Rights Practices for 1996.*

in the lives of Taiwan's and Singapore's citizens. It would be stating the obvious to observe that rising income levels and expectations have brought about corresponding changes in the way people perceive their status in state and society. I suggest that culture, as a determinant of attitudes toward human rights, has undergone a parallel evolutionary change.

The survey of cultural values and human rights previously referred to reveals that, although Singaporeans accord a much higher "value rating" to respect for authority than do their Western counterparts, it is not valued as highly as Singapore's political leaders would have us believe. In addition, although at least 50 percent of Westerners consider the right to freedom of speech and expression to be of the highest importance, the majority of Singaporeans also consider these rights to be among the top six most important values.[40] This is important because it indicates that values that people hold dear may change with time and in some cases with greater economic prosperity. At the societal level, perceptions are constantly being molded, not only by the influence of "Western" media, but by the very condition of modernity. These value changes may not, however, accord with what the state promotes as values worth protecting and safeguarding, as the "Asian values" debate demonstrates.

Clearly then, perceptions about human rights are being shaped differently at two levels. At the state-centric level, the leaders of Singapore and Taiwan disagree over whether there is an Asian version of human rights or whether there is a need to move toward a more liberal regime given the economic progress they have made. At the societal level, disagreement exists between what the people feel and what their rulers deem necessary and expedient, especially in Singapore. What then of prospects for greater liberalization and democracy?

I argue that, given the evident relationship between economic prosperity and political democratization elaborated by Lipset in the work cited at the beginning of this chapter, conditions for civil and political liberties will and must change. This change need not come in the form of institutionalized opposition parties: A change in the structure of civil society or the development of new social movements (as in the antinuclear movement in Taiwan, as discussed in Chapter 14, or the cooperatives in Japan) will engender political change. In Singapore, change at the ground level comes in the form of test-

---

40. See Ng, "Culture and Human Rights: An Empirical Study." Ng's survey revealed that 63 percent of "Westerners" placed freedom of speech and expression among their top two priorities (out of ten). In the survey, a total of 60.6 percent of Singaporeans considered freedom of speech and expression to be among their top six priorities. Although this figure is impressive, only 12.7 percent of Singaporeans surveyed considered freedom of speech and expression to be among their top two priorities, compared with 63 percent of "Westerners" surveyed.

ing of boundaries, or what Singaporean leaders term "OB markers" ("Out of Bounds" markers). In the literary and artistic fringe as well as in the mass media, Singaporeans are beginning to test the boundaries of what is possible within the state.

What has perhaps not changed is the deferential legal culture among the people. Although they may aspire to a greater degree of autonomy and civil and political freedoms, it is apparent that they do not feel sufficiently oppressed to embark on a mass-mobilization exercise to effect such a transformation. In an environment in which there is some grumbling but no widespread oppression, revolutionary change is not likely. The opportunity costs are simply too high. Singaporeans do not define themselves and their entire political culture and ethos with the idea of liberty, as do Americans. Their self-identification comes in the form of the material success of their tiny island state. So, although the people aspire to something better, there is little impetus for change emanating from the lower reaches of the political spectrum.

In the short term, the prospects for civil and political liberties in Singapore, and to an extent in Taiwan, are less than rosy. Threats to national security are often grounds that governments use to clamp down on civil and political rights. In Taiwan, the constant external threat of a belligerent China looms large. During the 1996 inaugural presidential elections in Taiwan, China launched six days of war games just off the coast of Taiwan in an attempt to frighten the Taiwanese people into abandoning the ballot boxes. Although this incident and the security threat it illustrates did not result in a government crackdown, that remains a lingering possibility.

The perceived threat to Singapore's security is an internal one, but the response to it in terms of civil liberties is similar. During the 1997 Singapore general elections, the PAP accused Workers' Party candidate Tang Liang Hong of being a "dangerous man" because of his views on Chinese culture and education. His views, they argued, could jeopardize ethnic harmony in Singapore. Although the "threat" Tang poses to the government's rule cannot be compared to that of China's war games, the point I wish to make is simple: Given the historical backgrounds of these two societies and the forging of their national identities — Taiwan through its confrontation with mainland China and Singapore through battles with communism and communalism — civil and political rights will be the first rights to be curtailed when the government perceives an imminent threat.

Despite all of these qualifications, however, there is a reasonable hope that Singapore's trajectory will follow that of other countries: that is, that prosperity will bring about a more open society. I agree with Singapore's former Prime Minister Lee Kuan Yew, one of the most outspoken proponents of soft authoritarianism, who had this to say in response to the question why he thought that in ten to twenty years a set of universal norms on human rights would be reached:

> Mainly because of communications. We are seeing each other in our own sitting rooms, and we are passing judgment on each other. And that is something new. You are not just passing a message to your representative at the UN urging a vote of condemnation, which is known only to a few leaders or people in the Foreign Ministry. Everybody is watching and saying, "My God, how can they do this?" So this will lead to drastic change.[41]

What is certain is that with each generational change, and with the increasing globalization of society, these changes will usher in new approaches and greater respect toward human rights in the region.

41. See Sandra Burton, "Society vs. the Individual," *Time* (June 14, 1993), p. 21.

CHAPTER 12

HUMAN RIGHTS ISSUES IN CHINA'S INTERNAL MIGRATION: INSIGHTS FROM COMPARISONS WITH GERMANY AND JAPAN

DOROTHY J. SOLINGER*

Migrant labor the world around unfailingly provides a fertile field for human rights abuse, as the following quotation by Gary Silverman of the *Far Eastern Economic Review* encapsulates cogently:

> To get their chance, migrants typically mortgage their human rights. . . . Many countries can't live without foreign workers – but don't want to live with them. The message to unskilled migrants is almost always: get the job done and get lost; citizenship is out of the question.[1]

Indeed, the problems of transient workers toiling outside their own home turf encompass a triple predicament from the perspective of human rights, as understood in the terms of international standards. First and most basic, their freedom of movement or migration and residence is at stake, violating Article 13 of the Universal Declaration of Human Rights. Second, their lack of possession of – and often of even the hope ever to possess – such civic or citizenship rights as the rights of assembly, association, and the vote; their minimal social security; and their negligible chance to enjoy a standard of living adequate for health and well-being, challenge, respectively, Articles 20 through 22 and 25 of this document.

Third, Articles 23 and 24 are overridden when their rights of employment, such as just and favorable conditions of work, equal pay for equal work, and reasonable limitation of working hours, are trampled upon. Phrased differently, freedom of movement, the right to citizenship and

*Full documentation of chapter sources is available from the author.
1. Gary Silverman, "Vital and Vulnerable," *Far Eastern Economic Review* (hereafter *FEER*), May 23, 1996, pp. 60–1.

accompanying civic and social rights in one's place of residence, and the right to decent treatment at work are all routinely ignored when sojourners subject themselves to labor markets outside their home territories.[2]

Moreover, the three forms of denial are intertwined. Simply put, the very fact of barriers to admission (or constraints on freedom of movement) implies difficulties in achieving first legal residence and later full (political, social, and economic) citizenship. Those so pushed into impropriety by their very presence are then barred from benefits when they pursue employment. This is the case because their illegal or nonlegal status severely limits their recourse to the law and so makes migrant labor vulnerable to exploitation and ill-treatment.

Though this problem of migrant labor is pervasive throughout East Asia, in China it takes on a peculiar form: The more economically developed areas of the country have since the economic liberalization beginning in the 1980s drawn upon the country's own domestic peasants to serve as drudges, in the process denying them the rights that international norms of justice decree should belong to all human beings.[3] I would underline a distinction here between China's transients and previously peasants working in the metropolises of other developing nations where they are, at a minimum, politically citizens, fully free to move, form associations, and vote, even though their working lives may be disadvantaged.[4]

Chinese leaders justify their stance by claiming that protection of rights includes guaranteeing people's right to subsistence and development.[5] The

---

2. See James F. Hollifield, *Immigrants, Markets, and States: The Political Economy of Postwar Europe* (Cambridge, MA: Harvard University Press, 1992), p. 3; Rogers Brubaker, *Citizenship and Nationhood in France and Germany* (Cambridge, MA: Harvard University Press, 1992), p. 21; and Shimada Haruo, *Japan's "Guest Workers": Issues and Public Policies,* Roger Northridge trans. (Tokyo: The University of Tokyo Press, 1994), pp. 40, 48.

3. I use the term "peasant" quite intentionally in this chapter. I do so because in designating Chinese people living in or newly from the countryside, these people themselves and Chinese urbanites both use the Chinese word *nongmin* to convey a meaning that is similar in its inexactness and pejorative bias to the English word "peasant."

4. In many other cities in the developing world in which competitive party systems exist, native migrant squatters have the ballot and so can sometimes bargain for city services and facilities in exchange for votes, at least around election time. See Ayse Gunes-Ayata, "Migrants and Natives: Urban Bases of Social Conflict," in Jeremy Eades, ed., *Migrants, Workers, and the Social Order* (London: Tavistock, 1987), pp. 234–48, on Turkey; Wayne Cornelius, "Urbanization and Political Demand Making: Political Participation Among the Migrant Poor in Latin American Cities," *American Political Science Review* vol. 68 (1974), pp. 1125–46; Wayne Cornelius, *Politics and the Migrant Poor in Mexico City* (Stanford: Stanford University Press, 1975), pp. 59–63 and 159–60; Bernard Gallin and Rita S. Gallin, "The Integration of Village Migrants into Urban Society: The Case of Taipei, Taiwan," in Robert N. Thomas and John M. Hunter, *Internal Migration Systems in the Developing World with Special Reference to Latin America* (Boston: G. K. Hall & Co., 1980), p. 170; Peter Lloyd, *Slums of Hope? Shanty Towns of the Third World* (Manchester: Manchester University Press, 1979), p. 32; and Bryan R. Roberts, *The Making of Urban Citizens: Cities of Peasants Revisited* (London: Arnold, 1995), p. 174, on Latin America.

5. As in *Xinhua* [New China News Agency] (hereafter *XH*), September 19, 1996, translated in *Summary of World Broadcasts* (hereafter *SWB*), FE/2725 S2/2, September 24, 1996.

implicit logic here appears to be that, because the cheap labor of peasants will speed up the course of such development on a national scale, the present oppression of urbanized farmers is just a temporary step on the road to rights that will be tendered later on.

This paper explores the Chinese situation, highlighting its idiosyncracies by comparing it to two other polities – Japan and Germany – in which "outsiders," who played a comparable role in economic growth, have been similarly placed beyond the pale. In all three countries, *jus sanguinis* determination of citizenship has sharply separated newcomers at work from the natives.

But critical distinctions in developmental and political trajectories among the three – namely, the place of labor in politics, the timing of immigration in relation to economic development in a country, and a nation's integration into certain international networks – appear in the long run to diminish the negative impact that ethnocentrism and developmental pushes place on granting rights. Thus, these factors could help account for China's current harshness to those it has made into aliens as well as pointing to a possibility that time and political change could alter these aliens' situation.

SIMILARITIES

The most fundamental similarity between the three cases is what one might term an "ethnocentric" underpinning for belonging and membership in all of them. If we extend Emily Honig's conception that – based on linguistic, lifestyle, custom, and self-perceptional grounds – ethnic Chinese native to the various regions of China are *in effect* members of separate ethnicities, we might say that, at least as a social construction, urban Chinese generally view rural Chinese as ethnically distinct, to stretch the usual meaning of the term a bit.[6]

If we then consider the package of benefits, privileges, and entitlements of city-born Chinese to be the equivalent of the rights of urban citizenship, from which the country-born are excluded, we can say that the Chinese government uses an ethnocultural foundation for granting this urban citizenship and denying it to ruralites, just as Japan and Germany do in the case of their own citizens and against foreign nationals.[7] For much as Japan and Germany ground citizenship on the principle of *jus sanguinis* – that is, on the basis of

---

6. Emily Honig, *Creating Chinese Ethnicity: Subei People in Shanghai, 1850–1980* (New Haven: Yale University Press, 1992).

7. Brubaker, *Citizenship and Nationhood in France and Germany,* p. 51, uses the term "ethnocultural understanding of nation-state membership" to describe the restrictiveness and the rootedness in descent of German policy on citizenship. On p. 123 he states: "An ethnonational self-understanding is one in which the nation is understood as an ethnic or ethnocultural community independent of the institutional and territorial frame of the state."

descent (sometimes called "blood") – so in China urban household registration is passed down hereditarily, in this case just via the maternal line.[8]

Germany (along with Switzerland) stands at an extreme pole among Western European nations in this regard, not counting even third-generation immigrants as citizens until they have themselves lived in the country for at least 10, or sometimes even as many as 15 years.[9] In Japan, a strong, historically derived ideology emphasizing racial homogeneity shores up the national bias against outsiders. This ideology, which boasts of the virtues of Japan's "single-race nation" or its "sage" society, has bolstered the nation's disinclination to open its labor market.[10] The source of the opposition lies in fears of polluting the cultural integrity of Japanese society.[11] Official documents prepared as recently as the late 1980s go so far as to attribute the country's economic miracle to its "one ethnic group, one language" society.[12]

In China, historically, even in the very cosmopolitan port of Hankow, according to William Rowe, domestic migrants in the form of squatters, whether laborers or beggars, were denigrated as rootless, people who summoned up distaste and even alarm among the town's permanent residents.[13] In contemporary

---

8. In Germany, only "ethnic Germans," those whose German parents or grandparents lived in the German Reich on December 31, 1937, can immediately become German citizens upon entering the country for residence. See Philip L. Martin, "Germany: Reluctant Land of Immigration," in Wayne A. Cornelius, Philip L. Martin, and James F. Hollifield, *Controlling Immigration: A Global Perspective* (Stanford: Stanford University Press, 1994), p. 216; and Brubaker, *Citizenship and Nationhood in France and Germany*, pp. 82–4 and 176, on Germany. In Japan, under the nationality law in effect up to 1985, Japanese nationality was handed down only through one's paternal lineage. But in that year, the government amended the law to permit nationality to be passed down through either parent. Wayne A. Cornelius, "Japan: The Illusion of Immigration Control," in Cornelius, Martin, and Hollifield, *Controlling Immigration*, p. 396.

   Citizenship based on descent is in contradistinction to *jus soli*, or soil, meaning birth within the national territory. See Hollifield, *Immigrants, Markets, and States*, p. 16; Brubaker, *Citizenship and Nationhood in France and Germany*, p. 32; and Yasemin Nuhoglu Soysal, *Limits of Citizenship: Migrants and Postnational Membership in Europe* (Chicago: University of Chicago Press, 1994), pp. 25–6. According to Brubaker, *Citizenship and Nationhood in France and Germany*, pp. 122–3, "*jus soli* defines the citizenry as a territorial community; *jus sanguinis* as a community of descent." For Chinese registration rules, see Sulamith Heins Potter and Jack M. Potter, *China's Peasants: The Anthropology of a Revolution* (Cambridge: Cambridge University Press, 1990), p. 296.

9. Brubaker, *Citizenship and Nationhood in France and Germany*, pp. 34, 81, 176; and Martin, "Germany: Reluctant Land of Immigration," p. 196. Soysal, *Limits of Citizenship*, p. 25, shows that the rate of naturalization in Germany was just 6 percent of total foreigners in the country, almost half the rate even in Switzerland, another *jus sanguinis* state. See also Hollifield, *Immigrants, Markets, and States*, p. 173; Ursula Mehrlander, "Federal Republic of Germany: Sociological Aspects of Migration Policy," in Daniel Kubat, ed., *The Politics of Migration Policies: Settlement and Integration – The First World into the 1990s* (New York: Center for Migration Studies, 1993), p. 196.

10. Saskia Sassen, *The Global City: New York, London, Tokyo* (Princeton: Princeton University Press, 1991), p. 33; Chalmers Johnson, "Studies of Japanese Political Economy: A Crisis in Theory," in *Japanese Studies in the United States, Part I: History and Present Condition*, Japanese Studies Series XVII (New York: The Japan Foundation, 1988), p. 109.

11. Shimada, *Japan's "Guest Workers,"* p. 47.

12. Cornelius, "Japan: The Illusion of Immigration Control," pp. 385, 396.

13. William T. Rowe, *Hankow: Conflict and Community in a Chinese City 1796–1895* (Stanford: Stanford University Press, 1989), p. 231.

China, in the wake of economic reforms after 1980 that permitted peasants to move out from the rural areas for the first time in several decades, the traditional discrimination for the outsider persists. Here it is probably at an even higher peak than in the past, given that large cities have suddenly had to adjust sometimes to a few million rustics newly residing within their midst. These quotations illustrate urbanites' scorn, and also indicate their certainty that these country people do not deserve the same rights that they themselves enjoy:

> Their [migrants'] thinking, morality, language, and customs are all different, their quality is inferior. The places they inhabit are very likely dirty places. . . . They lack a concept of public morality . . . so that behavior that harms prevailing social customs occurs time and time again. City residents are dissatisfied because they disturb normal life and livelihood.[14]

Similarly, a public security officer in Beijing is actually said to have pronounced that "[t]hese out-of-towners are no better than animals."[15]

A second key similarity between the three countries is this: all three have also all been the site for "economic miracles," the Japanese and the Germans in the postwar period, the Chinese just since economic reforms began in 1979. In Germany from the 1950s to the early 1970s, and in the Chinese special economic zones during the 1980s, rapid growth has been openly acknowledged to be the result of the cheaply recompensed drudgery of outsiders. In Germany, at the height of immigration in 1972, only 12 percent of the workforce has been said to have "made possible the remarkable economic recovery and expansion."[16] In China's Guangdong, the province made most prosperous by special governmental regulations meant to attract foreign capital, according to two roving Chinese journalists who traveled there in 1989,

> [a]t all levels of the Guangdong party and government, right down to the heads of the town and village enterprises, everyone highly praised the contribution of the peasant workers. Provincial Party Secretary [as of 1989] Lin Ruo said, "Without the peasant workers, Guangdong's prosperity wouldn't exist."[17]

14. Wang Jianmin and Hu Qi, "Pay Attention to Policy Research on Adjusting the Structure of the Outsider Floating Population," *Zhongguo renkou kexue* [Chinese Population Science] (hereafter *ZRK*) vol. 6 (1988), p. 72.

15. *South China Morning Post* (hereafter *SCMP*), Hong Kong, October 9, 1991, p. 10. Reprinted in U.S. *Foreign Broadcast Information Service, China Daily Report* (hereafter *FBIS*), October 10, 1991, p. 22.

16. Wayne A. Cornelius, Philip L. Martin, and James F. Hollifield, "Introduction: The Ambivalent Quest for Immigration Control," in Cornelius, Martin, and Hollifield, *Controlling Immigration,* p. 18. See also Martin, "Germany: Reluctant Land of Immigration," p. 198; Hollifield, *Immigrants, Markets, and States,* pp. 50, 58; and Ruth Mandel, "Ethnicity and Identity Among Migrant Guestworkers in West Berlin," in Nancie L. Gonzalez and Carolyn S. McCommon, *Conflict, Migration, and the Expression of Ethnicity* (Boulder, CO: Westview Press, 1989), p. 61.

17. Ge Xiangxian and Qu Weiying, *Zhongguo mingongchao: "mangliu" zhenxianglu* [China's Tide of Labor: A Record of the True Facts about the "Blind Floaters"] (Beijing: Chinese International Broadcasting Publishing Co., 1990), p. 175.

In Japan, granted, the postwar "miracle" emerged from the unstinting toil of the native people themselves, permitting them to do without outsiders for decades. But once the new boom of the mid- to late 1980s brought in outside laborers and built up a definite dependence upon them, there emerged within the country a growing recognition that foreign workers were supporting vital sectors of the Japanese economy and that their removal would have adverse economic impacts on businesses and communities.[18]

So in all three countries the response to outsiders – those from other countries in the case of Germany and Japan and those from the countryside in Chinese cities – starts from highly exclusionary, culturally superior, ethnocentrically informed stances. The heavy reliance of these places upon the brawn and the backbone of these outsiders, although somewhat pushing aside native distaste for their presence, still only marginally tempers a persisting and fundamental disdain for their persons.

We continue by reviewing what I will call the "migration regime" in each country, examining the three types of rights that are typically assaulted in the treatment of migrant labor: rules about entry (movement rights), extension of civic and social privileges (citizenship rights), and the treatment of migrant workers (labor rights). Following that, we explore the variation among the three societies and speculate about its effect for the human rights of migrants.

MIGRATION REGIMES IN GERMANY, JAPAN, AND CHINA

Germany

Rules about entry. "We are not a country of immigration," a slogan that is more a normative maxim than a descriptive statement, has been a repetitive theme in official German postwar policy toward foreigners.[19] The very name for nonnative workers, "guest worker," exposes the underlying belief that these people will be with the Germans only temporarily, never to become fully one of themselves. Even a more recent incarnation, the label "foreign fellow citizens," continues to communicate a sign of otherness.[20] And yet, we will find, of the three migration regimes to be considered in this chapter, Germany's is the most hospitable.

Rogers Brubaker traces the descent-based approach to citizenship and migrants at least to a 1913 law of citizenship – if not to an 1842 Prussian

---

18. Cornelius, "Japan: The Illusion of Immigration Control," pp. 378, 394.
19. Brubaker, *Citizenship and Nationhood in France and Germany,* p. 174.
20. Zig Layton-Henry, "The Challenge of Political Rights," in Zig Layton-Henry, ed., *The Political Rights of Migrant Workers in Western Europe* (London: Sage Publications, 1990), pp. 7–8.

law – which made domicile contingent on "membership" in the community, a status that was itself based on descent, marriage, or naturalization.[21] In the postwar period, reflecting this exclusivist posture, a minimum of 10 years' residence is typical for naturalization; one must also give up one's prior citizenship and fulfill a lengthy list of other requisites.[22] Even after meeting all of these conditions, an applicant is still subject to the discretion of local authorities, who frequently reject the request without explanation.[23]

The first postwar outsiders admitted into the country were mainly German refugees and displaced persons, encouraged to come for the purpose of working. With the erection of the Berlin Wall in 1961, foreigners from further away (Turkey, Italy, Spain, Portugal, Yugoslavia) were admitted during the 1960s and 1970s. But the recession and accompanying unemployment brought on by the oil crisis of 1973, along with wildcat strikes and threatening signs of permanent settlement, led the government to call a halt to recruitment.[24]

Since that time, the state has been pursuing a three-pronged policy: strict limits on further immigration, encouraging the voluntary repatriation of migrants, and integrating second-generation immigrants. This tightening up shows up in a new Aliens Law in 1990 and a decree in 1993, and in administrative measures taken since 1989 to bring in foreign workers geared specifically to prevent settlement.[25] At the popular level as well, in recent years, with the rise in Muslim inflow and renewed recession with its attendant steady and ominous unemployment, a threateningly xenophobic strain has appeared in the reactions to outsiders, marked by ugly incidents involving attacks on foreigners. And yet, as of the early 1990s, there were just seven million foreigners living in Germany, equal to a mere eight percent of the total population.[26]

Civic and social privileges. The Basic Law of West Germany, its constitution, reserved a few rights that would apply for citizens alone, such as the right to

---

21. Brubaker, *Citizenship and Nationhood in France and Germany,* pp. 52, 53, 64, 70–1, 136.

22. Brubaker, *Citizenship and Nationhood in France and Germany,* p. 77; Soysal, *Limits of Citizenship,* p. 26. Yet Martin, "Germany: Reluctant Land of Immigration," p. 196, claims that 15 years are required.

23. Gerard de Rham, "Naturalization: The Politics of Citizenship Acquisition," in Layton-Henry, ed., *The Political Rights of Migrant Workers in Western Europe,* pp. 162–3; and Martin, "Germany: Reluctant Land of Immigration," pp. 209–10.

24. Martin, "Germany: Reluctant Land of Immigration," pp. 198–99, 202; Brubaker, *Citizenship and Nationhood in France and Germany,* pp. 75, 172; and Catherine Wihtol de Wenden, "The Absence of Rights: The Position of Illegal Immigrants," in Layton-Henry, ed., *The Political Rights of Migrant Workers in Western Europe,* p. 31; and Hollifield, *Immigrants, Markets, and States,* p. 82.

25. Brubaker, *Citizenship and Nationhood in France and Germany,* pp. 76–8; Soysal, *Limits of Citizenship,* p. 26; Cornelius, Martin, and Hollifield, *Controlling Immigration,* p. 18; and Martin, "Germany: Reluctant Land of Immigration," pp. 194, 218–20.

26. Martin, "Germany: Reluctant Land of Immigration," pp. 189–202.

hold public meetings and form associations, but legislation later granted most of these to resident foreigners as well. Fundamental legal rights, such as equality before the law, due process, and appeal, however, were universally granted from the outset in the Basic Law. Although the Aliens Law of 1965 promised no freedom of occupation, place of work, or place of education, gradually foreigners did receive these rights.[27]

By the 1960s, pressure from the trade unions brought foreign children into the schools, obtained social services for them, and urged an end to discrimination.[28] And although the Federal Constitutional Court affirmed that giving local voting rights to noncitizens was unconstitutional, foreigners may at least join local advisory committees that local authorities can consult, are members of unions and work councils in the factories, and can serve as shop stewards. Foreigners are also in principle eligible for welfare money, though applying for it may be risky. As of the early 1990s, they were owning their own businesses and homes, renting government-subsidized apartments, forming political associations, and organizing protests; the lack of formal channels for interest representation (because of not having the franchise) would appear to be the only significant barrier to their effective, if not actual, citizenship.[29]

Treatment of migrant workers. The lot of the foreign worker in Germany would seem to be reasonably favorable. Though the government has focused more on his or her living conditions and on wages and fringe benefits, and not specifically on integration, this effort has so far surpassed that of the other two states. Their degree of unionization (about one third of them were members as of 1989) was more or less on a par with that of native workers; they have also been included in the apprenticeship system, which provides training for youths 16 to 19 years of age. Foreign workers amounted to about 5 percent of the workforce as of the early 1990s.[30] In general, then, the stigma of not belonging does hang somewhat heavily on noncitizens in Germany, but at

27. See Tomas Hammar, "The Civil Rights of Aliens," in Layton-Henry, ed., *The Political Rights of Migrant Workers in Western Europe,* pp. 79–85; and Soysal, *Limits of Citizenship,* pp. 122–30. Hammar notes that the right to assemble and demonstrate was granted foreigners in 1953; in 1964 they could form their own associations and in 1967 join political parties – but could still not create any of their own. See articles by Alan Cowell, the *New York Times,* May 15, 1996 and December 14, 1995, p. A6. After Germany unified in 1990, the migration regime of West Germany became the common regime of the whole of Germany.
28. Uwe Andersen, "Consultative Institutions for Migrant Workers," in Layton-Henry, ed., *The Political Rights of Migrant Workers in Western Europe,* pp. 116–17.
29. Soysal, *Limits of Citizenship,* pp. 88, 107–8, 124–9, 166; Layton-Henry, ed., *The Political Rights of Migrant Workers in Western Europe,* p. 24.
30. Jan Vranken, "Industrial Rights," in Layton-Henry, ed., *The Political Rights of Migrant Workers in Western Europe,* pp. 57, 61; Hollifield, *Immigrants, Markets, and States,* pp. 205, 208; Martin,"Germany: Reluctant Land of Immigration," p. 190.

least they might hope eventually to become a member, and while they wait and work – provided they escape the frustrated wrath of the new violence-prone xenophobes – life is more than tolerable.

Japan

Rules about entry. Like Germany's, Japan's official policy toward outsiders is explicitly exclusivist. Its three key provisions, though observed more in the breach than in reality, bear this out: to admit foreigners solely as a last resort, to prohibit the entry of the unskilled, and to keep all immigration purely temporary.[31]

The historical background to Japanese antiforeignism is unmistakable. Numbers of foreigners – for decades almost entirely Koreans and Taiwanese dragged in as forced labor under the reign of the empire, who themselves were compelled to take on Japanese nationality at that time, and later their descendants – remained low and stable until the 1980s, in part because immigration was actively resisted. In the years between 1950 and 1988 foreigners represented only 0.6 percent of the population.[32]

Starting in the late 1980s, however, a veritable surge of movement into the country – mainly migrants from Japan's South, East, and Southeast Asian neighbors – appeared: The numbers of foreigners overstaying their tourist visas to take up employment shot up (to about 280,000) while the ranks of legal immigrant workers doubled between 1986 and 1991. The demand was fed by domestic labor shortages driven by demographic trends unable to match a sudden economic boom as well as by a revaluation of the yen, which only served to increase the already sizable gap in income-earning potential between Japan and other Asian nations. As of the early 1990s, however, foreign workers, both legal and illegal, accounted for a mere one percent of the total workforce (500,000 to 700,000 of 65 million).[33]

The official response was an Immigration Control and Refugee Recognition

---

31. Cornelius, Martin, and Hollifield, *Controlling Immigration,* pp. 26–7.
32. Watanabe Susumu, "The Lewisian Turning Point and International Migration: The Case of Japan," *Asian and Pacific Migration Journal* vol. 3, no. 1 (1994), pp. 134–5; Sassen, *The Global City: New York, London, Tokyo,* p. 300; and Muto Matsatoshi, "Japan: The Issue of Migrant Workers," in Kubat, ed., *The Politics of Migration Policies,* p. 348; Cornelius, "Japan: The Illusion of Immigration Control," p. 375.
33. Sassen, *The Global City: New York, London, Tokyo,* p. 308; Watanabe, "The Lewisian Turning Point and International Migration," p. 135; and Morita Kiriro and Saskia Sassen, "The New Illegal Immigration in Japan, 1980–1992," *International Migration Review* vol. 28, no. 1 (1994), p. 154. Shimada, *Japan's "Guest Workers,"* states that in 1990, there were only 80,000 foreigners officially employed, less than one-third the number estimated to be there illegally. See also Cornelius, "Japan: The Illusion of Immigration Control," pp. 377–82; Muto, "Japan: The Issue of Migrant Workers," p. 348.

Law (1990), clearly aimed at limiting the inflow of the un- and the semi-skilled. Matching the mood of this legislation, the numbers of arrests and forced deportations of illegal residents rose, and a rotation system was used to cut down on the number settling down.[34]

Civic and social privileges. The situation for foreigners resident in Japan is not as fortunate at this point as it is for those in Germany. In the first place, the constitution does not even address the issue of the status of foreign workers. There appears, however, to be a general sense that foreigners have, among other rights, the rights to petition, of religious belief and assembly, and to reside where they wish, as well as freedom of thought and conscience, and are considered equal before the law. But the social consensus is that voting rights, and the rights to subsistence, education, and work apply to citizens alone. Though in many localities schools have in fact opened their doors to foreigners, this is not done by law, and housing discrimination is still serious.[35]

Treatment of migrant workers. The crux of the problem of treatment for migrant workers in Japan is that most of them are there illegally. This means that unfair treatment and abuses (by employers, the labor brokers – the *yakuza,* who dominate the underworld – who often manage them, immigration officers, and the police) are commonplace. There is neither any protective law to which the workers could appeal nor any guarantee of decent working conditions.[36]

The discrimination that fuels the situation is revealed in the following statistic: In a 1989 survey of 266 Tokyo firms, a mere 3 percent of employers expressed a belief that foreign workers should be treated like Japanese ones.[37] As for unions, even native temporary workers were not admitted into them historically.[38] Though specific programs have been designed to entice foreign workers into the country, these are generally not especially favorable to the workers. An April 1993 Ministry of Justice initiative titled the "Skills Work-Training System" for the first time permitted foreigners to do real

34. Morita and Sassen, "The New Illegal Immigration in Japan, 1980–1992," pp. 160–1; Shimada, *Japan's "Guest Workers,"* p. 164; Cornelius, "Japan: The Illusion of Immigration Control," pp. 387–400; and Sassen, *The Global City: New York, London, Tokyo,* p. 309.
35. Shimada, *Japan's "Guest Workers,"* pp. 161–2, 167–8.
36. Morita and Sassen, "The New Illegal Immigration in Japan, 1980–1992," p. 162; Muto, "Japan: The Issue of Migrant Workers," p. 348; and Shimada, *Japan's "Guest Workers,"* pp. 40–8.
37. Sassen, *The Global City: New York, London, Tokyo,* pp. 311–12.
38. However, they sometimes organized their own unions, and finally got some support toward regular status from the permanent workers in the 1950s. Andrew Gordon, "Conditions for the Disappearance of the Japanese Working-Class Movement," in Elizabeth J. Perry, *Putting Class in Its Place: Worker Identities in East Asia* (Berkeley: Institute of East Asian Studies, Center for Chinese Studies, University of California, Berkeley, 1996), p. 36.

work and to have their rights as workers guaranteed. Yet even here there are limitations.[39] Nonetheless, this system is clearly an improvement for the recipients over what went before.

As for benefits and protections, Japan did ratify the U.N. Agreement on Social Rights and pledges to guarantee all workers rights of social insurance and social security. There is also a pledge to all workers of a right to accident compensation. Although illegal workers are theoretically allowed these benefits, they would surely risk deportation if they tried to demand enforcement. Unemployment benefits are officially available to legal foreign workers, but even for them they are rarely granted; the illegals are not even eligible.[40]

A range of welfare benefits are supposedly open to illegal workers, such as child welfare, disability, and mental infirmity, but their application is spotty. Also, illegals cringe from even applying for medical insurance, because, again, of their fear of exposing their presence. And though in principle even those in the country illegally are entitled to enroll in pension plans, there are severe practical difficulties in receiving the pensions, even though most foreign workers are forced to pay into the schemes. As with education, some local governments have taken it upon themselves to offer basic social services, including assistance with medical bills, though this is by no means national policy.[41]

In sum, Japan's migration regime, although less humane than that of Germany, is at least informed by a sense of – if not yet a fulfillment of – internationally recognized rights and benefits. There has also been a development of potentially more humane work programs.

China

Rules about entry. Soon after the post-Mao regime of Deng Xiaoping launched the Chinese nation on a heady course of what was to become steadily intensifying marketization in 1979, the commune structure in the countryside was permitted to crumble, trading in the cities was legitimized, urban construction exploded, and, as a function of all these shifts, a "floating population" was born. This is a group comprised of those peasants lured away from the rural communities to which they had been confined for some 20 years and into the towns and cities by the promise of work and higher

39. Shimada, *Japan's "Guest Workers,"* pp. 73–7; Cornelius, "Japan: The Illusion of Immigration Control," p. 399; Morita and Sassen, "The New Illegal Immigration in Japan, 1980–1992," p. 161.
40. Shimada, *Japan's "Guest Workers,"* pp. 158–9, 164–5.
41. Shimada, *Japan's "Guest Workers,"* pp. 168–9; Cornelius, "Japan: The Illusion of Immigration Control," p. 406.

earnings. Varying accounts estimate as of the mid-1990s the total number of such transients as in the range of 60 million.[42]

But the increasing degree of freedom granted them to travel away from their original residence has not so far been matched by any meaningful right, once ensconced in the municipalities, to acquire what amounts to urban "citizenship." In fact, the hereditary distinction between those with a rural and those with an urban household registration (or *hukou*) remains nearly unscathed, despite the passage of over a decade since the first relaxation of restrictions on movement.[43]

It is important to note immediately that under the reign of the socialist system in China, urbanites, especially urban workers in state-owned and large "collectively" owned factories, were the recipients of a wealth of state-bestowed benefits, including full labor insurance, generous retirement and medical packages, housing, and lifetime job tenure, at a minimum.[44] In addition, all proper, permanent urban residents received dwellings at exceedingly low rents; almost gratis public transportation, home heating, and water; guaranteed jobs; and heavily subsidized grain, oil, and many other daily necessities.

Moreover, the cumbersome and uncertain procedure for attaining even *temporary* residence in the city – which cannot even confer citizenship – gives large numbers of these internal migrants (those who fail to register their presence in the city) a status that partakes of a legal limbo. Their consequent vulnerability in the face of local police and both domestic and foreign employers often renders their existence precarious to say the least.[45]

Although the residents of Chinese cities may historically have been hostile to sojourners – at least to those of the lower, working classes – governments prior to the Communist one by and large did nothing to restrict internal migration. Indeed, privately organized geographical mobility tended to predominate in both the late imperial and Republican (1911–49) periods,

---

42. Hein Mallee, "Agricultural Labour and Rural Population Mobility: Some Preliminary Observations" (unpublished paper prepared for the International Conference on Flow of Rural Labour in China, Beijing, June 25–27, 1996), p. 2.

43. The first State Council directive liberalizing peasants' right to be in towns came in October 1984. See "State Council Notification on the Question of Peasants Entering Towns and Settling," published in *Zhonghua renmin gongheguo guowuyuan gongbao* [State Council Bulletin] vol. 26, no. 447 (November 10, 1984), pp. 919–20.

44. See Andrew G. Walder, *Communist Neo-Traditionalism: Work and Authority in Chinese Industry* (Berkeley: University of California Press, 1986), pp. 40–3, 56–68.

45. Dorothy J. Solinger, "The Chinese Work Unit and Transient Labor in the Transition from Socialism," *Modern China* vol. 21, no. 2 (1995), pp. 155–83. In a 1996 survey, 79 percent of the transients queried had not registered in the cities. See Zhang Xiaohui, Zhao Changbao, and Chen Liangbiao, "1994: Nongcun laodongli kuaquyu liudong di shizheng miaoda [1994: A Real Description of Rural Labor's Cross-Regional Flow]," *Zhanlue yu guanli* [Strategy and Management] vol. 6 (Beijing, 1995), p. 28.

though most imperial rulers, at least, had the power to relocate their peoples if they so chose. Furthermore, in both eras, movement was common, widespread, and frequent.[46]

By contrast, under the PRC until the reform era, statist choices about population location prevailed in all but a very few years. No one moved freely, most of the time, at least not legally. The state struggled to check population movement beginning in the early 1950s, even if it did not succeed fully until 1960. By that point almost everyone in the countryside was harnessed tightly into a commune and the wherewithal for subsistence in the cities was locked securely in the grasp of the regime. Its purpose was to make of the peasantry a potential underclass, ready to be exploited to fulfil the new state's project of industrialization. The new state was prepared, as monopolist employer and owner (after coming into the possession of all of China's land, commercial, and industrial assets in the mid-1950s), to industrialize the cities ruthlessly; consequently, it was industrialization and its fiscal demands that dictated the pace of migration and that served to justify any abuses inflicted in its service.[47]

According to the plans of the leaders, this mission of modernization soon came to mean closing off the cities and attempting to keep them quiescent. This quiescence they hoped to achieve, in the face of generally strong and at times even acute pressure from peasants wanting to enter, by limiting city populations and supplying those within with the wherewithal for fairly comfortable subsistence. By barricading the cities against the peasants, the state rendered ruralites available for the big spurts of industrial growth, and disposable in tighter times.[48] Though earlier constitutions permitted movement,

46. James Lee, "Migration and Expansion in Chinese History," in William H. McNeill and Ruth S. Adams, *Human Migration: Patterns and Policies* (Bloomington: Indiana University Press, 1978), pp. 20–47; F. W. Mote, "The Transformation of Nanking, 1350–1400," in G. William Skinner, *The City in Late Imperial China* (Stanford: Stanford University Press, 1977), pp. 101–53; Gilbert Rozman, *Urban Networks in Ch'ing China and Tokugawa Japan* (Princeton: Princeton University Press, 1973); and R. J. R. Kirkby, *Urbanization in China: Town and Country in a Developing Economy, 1949–2000 A.D.* (London: Croom Helm, 1985), p. 34.

47. Zhang Qingwu, "A Sketch of Our National Migration Policy," *ZRK* vol. 2 (1988), p. 36; Chaoze Cheng, "Internal Migration in Mainland China: The Impact of Government Policies," *Issues and Studies* vol. 27, no. 8 (Taipei, 1991), p. 56; and Kirkby, *Urbanization in China*, pp. 14–21, 154. See especially Kam Wing Chan, *Cities with Invisible Walls: Reinterpreting Urbanization in Post 1949 China* (Hong Kong: Oxford University Press, 1994).

48. "Huji yanjiu" ketizu ["Household Registration Research" Task Force], "The Present Household Registration Management System and Economic System Reform," *Shanghai shehui kexueyuan xueshu jikan* [Shanghai Social Science Academy Academic Quarterly] (hereafter *HYK*) vol. 3 (1989), p. 86, states: "Controls over urban mechanical growth [i.e., immigration] are lax when economic development speed is fast and large amounts of rural and town population come in; when the economy is tense, controls on urban growth tighten." See also Kirkby, *Urbanization in China*, pp. 17, 21, 32; Potter and Potter, *China's Peasants*, p. 30; and Tiejun Cheng and Mark Selden, "The Origins and Social Consequences of China's Hukou System," *China Quarterly* vol. 139 (1994), pp. 644–68.

that right has not appeared in any version since 1975.[49] Thus, the larger economic aspirations of the authorities initially overrode not just any concern for the rights of ruralites to move about, but also their rights as coequal citizens and workers should they be summoned into town.

The legal basis for this division was first laid by a State Council directive of June 1955 on establishing a system of household registration, rules that were further elaborated in a set of January 1958 regulations on household registration.[50] With the order on household registration of mid-1955, each individual was required to register his or her place of residence officially, with records maintained by the public security offices at the brigade level (at that time) in the countryside and in the neighborhood in cities. Thenceforth, the individual's residence status became an ascribed, inherited one, determining his or her entire livelihood and welfare simply on the basis of where the registration was located. In accord with the industrialization imperative alluded to earlier, the system's rationale was to ensure that peasants remained on the land, producing the food that would enable the cities' residents to industrialize and modernize urban China.[51]

With the onset of the reform era after 1980, successively more and more permissive state policies on movement into urban areas were accompanied by a gradual relaxation of the state's control over the resources essential to daily life – namely, grain, housing, and employment. These developments made it possible for peasants to relocate, even into cities, in search of a more comfortable standard of living. Yet a closer look reveals that these migrants remain confined within the rubric of the state's persisting imperative: to marry urban growth and productivity with cost saving, and, as a "socialist" state, to provide for the city dweller while reserving the ruralite as docile, disposable trespasser and drudge.[52]

For instance, to be licitly resident in a city, a peasant is compelled to undergo a cumbersome process of seeking approval and credentials, one that, as

---

49. Ding Shuimu, "The Present Household Registration System and the Direction of its Reform," *Shehuixue yanjiu* [Sociological Research] vol. 6 (Beijing, 1992), p. 103. China has had five constitutions since the present regime was created in 1949: the Common Program of 1949, and the constitutions of 1954, 1975, 1978, and 1982.

50. Guowuyuan fazhiju, Zhonghua renmin gongheguo fagui huibian bianji weiyuanhui, bian [State Council Legal System Bureau, Editorial Committee of the Compendium of Legal Documents of the People's Republic of China, eds.], "Directive on Establishing a System for Registration of Permanent Households," *Zhongguo renmin gongheguo fagui huibian* [Compendium of Legal Documents of the People's Republic of China] (hereafter, *Compendium*), vol. 1 (Beijing: Falu chubanshe, 1956), pp. 197–200, and translated in Zhang Qingwu, "Basic Facts on the Household Registration System," *Chinese Economic Studies* vol. 22, no. 1 (1988), pp. 103–6. "Regulations on Household Registration in the People's Republic of China," published in *Compendium*, vol. 7 (Beijing: Falu chubanshe, 1958), pp. 204–16, and translated in Zhang, "Basic Facts," pp. 87–92.

51. Zhang, "Basic Facts," p. 74, presents this rationale; see also *HYK*, pp. 83–4.

52. Chan, *Cities with Invisible Walls*, chapter 4, makes the same argument.

suggested earlier, very few actually observe. Beyond requiring transients to make known their presence in the city, local authorities demand, just as for foreign workers in Western Europe, that they obtain labor permits.[53] As economic "reform" increasingly enshrined market values and profit considerations began to throw native urban workers' jobs into question, the legitimation for infringing rural migrants' rights shifted – the rationale became the need to protect the posts of city laborers. By early 1995, the Ministry of Labor was even considering establishing "a system similar to international passport and visa requirements, which will aim at curbing 'transprovincial migration,'" expressly for this purpose.[54]

Despite much discussion and debate, and even talk of fundamental reform, the *hukou* policy itself hangs on, with a few notable alterations. First, a new, "temporary" household registration, the *zhanzhuzheng*, has become available in the cities since the mid-1980s.[55] Another response has been a widespread resort to the sale of the urban *hukou*, both on black markets by the late 1980s, and, by the early 1990s, openly by the city administrations themselves in the form of a "blue *hukou*."[56] Finally, permission was granted for 450 hand-picked, highly developed county-level towns having a financial surplus to allow law-abiding peasants with stable employment to receive an urban *hukou*, complete with the right to send their children to school at subsidized rates and with eligibility for basic health and welfare benefits.[57]

The new, blue kind of registration became available in most larger cities for up to 10,000 yuan as of early 1993.[58] This clearly was a measure that, as its application proliferated, was to milk both the wealthier peasantry and the

53. Stephen Castles and Godula Kosack, *Immigrant Workers and Class Structure in Western Europe*, 2nd ed. (New York: Oxford University Press, 1985), p. 100. As in China, the residence permits are issued by the police and the labor permits by the labor market authorities.
54. Robert J. Saiget, "Beijing Exiles Floating Population," *Kyodo*, March 25, 1995, in *FBIS*, March 27, 1995, p. 33.
55. See Michael R. Dutton, *Policing and Punishment in China: From Patriarchy to "The People"* (New York: Cambridge University Press, 1992), p. 336. The regulations for Jiangsu province, in *Xinhua ribao* [New China Daily], March 5, 1994, p. 5, translated in *FBIS*, April 11, 1994, pp. 60–3, are typical. For discussion of fundamental reforms, see *FBIS*, January 31, 1994, p. 41, from *XH* of the same date, "Ministries to Reform the System of Household Registration."
56. On black market sales, see Anthony Kuhn and Lincoln Kaye, "Bursting at the Seams," *FEER*, March 10, 1994, pp. 27–8. Journal articles from the late 1980s speak of both black market and official prices, with the amounts varying with the prestige of the city. See, for instance, *HYK*, p. 85, and Ding Shuimu, "A Preliminary View of the Present Household Registration Management System," *Shehui* [Society] vol. 1 (Shanghai, 1987), p. 19. See also Cao Jingchun, "Some Deliberations on Household Registration as Temporary Residence Permit," *Renkou yu jingji* [Population and Economy] vol. 5 (1993), pp. 38–42; and Ma Chenguang, "Cities Set Looser Rules on Residency," *FBIS*, March 4, 1994, p. 22, from *China Daily* (hereafter *CD*) of the same date, p. 3.
57. "Gradually Reform Small Towns' Household Management System," *Baokan wenzhai* [Periodicals Digest] (Beijing), July 24, 1997, p. 1; SWB FE/2986 G/8 (August 1, 1997), from *XH*, July 30, 1997 and FE/2989 G3–4 (August 5, 1997), from *XH*, July 30, 1997; and *AFP*, August 16, 1997.
58. Cao Jingchun, "Some Deliberations on Household Registration as Temporary Residence Permit," p. 38.

countryside for the benefit of the cities. Its possession offered all the same rights as urbanites enjoyed at the time, except for the right to join the army. But the ongoing snobbish xenophobia that characterizes urbanites' attitudes toward the peasantry is illustrated by this: Even advocates of household registration reform were proposing in 1993 that the holder of this new type of registration, beyond disbursing the hefty fee, should yet have to wait a full 10 years before becoming the city's permanent resident![59]

For the most part, though national leaders welcome the peasant workers for their contribution to economic growth and their provision of services for the cities, the official viewpoint up through the mid-1990s has been, as ever, to protect the cities. Their opinion is that additional farmers in search of work should stay away from the municipalities and instead seek their livelihood in the vast countryside – by setting up township enterprises, by creating new small towns, by engaging in more intensive agricultural development, or by performing works of capital construction.

As for the managers and bosses who handle the migrants, this comment, casting aside a notion of rights, is illustrative of the form of justification they offer for doing so:

> Construction team leaders say the work of the laborers in their own team is more bitter than that of peasants, sometimes the living conditions at their work sites are inferior, what they eat is also inferior, but although it's like this, if you pay them and the wages come on time, the workers can tolerate it. Team leaders aren't concerned about the regulations in the [1994] Labor Law, since they think what their own workers are most concerned about is making more money.[60]

Yet there are signs of something else as time goes on: beginnings of mentions of rights, law, and protection for the migrants. For instance, the "Beijing City Regulations on the Management of Transient People Seeking Jobs in Beijing" of 1995 listed services migrant workers were to perform, protections they should enjoy, the fees they would be expected to pay, and the legal responsibilities to which they would be held accountable in the event of violating regulations.[61] And in mid-1995 Ren Jianxin, director of the Central Commission for Comprehensive Management of Public Security, announced:

> More should be done to intensify controls over residence and public order concerning the population who work in places other than their long-term residences.

59. Qin Qiuhong, "Reform the Present Household Registration System to Fit the Needs of the Market Economy," *Jingji gaige* [Economic Reform] vol. 5 (Xi'an, 1993), p. 46.
60. Yuan Yue, et al., *Luoren – Beijing liumin di zuzhihua zhuangkuang yanjiu baogao* [The Exposed – A Research Report on the Condition of the Organization of Migrants in Beijing] (Beijing: Beijing Horizon Market Research and Analysis Company, 1995), p. 35.
61. *FBIS*, April 19, 1995, p. 15, from *XH*, April 19, 1995.

In addition, such work should be linked to government efforts in educating and providing services for these people, which should be included in rules, regulations, or laws that relate to this population.[62]

Civic and social privileges. Like illegal foreign workers in Japan, many country-folk who come to town in China are forced to cobble together a coarse existence among the cracks and crevices of proper, permanent urban life, and even – if they fail to register – on the sly. Politically they are worse off, for given China's authoritarian polity, they suffer as do all workers in the country, only more so.

Trade unions in the PRC have until recently been heavily dominated by Party officials and far more responsive to Party directives and policies than to the workers themselves. In the case of the migrants, despite a national Trade Union Law of 1992 demanding that all firms set up branches of the trade union, the factories where they tend to concentrate, the foreign-funded firms, have been notoriously flagrant in not installing unions.[63] Perhaps in response to this lack of unions – as well as to the unrepresentative nature of the official unions – unauthorized unions, set up outside the party's aegis, had emerged in Guangdong province by early 1994. According to a Hong Kong journal, more than 800 such groupings existed at that time. But defenseless peasant workers feared openly joining them, because of the likelihood of being laid off as a result.[64]

True, the most recent version of the PRC Constitution grants the freedoms of speech, the press, assembly, association, procession, and demonstration to all citizens of the country, urban and rural alike, in its Article 35 (the right to strike, which was present in the 1978 version as Article 45, having been struck from this latest edition).[65] Yet many, if not most attempts at staging processions and demonstrations even by regular workers and proper urban residents – not even to mention the precariously situated urban "peasants" – do not receive the requisite advance approval from the authorities and, if carried out nonetheless, are therefore decreed illicit. Moreover, ever since the shoot down of June 1989 and the demonstrations that preceded it, all efforts at organization outside the Party have been declared ipso facto illegal.

Given this official posture toward even the mildest forms of assembly and protest by even the permanent residents of cities, it should be obvious that

---

62. *FBIS*, June 8, 1995, p. 17, from *XH*, June 7, 1995.
63. *XH*, September 12, 1994, and translated in *FBIS*, September 12, 1994, p. 51. As of the end of June 1994, only one third of the 52,000-plus foreign firms in the country had established trade unions (*CD*, October 27, 1994, p. 3, reprinted in *FBIS*, October 28, 1994, p. 31).
64. Reported in *Tangtai* [Contemporary Times] (Hong Kong), March 15, 1994, pp. 38–9, translated in *FBIS*, April 5, 1994, pp. 43–4.
65. *Beijing Review* (hereafter *BR*), March 17, 1978, p. 13; and *BR*, December 27, 1982, p. 16.

participation in such activities by temporary inhabitants would be all the more prohibited. As for voting (a practice that until the past few years has been without practical content or consequences even for those who have the right to engage in it), just as foreigners (noncitizens) are denied the franchise in Germany and Japan, anyone residing in a Chinese city for however long without official household registration in that city may not take part in elections.[66]

If we turn to other civic or social rights and prerogatives, such as the right to subsistence, education, employment, medical care, and nearly gratis housing, we find that migrants in the cities are in the main officially denied these as well. A document prepared by a researcher from the public security sector in the 1980s notes that "citizens" not in possession of a local *hukou* are barred from receiving education, gaining [state-provided] employment, health-care treatment . . . [and are] ineligible for state-allocated housing and grain allocation.[67]

Certainly these various deprivations and denials were experienced far more keenly before the late 1980s than thereafter. For by that time, bustling open markets in grain and produce were available to all takers alike and the low-quality rationed grain was rarely the choice of anyone. Urban schools began admitting outsiders, if for increasingly steep fees, as the size and prestige of the city rose. And peasants in town found shelter in rentals let by permanent residents, in newly opened guesthouses and hostels, and in the dormitories of the firms that hired them.

Also, a wider and wider nonstate labor market opened up as the 1980s progressed, with private entrepreneurs, self-employment, and foreign firms providing opportunities on a scale that had never before existed in the PRC, even as state-owned firms began employing peasants as temporary labor in far larger numbers and with more regular procedures than had been the case in the past. Private doctors also set up practices, and some of the state firms made medical care – if of a very rudimentary nature – available to their peasant workers.[68]

It must be pointed out, however, that of these five components of basic city living, four (grain, schooling, rentals, and health care) were provided either gratis or at exceedingly low cost to ordinary urbanites in the past, and the fifth (employment) was generally guaranteed for them. Even now (late 1997), though the employment picture is far less secure, costs of the first four for urbanites have risen only slightly. But for the peasant outsiders, the first four are obtainable only at relatively substantial cost, and the fifth must

66. Zhang, "Basic Facts," p. 8.   67. Zhang, "Basic Facts," p. 8.
68. Solinger, "The Chinese Work Unit and Transient Labor in the Transition from Socialism", pp. 162–4.

be arranged pretty much entirely by the migrants themselves (with the assistance of their friends and relatives).

Thus, as compared to foreigners in Germany and Japan, peasants in Chinese cities have a double disadvantage: First, like all Chinese nationals, they are subject to the authoritarian regimens of the still-Party-governed polity; second, they can acquire only at prices much elevated above those available to locals the basic necessities of daily urban living.

Treatment of migrant workers. For simplicity's sake, it is more or less accurate to state that peasant workers in Chinese cities are slotted into the same tier of the labor market as migrant labor is anywhere – that "secondary" niche in which work is dirty, dangerous, debilitating, and insecure. In many cases, it is also less well paid.[69] But, for accuracy's sake, at least two twists to the story should be specified. In the first place, migrant labor in many state-owned factories in Chinese cities appears to have received fairer treatment, better pay, shorter hours, and more welfare benefits than those in foreign-funded firms. It appears that they are generally housed in factory dorms (though placed up to 20 to a room, unlike the regular workers, each of whom gets at least a room to her or himself) and are often eligible at a minimum for some basic medical care, and sometimes for other benefits as well.[70]

The foreign firms (a fixture not present in Germany or Japan, but much courted in China for their famous boost to the economy), on the other hand, have often invested at the behest of local governments anxious for the extra taxes they will yield, and there state regulations are frequently ignored altogether. There have been numerous reports both in the Chinese and the foreign presses of the litany of abuses suffered by migrants in these overseas-financed enterprises. These range from sixteen-hour days to an absence of toilet breaks, kicking, beatings, lock-ins, and even to being penned up in a dog cage and being made to stand in the rain as penalties![71]

The second aberration from the stereotypical secondary sector of the labor market is that it is not uniformly wretched in China. For those with skills, capital, and connections (either to government or Party officials – presumably via blood or common place of origin – or to other country-siders from their native place who have already established an urban foothold), it is possible to

---

69. Michael J. Piore, *Birds of Passage: Migrant Labor and Industrial Societies* (Cambridge: Cambridge University Press, 1979).
70. Solinger, "The Chinese Work Unit and Transient Labor in the Transition from Socialism," pp. 161–5.
71. For detailed accounts and figures, see Liu Jinghuai and Zeng Mingzi, "Rights, Interests, and Dignity Brook No Infringement – Worries About Protection in Foreign-Invested Enterprises (Part 1)," *Liaowang* [Outlook] (Beijing), January 31, 1994, pp. 26–9, translated in *FBIS*, March 3, 1994, pp. 32–6; and "Part 2," *Liaowang*, February 7, 1994, pp. 15–17, translated in *FBIS*, March 3, 1994, pp. 37–41.

become a well-to-do private entrepreneur in the retail, service, or garment-manufacturing sectors. This chance for forming connections that bridge the barrier between local and outsider – possible, of course, because the Chinese migrants are, after all, nationals, unlike those in Japan and Germany – may actually privilege some Chinese migrant laborers in comparison with their fellow marginals in Germany or Japan.

To summarize, it would appear that Chinese farmers who come to town in their own country have been subject to at least as rigorous rules of entry, and have lesser formal civic and social privileges than their counterpart foreign migrant laborers in Germany and Japan. And for the most part, as migrant laborers, they probably fare about the same as foreign migrant workers in Japan, and not as well as those in Germany. With their nation beginning at a lower level of development than the other two, and as rulers of a staunchly authoritarian regime, China's leaders rely on a stringent developmental imperative that causes them to put peasant outsiders into a generally rightless realm. Yet, as we have seen, there are inklings of change – the move toward laws and protection (now mainly at the rhetorical level) noted earlier – on the horizon.

EXPLAINING DIFFERENCES

Three variables that distinguish the political economies of these three countries can each be shown to contribute to an explanation of the differences in the respective migration regimes of the countries, with implications for the rights migrant labor receives in each. The first of these is a set of issues connected with *developmental patterns* and the *associated timing* of demand for labor. Second is the *place of regular/native labor in the apolitical system*.[72] The third has to do with the *geopolitics of location*.

Development and Timing

An important distinction between Japan and Germany is that, when the massive postwar recovery thrust took off, almost half of the Japanese labor force was still in the agricultural sector; by 1970, this figure had dropped to just 19 percent. In the single decade between 1960 and 1970, the three major metropolises of Tokyo, Osaka, and Nagoya had raised their combined populations by a total of 10 million. This meant that, in addition to Japan's

---

72. Patrick R. Ireland, *The Policy Challenge of Ethnic Diversity: Immigrant Politics in France and Switzerland* (Cambridge, MA: Harvard University Press, 1994).
73. Sassen, *The Global City: New York, London, Tokyo*, p. 308; Muto, "Japan: The Issue of Migrant Workers," p. 350.

reliance on automation, the pool of ruralites migrating to the towns relieved the country from having to turn to foreigners for several decades.[73]

Germany, on the other hand, which had already begun to empty out its countryside much earlier, saw only about 3.5 million workers abandon the fields for the factories in the two decades between 1950 and 1970.[74] And so it was compelled to call in outsiders, albeit ethnic German resettlers at first, as early as the 1950s.

Note as well that neither of these countries devised a developmental agenda that locked the peasants onto the land in the interest of modernizing cities alone as China did; both of them, thus, had admitted their farmers as full-fledged workers as soon as the need arose. In the case of China, it was not until the early 1980s, just before Japan's surge of immigration also took off, that Deng Xiaoping's new market reforms ushered in an era of rural movement. As a result, policymakers and their municipally based publics in both China and Japan are only lately coming to terms with outsiders mixing into their fold, genuine foreigners in Japan, native-peasant foreigners in China.

Another difference in this category of developmentally governed timing has to do with unemployment figures in the 1980s. Unemployment in Germany – which had lingered in the range of 2 to 3 percent into the 1970s – was up to 8 to 10 percent by the 1980s. Indeed, beginning as early as the mid-1970s, following the oil price shock of 1973, high unemployment became the excuse for restricting immigration. Thus, as we have seen, the Germany of the 1990s began cutting back some of its more generous policies and its more open stance.[75] The important point here is that its relatively liberal migration regime was born in the early 1950s, when the economy craved migrant workers, long before these problems came to the fore, and it was by no means fully dismantled with this new thrust.

In Japan, to the contrary, unemployment rates remained around 2 to 3 percent into the 1980s.[76] Then, the mid-1980s saw a virtual economic boom that lasted into the first years of the 1990s, one that cried out for the entry of foreigners ready to work. This sequencing meant that even though the issue of competition in the labor market between outsiders and insiders had not

74. Jost Halfmann, "Social Change and Political Mobilization in West Germany," in Peter J. Katzenstein, ed., *Industry and Politics in West Germany: Toward the Third Republic* (Ithaca: Cornell University Press, 1989), p. 55.

75. Peter J. Katzenstein, "Stability and Change in the Emerging Third Republic," in Katzenstein, ed., *Industry and Politics in West Germany: Toward the Third Republic*, pp. 308–9; Brubaker, *Citizenship and Nationhood in France and Germany*, p. 176.

76. Watanabe, "The Lewisian Turning Point and International Migration," p. 122; Ronald Dore, *Flexible Rigidities: Industrial Policy and Structural Adjustment in the Japanese Economy 1970–80* (Stanford: Stanford University Press, 1986), p. 87.

emerged by the mid-1990s, neither had modes of integrating foreigners into this market yet evolved by then.

In China the prereform socialist system's pledge to grant a job to every urban worker held good in the main through the 1980s, largely because the labor market was kept manageable in size by excluding peasants.[77] Moreover, post-1980 economic liberalization stimulated the growth and legitimated the birth of brand-new components of this market, especially marketing and private and foreign business, all of which begged and bidded for hands, both "native" and peasant.

It was only in the years since the late 1980s – first because of a regime-engineered economic recession from 1988 to 1991, and then because of an acceleration of market-style reforms after 1992 – that city laborers actually began losing their positions. That latest bout of economic "reform" especially has led state firms, forced to be cost and profit conscious, to shed their permanent workforces.

So, not only did a regime of incorporation for transient labor fail to take root in China in the few short years between 1984 (when peasants first began populating the cities in sizable numbers) and 1988 (when recession and reform first joined in dispelling labor). Just on the heels of the entry of country-folk in significant numbers into the urban industrial workforce, urbanites under threat of loss of their jobs began to perceive – rightly or wrongly – a sense of competition with them. At the same time this encouragement to the incursion of market principles has seen increasing numbers of foreign investors and periurban communities open firms. These are enterprises for the most part operating outside the regimen of state-decreed benefits and fair treatment for migrant workers.

This may be comparable in effect to the case in Japan, where it is principally the small and medium construction and manufacturing firms, which derive their work from subcontracts with large corporations, that engage foreign labor.[78] These smaller firms handle their casual workforces, also in the secondary labor market, according to frameworks totally at odds with the regime of life-tenured, enterprise-trained employees that obtains in the major companies for which Japan is famous. In Germany, on the contrary, though foreign workers may stir antagonistic feelings among resident labor,

77. A limited number of peasants were recruited into the cities in the early 1960s and also in the early 1970s, but this was always carefully controlled, and voluntary individual migration was strictly forbidden.
78. Sassen, *The Global City: New York, London, Tokyo*, p. 315; Morita and Sassen, "The New Illegal Immigration in Japan, 1980–1992," p. 157.
79. Katzenstein, "Stability and Change in the Emerging Third Republic," pp. 350–1, implies that the less well-educated and unskilled native workers are vying for the same jobs taken by foreigners, even as another segment of German labor has fit into new high-skill, high-tech jobs since the 1980s.

the outsiders – who, as a collectivity, have been on the scene now for some decades – enter the same factories with native labor, and so are subject to similar rules of treatment.[79]

In sum, then, unlike in Germany, the presence of substantial rural reserves in China and Japan along with extremely low urban unemployment rates (both of which conditions were regime-manufactured outcomes in the Chinese case) delayed the importing of outside labor for decades, so that neither did any regime of incorporation develop nor did issues of competition come to the fore. Moreover, when migrant labor did appear, it was often shunted into firms that function in a realm set apart from, and so immune from, the comparative beneficence of the mainstream, primary labor market regulatory regime.

The Political Place of Labor

It is perhaps surprising that the place of native labor in the larger political econ-omy has definite implications for the reception accorded migrant labor: Where labor is coordinated at the national level by a powerful federation of unions and where it is bonded to a political party that is truly a player in national politics, migrant labor stands a better chance of receiving good treatment.

In Germany, workers lay claim to two distinct channels for the representa-tion of their interests: The first is via the works councils at the enterprise level, which are compulsory in private companies that employ at least five workers. These councils, in which foreign labor is also permitted to partici-pate, deal on an equal basis with management – via the practice of codeter-mination – on a range of important matters related to their own employ-ment. Second are the unions, also open to foreigners, in which workers can engage in collective bargaining.[80]

It is not just that regular workers are recognized. They have sometimes utilized their clout, paradoxically, for the benefit of the migrants: It was actually unionists who laid the foundation for the institution of migrant workers' rights and benefits in the 1950s and 1960s. Indeed, native workers fought migrants' early fights for them out of fear that the outsiders could potentially organize themselves into a competing, and presumably less demanding, union of their own. Also, beginning in 1986, the DGB (Federa-tion of German Trade Unions) campaigned – if, so far, fruitlessly – for voting rights for migrants at the local level.[81]

Respect for labor is probably enhanced by the concentration of its power

---

80. Peter J. Katzenstein, "Industry in a Changing West Germany," in Katzenstein, ed., *Industry and Poli-tics in West Germany*, p. 11; and Vranken, "Industrial Rights," p. 68.
81. Hammar, "The Civil Rights of Aliens," p. 88, and "Industrial Rights," pp. 57–8; Jan Rath, "Voting Rights," p. 133 – all in Layton-Henry, ed., *The Political Rights of Migrant Workers in Western Europe.*

in one mammoth federation at the federal level. This manifest strength, combined with the federation's close tie to a political party that is a genuine contender for power (the SPD, the socialist party), have probably together been responsible for the "relative equality in the distribution of power among [the] different actors" in the enterprise as between labor and business. They probably account as well for workers' power in the policy process at the central level.[82]

In Japan, labor – at least within the mainstream, large-scale corporations – is the beneficiary of the renowned lifetime employment system, is treated as valuable "human capital," is trained and educated on the job within the firm, and has been protected against the downsizing that might otherwise attend recessions, at least into the mid-1990s.[83] But although incorporated at the level of the plant, drawn into consultations with its own management there, and sheltered and promoted over time within long-nourished internal labor markets, this participation has essentially been one based just in the firm. It is thus workers as members of enterprise unions, limited to the bounds of their own companies, that have had a role in the Japanese industrial relations system. From the late 1940s until at least the late 1980s, when a national-level Japanese Trade Union Confederation (Rengo) was formed, labor as a whole was decentralized, fragmented, and scattered.[84] Even after the formation of Rengo, one scholar writing in the early 1990s still concluded:

> In short, although labor unions can and do participate in the policy process, their participation still falls short of being formalized in a neocorporatist structure involving the summit organs of functional interests.[85]

The other significant weakness of Japanese labor is its historical marginalization, which can be traced to the nature of its linkage with the party sys-

---

82. Katzenstein, "Stability and Change in the Emerging Third Republic," p. 348. On relations between labor and the SPD, see Vranken, "Industrial Rights," pp. 51–2.

83. Yamanaka Keiko, "Commentary: Theory versus Reality in Japanese Immigration Policy," in Cornelius, Martin, and Hollifield, *Controlling Immigration*, p. 413; Johnson, "Studies of Japanese Political Economy: A Crisis in Theory," pp. 96–110; Dore, *Flexible Rigidities* is a study of how protection from downsizing was accomplished in the 1970s and early 1980s. Note that the Japanese training system contrasts with the more nationally based system of vocational training that obtains in Germany. On this, see Katzenstein,"Industry in a Changing West Germany," p. 12.

84. Tsujinaka Yutaka, "Rengo and Its Osmotic Networks," p. 211, and Kume Ikuo, "A Tale of Twin Industries: Labor Accommodation in the Private Sector," p. 166, both in Gary Allinson and Sone Yasunori, eds., *Political Dynamics in Contemporary Japan* (Ithaca: Cornell University Press, 1993); and Lonny E. Carlile, "Party Politics and the Japanese Labor Movement: Rengo's 'New Political Force'," *Asian Survey* vol. 34, no. 7 (1994), pp. 617–20.

85. Mike Mochizuki, "Public Sector Labor and the Privatization Challenge: The Railway and the Telecommunications Unions," in Allinson and Sone, eds., *Political Dynamics in Contemporary Japan*, p. 196; see also Dore, *Flexible Rigidities*, pp. 88, 105, 123; and Sakakibara Eisuke, *Beyond Capitalism: The Japanese Model of Market Economics* (Lanham, MD: University Press of America, 1993), pp. 16–19.

86. Carlile, "Party Politics and the Japanese Labor Movement," pp. 609–19.

tem. Unlike in Germany, Japanese labor has been split in its allegiance to not one, but two, parties of the left: the Japanese Socialist Party for public-sector labor and, after 1960, the Democratic Socialist Party for the private sector.[86]

After a burst of the Socialist Party's energetic involvement at the core of power just following the war, mismanagement, combined with the United States "reverse course," quickly shut off a space for the left at the top until 1994, when the Socialist Party was arguably no longer leftist at all. Following that early taste of political centrality, the JSP's militancy and DSP's accommodating irrelevance over the years excluded both, along with their charges among labor groups, from the inner circles of power and policy.[87] This was a fragmentation already lent labor by the enterprise-centeredness of activism.

The upshot of these deficiencies from a political point of view was that, at least until the advent of Rengo, labor was relatively isolated at the top, its interests taken at best as secondary, certainly by no means "equal" as they were in Germany once the postwar era began. When foreign labor finally arrived in Japan in large numbers around 1986, it therefore entered a labor movement very different from the one that greeted the early "guest workers" of West Germany.[88]

This one was a movement at once too incoherent to accommodate this outside labor, and yet, with the foreigners entering only the subcontracting firms in the secondary labor market, it was also one whose own members were not really threatened. Thus, this movement was without a need to shackle foreign workers within some larger, homegrown union structure – a structure that, in 1986, was not yet even to exist for another three years. As of the mid-1990s, some smaller labor unions put forth a minimal call for legalizing unauthorized foreign workers, but Rengo, the new federation at the top, had so far failed to endorse this request, as of the mid-1990s.[89]

In the highly authoritarian Chinese case, the dominance of the Communist Party (CCP) and of its own agenda, both over individual laborers at the micro level and over the labor movement as a whole, meant that there was hardly a question of any genuine representation of labor's interests, either within the individual firm or via the national-scale All China Federation of Trade Unions.[90] There is thus a corporate federation at the top, but it has no independent power of its own. Chinese leaders have always justified both

---

87. Gary Allinson and Sone Yasunori, "Negotiating Labor's Role," in Allinson and Sone, eds., *Political Dynamics in Contemporary Japan,* pp. 156–7.

88. Carlile, "Party Politics and the Japanese Labor Movement," p. 620; Tsujinaka, "Rengo and its Osmotic Networks," p. 211.

89. Cornelius, "Japan: The Illusion of Immigration Control," p. 394.

90. On the modes of domination exercised by the party within the individual firm, see Walder, *Communist Neo-Traditionalism: Work and Authority in Chinese Industry.*

their larger economic, progrowth policies as well as their treatment of workers by couching their rule rhetorically as being "in the interests of the working class."

Again, because of the monopoly of power exercised by the CCPI it is so far meaningless to speak of a linkage between labor and one or another other party, for there is no other even potentially power-wielding entity. Even the efforts of underground labor organizers to mobilize independent unions among the peasant workers not only are devoid of an iota of influence within the present system, they have only led to arrests of the activists.[91]

Bringing these thoughts together, we can conclude the following: Where the power of permanent, resident labor is strong and its place more or less secure, both within the plant and at the apex of the political system, the fate of migrant labor is more promising. Both China's repressive political system and its continuing strategy of effectively sacrificing farmers' interests for untrammeled urban modernization have undercut any influence for outsider underdogs.

Geopolitical Location

One last variable is the influence of several facets of a nation's geographical location upon its migration regime. Here I refer to the impact a country's connections with its immediate neighbors might have on its policies; there may also be a relationship between the regime in place and the source of the migrants reaching its labor markets.

Several scholars have pointed to what they see as the effect of a progressively pervasive culture and global spread of conventions surrounding human rights internationally. According to them, the advance of values attached to human rights has begun to render the concept of "citizenship" nearly irrelevant in the granting of rights and privileges. Instead, they claim, citizenship is being replaced with a borderless "personhood," whereby entitlements are granted without regard to territory.[92]

Notably, however, among our three countries, such a movement appears to have taken root only in Germany. Indeed, it is Germany alone that has become incorporated into the liberal regime of the European Union, which is comprised of a set of rights-based countries, and in which European Community laws have become part of German law. As far back as 1957, in establishing the Union's predecessor, the European Economic Community, the Treaty

---

91. *FBIS*, May 17, 1994, p. 19, from *SCMP*, May 17, 1994, pp. 1, 8; *FBIS*, May 24, 1994, pp. 52–3, from *Eastern Express* (Hong Kong), May 23, 1994.

92. See Soysal, *Limits of Citizenship;* and Hollifield, *Immigrants, Markets, and States.* Cornelius, Martin, and Hollifield, *Controlling Immigration,* also refer to this literature.

of Rome guaranteed the citizens of all the member states the right to work in any EEC nation beginning in 1968.

In the early years, because Europe was unifying in other ways, receptivity in West Germany to foreign labor, virtually all of which was from Europe itself, if not always from EEC countries, was undoubtedly eased. As time went on, a growing harmonization of the judicial systems of the member states emerged, to which Germany falls subject.[93] This entails, among other matters, the laws governing both foreign as well as intra-EU labor.[94]

In Japan's case, the migration flows came from South, East, and Southeast Asian countries, and, more recently, China, a result in part of the Japanese economy's own internationalization, which involved much interaction with its neighboring economies.[95] Not only is there no liberal human rights regime impinging on this interchange; if anything, the societies from which the migrants hail – the Philippines, South Korea, Bangladesh, Pakistan, and Thailand – have certainly all been known to exhibit human rights abuses of their own.[96] Thus, neither Japan's location nor the homes of its sojourners exert a beneficial influence on its treatment of migrant workers.

In China, we are talking not about workers coming from the outside. Rather, the incoming masses are just the peasants from China's own countryside, so there is of course no question of any effect of a value system of some foreign country or grouping upon the migration regime that interests us here. Because inhabitants of the countryside have been downgraded for decades, there is no larger force involved here that could impose any more humane values than those held by China's own urban rulers and managers. There is, then, at this stage no legitimating framework issuing from the country's immediate surroundings, or from the homelands of its transients, that would counter the dominant paradigm within which most urban politicians are operating.

Insofar as the interaction with neighbors, trading partners, and homelands of migrants are concerned, it would appear that, James Hollifield and Yasemin Soysal to the contrary, it is so far just countries such as Germany, situated in and involved with Western European liberal and largely law-abiding regimes (and with the European Union itself) that are susceptible to

---

93. Martin, "Germany: Reluctant Land of Immigration," p. 199. On judicial systems, Miriam Feldman, "New Citizenship Strategies in Postwar Europe: Nationalist and Post-National" (unpublished paper presented at the American Political Science Association Meeting, September 2–5, 1993, Washington, DC), pp. 3–5.

94. Discussion with Alec Stone, Irvine, CA, February 15, 1996.

95. Sassen, *The Global City: New York, London, Tokyo*, pp. 32–3. According to Jonathan Friedland, "Immigration: Traffic Problem," *FEER*, August 4, 1994, p. 20, around 30,300 Chinese nationals were then living illegally in Japan, brought in by the *yakusa* in collaboration with organized criminal syndicates in Taiwan, Hong Kong, and China.

96. Morita and Sassen, "The New Illegal Immigration in Japan, 1980–1992," p. 151.

the power of the international human rights regime that is pervasive on that continent.

Migrant labor around the globe, insofar as its enjoyment of the human rights specified in international agreements is concerned, is in a sorry plight. Their problems are likely to be even worse in places such as Germany and Japan, where an ethnocultural bias is joined with a commitment to grow economically with no holds barred.

I have found disparities among these countries in three categories: in the timing of their absorption of migrant laborers and the connection of this with the health of the economy (because of the negative impact of high rates of native unemployment upon receptivity toward migrant workers), in the role of resident labor in the larger political arena, and in their geopolitical situations. I went on to point to ways in which these dissimilarities might be linked to differential outcomes in migration regimes.

This analysis yields the following relationships: Given relatively healthy economic conditions, the longer a society has had to cope with outsiders, the more likely it is that it will come to assimilate them.[97] The stronger, better organized, and more involved in governmental policy making domestic labor is, the more prone it will be to assist outsiders to gain a foothold and the more capable it will be of doing so, and the more entwined they are in exchanges with other liberal regimes, the more legalistic and rights-conscious states will become, with beneficial consequences for sojourners as well as for other minorities.

These conclusions, then, imply the following: First, over time, the Chinese floating population will likely be treated more benignly than it has been heretofore; there are already signs that this is underway. Second, if the regular, permanent workforce could gain new rights (and there was already in 1994 promulgated a Labor Law with many promises, though few yet realized in its first several years on the books) that would have positive side effects for the migrants as well.[98] And third, the more Western, law-based states engage China in their economic activities, the more the people of China, including the peasants in the cities, are apt, eventually, to gain good treatment.

---

97. This finding is consistent with Rita J. Simon and Susan H. Alexander, *The Ambivalent Welcome: Print Media, Public Opinion and Immigration* (Westport, CT: Praeger, 1993), p. 46: "The responses [in public opinion surveys] show that immigrant groups who have been in the United States longer tend to receive more positive evaluations than do recent immigrant communities . . . ."

98. This law was adopted on July 5, 1994, at the 8th Session of the Standing Committee of the 8th National People's Congress (translated in *FBIS*, July 19, 1994).

CHAPTER 13

THE ANTI–NUCLEAR POWER MOVEMENT IN TAIWAN: CLAIMING THE RIGHT TO A CLEAN ENVIRONMENT

MAB HUANG

INTRODUCTION

The question of whether human rights are innate has bedeviled legal and political philosophers for centuries in the West, but it has rarely been considered by Chinese philosophers. The idea of human rights was not introduced into China until the late nineteenth century. The rise of rights consciousness, both in China and in Taiwan, was closely tied to the emergence of liberalism. Many Chinese intellectuals of the 1920s and 1930s were dedicated to the promotion of liberty and human rights, although they were suppressed by the Nationalist government.

In Taiwan, one of the strongest historical examples of the relationship between awareness of rights and the emergence of participatory democracy is the anti–nuclear power movement in the 1980s. The movement took shape after decades of economic growth and against a background of political reform. Its leaders were not only concerned with the rights of freedom of speech and association and the right to participate in decision making – rights that had been promoted in earlier periods of liberal democratic aspiration by, for example, the Free China group in the 1950s[1] – they also promoted a new right: the right to a clean environment.

By any conventional criteria, East Asia has done a superb job of promoting economic growth.[2] Explanations of the causes of rapid growth in East Asia

---

1. For example, see Sechin Y. S. Chien, "Liberalism and Political Order: The Free China Semi-Monthly Revisited," in *Taiwan: A Radical Quarterly in Social Studies* vol. 1, no. 4 (Winter 1988).
2. The current economic crisis has obviously tempered some of this enthusiasm, but Taiwan in particular is still held up as an economic model. See Ben Dolven, "The Risk Taker: Why Taiwan Trumps Singapore as a Model for Asia," *Far Eastern Economic Review,* August 6, 1998, pp. 12–15.

vary from an emphasis on Confucian values to the rise of the middle class and the expansion of civil society. Only recently have debates about East Asian economic growth shown any concern with its impact on the environment. The conventional wisdom had been that the more economic growth the better. Not until the late 1980s did the idea of sustainable development – the need to manage economic growth – gain widespread acceptance, primarily through the efforts of the United Nations. The leadership of Taiwan's anti–nuclear power movement, which for all practical purposes dates from the same period, has been committed to this ideal.

In this chapter, the anti–nuclear power movement and the politics surrounding it will be used to explore the relationships among economic development, environmental protection, and human rights in Taiwan. The history of this movement illustrates how grassroots mobilization around the nuclear power issue, articulated as a question of the fundamental human right to a clean and safe environment, contributed to an increased level of political participatory rights during the period of liberalization in Taiwan. It also engendered a heightened awareness of human rights among the general population. This was distinctly influenced by the contemporary context of rapid political transition.

Focusing on the activities of the Environmental Protection Union over the past decade, this study will describe in some detail the political and economic factors that led to the rise of the environmental movement and the attendant rise in citizens' consciousness of their participatory rights and their right to a clean environment. It will also explain why, after a decade of efforts on the part of the Union, the right to a clean environment is still not recognized in Taiwan.

TAIWANESE POLITICS FROM THE 1970S TO THE 1990S

May 24, 1996, was a day of complicated maneuvers on the floor of the Legislative Yuan, Taiwan's law-making body, as tense confrontations between the police and the demonstrators took place outside. The Nationalist Party (KMT) and the two opposition parties, the Democratic Progressive Party (DPP) and the New Party, had been mobilizing for days, even bringing their sick and disabled supporters on stretchers to vote. The ballots were collected and, faced with solid opposition and a few defections from within its own ranks, the KMT went down in defeat. The cause was the passage of a resolution to ban all construction of nuclear power plants, which included halting the construction of the #4 Nuclear Power Plant.[3]

3. *China Times Daily*, May 25, 1996, pp. 1, 3.

It was a climax in the decade-long struggle against the government by the Environmental Protection Union (the Union), a group of intellectuals who had come together in 1987 to protest the construction of the new nuclear plant. The Union has been deeply involved in many environmental issues, from stopping nuclear power to banning the construction of golf courses to opposing the development of the cement industry on the eastern coast of Taiwan. But opposition to the construction of nuclear plants has been its greatest preoccupation.

The Union's victory in getting the resolution passed was short-lived, as the government announced the following day that it would ask for repeal of the resolution. According to Article 57 of Taiwan's Constitution, only one third of the votes in the Legislative Yuan were required for the administration to win.[4] Three months later the government succeeded, with the tacit support of the business community and the acquiescence of the population. Premier Lien Chien hailed the result as providing continuity of government policy, as well as a secure basis for further economic development.[5] The Environmental Protection Union was dealt a serious setback but vowed to fight on.

To understand the long, drawn-out struggle for environmental protection in general and the anti–nuclear power movement in particular requires an examination of the political situation in Taiwan, the position of the government, and how both changed after political reforms were initiated in the mid-1980s.

For the previous forty years Taiwan had been governed with an iron fist, first by Chiang Kai-shek, then to a lesser degree by his son, Chiang Ching-kuo. No political opposition was tolerated, and any dissident opinion was subject to severe punishment. The occasional challenge to authority was dealt with harshly.[6] Early on the ruling KMT was wedded to a political ideology of anticommunism and a pledge to reunify China by conquering the mainland, and thus its legitimacy was closely tied to the defeat of the Chinese communists. Economic development was not given priority, and consequently environmental damages were moderate compared to what would take place in later years. It was not until the 1970s that the KMT's claim to legitimacy began perceptibly to change to rapid economic development and

---

4. *China Times Daily,* May 26, 1996, p. 1.   5. *China Times Daily,* October 19, 1996, p. 2.
6. The demonstrations in Kao-hsuing in 1979 were the most serious challenge to the government since the Free China group in the 1950s. The opposition groups had been gaining strength both in organizational skills and popular support since the mid-1970s, moving toward the goal of forming an opposition party. The authorities reacted to the demonstrations with a sweeping crackdown, arresting all the important opposition leaders except one. This suppression was definitely a setback for the opposition: The Democratic Progressive Party was not formed until 1986. For a brief account of the demonstrations, arrests, and trials by the military court, consult *A Stormy Decade: The* Mei-li-tao *Affair,* edited by *Journalist,* Taipei, 1989. *Mei-li-tao* (literally, "the Beautiful Island") is the name of the journal published by the opposition groups at the time.

a more comfortable life for the people.[7] With this shift, the stage was set for a push for rapid industrialization, including the government promotion of nuclear power and the rise of the anti–nuclear power movement.

In this process, Chiang Ching-kuo's announcement in 1976 of the initiative that has come to be known as the Ten Construction Projects was a milestone, a bold move. Chiang committed his government to substantial investment in the creation of an infrastructure for an industrial society, pursuing an import-substitution strategy, especially in the steel and petrochemical industries. Later on, high-tech industries were targeted.

By all accounts Chiang's ambitious plan turned out to be highly successful, an "economic miracle," his supporters claimed. They included not only the economists, the entrepreneurs, and the rising middle class in Taiwan, but the World Bank, the international business community, and many governments throughout the world. A new entrepreneurial class emerged in Taiwan, and perceptibly living standards began to improve.

In March 1986, barely two years before his death, Chiang Ching-kuo decided that serious political reforms needed to be put into effect. The reform measures he proposed included ending governance by martial law and eliminating the ban on opposition parties. In part Chiang was convinced by pressures from opposition groups (*tang-wai*) that some kind of modus vivendi would be necessary to head off confrontations and assure the KMT's control of the political transition. It could also be argued, however, that he felt confident that economic success had given him a firm basis for major political reform. Opposition groups moved quickly to found the new political party, the DPP.[8] Political democratization had finally begun; social protest movements were not far behind.

Immediately after the death of Chiang Ching-kuo in January 1988, Lee Teng-hui, a native Taiwanese bureaucrat designated by Chiang to be his successor, took over as president of the republic and chairman of the KMT; the succession was achieved by intense maneuvers within the highest echelon of the government and the party. Hardly a year had gone by before Lee turned against his former ally, Prime Minister Lee Huan. In part to ease Lee Huan from his post and to remove the military strongman General Hao Po-ts'un from his position as commander of the armed forces, Lee Teng-hui appointed Hao to be his premier, thus ending a government impasse. Moving vigorously to reassert authority and push the economy ahead, Hao immediately initiated a Six-Year National Construction Plan, which gave priority to the construction of the #4 Nuclear Power Plant in northern Taiwan, a project

---

7. See, for example, Thomas Gold, *State and Society in the Taiwan Miracle* (New York: M. E. Sharpe, 1986).
8. See Mab Huang, "Political Ko'tung and the Rise of the Democratic Progressive Party: 1984–1986," *Political Science Journal* no. 5 (Soochow University, March 1996), pp. 133–58.

that had been shelved for many years. Hao was prepared to use force to suppress the challenge of the environmental protection groups, and he did so, creating an atmosphere of confrontation well into the 1990s.[9] After General Hao left his position as premier in early 1993, his ambitious Six-Year Plan was scaled down. Yet the struggle did not end.

How do we explain the attitude and policy of the government through the years and General Hao's decision to deliberately confront the environmental movement? To begin with, the shift in emphasis from anticommunism to economic growth was crucial. Once that decision had been made, it was not easy to deviate from it, especially when the economic development of Taiwan was widely judged to be a great success. Moreover, with the promotion of economic development came a new entrepreneurial class, which supported the government and in time received benefits from the government. As the process of democratization set in, the business community gained greater influence while the opposition groups were allowed more space to maneuver. The business community, working closely with the bureaucrats, was agitated by what it saw as the need to revive the faltering economy. It pointed to the environmental protection movement, the labor movement, and the rise in crime rate as the nemeses of economic prosperity in Taiwan. The government thus faced intense pressure to act. Finally, the international business community also played a part in shaping the policy of the government toward the environmental movement in Taiwan. For some years the United States had been urging the Taiwanese government to move more rapidly to open its market, and American firms were expected to secure large and lucrative contracts when the #4 Nuclear Power Plant was built.[10] Taiwan had become a place for the Western business community to make money.

THE BIRTH OF THE ANTI–NUCLEAR POWER MOVEMENT

For years it had been clear that environmental damage was getting out of control in Taiwan. According to the tabulations of the Union in 1992, there had been sixteen minor incidents at #1, #2, and #3 Nuclear Power Plants between October 1978 and October 1988; and thirteen employees had died of cancer at #3 Nuclear Power Plant in a span of a few years.[11] This information, of course, was not known to the public until much later. What could

9. Hui-jen Ong and Mau-kuei Chang, "The Anti–Nuclear Power Movement at Gong-liao: The Rebellion of a Fishing Village" (unpublished monograph, 1993). Also Mau-kuei Chang, "Anti–Nuclear Power Movement in Taiwan: State, Capital and Grass-Roots Protests" (unpublished paper presented at the American Sociology Association meeting, Miami, Florida, August 13–17, 1993).

10. Mau-kuei Chang, "Anti–Nuclear Power Movement in Taiwan."

11. Cited in Lin Pi-yao, "The Anti-Nuclear Movement in Taiwan," in Cheng Hsien-yu, ed., *Policy Decision on Nuclear Power Plant #4 and Radiation Damage* (Taipei: Vanguard Publishers, 1994), pp. 188–9.

not be kept secret was that people in local communities had been suffering from the pollution of the air and water and from food poisoning, and that self-help groups had emerged to seek redress. The case of Lin-yuan was the earliest disturbance. A foreign investigator describes it:

> In 1983, residents of Lin-yuan, near Kaohsiung in southern Taiwan, burned down an amino acid factory that had been polluting the air and water of their village, forcing the factory to move to another site. In 1985, threats of violence against pesticide plants in Hsinchu and Taichung counties led the management of both factories to agree to clean up their operations. These so-called self-salvation (*tzu-li chiu-chi*) actions were initiated by local residents, usually poor farmers and fishermen, who had suffered damages, demanded compensation, and acted alone, using the means at hand, without the benefit of allies or support groups in other parts of the island.[12]

Altogether, Taiwan witnessed 110 protest activities between 1980 and 1987, and 352 more actions between 1988 and 1991.[13] Time and again, the government and/or the businesses would buy off the protests, paying "compensation" to the local communities. The most encouraging case for the environmental movement was the fight against U.S. chemical giant Du Pont's plan to build a factory in Lukang in central Taiwan. After more than a year of tense confrontation, Du Pont decided in 1987 to abandon the site.[14]

With rising concern for environmental protection, the government was forced to take measures to ease the anxiety of the populace. The Environmental Protection Administration was elevated to a cabinet-level agency in 1987, and the Environmental Impact Assessment Act was enacted. Nevertheless, the government did not budge from its commitment to rapid economic development and its support of the entrepreneurial class, and thus the implementation of the new measures can only be described as halfhearted. For example, most factories, hospitals, and clinics are of moderate size and do not have the capacity to handle the toxic wastes they produce. A rational approach would stipulate that either they pool their resources or the government provide them with facilities and charge them for their use.[15] Yet the government has done nothing of the kind.

Similarly, as the Union has pointed out, the Nuclear Energy Commission is too closely tied to the Taiwan Power Company to be expected to supervise

12. James Reardon-Anderson, *Pollution, Politics, and Foreign Investment in Taiwan: The Lukang Rebellion* (Armonk, NY: M. E. Sharpe, 1992).
13. Michael Hsiao, "The Character and Changes of Taiwan's Local Environmental Protest Movement: 1980–1991," in Taiwan Research Fund, *Environmental Protection and Industrial Policies* (Taipei: Vanguard Publishing Co., 1994).
14. Reardon-Anderson, *Pollution, Politics, and Foreign Investment in Taiwan*.
15. Giin-Tarng Hwang, *Studies on Environmental Laws in Taiwan* (Taipei: Yeh Dan Publishing Company, 1994), pp. 28–30.

the latter effectively. Laws need to be revised, and a new and impartial supervisory body should be set up, but the Union has made these recommendations to no avail. The idea of incorporating the right to a clean environment into the state constitution was proposed by Professor Tsai Sung-lin of the Consumer Cultural and Educational Foundation in 1988.[16] However, it did not have much impact; the government and the business community were not receptive at all, and the scholarly community did not give it much support.[17] The *Far Eastern Economic Review* was not far from the truth when it reported in 1991 that

> Taiwan's Environmental Protection Administration (EPA) faces one of the most serious cases of ecological depredation in Asia as it attempts to clean up the results of several decades of rapid industrialization. Since it was established in 1987, the EPA has proposed fifteen major new laws concerning air, water and land pollution. But the Taiwan Government, in pursuit of rapid growth, has not demonstrated a serious commitment to environmental protection. Equally industry – in the absence of effective regulation – has no incentive to introduce environmentally sound practices.[18]

Against this background of environmental degradation, a few intellectuals began to make public statements about environmental deterioration, but they had to present their case cautiously, given the threat of punishment by the authorities. Professor Lin Chun-yi, a biologist at Tunghai University, was the first scientist to point out in 1980 the dangers of nuclear power plants. In April 1985 the Consumer Cultural and Educational Foundation, a newly established proconsumer organization, sponsored a seminar on the #4 Nuclear Power Plant and its social impact, attended by about fifty scholars and experts from related fields. In this public forum, the first of its kind and a symbol of the awakening of civil society, participants took the Taiwan Power Company to task for its many failures, ranging from mismanagement of the nuclear power plants, to withholding information concerning radiation, to being indifferent to energy conservation.[19] The Consumer Cultural and Educational Foundation also sponsored the publication of the *New Environment Magazine*.[20]

16. See Tsai Sung-lin, *Central Daily News*, September 8, 1988, p. 3.
17. Professor Lee Hung-hsi of the National Taiwan University was more sympathetic to the idea, whereas his colleague Professor Yeh Chun-yun was more skeptical. See Lee, "The Meaning of Environmental Rights as Human Rights," in his collection of essays, *Constitution and Human Rights* (unpublished, printed 1985), pp. 519–24; and Yeh, "Environmental Rights in Constitution," *National Taiwan Law Review* vol. 19, no. 1 (1990).
18. See Bill Savadove, "Something for the Children," *Far Eastern Economic Review*, September 19, 1991, p. 42.
19. Mau-kuei Chang, "Anti–Nuclear Power Movement in Taiwan."
20. Not to be confused with *Taiwan Environment* published by the Taiwan Environmental Protection Union.

In May 1985 a few members of the Legislative Yuan and the Censorial Yuan began to criticize the Taiwan Power Company for its laxity in managing the nuclear power plants. Then, fifty-five KMT members of the Legislative Yuan proposed to halt the construction of the plant, a motion that was passed. Premier Yu Kuo-hua reported Chiang Ching-kuo's decision that the plan to build the #4 Nuclear Power Plant be temporarily shelved until the public concern over its safety was dispelled. The plan remained on hold for five years.

The passage of the legislation must have had the tacit approval of Chiang Ching-kuo. Why Chiang chose to approve it is more difficult to discern. No doubt the opposition played a role. Yet at that time, nuclear power was not a controversial subject for the majority of people in the country. A survey conducted in 1986 is highly suggestive: 22.8 percent of the people polled did not know of the existence of nuclear power plants in Taiwan; among those with knowledge, 41.8 percent supported building more plants and only 20.9 percent opposed them. It was a resounding endorsement of government policy.[21] In other words, Chiang had not been under such severe pressure that he needed to make concessions. Could it be that in part he had anticipated his political reforms and chose to act in a statesmanlike fashion to enhance his chances of success? Speculation over Chiang's motives notwithstanding, the political reform measures he announced in 1986 opened the floodgate to political opposition and social movements.

Before long, the intellectuals and the local communities came together, and both became entwined in a symbiotic relationship with the DPP. The initiation of political reforms by Chiang Ching-kuo in 1986 made it possible for the environmental movement to challenge the government openly, which in turn helped speed the process of democratization. For a decade the anti–nuclear power activists spearheaded the entire environmental movement and emerged as its most militant and vital component. Gong-liao, a remote fishing village in northern Taiwan and the designated site for the #4 Nuclear Power Plant, was consecrated as the battleground of the movement.

The summer of 1987 was an exciting time. On April 6 of that year, under the planning and coordination of Professor Chang Kuo-long of the National Taiwan University, a group of intellectuals and scholars concerned with protecting the environment decided to stage a demonstration at Gong-liao to commemorate the first anniversary of the Chernobyl nuclear incident. About 200 persons participated in the activities. They began with a meeting and a protest demonstration in front of the Taiwan Power Company in Taipei. After that the protestors took buses to Gong-liao. It was raining when they

---

21. See Y. Y. Li, C. K. Hsu, and M. K. Chang, *Nuclear Power and Public Opinion* (Taiwan Power Co. and Tsing-hua University, 1987).

arrived, and few villagers took notice of them, for fear of the possible reper-
cussions of being associated with political activists. The professors proceeded
to make speeches at the Buddhist temple, attracting a few locals, most of
them elderly. When the group proceeded to walk to the designated site for
the Nuclear Power Plant #4, they were intercepted by the police on the
coastal highway.[22]

By November of that year, the Union was formally established. The DPP
seems to have been closely involved from the very beginning. Two active
members of the DPP, Chu Yi-ren, who later became the secretary-general, and
Lin Hsi-yao, had apparently discussed the formation of the Union with various concerned groups, and had urged Professor Shi Hsin-ming to organize and
lead it.[23] Professor Shi was well-known for his concerns for environmental
protection. He studied in Texas in the 1970s and was deeply impressed by the
environmental movement in the United States. In 1986, he and some of his
students had taken part in the activities against the Du Pont Corporation. In
the summer of 1987, he was invited to attend a conference at the University
of California at San Diego on "Man and His Environment," which inspired
the idea of creating an environmental organization in Taiwan. Professor Shi
and his colleagues reached a consensus to mobilize the academic community
and politicians with ties to the local communities in a joint effort.

Thus, from its inception the environmental movement was highly sympathetic to the opposition DPP. In those areas where the opposition party dominated the local branches of government, it exercised a great deal of influence
over the Union's activities. This ideological bias toward the opposition party
was natural. For many of the leading participants in the Union at this early
stage – both university professors and students – to be concerned with the
environment and the country was to identify with Taiwan, to work for its
political independence. Nevertheless, this theme was deliberately down-
played, if for no other reason than for its potential to invite persecution from
the government and unfavorable reactions from society.[24]

This is not to imply that the emphasis on the rights of the people was in
any sense a pretense. The movement was genuinely committed to the right
to a clean environment as well as to the rights of freedom of speech and association and the right to participate in making decisions that seriously
affected their lives, a fact made clear by the rights discourse of the Union
Charter. Article 3 of the charter declares (1) that the right to a clean environ-

22. Hui-jen Ong and Mau-kuei Chang, "The Anti–Nuclear Power Movement at Gong-liao."
23. Hsu Chun-dan, "Interview with Professor Shi Hsin-ming," *Taiwan Environment* no. 52 (October 31, 1992), p. 25.
24. See Cheng Kun-chong, *A Framework for Analyzing the Anti-Nuclear Movement in Taiwan: A Case Study of the Taiwan Environmental Protection Union, 1988–1995* (M.A. thesis, Political Science Department, Soochow University, 1996), pp. 27–8.

ment is a basic human right: It can neither be bartered away nor abandoned. To achieve a sustainable environment, the people have the right to oppose any law and policy that is detrimental to the environment, as well as the right to decide upon and supervise development projects within their communities. (2) Humankind must depend on the natural environment for its survival; sustainable use of natural resources, along with a harmonious interdependence of people and nature, is not only the guiding principle of social, economic, scientific, and technological development, but also the guarantee of the survival of humankind. (3) Preserving the environment is the responsibility of all people, without any distinction of nation, race, religion, or political party; all individuals and groups concerned must work together to realize this goal.

To implement this basic creed, the Union dedicated itself to being a "knowledge-based, action-oriented, grass-roots" organization. "Knowledge-based" refers to the reliance on the expert knowledge of concerned professors and scientists. "Action-oriented" and "grass-roots" signify the active participation of local communities. Since its founding, the Union has been militant and vigorous, a thorn in the side of the government. Tactics have included sponsoring lectures and forums to propagate the idea of environmental protection, mobilizing local communities to petition and demonstrate against the government, organizing hunger strikes, and confronting the police on the construction sites.

The day-to-day operation of the Union is in the hands of the Executive Committee, which includes the presidents of all local branches and some members of the Expert (*hsueh-shu*) Committee. By consensus, the post of president of the Union is a prerogative of university professors, who are deemed best able to serve the Union's cause given their impartiality and respect within Taiwanese society. Almost without exception, they had been educated in the United States, and many of them, including Professors Shi Hsin-ming and Chang Kuo-long, mentioned earlier, had been influenced by the efforts of U.S. governmental and nongovernmental groups to protect the environment.

By 1995, about sixty scholars had served as members of the Expert Committee, which had played an influential role in charting the direction of the Union, especially in presenting the Union's position vis à vis that of the government and the business community. Altogether, ten branches had been established in different parts of the country in accordance with the ecological problems confronting the local communities. For example, the Northeastern Corner Branch, which had evolved from the Gong-liao Anti–Nuclear Power Self-Help Association, was primarily concerned with opposing the #4 Nuclear Power Plant, and the branches of Yun-lin and Yi-lan were dedicated to fighting against the building of the #6 Naphcracker Factory by the Taiwan Plastic Company.[25]

In this connection it is interesting to note that the Gong-liao Anti–Nuclear Power Self-Help Association was formed in 1988, a year after the visit to Gong-liao by the university professors in their attempt to link up with local communities. The mobilization techniques were traditional to their core – the use of connections of families and friends. Indeed, the traditional ties were so strong that hardly anyone dared openly to declare themselves in favor of nuclear power. Behind the solidarity of the community were long years of economic deprivation caused by government policies. For example, in developing Gong-liao and its adjacent areas as a tourist attraction, the government had begun to restrict the use of space, enforcing strict building codes. Later, during 1978–80, the government prohibited the villages from making money by investing in hatcheries for *chiu-kung,* a high-priced shellfish. Still later, smuggling and trade with mainland China were punished by the government.[26] Many other branches of the Union, however, were not very effectively run because they were closely intertwined with the leadership of the DPP in the local communities and could not avoid being ensconced in all its political maneuvers and dissensions.

Through the years, the Union was forever in need of more personnel, and many of the students had to step in and do the chores of the secretariat. In the early 1990s the student organization affiliated with the Union acted as its fighting brigade, handling both organizational and propaganda work. The Union's lack of adequate funding was in part caused by its refusal to accept any contributions from large corporations associated with environmental degradation, nor would it do research projects for the government. As a result, its money primarily came from small contributions. Not until 1995, after the DPP captured the mayor's office in that year, did the Union register with the city government of Taipei. Before that, it was not permitted to register because of its use of the word "Taiwan" in its name.[27]

A SERIES OF SKIRMISHES

The Union from the very beginning assumed a leadership position in the environmental coalition. It convened a meeting in January 1988 of some thirty groups, including women's organizations, human rights groups, and church groups, to chart a strategy for opposing nuclear power. The Union also moved quickly to support the Yami – the indigenous people of Lan-yu – in their

25. Cheng Kun-chong, *A Framework for Analyzing the Anti-Nuclear Movement in Taiwan,* pp. 30–1.
26. Hui-jen Ong and Mau-kuei Chang, "The Anti–Nuclear Power Movement at Gong-liao."
27. Cheng Kun-chong, *A Framework for Analyzing the Anti-Nuclear Movement in Taiwan,* p. 28.

efforts to remove the low-intensity nuclear waste sites at their islets. Both the president of the Union, Professor Shih Hsin-min, and the chairman of the Expert Committee took part in demonstrations to drive out "the evil spirit" in Lan-yu.[28] Over the ensuing decade the Union has developed a discernible pattern of shifting strategy and maneuvers, in part as responses to actions taken by the government. In this process the Union has succeeded in asserting the rights of expression, assembly, and association and has managed to raise the consciousness of a right to a clean environment for a fairly large group of people.

From 1987 to 1990, the Union was determined to attack the "myth" of nuclear technology through an educational campaign. For years, the government had promoted nuclear power as a "clean, safe, and cheap" energy source absolutely necessary for the economic development of the country.[29] Although the construction of the #4 Nuclear Power Plant had been shelved due to intense criticism of the management of the Taiwan Power Company, most Taiwanese were not aware of the dangers of nuclear power. To counter the propaganda of the government, the Union set out to argue that nuclear power was neither safe nor economical. The population density and ecological vulnerability of the island, it asserted, could not possibly absorb the impact of a nuclear accident. The Chernobyl nuclear explosion in 1986 was cited prominently to drive home the point. In the Anti-Nuclear Declaration of 1988, the Union demanded that, among other things, the plan to build the #4 Nuclear Power Plant should be immediately canceled, the measures for preventing pollution by the operating nuclear plants should be strengthened, and the plan to expand the facilities for storing nuclear wastes in Lan-yu, home of the indigenous Yami people, should be halted.[30] Although in this initial period the Union was preoccupied with educating the people and establishing its branches, this did not exclude more forceful action. On March 26 and 27, in commemoration of the ninth anniversary of the Three Mile Island incident, more than four thousand people took part in demonstrations against nuclear energy at the sites of existing nuclear power plants and in Gong-liao. The height of this event was reached on April 24, when more than two thousand people from all over the country converged in Taipei to demonstrate against the Taiwan Power Company.[31] As of that date the Union had not attacked the government directly.

The situation abruptly changed when General Hao assumed the post of

28. Cheng Kun-chong, *A Framework for Analyzing the Anti-Nuclear Movement in Taiwan*, p. 114.
29. Taiwan Power Company, *Handbook on Possible Questions by the Members of Legislative Yuan and Their Answers (Nuclear Energy)* (1995), p. 3.
30. In the next chapter, Benedict Kingsbury discusses the case of Lan-yu and its impact on the rights of indigenous peoples.
31. Cheng Kun-chong, *A Framework for Analyzing the Anti-Nuclear Movement in Taiwan*, p. 114.

premier in March 1990 and insisted that the #4 Nuclear Power Plant be built in Gong-liao. This was the story of a period of bitter and violent confrontation between the government and the Union. Hao stated that the decision should be based on the testimony of experts alone, not on the views of the public or the opposition politicians.[32] Plainly, he would not tolerate any challenge to the government's authority. Under his probing, the government rushed through the review of the plan proposed by Taiwan Power Company. In September 1991, the Atomic Energy Commission (AEC) approved the plant's environmental impact assessment report, requiring only technical revisions. Two months later the Review Committee of the AEC, acting without the participation of some members who were sympathetic to the Union, accepted the reply concerning the technical matters from Taiwan Power Company. By spring 1992, first the Ministry of Economic Affairs and then the Executive Yuan approved the plan for the construction of #4 Nuclear Power Plant, setting an unusual example of government expediency and determination.

The Union did not, and in a sense could not, sit by while Hao was moving fast on the attack. On May 5, 1991, it mobilized a street demonstration that drew more than 20,000 people, including some 2,000 students. It concluded with a petition to the Executive Yuan and to the Presidential Palace to end nuclear power. The day after the AEC approved the environmental impact report, September 25, 1991, the Gong-liao Anti–Nuclear Power Self-Help Association (now the Northeast Branch of the Union) began to mobilize and set up tents for a protracted confrontation with the government at the designated site. On October 3, the police went back on their word and moved to dismantle the tents, provoking a violent clash. Several dozen people were hurt; one policeman was killed.[33]

This event became known as the October 3 Incident. The confrontation between the government and the Union had reached its height. The government quickly decided on a two-front attack. First, it moved to prosecute the people involved in the clash. Seventeen persons from Gong-liao were charged with various crimes. By early March 1992, they were sentenced by the district court to serve terms of imprisonment; Lin Hsun-yuan, the driver of the car that killed the policeman, received a life sentence. A long process of appeal to the higher court ensued. Again in May, during a twenty-four-hour hunger strike by more than a hundred university professors that lasted twenty-three days, an unidentified person distributed a propaganda sheet accusing the Tai-

---

32. *Economy Daily,* December 12, 1990; also *United Evening News,* March 19, 1991.
33. Chu Chia-yi, "Report on the Tragedy of Gong-liao," in Liao Pin-liang, ed., *The True Record of the Anti-Nuclear Movement in Taiwan* (Taipei: Vanguard Publishing Co., 1993), pp. 115–19.

wan Power Company officials of bribing KMT members of the Legislative Yuan. Later, it was discovered that this person was a member of the Union, and he and the secretary-general of the Union were also prosecuted.[34]

The authorities proceeded to wage a propaganda war against the Union, using the mass media that was at the government's command. Union activists were condemned as "environment ruffians" bent on creating troubles for the government and society. This assault by Hao was apparently effective. Professor Cheng Hsien-yu, the president of the Union, was forced to resign as a result of the violent clash in March, and the secretary-general gave up his post in September. Many people, especially those from the middle class who were just beginning to identify with the anti–nuclear power movement, were frightened by the violence. The anti–nuclear power movement was dealt a severe setback.

Meanwhile, the government stepped up its maneuvers in the Legislative Yuan to approve the budget for the #4 Nuclear Power Plant. The Central Executive Committee of the KMT went so far as to threaten its members in the Legislative Yuan with denial of party nomination in the next elections if they did not declare their support for the project.[35] Under these circumstances, the government plan and budget were adopted in 1994, despite the testimony against the #4 Nuclear Power Plant by opposition party members of the Legislative Yuan.

Throughout this period the Union had continued to campaign vigorously against the power plant. For example, from July 6 to August 23, 1992, in a span of two months, more than fifty Union officials and supporters toured the island, visiting sixteen cities and towns. Usually they would hold public meetings at the railroad stations, giving speeches and distributing propaganda pamphlets. Sometimes they showed videos and sang Taiwanese folk songs. In 1993 and 1994, the Union protested the planned participation of the American multinationals General Electric and Westinghouse in building the plant, as well as that of a French firm, staging demonstrations at their Taipei offices.[36] None of these efforts swayed the government. It seemed that the government had scored its final victory.

With the struggle's escalation in violence, the Union's ideological position became openly politicized in the early 1990s. The Union articulated two new themes. First, it drew attention to the collusion between the government and the entrepreneurial class, including foreign corporations positioned to reap substantial financial benefits from the building of the plant. Second,

---

34. Cheng Kun-chong, *A Framework for Analyzing the Anti-Nuclear Movement in Taiwan*, p. 74.

35. Cheng Kun-chong, *A Framework for Analyzing the Anti-Nuclear Movement in Taiwan*, p. 66.

36. See, for example, "A Letter of Protest to Westinghouse," *Taiwan Environment* no. 73 (June 22, 1994), p. 110.

it asserted that the attitude and policy of the government under the steward-ship of General Hao was a political dictatorship; the decision to build the #4 Nuclear Power Plant had been reached in opposition to the will of the peo-ple. As the Union's #5 Anti-Nuclear Declaration of 1992 asserted, "To oppose nuclear power is not only for the survival of our children and our chil-dren's children, it is nothing less than opposition to dictatorship and totali-tarianism."[37] In a word, the antinuclear position became more and more identified with opposition to antidemocratic rule and with appeals to Tai-wanese independence. The Union did not, and apparently could not, uphold its earlier neutral posture.

During 1994 and 1995, the Union worked for the recall of some members of the Legislative Yuan who had supported the nuclear power project and demanded that a plebiscite be held to decide the fate of the #4 Nuclear Power Plant. The idea of a plebiscite had been around for some time. Profes-sor Wang Tu-fa and many other Union leaders proposed a two-stage plebiscite: First, the residents of Gong-liao were to decide whether they would agree to the construction of the nuclear plant; if they agreed, the peo-ple of Taiwan were to hold a plebiscite islandwide. Thus, the consent of both the residents of Gong-liao and all of the people of Taiwan would be necessary to legitimize the decision.[38]

The plebescite was proposed as early as 1989 by the residents in Gong-liao and was endorsed by the Union the next year.[39] However, little action was taken over the ensuing years. This was in part due to obstacles surrounding arranging a plebiscite: The Legislative Yuan was controlled by the KMT, so it could not be expected to adopt the laws needed for such an undertaking. For its part, the Union had been preoccupied with so many other activities that it simply did not have the resources to pursue this strategy. It was not until May 22, 1994, that the local administration of Gong-liao, with the support of the government of the County of Taipei which was under the con-trol of DPP, held a plebiscite. The result was that 58.36 percent of the vil-lagers turned out to cast their ballots; among them an overwhelming 96.12 percent opposed the construction of a nuclear power plant in their area.

After the adoption of the budget for building the #4 Nuclear Power Plant by the Legislative Yuan on July 12, 1994, the national plebiscite was given powerful impetus by two opposition leaders, Lin Yi-hsiung and Chen Shui-bian. In anticipation of the decision by the Legislative Yuan, Lin declared a

37. In Liao Pin-liang, ed., *The True Record of the Anti-Nuclear Movement in Taiwan*, p. 150.
38. Wang Tu-fa, *Exposing the Myth of Nuclear Power Economy* (Taipei: Vanguard Publishing Co., 1993), p. 21.
39. See "Statement by the North-East Corner Branch Urging Plebiscite," *Taiwan Environment* no. 14 (July 20, 1989), p. 3.

hunger strike and called for 100,000 signatures for a petition to urge a plebiscite to decide the fate of the #4 Nuclear Power Plant. His action was significant because of his high stature in the opposition camp and his influence in society.[40] Within a week, more than 200,000 signatures were secured and Lin ended his strike.

Given the lead taken by Lin Yi-hsiung, the Union and other environmental protection organizations supported the idea of a plebiscite and sought to implement it. In September 1994, the Association for Promoting a Plebiscite, with Lin at its helm, sponsored a month-long Thousand-Mile Walk Campaign to propagate the idea.[41] They walked from one end of the island to the other.[42]

The second source of support for the idea of a plebiscite came from Chen Shui-bian, the DPP candidate for mayor of Taipei. During his campaign, he pledged to hold a plebiscite in Taipei if elected. However, after being elected he postponed the plebiscite until 1996 to coincide with the presidential elections.[43]

Simultaneously with the promotion of a plebiscite, the Union moved to recall some members of the Legislative Yuan who had supported the nuclear power project and who were considered vulnerable. The targets were some of the legislators elected from Taipei City and Taipei County. The KMT countered by revising the laws on elections and recalls of governmental officials, making it more difficult for the Union to succeed. The number of signatures of voters needed for petitioning the Central Electoral Commission to set up the procedures were quickly surpassed, and the recalls were duly held in the end of 1994 in Taipei County, and in January 1995 in Taipei City. Yet in both places the Union failed miserably, for the turnout for the recalls had not reached the threshold stipulated by the new law.[44] President Lee apparently had used his tremendous prestige to urge against the recalls, and by doing so he prevailed.

Judging by the results, the plebiscite and the recalls were serious setbacks

---

40. Lin is one of several activists who was arrested and tried after the Human Rights Day demonstrations in Kao-hsiung in 1979. During Lin's trial on February 28, 1980, his aged mother and two teenage daughters were brutally murdered. Rumor had it that they were murdered by the secret police in retaliation for a telephone conversation between Lin and his mother in which Lin revealed that he had been tortured. Despite repeated assurances from the police that they are investigating these murders, the case still has not been solved. After these tragic events, Lin withdrew from politics and spent several years in the United States. In a sense, he became a spiritual leader for the opposition. It is not surprising that he evoked an outpouring of sympathy with his hunger strike.

41. Kao Chen-yen, "The History and Prospect of the Anti–Nuclear Power Movement," *Taiwan Environment* no. 80 (April 25, 1995).

42. See the Association for Promoting a Plebiscite, ed., *Plebiscite on #4 Nuclear Power Plant Thousand Mile Walk Campaign* (Taipei: Yu Shan Publishers, 1995).

43. Cheng Kun-chong, *A Framework for Analyzing the Anti-Nuclear Movement in Taiwan*, p. 85.

44. Hsu Wen-ping, "The Old Law Should Be Applied in the Case of Recalling the Legislators," *Taiwan Environment* no. 78, pp. 6–7.

for the Union. Nonetheless, they have contributed to raising the consciousness of the people about the environmental dangers of nuclear power. In the process, the Union became even more entangled with the DPP and to a lesser degree with the New Party, a splinter group from the KMT. It was a simple fact that the Union needed the support of the political parties to mobilize the people. Some Union leaders maintained that they were struggling for genuine democratic reforms, in contrast to the sham political reforms promoted by the government, and for the people in Taiwan to take their destiny into their own hands.[45]

Through the decade of struggle against the government and the business community, the Union made a serious effort to draw support from abroad, and it has become increasingly connected with a global network of organizations working to protect the right to a clean environment. During the 1980s, the Union often invited foreign visitors to participate in its activities; for example, in 1988 it gained encouragement and publicity from the visit of two prominent members of the German Green Party. The international dimension of its activities was peripheral in the early years, but now, partly because of its growing experience with international networking, the Union has become more and more a part of the worldwide movement. In May 1995, when the French government carried out a series of nuclear tests in the South Pacific, the Union engaged actively in protest.[46] It also severely condemned tests conducted by the Chinese government. In both cases, the Union urged consumers to boycott goods from France and mainland China.

The height of its international involvement to date was reached in September 1995, when the Union sponsored the No Nukes Asia Forum in Taipei. In anticipation of the forum, an international antinuclear demonstration was held on September 3, with an estimated 30,000 people taking part. For three days international visitors were taken to see the nuclear power plants in operation as well as the designated site for the #4 Nuclear Power Plant. They also visited Lan-yu Island, where the resident Yami people had been protesting for some years, to inspect the site for nuclear wastes.[47] On the whole, the influence exerted by the international nongovernmental groups was positive and deeply appreciated. Union leaders were able to learn from what had been done in other, more industrialized countries. The liaison provided a sense of comraderie and reduced the feeling of isolation. The future of the environmental protection movement in Taiwan became tied to that of its counterparts in the international community.

45. Cheng Kun-chong, *A Framework for Analyzing the Anti-Nuclear Movement in Taiwan,* p. 86.
46. It not only protested at the French office in Taipei, it also urged the Ministry of Foreign Affairs to condemn the tests.
47. See "Statement of the Third No Nukes Asia Forum," *Taiwan Environment* no. 84, p. 3.

A SUMMARY OF THE OPPOSING POSITIONS

A decade of confrontation between the Union and the government on so many fronts makes it difficult to sort out the points of contention between the two antagonists. At times they seemed to be not only disputing the facts, but arguing about which facts were relevant. Nevertheless, a summary of the positions of both sides on the #4 Nuclear Power Plant will help to put the struggle in perspective.

To begin with, the debate centered on the need for nuclear power and what an appropriate energy policy should be. The government through its agent, the Taiwan Power Company, argued forcefully that to keep up with economic growth and further improve living standards, nuclear energy was essential. Indeed, nuclear energy turned out to be the most stable, most economical, and cleanest source of energy. Assuming that the first two units of the Nuclear Power Plant #4 were completed by 2003, nuclear energy would account for 21.1 percent of the entire power system; without #4 Nuclear Power Plant, it would have accounted for 15.1 percent. In other words, the government's energy policy was one that emphasized reliability and diversity in energy sources.[48]

The position held by the government met with immediate challenge from the Union and many scientists sympathetic to its cause. They argued that the need for increased electric power as estimated by the Taiwan Power Company – 7 percent per year for the next decade – was far too high; moreover, it was possible to think about conserving energy while developing alternative sources of energy. For many experts and scientists in the opposition camp, the favored energy source was natural gas.[49] The government and the Taiwan Power Company, however, disagreed that natural gas was a reliable source, citing the world market situation.

Next, the controversy centered on whether the #4 Nuclear Power Plant would be safe, economical, and clean. The government insisted that it was safe because it was American designed and thus could not be compared with the one at Chernobyl and that the Taiwan Power Company had learned through long years of experience how to operate the plant successfully.[50] But the Union did not agree. It argued that, given the ecological vulnerability and the high density of population, Taiwan simply could not afford nuclear

---

48. Taiwan Power Company, *Handbook on Possible Questions*, pp. 1–3. Also, see the statement by the president of Taiwan Power Company, Chang Shih-min, in a forum discussing the future of the #4 Nuclear Power Plant, in *Independence Evening News*, June 14, 1993.
49. See, for example, statements by Professor Yang Chao-yeh and Liu Chi-chen, president of the Union, *Independence Evening News*, June 14, 1993.
50. Taiwan Power Company, *Handbook on Possible Questions*, pp. 5–8. See also a statement by Chang Shih-min in the forum cited earlier, *Independence Evening News*, June 14, 1993.

power because it was far too dangerous. The track record of the Taiwan Power Company did not warrant any confidence in its management. To pursue more nuclear power plants after Three Mile Island and Chernobyl was irresponsible and should not be sanctioned.[51]

As for the dispute over whether the #4 Nuclear Power Plant would be economical, the two antagonists simply could not agree. The government asserted that it was cheaper per unit compared to coal, oil, or natural gas. It also refused to give much weight to the social costs of using nuclear power.[52] In contrast, the Union and its supporters emphasized those social costs, including the costs in case of accidents or disasters as well as that of the disposal of nuclear wastes.[53]

Similarly, regarding the impact on the environment, there was little common ground between the opposing camps. The government insisted that many studies on the use of nuclear energy indicated that its environmental impact is negligible, and it claimed that its methods of disposal of nuclear wastes, including the construction of low intensity radioactive waste sites in Lan-yu, were competent.[54] The Union did not agree with the government assessment. As early as 1988, Professor Chang Kuo-long had argued that given the track record of the Taiwan Power Company, it was far too dangerous to go ahead with the building of #4 Nuclear Power Plant.[55] As for using Lan-yu as the site for low-level nuclear wastes, it provoked immediate opposition from the indigenous Yami who reside in the area. In February 1988 the Yami began mobilizing to oppose the use of their territory for disposal of nuclear wastes. As they saw it, the government policy directly threatened their cultural heritage and their unique way of life.[56] The controversy has persisted, and it is far from being resolved.

Finally, the question of who should have the right to decide whether the nuclear plant would be built revolved around different interpretations of

51. Liu Chi-chen's statement, *Independence Evening News,* June 14, 1993. Also Wang Tu-fa, *Exposing the Myth of Nuclear Power Economy,* pp. 17–19.

52. See, for example, Yeh Mann-shen, the deputy commissioner of State Enterprises Commission, and Chang Shih-min, in the forum cited above, *Independence Evening News,* June 14, 1993. See also Taiwan Power Company, *Handbook on Possible Questions,* p. 80.

53. See, for example, Wang Tu-fa, *Exposing the Myth,* pp. 23–5.

54. See, for example, Taiwan Power Company, *Handbook on Possible Questions,* pp. 19, 25–32. Also, see statements by Chang Shih-min and Yeh Mann-shen, *Independence Evening News,* June 14, 1993.

55. Kang Chao, "Nuclear Power Plant #4: Everyone Takes Action to Oppose Nuclear Energy," in *Taiwan Environment* no. 2, p. 9. See also *Union's Anti-Nuclear Declaration of 1988,* p. 10. Professor Lin Pi-yao also emphasizes the incompetence of the Taiwan Power Company in handling crises. Lin Pi-yao, "Taiwan Does Not Have the Ability to Handle Technological Disasters," *Independence Evening News,* June 27, 1993.

56. For a discussion of the destruction of the cultural heritage of Lan-yu, see *Proceedings of a Series of Conferences on Intergenerational Justice and Environmental Protection* (unpublished; conferences held from January to May 1997 as part of the research project sponsored by the National Science Council and coordinated by this writer, Taipei, 1997), pp. 52–75.

legitimacy. As indicated earlier in this chapter, during the long years when Chiang Kai-shek and his son were in power, the people had little say in policy decisions. As late as the early 1990s, General Hao still insisted that only the opinion of experts should be taken into account, not that of the politicians or the local communities. Nevertheless, the Taiwan Power Company took the position that the decision of the Legislative Yuan should be the ultimate authority because it was the manifestation of the will of the people.[57] The Union countered with the idea of a plebiscite, arguing that it would hold greater legitimacy than the decisions of the elected national legislature.

THE FUTURE OF THE MOVEMENT

The construction of the #4 Nuclear Power Plant has been proceeding according to the government's plan with the clearing of the grounds.[58] The Union's fortunes are at a low ebb. And the close relations between the Union and the DPP in the past decade have been severely tested as the DPP and the KMT move toward rapprochement. Collaboration between the two political parties culminated when they succeeded in amending the state constitution in July 1997, against widespread opposition from the New Party and a substantial body of public opinion. Two important leaders of the Union, Professors Kao Chen-yen and Shi Hsin-min, formed the Green Party in May 1996, sharply condemning the DPP for having betrayed its early idealism. According to Professor Kao, the Green Party is a permanent opposition party dedicated to challenging the authorities from without.[59] By its Charter, the Green Party is committed to opposing nuclear power and to advocating a constitutional right to a clean environment, among other things. The Union is clearly going through a period of reorganization and adaptation. Nevertheless, it has not been inactive. For example, in January 1997 it was approached by and gave support to South Korean environmental groups when they came to Taiwan to protest against the government for its decision to ship low-level radioactive materials to North Korea.

As for the environmental movement as a whole, it has certainly made progress in the past decade, albeit slowly. Not only is there more diversity of organizations and interests, ranging from bird watching to animal rights, almost every local community has its environmental group. Many of these organizations are poorly financed and must fight both government bias in

---

57. See Chang Shih-min, *Independence Evening News*, June 14, 1993.
58. In 1996–8 the annual budget was a moderate 100 million Taiwan dollars. The Union attempted and failed in the Legislative Yuan to cancel the appropriation.
59. *China Times Daily*, January 24, 1997, p. 3.

favor of development and the ignorance and prejudice found in their own communities; nonetheless, they are here to stay.[60]

CONCLUSION

The anti–nuclear power movement and the Environmental Protection Union were made possible by the political reform of an authoritarian government, which became more tolerant of opposition and social movements. This by no means denigrates the courage and hard work of the university professors from the cities and the people in the local communities. Indeed it was only when the two groups converged in their efforts that the Union became possible. The former group was motivated by a sense of idealism and patriotism, and in many cases by the desire for Taiwan's political independence; the latter became involved primarily because of their experience of neglect and suffering at the hands of the government.

From a historical perspective, the antinuclear movement was part of a continuous struggle for rights against an authoritarian government. What makes it different from the previous contests has much to do with the stage of economic development and technological advancement, which placed the nuclear power issue on the political agenda. It is also related to the close liaison between the movement and the political opposition, which led to an intermingling of politics and environmental concerns. The connection between the Union and the opposition parties, especially the Democratic Progressive Party, was a natural alliance based on mutual interests in the early years, yet it turned out to be a double-edged sword. The Union had gained much from this liaison, but it was left vulnerable when the DPP moved into collaboration with the KMT. In reaction the movement accused the DPP of betrayal and formed the Green Party. Many people in the environmental movement had learned a lesson: A viable environmental movement must be autonomous, independent of any political party.

Underlying its activities was the Union's bold claim that the right to a clean environment was a fundamental human right, never to be bartered away. The Union further asserted that the people have the right to oppose

---

60. Indeed, a new coalition has emerged, the Ecological Conservation League, which includes the Environmental Protection Union in its membership. In contrast to the Union, the League eschews militant actions, preferring instead to work with the government. Neither does it believe, like the Green Party, that by becoming a political party it would contribute to the cause of environmental protection. During the past two years, the Ecological Conservation League has held two national conferences. The first was convened in 1995 on the theme of wetlands protection. The second conference was convened in October 1997 and was jointly sponsored by twenty-seven environmental groups, including the Union. The theme of a Sustainable Taiwan was chosen for the two-day meeting.

any law or policy that is detrimental to the environment as well as the right to decide and supervise the development projects within their communities. It spoke of the use of natural resources in a sustainable way and of a harmonious interdependence between man and nature, as well as saving the environment for future generations, and was committed to sustainable development, to international cooperation, and to nonviolence in its struggle against the government. In other words, the leadership of the Union was in sync with the new wave of thinking of the Western nations.

Through the efforts of the Union, a large part of the Taiwanese population has been educated regarding the dangers of nuclear power and environmental degradation. However, the government and the business community remain committed to rapid economic development and have not given indications that they are prepared to compromise. The Taiwan government, belatedly, has embraced the rhetoric of sustainable development. In his inaugural address on May 20, 1996, President Lee pointedly asserted that "sustainable development" would guide his policies. The government's Commission on Economic Construction immediately set up a public forum and invited the business community to contribute ideas. In this sense the environmental movement and the government have finally found in sustainable development a common language to discuss economic development and environmental protection, but a genuine dialogue does not appear to be emerging from it.

Similarly, neither the movement nor the government have confronted the issue of intergenerational justice in environmental protection. This can be partially explained by the fact that it is a relatively new issue, seriously raised in the West only since the 1970s.[61] More to the point, however, the leadership of the Union has been too preoccupied with mobilization and its political struggles to pay much attention to it. Neither the government nor the business community has adequately addressed the issue; but to the extent they have, the Taiwan Power Company spokesmen and scholars sympathetic to nuclear power have insisted that the interests of future generations demand the use of nuclear power; they may be wrong, but they seem to be addressing the issue directly.[62]

To conclude, the Union and the anti–nuclear power movement have succeeded in making the right to a clean environment part of the political agenda in Taiwan, increasing the level of awareness of a fairly large portion of Taiwan's population. In the process, environmental activism has also con-

---

61. See Mab Huang, "A Preliminary Report on the Idea of Justice Between Generations," *Soochow Journal of Political Science* no. 7 (March 1997).
62. See *Proceedings of a Series of Conferences on Intergenerational Justice and Environmental Protection*, pp. 17–18, 21, 39.

tributed to securing the rights to free expression, assembly, and association, indirectly adding impetus to Taiwan's democratization and the strengthening of civil society. Despite these ancillary benefits, the enjoyment of the Taiwanese people's right to a clean environment still remains problematic, owing to the intransigence of government officials serving the perceived needs of the business sector at the expense of the general population, both present and future.

CHAPTER 14

THE APPLICABILITY OF THE INTERNATIONAL LEGAL CONCEPT OF "INDIGENOUS PEOPLES" IN ASIA

BENEDICT KINGSBURY

Over a very short period, the few decades since the early 1970s, "indigenous peoples" has been transformed from a prosaic description without much significance in international law and politics into a concept with considerable power as a basis for group mobilization, international standard-setting, transnational networks, and programmatic activity of intergovernmental and nongovernmental organizations (NGOs).[1]

Following the pattern of group mobilization established in states dominated by European settlement – in the Americas, Australasia, and the Nordic countries – groups based in different Asian states have more recently begun to participate in international institutions and gatherings of "indigenous peoples," and transnational networks have been formed in Asia under the rubric "indigenous peoples."[2] The concept of "indigenous peoples," or its

---

1. For overviews see, for example, Douglas Sanders, "The Re-Emergence of Indigenous Questions in International Law," *Canadian Human Rights Yearbook* vol. 1 (1983), p. 3; Chris Tennant, "Indigenous Peoples, International Institutions, and the International Legal Literature from 1945–1993," *Human Rights Quarterly* vol. 16 (1994), pp. 1–57. The history of international activity involving or relating to indigenous peoples is much longer, encompassing inter alia bilateral diplomacy by indigenous peoples as well as attempts to petition and appear at the League of Nations, transnational operations of church groups and NGOs such as the Aborigines Protection Society and the Anti-Slavery Society in the nineteenth century, and the long history of International Labour Organization activities.

2. For example, the Pacific-Asia Council of Indigenous Peoples, which has connections with the pioneering World Council of Indigenous Peoples, and the Asia Indigenous Peoples Pact (AIPP), established in the early 1990s and active as an international network. In 1996 the primary membership of the AIPP numbered 18 organizations, including the Naga Peoples Movement for Human Rights, BIRSA (Ranchi, India), Nepal Federation of Nationalities Federal Council, Chittagong Hill Tracts Peoples Council, Inter Mountain Peoples Education and Culture in Thailand Association (IMPECT), Partners of Community Organization (PACOS, Sabah), Arakhan Human Rights Centre, Kachin Land Foundation, Cordillera Peoples Alliance, National Federation of Indigenous Peoples of the Philippines (KAMP), Lumad Mindanaw (Mindanao), Homeland Mission 1950 Maluku (Amsterdam), Alliance of Taiwan Aborigines, Adivasi Solidarity (Bombay), Centre for Orang Asli Concerns (Petaling Jaya).

local cognates, has become an important unifying connection in transnational activist networks, linking groups that were hitherto marginal and politically unorganized to transnational sources of ideas, information, support, legitimacy, and money.[3] International institutions increasingly apply to parts of Asia policies, programs, and specific rules concerning "indigenous peoples." The World Bank, for example, first adopted a policy on tribal peoples arising out of the dismal experience of projects in Latin America, but as a global organization seeks to apply its current policy on indigenous peoples to some of its projects in Asia; the relevant World Bank policies have also provided an influential model for the Asian Development Bank. The international activity has begun to shape national practice in many states, influencing political discourse, government policy, and some judicial and legislative action. The attitudes of governments in Asia to application to their states of the concept of "indigenous peoples" differ considerably, but strong opposition has been expressed by the governments of China, India, Bangladesh, Burma, and (for the most part) Indonesia.

The political salience of debates about the concept of "indigenous peoples," and much of the legal controversy, has been heightened by conflicts over land, forests, mineral resources, fishing rights, and other valuable natural resources. These conflicts arise in the context of rapid economic change, often precipitated by government-supported "development" projects. If "indigenous peoples" are deemed in international practice to have particular entitlements to land, territory, and resources, based on historical connections, customary practices, and the interdependence of land and culture, the question whether a particular group is an "indigenous people" may take on great political and legal importance. Even where governments do not accept that any of the groups in their states are "indigenous peoples," international agencies, multinational corporations, and the governments of foreign states may continue to press a particular case on the basis that relevant international standards apply.

This chapter will address the important practical problem of whether and how the concept of "indigenous peoples," formed and shaped in areas of the world dominated by the history and effects of European settlement, might or should be adapted and made applicable in Asia and elsewhere. Both elements of the term – "indigenous" and "peoples" – are contentious, but the discussion here will focus mainly on indigeneity.

A caveat must be entered about the scope and generality of this chapter. It focuses on issues arising in Asia, loosely encompassing, without particular

---

3. R. H. Barnes, Andrew Gray, and Benedict Kingsbury, eds., *Indigenous Peoples of Asia* (Ann Arbor, MI: Association for Asian Studies, 1995).

distinction, east, southeast, and south Asia. This region is so diverse as to issues pertaining to "indigenous peoples" that generalizations must be treated with the utmost caution.[4] There are overlapping themes, as well as considerable variation, between Asia and Africa with respect to these issues, and the question of the relevance or irrelevance of the concept of "indigenous peoples" in Africa is of great importance. Although to a lesser extent than Asian groups, representatives of a small number of African groups have become involved in the international indigenous peoples movement,[5] and governments of a few African states have expressed concerns similar to those of Asian governments considered in this chapter.[6] For clarity, specific issues concerning the concept of "indigenous peoples" in Africa are not considered in this chapter.

DOES THE INTERNATIONAL CONCEPT OF "INDIGENOUS PEOPLES" APPLY IN ASIA? SEPARATING INSTITUTIONS, NORMS, AND JUSTIFICATIONS

This section will address one of the central questions in the current controversy: Does the concept of "indigenous peoples" have any application to people in the group of major Asian states whose governments deny its relevance? The core of the international controversy may be captured by juxtaposing two quotations, both originating in the context of ongoing efforts in the United Nations to draft a normative Declaration on the Rights of Indigenous Peoples. Each is representative of strongly held recurrent positions.

4. See the thoughtful discussion in Yash Ghai, "Human Rights and Governance: The Asia Debate," *Australian Year Book of International Law* vol. 14 (1994), pp. 1–34.

5. A Member of the Tanzanian Parliament, Moringe Parkipuny, made a statement on "The Indigenous Peoples Rights Question in Africa" at the U.N. Sub-Commission Working Group on Indigenous Populations in 1989 (*IWGIA Newsletter* no. 59 (1989), pp. 92–4), and an increasing number of groups from Africa have attended subsequent meetings of the Working Group. Among the most prominent African participants in the international indigenous peoples movement has been Ken Saro Wiwa, whose writings include *Genocide in Nigeria: The Ogoni Tragedy* (Port Harcourt: Saros, 1992) and collections of short essays such as *Nigeria: The Brink of Disaster* (Port Harcourt: Saros, 1991). He was a vice-president of the Netherlands-based Unrepresented Nations and Peoples Organization. He was executed, with other Ogoni, by the Nigerian government in 1995. In a solemn session that year at the U.N. Commission on Human Rights Inter-Sessional Working Group on the draft declaration on the rights of indigenous peoples, "the Chairperson-Rapporteur, at the request of many governmental and indigenous delegations, paid tribute to the Nigerian writer and human rights activist, Mr. Ken Saro Wiwa, who had given his life for the cause of human rights." *Report of the Working Group Established in Accordance with Commission on Human Rights Resolution 1995/32 of 3 March 1995 (first session)* (U.N. Doc. E/CN.4/1996/84, January 4, 1996), para. 17.

6. It may be indicative that the Nigerian government is the only sub-Saharan state not then a member of the Commission on Human Rights to have chosen to participate in both the first and second sessions of the intersessional working group. For an example of express governmental concern, see the comment of Niger on a U.N. report: "the absence of a definition of 'indigenous people' invited subjective interpretations, which poses dangers for those emerging nation-states in Africa that face recurrent tribal conflicts." Erica-Irene Daes, "Protection of the Heritage of Indigenous People: Final Report" (U.N. Doc. E/CN.4/Sub.2/1995/26, June 21, 1995), para 6.

The first quotation is from a statement made in 1991 to the U.N. Working Group on Indigenous Populations in the names of members of the West Papuan Peoples' Front, Karen National Union, Jumma Network in Europe, Indian Council of Indigenous and Tribal Peoples, Alliance of Taiwan Aborigines, National Federation of Indigenous Peoples of the Philippines (KAMP), Lumad-Mindanao, Cordillera People's Alliance, Ainu Association of Hokkaido, Asia Indigenous Peoples Pact, Naga Peoples Movement for Human Rights, Homeland Mission 1950 for South Moluccas, and Hmong People.[7]

> First and foremost, we want to bring to your attention the denial of some Asian governments of the existence of indigenous peoples in our part of the world. This denial presents a significant obstacle to the participation of many indigenous peoples from our region in the Working Group's deliberations. The denial also seeks to withhold the benefits of the Declaration from the indigenous, tribal, and aboriginal peoples of Asia. We hereby urgently request that peoples who are denied the rights to govern themselves, and are called tribal, and/or aboriginal in our region, be recognized, for purpose of this Declaration, and in accordance with I.L.O. practice, as equivalent to indigenous peoples.

The second quotation is from comments sent in 1995 by the government of the People's Republic of China to a working group of the U.N. Commission on Human Rights.[8]

> The Chinese Government believes that the question of indigenous peoples is the product of European countries' recent pursuit of colonial policies in other parts of the world. Because of these policies, many indigenous peoples were dispossessed of their ancestral homes and lands, brutally oppressed, exploited and murdered, and in some cases even deliberately exterminated. To this day, many indigenous peoples still suffer from discrimination and diminished status, and they cannot in fact exercise on an equal footing or to the full the economic, social, cultural, civil and political rights enjoyed by other citizens of the countries where they live. . . . As in the majority of Asian countries, the various nationalities in China have all lived for aeons on Chinese territory. Although there is no indigenous peoples' question in China, the Chinese Government and people have every sympathy with indigenous peoples' historical woes and historical plight. China believes it absolutely essential to draft an international instrument to protect their rights and interests. . . . The special historical misfortunes of indigenous peoples set them apart from minority nationalities and ethnic groups in the ordinary sense. For this reason, the draft declaration must clearly define what indigenous peoples are, in order to guarantee that the special rights it establishes are accurately targeted at genuine communities of indigenous people and are not distorted, arbitrarily extended or muddled. In the

---

7. Reproduced in *Newsletter of the International Work Group for Indigenous Affairs* no. 2 (1991).
8. *Consideration of a Draft United Nations Declaration on the Rights of Indigenous People* (U.N. Doc. E/CN.4/WG.15/2, October 10, 1995).

materials it prepared for the World Conference on Human Rights, the [U.N.] Centre for Human Rights presumptuously categorized ordinary minority nationalities in many Asian countries as "indigenous peoples" and refused, despite collective and individual clarifications from the Asian countries, to rectify its mistake. This example amply demonstrates the necessity of an established definition of an indigenous people.

As the first quotation indicates, representatives of a large number of groups in Asia are actively participating in international activities of indigenous peoples and take the view that their groups are within the international rubric of "indigenous peoples" even if a cognate expression has not hitherto been used in local politics. Conversely, several governments of Asian states argue that the concept of "indigenous peoples" is so integrally a product of the common experience of European colonial settlement as to be fundamentally inapplicable to those parts of Asia that did not experience substantial European settlement. The dispute as to the meaning and scope of the concept of "indigenous peoples" is of considerable importance to contemporary efforts in the United Nations to negotiate a declaration on the rights of indigenous peoples, and it has important implications for operational policy in institutions ranging from the World Bank to the Biodiversity Convention.

The use of "indigenous peoples" or cognate terms in political discourse and attitudes of state governments toward the concept vary considerably among Asian countries. Differences in the impacts and legacies of European, Japanese, and U.S. colonialism, political dynamics, nationalist ideologies, and understandings of history all contribute to this variation. The concept of "indigenous peoples" has multiple lineages. In the era of decolonization, the term "indigenous peoples" was regularly used by Afro-Asian state governments and by colonial governments to refer to the non-European majority populations of European colonies in Asia and Africa; the international indigenous peoples' movement draws, in part, on the discourses and legal principles (especially self-determination) given currency by the Afro-Asian decolonization movement.[9] The concept of "indigenous peoples" has roots also in the practice of colonial administrators establishing special laws and

9. The general association between the Afro-Asian decolonization movement and contemporary U.N. activity concerning "indigenous peoples" has become more attenuated, but the anticolonial and antidiscrimination elements of the "indigenous peoples" program have continued to find some resonance with governments of states active in the decolonization movement. For example, the Zambian government stated in 1994 that it "welcomes the establishment of a permanent forum in the United Nations for indigenous peoples. At the international level Zambia has traditionally been a strong supporter of the rights of indigenous peoples. This is evidenced by action taken in respect of the liberation of southern Africa and the eradication of apartheid in South Africa" (U.N. Doc.E/CN. 4/Sub. 2/AC. 4/1995/7/Add. 1, June 14, 1995). Whether such support will endure if it appears that the concept of "indigenous peoples" is being used to confer international legitimacy on groups and activities within such states is another matter.

policies relating to distinct nonmajority groups. Security, and the pursuit of cost-effective if very rough governance, were often major reasons for establishing inner lines, scheduled areas, frontier zones, and other special arrangements,[10] although the conscious motives of such administrators were in some cases also welfarist or religious.[11] In the nineteenth and early twentieth centuries especially, standards of good colonial administration were identified, espoused, and disseminated to different parts of the world through metropolitan colonial offices and legislatures, missionary societies, NGOs such as the Aborigines Protection Society, and intergovernmental activity such as the 1884–5 Berlin Conference and the 1889–90 Brussels Conference. The impact of this diffusion of norms is evident in, for example, Japan's apparently mimetic colonial programs relating to aborigines during its rule in Formosa, which Japanese authorities publicized in a carefully produced English-language publication.[12] Such norms became more formal under the League of Nations mandate system and the rarely invoked provision in Article 23(b) of the League of Nations Covenant requiring just treatment of native inhabitants.

Colonial policies had enduring impacts on understandings of ethnicity and patterns of ethnic relations in postcolonial states.[13] Benedict Anderson defines a polar position in his contention that in contemporary Southeast Asia "the politics of ethnicity have their roots in modern times, not ancient history, and their shape has been largely determined by colonial policy."[14] According to this thesis, the concept of ethnic minority was virtually introduced, and many ethnic identities largely created, by the imaginings of European colonial powers concerned in the late nineteenth and twentieth centuries with building majority coalitions to assuage their own vulnerable positions as minority rulers in an age where majority rule was increasingly a principle of legitimacy. Thus groups favored by European rulers in the eighteenth century on the ground of having elevated themselves from others through embracing Christianity were by the late nineteenth century favored instead in census-

---

10. For example, British designation of Scheduled Tribes and Scheduled Areas in India – as to which, see, for example, Christoph Von Fürer-Haimendorf, *Tribes of India: The Struggle for Survival* (Berkeley: University of California Press, 1982) – Scheduled Areas in Burma, and the Frontier Districts subject to the Frontier Crimes Regulations in what is now Pakistan.

11. See, for example, Verrier Elwin, *India's North-East Frontier in the Nineteenth Century* (London: Oxford University Press, 1959); Verrier Elwin, *A Philosophy for NEFA*, 2nd ed. (Shillong: J. N. Chowdhury, 1959); and Peter Robb, "The Colonial State and Constructions of Indian Identity: An Example on the Northeast Frontier in the 1880's," *Modern Asian Studies* vol. 31 (1997), pp. 245–83.

12. Government of Formosa, *Report on the Control of the Aborigines in Formosa* (Taihoku, Formosa: Bureau of Aboriginal Affairs, 1911).

13. For a detailed survey see Donald Horowitz, *Ethnic Groups and Conflict* (Berkeley: University of California Press, 1985).

14. Benedict Anderson, "Introduction," in *Southeast Asian Tribal Groups and Ethnic Minorities* (Cambridge, MA: Cultural Survival, 1987), pp. 1–15.

defined ethnicities as Moluccans or Karens. Such groups were cast stereotypically as honest and loyal, as opposed to larger and more threatening groups stereotyped as treacherous, feudal, and so on. As evidence for the thesis that ethnic classifications were designed to further the coalition-building goals of European colonists, Anderson asserts that in the last years of colonial administration, ethnic minorities were accorded disproportionate numbers of seats in "representative" bodies, these being occupied by individuals likely to act consistently with the preferences of colonial power.

The legacy of colonial experiences has been distinctive identification of "alien" minorities (particularly Chinese, who have integrated into non-Chinese elites much more easily in uncolonized Thailand than in Indonesia), the presence in many states of local "coalition minorities" with modern and evolving identities able to exercise influence in statewide coalition building, and a category of what in international terms might now be called "indigenous peoples." These are "groups which, because they are small in numbers, geographically remote from the political center, marginal to the national economy and lacking in Western education, are insignificant to any conceivable majority."[15] In some cases these groups were mobilized by the colonial power to resist advancing nationalist causes, though more often they were left unincorporated into the coalition-building arrangements. Whether wholly unincorporated or belatedly mobilized and ineffectually incorporated, the colonial legacy continues to the present in their pronounced underrepresentation in military officer corps, universities, large state enterprises, private corporations, and the senior civil service. Their leverage with the state government and elites is small. One strategy for such groups is to combine forces with other local groups and form a larger ethnic identity, but willingness to do this may be inhibited by the necessity of religious conversion (e.g., to Islam to join the broad Malay identity in Malaysia, to Buddhism to integrate with Thai identity, or to Christianity to build other coalitions) and reluctance to accept cultural fusion and a surrender of autonomy.[16] Another possible strategy, pursued in tandem with or instead of this larger ethnic strategy, is to join the international category of "indigenous peoples." Whether this international movement provides sufficient legitimation and leverage to shape national political outcomes varies with the state and groups involved, but in some circumstances this alternative has begun to prove attractive.

The controversy about the meaning and application of "indigenous peoples" as an international concept encompasses struggles over the potentially potent roles of *international institutions,* conflicting views as to the *norms* applic-

15. Anderson, "Introduction," pp. 10–11   16. Anderson, "Introduction," pp. 1–11.

able to indigenous peoples and their relationships with states and with individuals, and fundamental differences as to the *justifications* for institutional and normative programs based on recognition of a distinct category of "indigenous peoples."[17] It will be argued that the best possibility of progress toward broad international agreement among different states and groups – an agreement that by no means exists at present – will be through the continued evolution of distinct practices in different types of institutions, continuing bargaining on norms applicable to indigenous peoples, and a definition of "indigenous peoples" that is sufficiently flexible to accommodate a range of different justifications. This view is animated by an understanding of "indigenous peoples" not in positivist terms as a sharply defined universal set of right holders, but in constructivist terms as a legal concept continuously abstracted from a vast range of specific cases, but itself made specific from the abstract when it comes to be applied in each concrete setting or dispute.

In the area of international human rights, diplomatic negotiations have long utilized distinctions between institutions, norms, and justifications as a means to facilitate consensus. A recurrent feature of international human rights instruments since 1945 has been the articulation of norms in universal terms, albeit with margins for different local interpretations and some acknowledgment of the relevance of cultural difference, accompanied by acceptance of wide discretion for states in choices of national and international institutional mechanisms to protect and promote human rights, and openness of international normative texts to divergent justifications of the norms of human rights. At the same time, this pattern has been continuously contested by those seeking universality through convergence around tightly drafted norms, standardized court-centered national and international institutions for enforcement, and explicit endorsement of Enlightenment-type justifications to be used to enhance the interpretation of norms and the effectiveness of institutions.

In relation to questions concerning indigenous peoples, I argue that although there are conflicts of interests on institutions and norms, the most fundamental and problematic disagreement is over the justifications inherent in the concept of "indigenous peoples" as currently understood. Controversy arises in particular from the implication that distinctive rights of "indigenous peoples" are justified by the destruction of their previous territorial entitlements and political autonomy wrought by historic circumstances of invasion and colonization. The best possibility of progress is to make the concept sufficiently flexible to make clear

---

17. This distinction is used in a somewhat different way in Charles Taylor's stimulating Chapter 5, "Conditions of an Unforced Consensus on Human Rights."

that it accommodates a wider range of justifications. This argument depends on a particular – and contested – constructivist view of how such international legal concepts work. The argument for broadening the concept of "indigenous peoples" to accommodate a wider range of justifications is delicate, in that there is a significant risk for the indigenous peoples movement that the existing and highly functional international political distinction between "indigenous peoples" and ethnic and other minorities will erode, galvanizing opposition to claims of "indigenous peoples."

International Institutions and Legal Norms
Relating to "Indigenous Peoples"

The global intergovernmental institutions specifically concerned with indigenous peoples issues range from the World Bank, in which policies are drafted mainly by Bank staff and focus directly on the lending and other development-related functions of the World Bank Group, to the United Nations, a body of general political competence in which drafting and adoption of normative instruments and work programs ordinarily are heavily influenced by member states and, increasingly, other actors such as NGOs and indigenous peoples' groups. The International Labour Organization (ILO), a tripartite body involving governments and representatives of employers and trade unions, has a specialized mandate but for historical reasons has become involved with a broad range of indigenous peoples issues that extends beyond the scope of other ILO activities. The World Bank and the ILO have each been able to adopt broad and flexible indicative definitions of "indigenous peoples" in terms that have met the practical needs of these agencies without provoking unmanageable state opposition. Nevertheless, each of the functional agencies has found issues of "indigenous peoples" to pose distinctive challenges in the practical operations of the institution. Each is required to engage in difficult negotiations with recalcitrant state governments while endeavoring to be somewhat responsive to constituencies of indigenous peoples and their supporters. The leverage available to the Bank is typically greater, but the Bank often has conflicting interests, especially in dealing with very large borrowers needed by the Bank, above all China. Neither in the World Bank nor even in the ILO have indigenous peoples been nearly as fully involved in the processes of formulating and implementing normative standards as many such groups would wish. In the U.N. Working Group on Indigenous Populations, by contrast, indigenous peoples have been more extensively involved along with state governments, but the highly politicized setting and realization that any definition adopted could have very wide ramifications have hitherto rendered impossible any serious negotiation on the question.[18] With regard to issues concerning indigenous peoples, the United Nations as an institution enjoys less autonomy from both the member states and indigenous peoples, and its practice concerning a definition potentially has more potent political implications. Hence no U.N. definition of "indigenous peoples" has been adopted, although U.N. practice has been guided by a working definition in the 1986 report of U.N. Special Rapporteur Martínez Cobo:

> Indigenous communities, peoples and nations are those which, having a historical continuity with pre-invasion and pre-colonial societies that developed on their territories, consider themselves distinct from other sectors of the societies now prevailing in those territories, or parts of them. They form at present non-dominant sectors of society and are determined to preserve, develop and transmit to future generations their ancestral territories, and their ethnic identity, as the basis of their continued existence as peoples, in accordance with their own cultural patterns, social institutions and legal systems.

> This historical continuity may consist of the continuation, for an extended period reaching into the present, of one or more of the following factors:

> (a) Occupation of ancestral lands, or at least of part of them;
> (b) Common ancestry with the original occupants of these lands;
> (c) Culture in general, or in specific manifestations (such as religion, living under a tribal system, membership of an indigenous community, dress, means of livelihood, lifestyle, etc.);
> (d) Language (whether used as the only language, as mother-tongue, as the habitual means of communication at home or in the family, or as the main, preferred, habitual, general or normal language);
> (e) Residence in certain parts of the country, or in certain regions of the world;
> (f) Other relevant factors.[19]

The definition proposed in 1986 under Special Rapporteur Martínez Cobo takes a potentially limited, and controversial, view of "indigenous peoples" by requiring "historical continuity with pre-invasion and pre-colonial societies that developed on their territories." The ILO has modified the historical requirement and broadened its legal definition to an additional category of

---

18. The chair-rapporteur of the U.N. Working Group on Indigenous Populations, Erica-Irene Daes, has suggested that the solidarity and experience built up in gatherings of indigenous peoples, states, and working group members since 1982 may provide a platform on which that body might construct an agreed definition in the future. Erica-Irene Daes, *Note on Criteria Which Might be Applied when Considering the Concept of Indigenous People* (U.N. Doc. E/CN.4/Sub.2/AC.4/1995/3, June 21, 1995). It is most improbable that the Working Group would confine the concept of "indigenous peoples" to areas of European settlement. Daes, *Working Paper on the Concept of "Indigenous People"* (U.N. Doc. E/CN.4/Sub.2/AC.4/1996/2, June 10, 1996).

19. Jose Martínez Cobo, *Study of the Problem of Discrimination Against Indigenous Populations* (Geneva: U.N. Doc. E/CN.4/Sub.2/1986/7/Add.4, 1986), paras. 379–80.

"tribal peoples," and has firmly established the applicability of its treaties in all regions. The World Bank has dispensed altogether with criteria based on historical continuity and colonialism, instead taking a functional view of "indigenous peoples" as "groups with a social and cultural identity distinct from the dominant society that makes them vulnerable to being disadvantaged," an approach clearly applicable in much of Asia.

Indigenous peoples' groups have invoked human rights but have not been content to rest on the human rights program, nor have they been willing to equate themselves with "minorities." Particular legal and political norms concerning indigenous peoples have evolved in many states, but the global development of a distinct program of "hard" international legal norms relating to indigenous peoples has been slower than some activists suggest. Partly this reflects the constraints imposed by state power in the law-making process. This has been focused particularly on the most important issues for indigenous peoples, self-determination, autonomy, control of land and territories, and access to and veto power over resources. This state reticence reflects uncertainties (or antagonisms) in many states about how to accommodate the claims of indigenous peoples with the claims of others, including claims of the state.[20]

As international law stands at present, many claims made by individuals or groups who are "indigenous peoples" do not rest on the group being an "indigenous people." For example, slavery, discriminatory dispossession, military brutality, genocide, and other atrocities are prohibited by well-established principles of the generally applicable international law of human rights, and the relevant international supervisory bodies frequently address claims by indigenous peoples in variants of these standard terms. In international law, claims made by nonstate groups may draw upon at least five principal domains of discourse (and many claims simultaneously invoke several of these): human rights claims, minority rights claims, self-determination claims, claims to revendication of historical sovereignty, and claims based on particular attributes of indigenous peoples.[21] Histories of dispossession and abuse, and current vulnerability and aspirations, are all relevant to the international law applicable to particular "indigenous peoples," as are specific issues concerning historical entitlements and treaty promises. Nonetheless, the category of "indigenous peoples" is assuming increasing normative importance as negotiations continue in the United Nations and as international and national practice evolves.

20. United Nations, *Report of the Working Group on Indigenous Populations on its Fourteenth Session* (U.N. Doc. E/CN.4/Sub.2/1996/21, August 16, 1996), paras. 28–45; United Nations, *Report of the Second Session of the Working Group Established in Accordance with the Commission on Human Rights Resolution 1995/32 of 3 March 1995* (U.N. Doc. E/CN.4/1997/102, December 10, 1996), passim.
21. Benedict Kingsbury, "Claims by Non-State Groups in International Law," *Cornell International Law Journal* vol. 25 (1992), pp. 481–530.

Justifications: Nationhood, Historical Continuity, and Colonialism

The fundamental and difficult issues concerning the range of justifications admitted by the concept of "indigenous peoples" as presently constructed may be illuminated by considering the justifications embraced by the international indigenous peoples' movement, and by Asian state governments opposing the concept.

"Indigenous peoples" as a justificatory self-conception. The choice and evolution of an overarching self-conception to unify the international political movement of indigenous peoples has necessarily involved abstracting from a highly diverse range of self-understandings and political discourses held among different groups. The social and political concepts available to the movement are influenced by the concepts carried in its principal working languages. "Indigenous peoples" is now a well-established usage in English and Spanish, but it has an element of novelty even in French and is difficult to capture nonpejoratively in Chinese, Japanese, or Thai except by new usages or translation from other languages. In ordinary language "indigenous peoples" connotes priority in time, if not immemorial occupancy. It suggests also a continuity of group identity over a very long period, even as conditions have changed with colonialism, influx, migration, or the frequent changes in group structures and ethnic identities.[22] These elements of historical priority and group continuity have acquired significance as "indigenous peoples" has evolved from ordinary language into a specialized term in transnational mobilization and normative instruments.

A comparison of two texts from the international indigenous peoples movement illustrates the point, notwithstanding that the texts themselves proved evanescent. A preparatory meeting in 1974 to plan the 1975 conference that established the World Council of Indigenous Peoples (WCIP) used a provisional working definition (for determining who qualified as delegates) that has in it elements of priority and historical continuity but seems also to acknowledge the fluidity and imprecision of these elements:

> The term indigenous people refers to people living in countries which have a population composed of differing ethnic or racial groups who are descendants of the earliest populations living in the area and who do not as a group control the national government of the countries within which they live.[23]

By 1984, the developing collective political consciousness and confidence of the international indigenous peoples movement produced, in the draft International

---

22. *The Concise Oxford Dictionary,* 9th ed. (Oxford: Oxford University Press, 1995), p. 692, defines "indigenous": "1. *a* (esp. of flora or fauna) originating naturally in a region; *b* (of people) born in a region. 2. (foll. by to) belonging naturally to a place."

23. Douglas Sanders, *The Formation of the World Council of Indigenous Peoples* (Copenhagen: International Work Group for Indigenous Affairs, 1977).

Covenant on the Rights of Indigenous Peoples prepared for the WCIP, a sharpened and more reified view of these elements. An indigenous people is one:

(a) who lived in a territory before the entry of a colonizing population, which colonizing population has created a new state or states or extended the jurisdiction of an existing state or states to include the territory, and
(b) who continue to live in the territory and who do not control the national government of the state or states within which they live.[24]

This construction of a collective self-representation simultaneously challenges dominant conceptions of the state as the political embodiment of a nation comprising all of the people within the state and emulates the representation of historical "nations" connected to particular territory as a foundation for many modern "nation-states."

The impacts on political consciousness of the modern territorial state and the concepts of "nation" that have buttressed it have been so strong that it is scarcely surprising that in some usages the concept of "indigenous peoples" has taken on a parallel structure. "Indigenous peoples" challenges totalizing views of "nation" and the "nation-state" that have frequently made it difficult for identities other than the "nation" to secure recognition and acceptance. "Indigenous peoples" would legitimize such cultural and political units in the way nation-states have been legitimized by "nations." "History" has often seemed to leave indigenous peoples not so much as participants and subjects but as marginal objects contained within a much broader account of the nation, prominent perhaps as to customs and folk dances but peripheral in national politics and national law.

In a reaction against this, the rhetoric of some international conceptions of "indigenous peoples" would imply an approach to history similar to those histories of "nations" probed skeptically by Elie Kedourie, Benedict Anderson, and many others.[25] Such approaches to history have proved highly functional

---

24. World Council of Indigenous Peoples (mimeo, 1984).
25. See, for example, Elie Kedourie, *Nationalism,* 4th ed. (Oxford: Blackwell, 1993); Benedict Anderson, *Imagined Communities: Reflections on the Origin and Spread of Nationalism,* rev. ed. (London: Verso, 1991). The Solemn Declaration adopted at the 1975 WCIP meeting has a striking narrative line. "We the Indigenous Peoples of the world, united in this corner of our Mother Earth in a great assembly of men of wisdom, declare to all nations: We glory in our proud past: when the earth was our nurturing mother, when the night sky formed our common roof, when Sun and Moon were our parents, when all were brothers and sisters, when our great civilizations grew under the sun, when our chiefs and elders were great leaders, when justice ruled the law and its execution. Then other peoples arrived: thirsting for blood, for gold, for land and all its wealth, carrying the cross and the sword, one in each hand, without knowing or waiting to learn the ways of our worlds, they considered us to be lower than animals, they stole our lands from us and took us from our lands, they made slaves of the Sons of the sun. However, they have never been able to eliminate us, nor to erase our memories of what we were, because we are the culture of the earth and the sky, we are of ancient descent and we are millions, and although our whole universe may be ravaged, our people will live on for longer even than the kingdom of death. . . . We vow to control again our own destiny and recover our complete humanity and pride in being Indigenous People." (Quoted in Sanders, *The Formation of the World Council of Indigenous Peoples,* p. 17.)

for certain purposes. As Prasenjit Duara argues in a discussion concerned particularly with elements of Chinese historiography:

> National history secures for the contested and contingent nation the false unity of a self-same, national subject evolving through time. . . . It allows the nation-state to see itself as a unique form of community which finds its place in the oppositions between tradition and modernity, hierarchy and equality, empire and nation. Within this schema, the nation appears as the newly realized, sovereign subject of [Enlightenment] History embodying a moral and political force that has overcome dynasties, aristocracies, and ruling priests and mandarins, who are seen to represent merely themselves historically. In contrast to them, the nation is a collective subject poised to realize its destiny in a modern future.[26]

James Clifford captures exactly this element in his observation of the trial of a Native American land rights claim that under U.S. law was deemed to depend on establishing a simple linear historical continuity of the group over hundreds of years – a romanticized continuity demanded by Western history with little regard to tribal history. In history,

> [tribal] societies are always either dying or surviving, assimilating or resisting. Caught between a local past and a global future, they either hold on to their separateness or "enter the modern world.". . . But the familiar paths of tribal death, survival, assimilation, or resistance do not catch the specific ambivalence of life in places like Mashpee over four centuries of defeat, renewal, political negotiation, and cultural innovation.[27]

In struggles to put into question totalizing views of the "nation," it may be inevitable that the concept of "indigenous peoples" takes on some of the same characteristics, but such approaches risk some of the same hazards as extreme varieties of nationalism and are likely in the future to meet with similar skeptical reconsideration. Just as national projects have evolved or metamorphosed in many places, however, so the concept of "indigenous peoples" is often espoused flexibly both in international institutions and in more local politics.

LEGAL AND POLITICAL POSITIONS OF VARIOUS ASIAN STATE GOVERNMENTS WITH RESPECT TO "INDIGENOUS PEOPLES"

The major controversy in the United Nations concerns the proposed requirement of historical continuity with a preinvasion or precolonial society established on the territory. Since the establishment of the U.N. Working Group

---

26. Duara, *Rescuing History from the Nation* (Chicago: University of Chicago Press, 1995), p. 4.
27. Clifford, *The Predicament of Culture* (Cambridge, MA: Harvard University Press, 1988), p. 342.

on Indigenous Populations in 1982, India has espoused the position that the concept of "indigenous peoples" does not apply within its borders.[28] Bangladesh and Burma/Myanmar have also followed this line.[29] The People's Republic of China has begun recently to take more assertive public positions against the applicability of the concept of "indigenous peoples" in China. Maintenance of a strict requirement of historical continuity from preinvasion or precolonial societies – a requirement that owes at least part of its inspiration to perceptions and experiences in areas of European settlement areas – would be likely both to complicate and to restrict,[30] without altogether excluding, the applicability of the concept of "indigenous peoples" in other parts of the world.

The precise grounds for opposition among Asian governments vary and have not all been made fully explicit. At least three kinds of arguments are involved: definitional, practical, and policy. The definitional arguments are lexical, resting on a view of "indigenous" as entailing prior occupancy, and stipulational, associating "indigenous peoples" with the deleterious effects of European colonialism. The practical argument is that it is impossible or misleading to seek to identify the prior occupants in countries and regions with such long and intricate histories of influx, movement, and melding. The policy argument is the powerful one that recognizing rights on the basis of prior occupation for particular sets of groups will spur and legitimate group mobilization and claims by a vast range of groups, undermining other values with which the state is properly concerned.

Definitional Arguments

The views and approach of the PRC government on the meaning of the concept of "indigenous peoples" are exemplified by its 1995 comments concerning consideration by the U.N. Commission on Human Rights' Inter-Sessional Working Group of a draft U.N. declaration, quoted earlier. China's position is that the concept of "indigenous peoples" is inextricably bound up with, and indeed a function of, European colonialism. This is in one way a continuation of the U.N. General Assembly practice of treating the entire nonsettler or non-European population of European colonies (e.g., the entire population of Mozambique under Portuguese rule) as "indigenous peoples." In this respect, "indigenous peoples" are those who, not having obtained lib-

28. See, for example, Lakshmi Puri, *Statement on Behalf of the Delegation of India to the United Nations Working Group on Indigenous Populations, 12 August 1983* (Geneva: U.N. files, mimeo).

29. U Win Mra, *Statement on Behalf of the Delegation of Myanmar to the United Nations Working Group on Indigenous Populations, 31 July 1991* (Geneva: U.N. files, mimeo).

30. Alternatively, the Bangladesh government has begun to argue that all Bangladeshis are indigenous people who existed in the territory prior to British colonialism and are now, fortunately, liberated.

eration from European rule, are continuing victims of sufferings caused by European settler colonialism – the losers, in a sense, in the process of the formation by Europeans of states outside Europe. China has thus supported in general terms a definition under which indigenous peoples were "living on their lands before settlers came from elsewhere; . . . descendants . . . of those who inhabited a country or a geographic region at the time when peoples of different cultures or ethnic origins arrived, the new arrivals becoming dominant through conquest, occupation, settlement or other means."[31]

India, Bangladesh, and Myanmar have also made similar arguments, stressing that indigenous peoples are descendants of the original inhabitants who have suffered from conquest or invasion from outside.[32] There is no express reference to the notion of "saltwater colonialism," used by the Group of 77 developing nations to distinguish European colonialism outside Europe from practices by non-Europeans that might share some characteristics with European colonialism, but China's approach strongly suggests that the "historical misfortunes of indigenous peoples" that set them apart are the misfortunes of saltwater settler colonialism. China's position is in one sense a continuation of the rejection by G77 states of the "Belgian thesis," which was an assertion in the early 1950s that U.N. scrutiny of the treatment of non-autonomous peoples under Chapter XI of the U.N. Charter should not be confined to the indigenous inhabitants of European colonies but ought also to extend to indigenous peoples in independent states, who were just as deserving of international protection. Peoples in many of the anticolonial states, including India, Indonesia, the Philippines, and the USSR, were described by Belgium to fall within this category.[33] The Belgian thesis was plausibly regarded at the time as a somewhat cynical part of the rearguard defense of European colonialism.[34]

There is implicit in the contemporary position of China and other Asian states the suggestion that the attempt to impose the concept of "indigenous peoples" upon various Asian states is a form of neocolonialism. In this view, the concept of "indigenous peoples," made relevant and necessary in Western states (including Latin America) by the enduring human consequences of the

31. People's Republic of China, *Consideration of a Draft United Nations Declaration on the Rights of Indigenous Peoples* (U.N. Doc. E/CN.4/WG.15/2, October 10, 1995); *Report of the Second Session of the Working Group Established in Accordance with Commission on Human Rights Resolution 1995/32 of 3 March 1995* (U.N. Doc. E/CN.4/1997/102, December 10, 1996), para. 106.

32. Government of India, *Observations* (U.N. Doc. E/CN.4/Sub.2/1984/2/Add.2., 1984); Government of Myanmar, *Observations* (U.N. Doc. E/CN.4/Sub.2/1989/33/Add.1., 1989). For Bangladesh, see *Report of the Working Group on Indigenous Populations on its Fourteenth Session* (U.N. Doc. E/CN.4/Sub.2/1996/21, August 16, 1996), para. 34.

33. Belgian Government Information Center, *The Sacred Mission of Civilization: To Which Peoples Should the Benefits Be Extended? The Belgian Thesis* (New York: Belgian Government Information Center, 1953).

34. Inis Claude, *National Minorities: An International Problem* (Cambridge, MA: Harvard University Press, 1955), p. 172.

European incursion and majority settlement that gave these states much of their present form and character, is now applied at the initiative of these Western states to Asian states that either staved off Western colonialism or rid themselves of its most direct effects in the struggle for decolonization.

Practical Arguments

Building on the notion of indigenous peoples as the peoples who came first (or at least earlier than the others who are now dominant), representatives of the government of India have made the practical argument that the concept cannot apply in India because after centuries of migration, absorption, and differentiation it is impossible to say who came first. (This is echoed in China's argument that all of the nationalities in China have lived there for eons.) Thus, in 1991 the representative of India in the Working Group on Indigenous Populations commented that most of the tribes in India share ethnic, racial, and linguistic characteristics with other people in India, and that 300 to 400 million people there are distinct in some way from other categories of people in India.[35]

Prescription of ethnicity by administrative fiat or by self-designation involves numerous problems and is open to much criticism, and there are difficult cases under any approach. Nonetheless it has proved possible as a practical matter to enumerate detailed lists of Scheduled Tribes under the Fifth and Sixth Schedules to the Indian Constitution; these constitutional categories have provided a practical starting point for identification of groups to whom policies of international agencies relating to "indigenous peoples" have been applied in India. Similarly in China, in a major project conducted largely in the 1950s, the Nationalities Commission has identified 55 minorities to whom various preferential policies are supposed to apply. Whether it has always proved beneficial to groups to be so identified, or to have an identity created, and to then be subject to distinctive treatment is a serious question, but it is one of policy rather than practicalities. This is not to downplay the practical problems, which in many areas may be severe, but the practical objections seem to reflect objections to imposition of a foreign concept to which strong policy objections are made.

Policy Arguments

There is implied also in the Indian government's position an argument that a forensic inquiry into who came first in India would be unhelpful and

---

35. Prabhu Dayal, *Statement on Behalf of the Delegation of India to the United Nations Working Group on Indigenous Populations, 31 July 1991* (Geneva: U.N. files, mimeo).

undesirable, for two reasons. First, some groups meriting particular protection would be excluded, whereas others not in need of particular protection might be included. Second, recognition of special rights and entitlements on the basis of being the earliest or original occupants might spur and legitimate chauvinist claims by groups all over India, many of which may be very powerful locally although in some sense "nondominant" nationally. Claims to historical priority already feature in some "communal" conflicts, and incipient chauvinist movements abound, as with the pro-Marathi, Hindunationalist Shiv Sena party in Maharashtra.[36] In effect, if some people are "indigenous" to a place, others are vulnerable to being targeted as nonindigenous, and groups deemed to be migrants or otherwise subject to social stigma may bear the brunt of a nativist "indigenist" policy. Once indigenousness or "sons of the soil" becomes the basis of legitimation for a politically or militarily dominant group, restraints on abuses of power can be difficult to maintain.[37]

This has been a crucial issue in the national politics of states such as Malaysia and Fiji, and is a potential source of bitter division in many other polities. Perhaps because of the sensitivity of what is involved, this second point is not often developed explicitly in government statements, but it seems to have animated India's long-standing concern to keep the concept of "indigenous peoples" at a safe distance. This underpins the point that a functional concept of "indigenous peoples" applicable in all regions will be viable only if it is broad enough to permit alternative justifications. A concept that is integrally dependent on arguments of priority in time and historical continuity from ancient times to the present may work well enough in some regions but is unlikely to be adequate and workable in all regions.

The Evolving Domestic Politics of Indigenous Identity

In the Philippines, Spanish colonial rule left a significant number of groups "un-hispanicized" or "non-Christian," and distinctions of this sort were reinforced by the U.S. regime, which established a Bureau of Non-Christian Tribes and drew on administrative policies relating to Indians in the United States. The category of indigenous cultural communities (ICCs), covering somewhat more than 10 percent of the population, has become well established in Philippines politics. Resistance by indigenous groups in northern Luzon to large Marcos-era projects such as the Chico dams (which were eventually canceled) and the Cellophil pulp and processing operations in Abra increased political

36. Mary Fainsod Katzenstein, *Ethnicity and Equality: The Shiv Sena Party and Preferential Policies in Bombay* (Ithaca: Cornell University Press, 1979); Clare Talwalker, "Shivaji's Army and Other 'Natives' in Bombay," *Comparative Studies of South Asia, Africa and the Middle East* vol. 16 (1996), pp. 114–22.
37. Horowitz, *Ethnic Groups in Conflict*, pp. 201–16.

mobilization among Kalinga, Bontoc, Tinggians, and others[38]; these projects were also associated with militarization of the region, considerable brutality, and some tribal support for the New Peoples Army.[39]

The political and legal dynamics of issues concerning indigenous peoples have changed somewhat since the Marcos period, and numerous highly effective civil society organizations involving indigenous peoples are flourishing, including the internationally prominent Cordillera Peoples' Alliance and other northern organizations, Lumad Mindanaw and several other organizations in Mindanao, and national organizations such as the National Federation of Indigenous Peoples of the Philippines (KAMP). Bitter disputes about development projects continue, as with opposition of Cordillera groups to the Newcrest and Newmont mining explorations, the controversy concerning the Western Mining Corporation operation in Mindanao, and resistance to forced land sales and exclusion of indigenous peoples in commercial plantation projects.[40] The international concept of "indigenous peoples" is currently influential and is accepted by the government as applicable to the ICCs. Under the Ramos administration the process of issuing Certificates of Ancestral Domain Claims to groups among the ICCs has proceeded apace; although beset with problems, this is potentially an important step to recognition of land rights for numerous groups.[41]

Substantial Japanese northward movement in Hokkaido in the Tokugawa and Meiji periods had a major impact on Ainu. An assimilationist philosophy was embodied in the principal legislation, the Hokkaido Former Indigenes Protection Act of 1899. This statute continued in force for almost a century; new legislation was adopted in 1997, but it did not satisfy all concerns expressed by Ainu groups. Until the late 1980s the government of Japan remained unwilling to accept that Ainu constituted even an ethnic

---

38. See, for example, Richard Dorall, "The Dialectic of Development: Tribal Responses to Development Capital in the Cordillera Central, Northern Luzon, Philippines," in Lim Teck Ghee and Alberto G. Gomes, eds., *Tribal Peoples and Development in Southeast Asia* (Kuala Lumpur: University of Malaya, 1990), pp. 37–67.

39. For a historical survey, see Ma. Elena R. Regpala, "Resistance in the Cordillera: A Philippine Tribal People's Historical Response to Invasion and Change Imposed from Outside," in Ghee and Gomes, eds., *Tribal Peoples and Development in Southeast Asia*, pp. 112–40.

40. The Philippine Mining Act of 1995, the 1996 Implementing Rules and Regulations of the Philippine Mining Act, the Financial or Technical Assistance Agreement made with Western Mining, and other instruments were challenged on constitutional and other grounds in judicial proceedings launched in Philippines Supreme Court in 1996–7.

41. Owen Lynch and Kirk Talbott, *Balancing Acts: Community Based Forest Management and National Law in Asia and the Pacific* (Washington, DC: World Resources Institute, 1995); David Daoas, "The Rights of Cultural Communities in the Philippines," in Christian Erni ed., "... Vines That Won't Bind ...": *Indigenous Peoples in Asia* (Copenhagen: International Work Group for Indigenous Affairs, 1997), pp. 97–107; United Nations, *Report of the Second Session of the Working Group Established in Accordance with Commission on Human Rights Resolution 1995/32 of 3 March 1995* (U.N. Doc. E/CN.4/1997/102, December 10, 1996), para. 314.

minority under the International Covenant on Civil and Political Rights.[42] In subsequent years the government acquiesced to interacting domestic and international pressures and abandoned the insistence on the homogeneity of Japan, and de facto it has accepted that the Ainu people are a distinct group properly associating themselves with the international indigenous peoples' movement. In an important decision in 1997 finding that Ainu land had been illegally expropriated for a dam, the Sapporo District Court accepted that Ainu are an indigenous ethnic group and found this potentially to have legal significance in Japan. However the legislation that followed in 1997, although charting a clearly nonassimilationist policy, reflected the government's continuing reluctance formally to accept that Ainu should be regarded as "indigenous" or an "indigenous people."

In Malaysia a concept of indigenousness features prominently in political discourse as an underpinning for the *bumiputra* ("son of the soil") policy. In peninsular Malaysia this policy is designed to maintain and advance the position of Malays. "Malay" is defined in the Constitution as "a person who professes the religion of Islam, habitually speaks the Malay language, conforms to Malay custom" and traces descent to one who at the date of Independence had been born in or was domiciled in the Federation. In a separate constitutional category are "aborigines" of the peninsula, usually known collectively as Orang Asli, whose legal status has been regulated (in the exercise of federal rather than state power) primarily by a series of Aboriginal Peoples' Acts.[43] The philosophy of the legislation and of the administration of the relevant government agency, the Jabatan Hal Ehwal Orang Asli, has been protectionist, with some aspiration of long-term assimilation of Orang Asli into Malay communities and very little endorsement of active self-determination. However, political activity by Orang Asli organizations, led in particular by members of the growing cadre of Orang Asli who have gone through state educational institutions but supported also by non–Orang Asli concerned with the issue, has begun since the 1980s to urge new approaches and initiatives.[44]

As to East Malaysia, the Constitution identifies a category of "natives" of

42. Article 27 of the ICCPR refers to ethnic, religious and linguistic minorities. The Japanese government stated in 1980 that "minorities of the kind mentioned in the covenant do not exist in Japan" (U.N. Doc. ICCPR/C/10/Add.1, 1980). In 1988 the government adopted a delicate formulation stating with respect to "the people of the Ainu" that "it is recognized that these people preserve their own religion and maintain their own culture" (U.N. Doc. ICCPR/C/42/ Add.4, 1988).

43. For a brief overview see Sothi Rachagan, "Constitutional and Statutory Provisions Governing the Orang Asli," in Ghee and Gomes, eds., *Tribal Peoples and Development in Southeast Asia*, pp. 101–11. See also I. Carey, *Orang Asli: The Aboriginal Tribes of Peninsula Malaysia* (Kuala Lumpur: Oxford University Press, 1976).

44. Several works of Colin Nicholas address this issue. See, for example, his "In the Name of the Semai? The State and Semai Society in Peninsular Malaysia," in Ghee and Gomes, eds., *Tribal Peoples and Development in Southeast Asia*, pp. 68–88.

Sabah and Sarawak, and in the case of Sarawak lists a large number of "races . . . indigenous to Sarawak" who count as "native." This category includes Malays, and formally these "native" groups are on much the same footing as Malays in Malaysia as a whole. In practice the legal and political dynamics in East Malaysia have been quite distinct from those pertaining in the center of federal power on the peninsula, and there has emerged considerable opposition to deforestation and land alienation, involving numerous organizations including the Sarawak Indigenous Peoples' Alliance,[45] as well as debate about the direction and effects of rapid economic development.[46] Constitutional recognition of the Orang Asli and natives of Sarawak and Sabah as indigenous is in some respects a continuation of British practice, overlain by the *bumiputra* policy, which actively privileges on grounds of indigenousness a Malay group that is politically dominant and economically influential and confers juridical recognition if more limited practical benefits on native groups in Sabah and Sarawak who are in aggregate numerical majorities in those states but whose political influence and economic power are uneven. Against this complex background, it is not surprising that the final position of the Malaysian government on the developing concept of "indigenous peoples" in the United Nations has yet to emerge.

A category of "hill-tribe" people in the north and northwest of Thailand has been recognized and actively addressed as a subject of government policy since the 1950s, initially in response to concerns about opium cultivation and insurgency related to the Cold War, and more recently as part of forest policy and community development schemes. The complex demography of the hill regions includes many groups who moved into the forest areas they now occupy within historical memory, often during the past century, coming mainly from areas in present-day Burma, Laos, and in some cases China. Large numbers of these people are not registered as citizens of Thailand but would like to be in order to secure political rights and access to government services. There is thus a radical contrast with the claims of some Native American groups in the United States, who assert a continuing separate tribal sovereignty as against the jurisdiction of the United States and issue their own passports.

Such divergences make difficult the formulation of positions in the interna-

---

45. See, for example, remarks by a leader of this organization: Anderson Muutang Urud, "Statement to the United Nations General Assembly, 10 December 1992," in *Voice of Indigenous Peoples: Native People Address the United Nations* (Santa Fe, NM: Clear Light Publishing, 1994), pp. 103–7. For a summary by a community organizer from Partners of Community Organizations (PACOS) in Sabah, see Jannie Lasimbang, "Juridical Rights of Indigenous Peoples and Their Relations to the State and Non-Indigenous Peoples: The Case of Sabah," in Erni ed., ". . . *Vines That Won't Bind . . . ,*" pp. 109–14.

46. Victor King, "Indigenous Peoples and Land Rights in Sarawak, Malaysia: To Be or Not to Be a *Bumiputra,*" in Barnes, Gray, and Kingsbury, eds., *Indigenous Peoples of Asia,* pp. 289–306.

tional indigenous peoples' movement and illustrate the need for care in identifying the sources and representativity of normative pronouncements by international networks. At present the discourse of "indigenous peoples" appears scarcely to figure in national politics or in claims made by non-ethnic-Thai tribal groups. Nevertheless, there are many points of similarity between issues in northern Thailand and those arising in other parts of the world. A major concern in northern Thailand is lack of recognized rights to the land that a particular group may have occupied or used for many decades; often the state has purported to obliterate such land claims through proclamation of forest reserves or national parks.[47] Chayan reports that a 1995 demonstration by hill-tribe people, mainly Karen, against Forest Department programs to exclude people from watershed areas and relocate them was "the first such event in modern Thai history."[48] In 1992 the government of Thailand indicated to the United Nations its view that hill tribes are ethnic groups but "are not considered to be minorities nor indigenous people but as Thais who are able to enjoy fundamental rights . . . as any other Thai citizen."[49] However, the government seems not to have taken a final position on the application to Thailand of the international concept of indigenous peoples.

The Implications of Government Attitudes for U.N. Negotiations

The opposition of several major Asian state governments to application of the concept of "indigenous peoples" in their territories has obvious significance in the politics of issues relating to indigenous peoples in the United Nations. Having called for a clear, scientific, objective, and practical definition of indigenous peoples that can clearly be interpreted as not applying to any groups in the PRC, China comments: "Until a clear definition of indigenous peoples has been established, the Chinese Government cannot formulate specific opinions on individual clauses of the draft declaration."[50] The position of the PRC makes clear what is implicit: At least some Asian states may support – or at least not block – stronger provisions in the U.N. draft declaration if they are reasonably confident that such provisions will not be applied to groups within these states. A negotiating position is thus indicated: A draft declaration with a wide or open-ended definitional provision,

---

47. See the powerful 1973 statement against this government practice by His Majesty King Bhumibol, quoted in Lynch and Talbott, *Balancing Acts*, p. iii.
48. Chayan Vaddhanuphuti, "The Present Situation of Indigenous Peoples in Thailand," in Erni, ed., ". . . *Vines That Won't Bind* . . . ," p. 83.
49. Thailand Government statement, *Hill-Tribe Welfare and Development* (U.N. Doc. E/CN.4/AC.2/ 1992/4, May 12, 1992).
50. People's Republic of China, *Consideration of a Draft United Nations Declaration on the Rights of Indigenous Peoples* (U.N. Doc. E/CN.4/WG.15/2, October 10, 1995).

or with no definitional provision at all, may well meet with opposition or proposals for severe attenuation, whereas a draft declaration with a narrow and precise definitional provision may well be supported.

The initial hesitancy among leaders of some groups in the areas of European settlement, particularly in the Americas, about extending the category of "indigenous peoples" to Asia still recurs, and the temptation to acquiesce in a narrower definition in order to attain the agreement of Asian states to stronger substantive provisions in a U.N. declaration is undoubtedly present. It seems most likely, however, that such temptations will continue to be overwhelmed by the commitment to universality and solidarity within the internationally active indigenous peoples' movement, especially in view of the global scope of the agencies of the U.N. system and the presumptions of universality inherent in the U.N. human rights culture.

FIVE ILLUSTRATIVE CASES OF INDIGENOUS PEOPLES' MOBILIZATION

The early effort to build a vibrant international "indigenous peoples" movement in the 1970s was driven primarily by groups from areas of European invasion and settlement. The World Council of Indigenous Peoples (WCIP), for example, was founded in 1975 at the initiative of George Manuel of the National Indian Brotherhood of Canada: its initial scope and the sources of its momentum are indicated by its early five-region structure, covering North, Central, and South America, the Nordic region, and Australasia.[51] The inclusion of Asian groups under the umbrella of the international indigenous peoples' movement was accomplished as such groups became more organized and active in international fora. There was initial hesitation about this among some individuals active in the "founding" regions of the World Council of Indigenous Peoples – thus people living in Japan, India, and Thailand were permitted to speak only as observers at the Third General Assembly of the WCIP in 1981[52] – but the WCIP subsequently decided to broaden its geographic scope, and a Pacific–Asia Council of Indigenous Peoples was established. The WCIP is no longer as active as in its early years, but the international "indigenous peoples" movement is very active, with numerous networks and loose organizational structures in which many groups from Asia are now involved.

The existence of an "indigenous peoples" movement is a major factor in the diffusion and impact of "indigenous peoples" as an international legal

---

51. See generally Sanders, *The Formation of the World Council of Indigenous Peoples.*
52. *Newsletter of the International Work Group for Indigenous Affairs* no. 27 (1981), p. 5.

concept. Groups and individuals participating in this movement have focused on elements of commonality that have helped the movement to cohere: connections with land and territory, aspirations for autonomy and self-determination, renewed interest in distinct cultures and languages, historical experience of incursions by other groups, continuing consequences of dispossession and subordination, concerns over health and education, and relative disadvantage in child welfare, mortality, nutrition, and poverty levels. A further element is the shared effects of modernity.[53] Although the "indigenous peoples" movement is in some respects made possible by these modern developments, it is also a form of resistance to them, particularly to the convergence and homogenization they threaten to bring with them. All of this has made possible the formulation of international normative programs and credos by various groups of organizations participating in the "indigenous peoples" movement. It is not surprising that in structured political settings such as the U.N. effort to draft a Declaration on the Rights of Indigenous Peoples, these normative programs have been heavily influenced by agendas and demands formulated by a smaller number of representatives of politically dominant groups skilled in the methods, politics, and working languages of the United Nations, relatively few of whom are from Asia.

Historical circumstances and contemporary conditions vary immensely among participants in the international "indigenous peoples" movement, and there are huge differences in contemporary political opportunities and in the types of threats currently faced by groups and individuals. One experience shared by many groups[54] that has spurred much mobilization and transnational activity of local groups has been large-scale development projects designed and imposed by others. Experience with such projects illustrates many of the themes of this chapter; five examples from Asia will be mentioned briefly here.

53. These include the ubiquity of state interests in economic modernization and exploitation of resources, often in response to global demands for such commodities as timber, electricity, copper, and gold; commonalities through the transnational operation and global technologies of industries such as mining, nuclear power, large dams, tropical forestry, or oil recovery; similarities among modern monetarized economies, and their connections through markets, brand names, and tastes fostered by advertising; shared social technologies for the organization of important sectors from educational institutions and censuses to banking and insurance; and the global communications that simultaneously facilitate transnational connections of markets and networks of indigenous peoples.

54. For works on a small sample of the many similar issues that have arisen in the states dominated by European settlement, see Thomas Berger, *Northern Frontier, Northern Homeland: The Report of the Mackenzie Valley Pipeline Inquiry,* 2 vols. (Toronto: James Lorimer and Co., 1977); Thomas Berger, *Village Journey: The Report of the Alaska Native Review Commission* (New York: Hill and Wang, 1985); Dave Treece, *Bound in Misery and Iron: The Impact of the Grande Carajas Programme on the Indians of Brazil* (London: Survival International, 1987); Carmen Junqueira and Betty Mindlin, *The Aripuana Park and the Polonoreste Programme, Brazil* (Copenhagen: IWGIA, 1987); Shelton Davis, *Victims of the Miracle: Development and the Indians of Brazil* (Cambridge: Cambridge University Press, 1977); Robert Paine, *Dam a River, Damn a People?* (Copenhagen: IWGIA, 1982).

The Narmada Dam and Canal Projects

In western India, the Sardar Sarovar dam and canal project, together with related projects in the Narmada river basin, has met with strong opposition from a wide variety of groups since the projects began to take clear shape in the early 1980s.[55] Groups subjected to or threatened with involuntary displacement, particularly tribal people whose undocumented customary land holdings did not meet the requirements to prove title in state legal systems and who were thus deemed ineligible for land-for-land compensation, have engaged in direct protests such as peaceful occupations and hunger strikes.[56] Investigations, reports, and litigation have been organized by these and many other Indian groups, including well-known social activists, students, and environmental NGOs, as well as numerous foreign NGOs and transnational networks.

The World Bank initially played a major role in international financing of the Narmada projects. Following intense criticism in India and abroad, withdrawal of support for the project by the government of Japan, and the 1992 report of an independent review commissioned by the World Bank that found the project to fall far short of the Bank's own policies regarding resettlement of oustees, compensation to project-affected people, and environmental protection, the Bank in 1993 ceased further participation.[57] The authors of the review took the position that the Bank has adopted explicit policies for the benefit of indigenous and tribal peoples in development projects, that "[c]oncern for such groups is an aspect of the world's increased awareness of how isolated cultures have all too often paid an appalling price for development," and that as a functional matter many aspects of tribal culture posed distinctive problems of project implementation that required special consideration in the project.

A basic disjunction was at the heart of this element of the project:

> From the point of view of the people themselves, the intent of the Indian Constitution, basic anthropological findings, and the criteria embedded in World Bank policy directives for tribals and indigenous peoples in Bank-aided projects, a substantial

55. The way was cleared for the projects after the 1979 decision of the Narmada Water Disputes Tribunal allocated water rights among the interested riparian and nonriparian states. The Tribunal also set a basic requirement of land-for-land compensation as well as modest compensation for "landless" oustees.
56. For example, the Bargi Bandh Visthapit Aur Prabhavit Sangh (an association of oustees displaced by the already-complete Bargi Dam) organized a *satyagraha* on the banks of the reservoir to try to prevent a further rise in its level in 1996, and litigation has been pursued by the Narmada Bachao Andolan (NBA). Groups organized around the issues of displacement and resettlement take a wide range of positions – many do not oppose, or indeed support, the dam and canal projects, but are concerned with specific features of the projects or with gross inadequacies in implementation.
57. This followed a request from the government of India to end further disbursements, made in the context of the Bank's concerns about the project and of the government's concerns about external pressure.

proportion of those likely to be affected by Sardar Sarovar Projects are tribal people and entitled to the benefit of special measures that will defend and secure their distinctive interests . . . [yet] no policies have been devised by the Governments of Gujarat, Maharashtra, or Madya Pradesh that pay attention to the particular needs and concerns of Sardar Sarovar tribals.[58]

In a bold decision, assisted by the expertise of the Indian NGOs in gathering data and presenting arguments, and perhaps facilitated somewhat by the previous developments in international bodies, the Supreme Court of India in December 1995 issued a temporary order restraining continued construction of the Sardar Sarovar dam pending full judicial consideration of resettlement, environmental impact, and other issues, although the government of India and the state governments remained more or less committed to the scheme.

Settlement in the Chittagong Hill Tracts

A Bangladesh government program to resettle in the Chittagong Hill Tracts (CHT) large numbers of people from other parts of Bangladesh has met with fierce resistance by members of tribal groups who regard the land as theirs and see their economic circumstances deteriorating in the transformation from swidden agriculture to plantation wage-labor. The conflict became heavily militarized, causing large refugee flows and numerous deaths before a peace agreement was finally reached in December 1997.[59] Deliberately isolated from Bengali settlement during British rule, the diverse groups who have long inhabited the area have sought to build unity among themselves in the face of increasing interactions with the Pakistani and Bangladeshi states and massive Bengali settlement since the early 1970s. This unity has been constructed around the term *jumma* as a new collective self-designation of these inhabitants of the CHT, and there are now frequent references among CHT people to the *jumma* people or the *jumma* nation.

In Van Schendel's assessment, *jumma*, "[a]n old pejorative term for a swidden cultivator in the Chittagonian dialect of Bengali," was appropriated by the Jana Samhati Samiti (the main nonsettler CHT political organization, whose military wing is the Shanti Bahini) "in an attempt to unify all the hill

---

58. Bradford Morse and Thomas Berger, *Sardar Sarovar: Report of the Independent Review* (Ottawa: Resource Futures International, 1992), pp. 77–9. The two authors of the review are respectively a U.S. citizen who served as a prominent international civil servant and former head of the U.N. Development Programme and a well-known Canadian jurist who has been involved extensively in indigenous issues relating to development projects in North America.

59. Peace agreement between the government of Bangladesh and the Parhatya Chattagram Jana Sanghati Samiti, December 3, 1997, *Daily Star* (Dhoka), December 3, 1997. On the conflict see Chittagong Hill Tracts Commission (a nongovernmental outside group), *Life Is Not Ours: Land and Human Rights in the Chittagong Hill Tracts, Bangladesh* (London: Calverts, 1991).

people under one social umbrella."[60] Externally, however, the issues raised by the CHT groups are increasingly being couched as issues of indigenous peoples. As one CHT activist put it prior to the peace agreement:

> The Government of Bangladesh does not recognize us as indigenous peoples in the constitution. We have no constitutional rights as indigenous peoples. The government is very carefully trying to avoid the international recognition of indigenous peoples in Bangladesh. The constitution has recognized the rights of citizens in general, but we have clear linguistic, cultural and sociopolitical distinctiveness from the majority Bengali people. That is why we want the right to a "separate status" in the constitution as indigenous peoples.[61]

The Yadana Pipeline in Myanmar

In Burma, the complex military conflicts that have waxed and waned since the final days of British rule, the political positions of the Ne Win regime and its successors, and in recent years the political conflicts between the State Law and Order Restoration Council (SLORC) and its opponents, have limited the number of large-scale development projects and have to some extent overshadowed concern about adverse impacts of deforestation and other forms of "development." Thus opposition since the mid-1990s to the projected Yadana natural gas pipeline, running from the Yadana offshore field under the Andaman sea and through the Tenasserim region of Burma to the Thai border, where it will meet projects on the Thai side, has been bound up with opposition to SLORC and calls for international prohibition of new investments in Burma.[62] Although the onshore portion of the pipeline runs through areas populated by non-Burman ethnic groups that have often been in conflict with SLORC, the civil suit brought in the United States against the oil company Unocal focuses not on issues particular to indigenous peoples but on general human rights violations related to the project, particularly the use of forced labor and the issue of forced relocation.[63] Members of Karen and other groups in Burma have participated in U.N. fora and other

---

60. Willem Van Schendel, "The Invention of the 'Jummas': State Formation and Ethnicity in Southeastern Bangladesh," in Barnes, Gray, and Kingsbury, eds., *Indigenous Peoples of Asia*, p. 121, 139ff. Van Schendel notes: "It is remarkable that this term was adopted at a time when many hill people had been forced to give up swidden cultivation."

61. Sanchay Chakma, "The Legal Rights Situation of the Indigenous Peoples in Bangladesh," in Erni ed., *". . . Vines That Won't Bind . . . ,"* p. 151. Sanjay Chakma, a student in Dhaka, is General Secretary of the Greater Chittagong Hill Tracts Hill Students' Council.

62. See, for example, *Total Denial* (July 1996), a critical report on the pipeline by two anti-SLORC NGOs, EarthRights International and the Southeast Asian Information Network.

63. John Doe I, et al. *v.* Unocal Corporation, et al., Orders of Judge Richard Paez of March 25, 1997 and April 24, 1997, 1997 WL 218807 (U.S. District Court, C.D. California).

international activities relating to indigenous peoples,[64] but this participation has been modest in relation to the numerical size of such groups and the scale of the issues involved, and the specific impact of the international concept of indigenous peoples in Burma does not appear to have been great.

The Lanyu Island Nuclear Waste Dump

In Taiwan, the Taiwan Power Company began in the early 1980s to use Lanyu Island to store nuclear waste from power generation, but a vigorous campaign by some of the Yami indigenous people succeeded in turning away a ship bringing more waste in 1996, and Taipower promised to remove all the waste by 2002.[65] This achievement of such a small group – fewer than 4000 people are officially classified as Yami – reflects the growing political salience of environmental activism in Taiwan, reinforced to some extent by the involvement of international NGOs such as Greenpeace. It illustrates also the gradual change in the position of indigenous peoples in Taiwan since the end of martial law, evidenced by the recent proliferation of indigenous organizations.

Among the oldest (founded in 1984) is the Alliance of Taiwan Aborigines (ATA), organized to coordinate political action among nine major indigenous groups whose combined populations by official estimates exceed 350,000.[66] Although specific results have been modest in comparison to their objectives, the ATA has lobbied and mobilized protests on such issues as land rights and land use, political status and representation, education, cultural protection and autonomy, economic opportunities, sexual exploitation of women and girls, requirements to sinify names (reversed by the government in 1995), and nomenclature. In 1994 the ROC Constitution was amended to excise references to *shan-pao* (mountain compatriots, also *shan-ti tung-pao*); the official constitutional usage is now *yuan-chu min* (the people who lived here first). The ATA has made a similar argument in the United Nations, challenging the U.N.'s translation of indigenous peoples as *tuzu renmin,* a usage apparently supported by the PRC Government in the United Nations but widely regarded as connoting "primitive" or "low cultural level." The ATA

---

64. See, for example, the statement by a Chin student, Zo Tum Hmung, "The Juridical Rights of the Indigenous Peoples in Burma," in Erni ed., ". . . *Vines That Won't Bind . . . ,"* pp. 89–95.

65. Taipower's 1997 proposal to export the waste to North Korea, a country in desperate need of revenue but unlikely adequately to manage such waste, led to strong protests in South Korea and from international NGOs, and caused disquiet among Yami and other campaigning groups in Taiwan. A further contentious issue for Yami arises from plans to turn a cleaned-up Lanyu into a national park, threatening to limit Yami economic opportunities and to promote a commodified tourist culture.

66. Also increasingly active is the Union of Native Taiwanese Villages, founded in 1994, and other social movements.

has instead urged the United Nations to adopt *yuanzu minzu* (indigenous peoples) or *yuanzu min* (indigenous people).[67] The ATA has participated actively in international organizations of indigenous peoples, and there are clear connections between the developing international concept of indigenous peoples and political and legal demands made by the ATA and other groups in Taiwan.[68]

The Freeport–McMoRan Mine and Mill at Grasberg

The Freeport–McMoRan mining and metal milling operation at Grasberg, and related mineral activities in other parts of West Irian, have attracted severe international criticism. The western portion of Papua, a generally Melanesian area colonized by the Netherlands but not greatly developed under Dutch rule, was incorporated into Indonesia only during the 1960s, by which time a distinctive self-identity had begun to evolve. The Indonesian government has promoted various economic projects and organized some resettlement of local people, raising for local people conflicts between preservation of autonomy and the appeals of development. Parts of the area have become highly militarized, with armed conflict between the Indonesian army and the Free Papua Movement (Organisasi Papua Merdeka); large projects such as the Grasberg copper, gold and silver mine have been accompanied by heavy security deployments. Civil conflicts connected in some way to the project have been frequent, and concerns about human rights abuses and environmental problems have been expressed within Indonesia by groups such as the Indonesian Human Rights Commission and church organizations, but the main pressure has come from outside. The U.S. government investment promotion agency, the Overseas Private Investment Corporation (OPIC), terminated its political risk guarantee to Freeport in 1995, reinstating it temporarily in 1996 with some encouragement from environmental NGOs keen to see Freeport held to stronger environmental conditions. Lawsuits against Freeport–McMoRan alleging human rights violations were filed in state and federal courts in Louisiana (where Freeport's corporate head office is located) in 1996 and 1997.[69]

---

67. "Statement by the Delegation of Taiwan Aborigines," United Nations Working Group on Indigenous Populations, 11th Session (U.N. files, July 1993, mimeo). Although the Romanization differs, the Chinese characters in *yuan-chu min* and *yuanzu min* are identical.

68. See, for example, Alliance of Taiwan Aborigines, I Chiang, Lava Kau, "Report on the Human Rights Situation of Taiwan's Aborigines," in Barnes, Gray, and Kingsbury, eds., *Indigenous Peoples of Asia*, p. 357.

69. Yosofa Alomang *v.* Freeport-McMoRan, Decision of October 17, 1996, 1996 U.S. Dist. Lexis 15908 (U.S. District Court, E.D. Louisiana) (declining Freeport's motion to remove the case from state court to federal court); Tom Beanal *v.* Freeport-McMoRan, Decision of April 10, 1997, 1997 WL 178637 (U.S. District Court, E.D. Louisiana) (dismissing plaintiff's claim). An amended complaint was thereafter filed in the latter case in which an Amungme tribal organization, Lembaga Musyawarah Adat Suku Amungme (LEMASA) is also a plaintiff.

Themes Drawn from the Illustrative Cases

A number of general themes bearing on the subject to this chapter may be drawn from these illustrative examples. First, every controversy is about weighing the competing interests and/or preferences of those who stand to gain or lose from a project, but there is particular disagreement as to how to weigh the interests of local people and whether to accept that these interests are sufficiently represented by statements of preferences. Their interests are often concentrated, potentially a political strength vis-à-vis the more diffuse interests of some classes of distant beneficiaries, but in many political and legal systems they lack the leverage to contend with proproject interests. Thus, enhancing the salience of the interests of local residents has been a major strategy in the field of international development, advocated even by environmental NGOs whose preferences and priorities may diverge sharply from those expressed by local people.[70]

The concept of "indigenous peoples" fits well in this strategy. Thus ILO Convention 169 provides that indigenous and tribal peoples "shall have the right to decide their own priorities for the process of development as it affects their lives, beliefs, institutions and spiritual well-being and the lands they occupy or otherwise use." The 1993 U.N. Draft Declaration on the Rights of Indigenous Peoples goes further:

> Indigenous peoples have the right to determine and develop priorities and strate-
> gies for the development or use of their lands, territories and other resources,
> including the right to require that States obtain their free and informed consent
> prior to the approval of any project affecting their lands, territories and other
> resources, particularly in connection with the development, utilization or
> exploitation of mineral, water or other resources. Pursuant to agreement with the
> indigenous peoples concerned, just and fair compensation shall be provided for
> any such activities and measures taken to mitigate adverse environmental, eco-
> nomic, social, cultural or spiritual impact.[71]

The international concept of "indigenous peoples" carries with it particular emphasis on self-determination and the role of groups in decisions affecting them, respect for different cultures shaped over long periods of history, recognition of special relations with land and territory, and unique knowledge

---

70. Note, for example, Haripriya Rangan's observation of differences in the Garhwal Himalayas, home of the Chipko tree-protection movement made famous and celebrated by international environmentalists, between "images of self-contained village communities living in harmonious ecological utopias" and the desire of many residents to resume their long-standing involvement in commercial use of the forests and other activities necessary to make a living. "Romancing the Environment: Popular Environmental Action in the Garhwal Himalayas," in John Friedmann and Haripriya Rangan, eds., *In Defense of Livelihood: Comparative Studies on Environmental Action* (Westport, CT: Kumarian Press, 1993), p. 162.

71. U.N. Doc. E/CN.4/Sub.2/1993/29, Annex 1, 1993.

about the use and management of these, and awareness of the disastrous consequences for these peoples of many prior policies of states and international institutions. The concept thus has a range of justifications, variously based on equity, history, the value of diversity, functional criteria, politics, and law. Where support for recognition of rights or entitlements of "indigenous peoples" is offered strategically on functional grounds as a means to enhance local influence, however, it is in some cases tempered by concerns that the category of "indigenous peoples" is underinclusive or inequitable. Thus, in a village in India affected by land encroachments from a coal mine, people from one or more "scheduled tribes" may be living interspersed with nontribal Hindus, some of whom are almost equally disadvantaged in economic vulnerability and social status in the caste system.[72]

There may exist special factors relating to means of consultation and to compensatory development initiatives that apply to tribal families but not to others, but many of the economic and social issues may be similar. Tania Murray Li comments with reference to Indonesia that most "rural areas, both on and off Java, are complex mosaics of cultural groups and social classes, products of diverse agrarian histories and centuries of interaction with market and state."[73] Reacting to concerns that "indigenous" or "tribal" are too narrow for certain functional purposes, some practitioners and policy activists concerned with sustainable development in Asia advocate emphasis on the role of local "communities" in such activities as development planning, common property management, and sustainable forestry.[74] As a practical matter, in many situations local "communities" are in much the same position vis-à-vis the state or vis-à-vis development projects whether or not the communities or portions of them might be described as "indigenous." In practice there will often be no sharp line between policies applicable wherever indigenous peoples are involved and policies applicable in cases of similarly situated "communities." Common to the concepts of "indigenous people" and of a defined "commu-

---

72. Issues of this sort have arisen in the operations of Coal India Ltd. covered by the World Bank's India Coal Sector Rehabilitation Project. For comments on this project see Ratnakar Bhengara, "Coal Mining Displacement," *Economic and Political Weekly*, March 16, 1996, pp. 647–9.

73. Tania Murray Li, "Images of Community: Discourse and Strategy in Property Relations," *Development and Change* vol. 27 (1996), pp. 501–27, 508.

74. See, for example, the debate between Owen Lynch and James Anderson in Dolores Flamiano and Donald Goertzen, eds., *Critical Decade: Prospects for Democracy in the Philippines in the 1990's* (Berkeley, CA: Philippine Resource Center, 1990). See also Lynch and Talbott, *Balancing Acts*. Their "definition" of "community" seems underspecified for many practical purposes; it is so broad as to encompass virtually any enduring mutual benefit arrangement. The relevant features are (p. 23): "1) extensive participation by its members in the decisions by which its life is governed; 2) the community as a whole takes responsibilities for its members; and 3) this responsibility includes respect for the diverse individuality of these members." See further, Herman Daly and John Cobb, *For the Common Good: Redirecting the Economy Toward Community, the Environment, and a Sustainable Future* (Boston: Beacon Press, 1989), pp. 168–75.

nity" are the deep problems of how such abstract concepts are rendered operational in practice. As Li notes, the interests and voices of women, distressed migrants, and underclasses may be submerged in a focus on community that "leaves begging the central question of who is enabled or constrained: whose economic circumstances or security of tenure is at stake."[75]

Evaluating the campaign by national and international NGOs that led to cancellation in 1995 of the enormous Arun III dam project in Nepal, notwithstanding the apparent support of most residents of the very remote Arun valley for the roads and communications the project would bring, Ann Armbrecht Forbes comments that "the search for the real 'local' is an incomplete and thus a potentially misguided search. . . . Factors such as who speaks up, who claims to speak for whom, who chooses to remain silent and why, all influence which voice is eventually labeled as the 'local'."[76] In many large projects, some members, on occasion even most members, of indigenous groups have supported the whole project or elements of it, whether because of inevitability, a view of the best interests of the community, or more personal benefits realized or hoped for. Complex issues arise as to decision making and representation in communities that may be undemocratic in structure, poorly informed about the long-term consequences of proposed projects, diverted by disputes with other groups, and vulnerable to suborning and coercion.[77]

Issues also arise as to who knows best and whose voice counts, raising problems of representation, accountability, and decision making in NGOs and in overseas lawsuits, as well as in governments and international organizations. For some purposes it is not very helpful to rely on an underspecified unit of "community" as somehow bounding legitimate involvement and concern. The sheer scale of such projects and the transformations they effect can overwhelm not only small groups with distinctive cultures, but much larger and more distant communities as well. As Forbes argues with respect to Nepal, a small country subject to enormous impact from such a project: "A 'local' in the Arun controversy . . . includes those living within an hour's walk of the dam site, as well as those in Kathmandu whose work is disrupted by electric shortages, as well as those worried about Nepal's foreign debt."[78]

The second theme that emerges from these cases is that large-scale economic development projects typically have a unity of identity and a structure

---

75. Tania Murray Li, "Images of Community," p. 505, quoting Melissa Leach, "Endangered Environments: Understanding Natural Resource Management in the West African Forest Zone," *IDS Bulletin* vol. 22, no. 4, p. 18.

76. Ann Armbrecht Forbes, "Defining the 'Local' in the Arun Controversy: Villagers, NGOs, and the World Bank in the Arun Valley, Nepal," *Cultural Survival Quarterly* (Fall 1996), p. 31.

77. Marcus Colchester, "Indigenous Peoples' Rights and Sustainable Resource Use in South and Southeast Asia," in Barnes, Gray, and Kingsbury, eds., *Indigenous Peoples of Asia,* pp. 73–6.

78. Forbes, "Defining the 'Local' in the Arun Controversy," p. 31.

of control that makes them ready focal points for local and transnational mobilization to a much greater extent than more incremental or diffuse sources of equally profound and disruptive changes. When large projects draw on capital and support from intergovernmental agencies or foreign corporations, international campaigners have found points of leverage outside the host state that generate publicity and intensify pressure. High-visibility transnational campaigns against development projects attract the attention of many outside the area directly affected, but the objectives of such campaigns and their criteria of success may be radically different for national NGOs, for transnational groups, and for local residents. In some cases campaigns of national and transnational NGOs and foreign governments on a specific development issue may be part of a wider political struggle concerning national leadership, in which indigenous peoples may or may not be active participants and in which their claims may be used to further quite different interests of others. National groups may be focused on achieving victories in national courts, thereby setting precedents requiring public access to environmental information or obliging the government to ensure that affected groups are consulted. Transnational groups may seek to secure critical rulings from bodies such as the World Bank Inspection Panel and courts in the United States and elsewhere, and to change the broad policies of institutions such as the World Bank, the Exim Bank, and the Overseas Private Investment Corporation (OPIC). Campaigns are often directed at the cancellation of projects, but it is much more difficult for campaigners to promote and deliver positive alternatives that meet development needs of local people. The actual consequences of a court victory, a policy change, or cancellation of a project are not necessarily experienced in the same way by the local populace as by more distant NGOs, who can declare the battle over and move on.

Third, the significance of "indigenous peoples" as a salient category in political discourse about these projects varies considerably. The existence and recognition of "indigenous peoples" in international and transnational practice provides a legitimacy, perhaps even a language, for pursuit of aspirations and grievances that may otherwise struggle for purchase or vocabulary. It provides access to transnational benefits supplied by private groups such as Oxfam, intergovernmental agencies such as the Asian Development Bank, and foreign governments such as the Netherlands and Norway, which have policies specifically targeted to overseas indigenous peoples[79] and to political and institutional fora such as the United Nations, , the U.N. Commission on Sustainable Development, the Conference of the Parties to the Biodiversity

79. *Indigenous Peoples in the Netherlands Foreign Policy and Development Cooperation,* English trans. (Memorandum of the Minister of Foreign Affairs, P. H. Kooijmans, and the Minister of Development Cooperation, J. P. Pronk, to the Netherlands Parliament, March 29, 1993, mimeo).

Convention, or associations of museum directors and national parks administrators. The category certainly has international purchase: Publications and
Internet postings of NGOs seeking to appeal to a Western/OECD audience
regularly emphasize adverse impacts of projects on ethnic minorities or
indigenous groups with distinct cultures. What exactly the appeal is based
on is a more complex matter.

There has long been a popular image, particularly in the West, of indigenous peoples as "victims" of "development,"[80] and a romantic attachment to
cultural diversity and saving indigenous peoples from "vanishing." In practice
indigenous peoples may have as much cause to feel themselves victims of
"conservation" – the restrictions on swidden agriculture introduced in most
Southeast Asian countries, the displacement of people to make room for
national parks, the blanket protection of depleted wildlife stocks, denial of
access to minor forest produce to prevent deforestation. In either case the
imagery of passive victims living at one with nature and beset by unwelcome
modernity is misleading as a general account of the practices and aspirations
of groups participating in the "indigenous peoples" movement. Most of these
groups are active agents and practitioners of "development" and "conservation," and vary considerably in their practices and attitudes relating to
resource exploitation and environmental maintenance.[81] This reality is explicitly recognized in programs ranging from community forestry and biodiversity maintenance to opium crop substitution and peoples-and-parks, and in
ameliorative doctrines such as the World Bank's policy requiring "informed
participation" and "culturally compatible social and economic benefits" for
indigenous peoples in development projects.[82] Nevertheless, although aspirations for self-determination and a substantial role in development decisions
seem to be widely shared by indigenous groups, they are often far from being
realized in practice. There remains, in Asia as elsewhere, a gulf between the
"self-determination" advocated by indigenous peoples in the United Nations
– or even the doctrines of consultation, participation, and choice espoused in

---

80. For example, John H. Bodley, *Victims of Progress,* 2nd ed. (Palo Alto, CA: Mayfield Publishing, 1990);
    and John Bodley, ed., *Tribal Peoples and Development Issues: A Global Overview* (Mountain View, CA:
    Mayfield Publishing, 1988).
81. For a mixture of assessment and advocacy, see Peter Brosius, *After Duwagan: Deforestation, Succession
    and Adaptation in Upland Luzon, Philippines* (Ann Arbor, MI: Center for South and Southeast Asian
    Studies, 1990); Marcus Colchester and Larry Lohmann, eds., *The Struggle for Land and the Fate of the
    Forests* (Penang: World Rainforest Movement, 1994); and Elizabeth Kemf, ed., *Indigenous Peoples and
    Protected Areas* (London: Earthscan, 1993). The image of indigenous peoples as active consumers is evi-
    dent in advertising in many of the places where the cash economy and mass commercial communica-
    tion reach. See, for example, Robert J. Foster, ed., *Nation Making: Emergent Identities in Postcolonial
    Melanesia* (Ann Arbor: University of Michigan Press, 1995), and Foster's forthcoming work on adver-
    tising in Papua–New Guinea and other parts of Melanesia.
82. World Bank, *Operational Directive 4.20: Indigenous Peoples* (Washington, DC: World Bank, 1991).
    Reproduced in *Newsletter of the International Work Group for Indigenous Affairs* no. 3 (1991).

some international institutions – and the actual experiences of "indigenous peoples" with externally driven "development" and "conservation."

A PROPOSAL CONCERNING DEFINITION:
REQUIREMENTS AND INDICIA

Representatives of both states and nonstate groups in Asia continue to suggest, albeit in radically different ways, that the international concept of "indigenous peoples" as commonly understood does not adequately incorporate their interests or their social realities. Thus, depending on one's viewpoint, either the concept cannot sensibly be applied or it is not at present likely to be applied without outside pressure.

Undoubtedly there are elements of cynicism and opportunism in the debate. The total refusal or failure of some state governments to recognize and take account of distinctive histories, needs, vulnerabilities, and aspirations of indigenous peoples has long been a cause of immense destruction, dispossession, misery, and death for a great many people. In some cases such nonrecognition is part of a deliberate strategy of denial to facilitate outrages against clear international and national legal standards. Nonrecognition may also be designed to cut groups off from the kinds of transnational and international support (not all of it benign), identity, and solidarity increasingly associated with "indigenous peoples." Some states pursue an international policy of denial even while agencies of these same states operating at the level of national rather than foreign policy recognize distinctive identities of particular indigenous groups.

Nevertheless, there are genuine problems in many societies with continuity on the basis of historical priority as the foundation for a locally applicable concept of "indigenous people," and in such circumstances nonrecognition is not necessarily motivated by malevolence, particularly when other bases of social identity and recognition of distinctive cultures, histories, and needs are resonant and well established within the polity. Each of the main positions in this debate encompasses persuasive substantive concerns that must be addressed if the concept of "indigenous peoples" is to evolve and have sustained useful application in situations when colonial settlement or invasion are not such clear parts of the social context.

Like any legal concept, "indigenous peoples" is a construct that itself has a shaping effect on social meanings and legal development. The international concept of "indigenous peoples" may be understood as an abstraction from a vast set of complex particular realities. These realities involve divergent self-perceptions and political discourses of groups and national societies, and diverse state–society relations. The abstract international concept of indigenous peoples has the potential to be drawn from international society back into national society; the abstract concept is worked out and made particular in a specific context.[83] This happens most obviously in those national societies in which legal and political decision making gives weight to international practices and texts referring to indigenous peoples, and to decisions and models in other countries that are understood as involving indigenous peoples.[84] In different ways this happens also when groups draw upon the international concept of "indigenous peoples" in constructing their own identities: thus groups whose self-concept might not have centered on prior possession may come to identify themselves as indigenous peoples with experiences and worldviews shared with other indigenous peoples. Questions about the applicability of the international concept in various Asian states are in part questions about the suitability of the international concept in the context of competing visions of identities of particular groups and of national societies and polities.[85]

For the purposes of international legal instruments intended to have general rather than regional or highly specific application, four factors seem relatively unproblematic as requisites for a group to be an "indigenous people": self-identification as a distinct ethnic group; historical experience of, or contingent vulnerability to, severe disruption, dislocation, or exploitation; long connection with the region; and the wish to retain a distinct identity. These four criteria establish a set narrower than "ethnic group" and more focused than "ethnic minority," but still overly broad to delimit the category of "indigenous peoples" as it is employed in contemporary practice. Three further criteria are highly relevant, but in each case some flexibility is required in order not to arbitrarily exclude special cases.

The first of these is nondominance in the state or region. This is virtually a requisite, but the exact meaning of "dominance" is difficult to capture in many situations. Most obviously, numerical dominance is not ipso facto exclusionary when a group has little political or economic power. More complex situations arise when small groups are part of uneasy ruling political coalitions but have little power or when a very few members of a group exercise considerable national political power but most members of the group are entirely marginal to this process. Even when a group is numerically and politically dominant in a state, the state may be so extremely small that vis-à-vis international lending

83. Philip Allott, *Eunomia: New Order for a New World* (Oxford: Oxford University Press, 1990), chapters 10, 16.
84. On Australia, Canada, and New Zealand, see Benedict Kingsbury, "Whose International Law? Sovereignty and Non-State Groups," *Proceedings of the American Society of International Law* vol. 88 (1994), pp. 1–13.
85. See, for example, Li, "Images of Community," pp. 501–27.

agencies, the blandishments of transnational mining and logging corporations, dumpers of hazardous waste, foreign fishing fleets, mercenaries, and other powerful actors, the people of the state may face many of the same problems as "indigenous peoples" within states.

Second is the requirement that a group have close cultural affinity with a particular territory or area of land. Many indigenous peoples regard this as a fundamental feature of their own identities. It is not required that the group have been associated with the particular land or territory for countless generations; groups have often moved, joined with other groups, or been forcibly relocated. Nevertheless, to make this a strict requirement would render injustice in some cases. Some groups have been displaced from traditional land areas and lost touch altogether with these, or have formed in new circumstances, living perhaps in urban centers. Nevertheless, their relations with land and natural resources in general, and their outlooks and lifestyles, may be almost indistinguishable from other indigenous groups in the area. For example, the Seaman Commission in Western Australia discussed the case of the urban or periurban Nyungars: "Although they cannot now identify particular areas of land as being owned in traditional law by particular ancestors they feel a great passion about their ties to land and their concern over diminishing access to lands, rivers and coast for hunting and fishing."[86]

Third, the definitional requirement of historical continuity with preinvasion or precolonial societies is important in many contexts and is often seen as a central requirement. It may also be seen, however, as a product of one foundational phase in the continuing social process of the construction and elaboration of the international concept of "indigenous peoples." During this phase, the international concept of "indigenous peoples," with its emphasis on historical continuity, did not necessarily reflect the full range of social categories and realities in many parts of Asia (or, indeed, in other areas of the world).[87]

An approach to the problematic requirement of historical continuity from preinvasion or precolonial peoples, and to the question of connections with land, has been proposed by the experienced chairperson-rapporteur of the U.N. Working Group on Indigenous Populations, Erica-Irene Daes. She would eliminate the implication that "indigenous peoples" are the original inhabitants of a state in contradistinction to groups of "immigrants" or "settlers" in the country and would recognize that "indigenous" and "nonindigenous" groups in Asia and elsewhere may well have been neighbors for mil-

---

86. Commissioner Paul Seaman, QC, *The Aboriginal Land Inquiry* (Perth: Government of Western Australia, 1984), paras. 3.16ff.

87. Note the comments of Erica-Irene Daes, *Working Paper on the Concept of "Indigenous People"* (U.N. Doc. E/CN.4/Sub.2/AC.4/1996/2, June 10, 1996).

lennia. She argues that "indigenous peoples" are "groups which are native to their own specific ancestral territories within the borders of the existing State, rather than persons that are native generally to the region in which the State is located."[88] Thus one of the requisites for a group to be an indigenous people would be priority in time with respect to the occupation and use of a specific ancestral territory, even if the group has in recent times been displaced from some or all of this territory.[89] This broad argument is powerful, but the practice of international institutions dealing regularly with Asia and Africa, such as the World Bank and the ILO, suggests that the element of historical continuity – of "being there first" – in a region or on a specific territory, has not been seen, from a functional standpoint, as an essential and rigid requirement.

To make this criterion a strict requirement in the United Nations unduly narrows the range of justifications that must be kept open if the concept of "indigenous peoples" is to have real prospects of widespread and satisfactory application. A requirement such as that proposed by Erica Daes would also create difficulties in situations when priority in a particular territory is contested, when groups are known to have resettled into new "ancestral" territories that may also be claimed by others, when ethnogenesis or changes in group identity make connections with particular territory unclear, and when a group with a clearly "indigenous" identity has become so displaced or urbanized as not to have connection with particular "ancestral" land.

For the reasons given, the three criteria of nondominance, special connections with land or territories, and continuity based on historical priority, should not be treated as rigid requirements. Not only must these criteria be interpreted flexibly, they should be regarded as indicia the presence of which strongly supports categorization as an "indigenous people." Absence of all three would raise very strong doubts, and absence of either of the first two would raise doubts that may be rebutted in special circumstances of the types mentioned.

Other indicators may also be of assistance in understanding and applying the concept of "indigenous peoples," their presence adding to the case, without being in any sense requisites.

A more flexible approach to definition may provide scope to promote the fundamental values underlying the concept of "indigenous peoples" while recognizing both its changing nature and the need to work out the applica-

---

88. Daes, *Working Paper on the Concept of "Indigenous People,"* para. 64.
89. Daes, *Working Paper on the Concept of "Indigenous People,"* para. 69; Daes, *Note on Criteria Which Might Be Applied when Considering the Concept of Indigenous Peoples,* para. 12; The Other Media, *Summary of Resolutions of Workshops on Indigenous and Tribal Peoples' Struggle for Right of Self-Determination and Self-Government in India* (U.N. Doc. E/CN.4/Sub.2/AC.4/1994/4/Add.1, June 21, 1994).

tion of the concept in a vast range of situations.[90] Adoption of a flexible approach to the meaning of "indigenous peoples" is consistent with the functions of the concept in international law and institutions. A flexible approach might involve compilation of a list of indicia, some of which would be requisites, others strongly indicative but not required in special circumstances, others simply relevant factors to be evaluated and applied in cases of doubt or disagreement. Such a list might resemble the following.

Essential Requirements:
1. Self-identification as a distinct ethnic group
2. Historical experience of, or contingent vulnerability to, severe disruption, dislocation, or exploitation
3. Long connection with the region
4. The wish to retain a distinct identity

Relevant Indicia:
1. Strong Indicia
   - nondominance in the national (or regional) society (ordinarily required)
   - close cultural affinity with a particular area of land or territories (ordinarily required)
   - historic continuity (especially by descent) with prior occupants of land in the region
2. Other Relevant Indicia
   - socioeconomic and sociocultural differences from the ambient population
   - distinct objective characteristics: language, race, material or spiritual culture, etc.
   - regarded as indigenous by the ambient population or treated as such in legal and administrative arrangements.

CONCLUSION

The challenge offered by some Asian states to the application of the concept of "indigenous peoples" is in some respects an exemplar of continuing contests concerning the transplantation and adaptation of West-originated but internationally defined concepts. It is unsurprising that there is resistance to international and transnational processes that are seen largely (if not always

90. Daes, *Working Paper on the Concept of "Indigenous People."*

accurately) to entail one-way projection of concepts and values from a dominant group of Western countries to others.

The argument that proposals to universalize the concept of "indigenous peoples" are another variant of the multifaceted tendencies to "eurocentrism" in international law has sometimes been made in sweeping terms similar to those employed for the cognate argument about the concept of "human rights." Like the human rights argument, the charge of "eurocentrism" is politically colorable when made against aggressive global assertion of Western concepts by governments and transnational networks based in the West, but depends on notions of false consciousness, manipulation, or opportunism when made against claims by local groups claiming to be "indigenous peoples."

The complexity of issues raised by indigenous peoples is reflected in the range of national, transnational, and interstate institutional mechanisms deployed, including formal judicial or rule-governed approaches, special commissions, fact-finding and mediating bodies, and negotiating fora. The international institutional mechanisms overlap with those operating in the field of individual human rights, and additional mechanisms confer status on nonstate groups.[91] It is not surprising that there is some objection, especially from China and Myanmar, to the institutional elements, particularly the availability of international platforms to criticize the state, the perception that international agencies are "meddling in internal affairs," the energetic activities of extensive transnational networks of indigenous peoples and interested NGOs, and "extraterritorial" proceedings in foreign courts.[92] But the give and take of bargaining within such institutional structures is the ordinary stuff of international law and politics, and it is to be expected that practical accommodations (however much open to criticism) can be reached, as has been demonstrated in the practice of some of the functional agencies such as the ILO and the World Bank, and in the evolution of the innovative practices of the UN Working Group on Indigenous Populations.

The normative program has resulted in the formulation of legal texts asserting rights of indigenous peoples, or rights of individuals members of indigenous peoples, and related duties of states and other obligees. Objections to the norms by Asian states pertain mainly to self-determination and to rights to land and resources, but these are unlikely to be more severe than those of some European settler states in which the concept of "indigenous peoples" is now uncontested (e.g., Brazil). The normative program does not formally depend at the global level on a precise specification of the meaning

91. Kingsbury, "Claims by Non-State Groups in International Law," pp. 481–530.
92. Ralph Litzinger, *The Work of Culture and Memory in Contemporary China* (Durham, NC: Duke University Working Papers in Asian/Pacific Studies 95–03, 1995), pp. 7–8.

of "indigenous peoples": The disputes concerning relevant norms of land and resource rights, autonomy and self-determination, equality and equity, involve clashes of interests and values within states in all regions. Nevertheless, some formulations of elements of the normative program are bound up with particular views as to justifications of the norms that are deeply contested.

The concept of "indigenous peoples" carries within it grounds of justification related to prior occupancy, dispossession, and group identity. Although conceptual issues and more instrumental political and legal concerns are inevitably mixed, the principled objection of the Indian government to applying to India international instruments concerning "indigenous peoples" is above all an objection to a particular justification perceived to be inherent in the concept of "indigenous peoples," a justification that is not simply a product of European expansion but that nevertheless does not capture well the identities and outlooks in some regions not structured by waves of recent invasion and migration.[93] Two paths are currently open. One is to adhere to the requirement of historical continuity, thus assuring the political viability of the international concept of "indigenous peoples" and perhaps opening the way for greater normative and institutional development while avoiding some of the serious policy problems of a potent but uncircumscribed and open-ended category.

The other is to treat historical continuity as an indicator rather than a requirement. This approach emphasizes the commonality of experiences, concerns, and contributions made by groups in many different regions, and argues that functional matters such as dispossession from land, cultural dislocation, environmental despoliation, and experiences with large development projects establish a unity that is not dependent on the universal presence of historical continuity. This approach recognizes that the concept of "indigenous peoples" must be circumscribed to be useful, but proposes to achieve this through a different means of definition as set forth in this chapter. Where a broader range of groups is potentially involved, normative and institutional development will be more complex and more flexibility may be necessary, but the ILO and the World Bank have established that such an approach is, at a minimum, possible.

The flexible approach to definition advocated here would be problematic if the concept of "indigenous peoples" were understood as operating primarily in the positivist sense of defining and delimiting a category of right holders, but, although this is one of its functions, the concept must not be viewed simply in static terms. The basic question is how a single concept of "indige-

---

93. This argument about India may well apply also to the position of the Chinese government, and the views of the governments of Bangladesh and Myanmar may follow this track but are difficult to analyze independent of issues of insurgency, state building, and central political/military control.

nous peoples," potentially global in scope, is both abstracted from and germane to the enormous variety of local self-conceptions and political contexts and the abstraction to which its relevance is asserted. It has been argued here that concepts such as "indigenous peoples" are better understood in the constructivist fashion sketched in this chapter, and that on balance more is gained than lost by adopting a flexible approach. This chapter therefore advocates setting forth flexible international criteria as to the meaning of "indigenous peoples," with a combination of requirements and indicia, and relying on the dynamic processes of negotiation, politics, legal analysis, institutional decision making, and social interaction to work out the application of these criteria to the innumerable nuances of specific cases.

INDEX